Praise for
Verdict for America

Bill Ponath's common sense wisdom provides refreshing, keen insight for people with moral longings towards the major issues of the day.
> **–Dr. Cornell Haan,** Mission America Coalition

Verdict for America is a wonderful tool for both legislators and the voting public. The Abortion chapter gives insight to the legal environment and the gaps that currently exist. It directs us to work to overcome these barriers and pass laws that protect the unborn.
> **–Rep. Nancy Barto,** Arizona House of Representatives

When Bill Ponath served on my court's bench, I always knew that it was in good hands. *Verdict for America* is an extension of that ability to reason and will serve its readers well.
> **–The Honorable Michael Orcutt,** retired Justice of the
> Peace, Maricopa County, Arizona

William Ponath's chapter on abortion holds the reader's attention on this difficult and complex subject. It contains a masterful and concise review of the major legal strategies and court decisions over the past nearly 40 years since abortion on demand changed America. More importantly, this history gives credence to Ponath's point that, if we unite behind smart political and legislative strategies, there is great hope that we can reverse our country's destructive course. Ponath's optimism is inspiring and he offers a practical course for the future.
> **–Peggy H. Hartshorn,** Ph.D., President, Heartbeat International

Our society is at a major crossroads--a time when wisdom is so vitally necessary. In the Bible, I Chronicles 12:32 mentions the sons of Issachar who had an understanding of the times and knew what to do. Bill Ponath is a modern day equivalent, possessing special wisdom we need at these pivotal times. If you want researched facts and informed insights, *Verdict for America* needs to be at the top of your reading list.
> **–Sara J. Moulton Reger,** Transformation Program
> Executive, IBM; Author of *Can Two Rights Make a*
> *Wrong?* and Lead and Succeed

Bill Ponath's chapter on abortion is an accurate and well-documented analysis of the past, present, and potential future of abortion laws in Arizona and the United States. His "laymen's language" makes navigating the stormy and muddy waters of abortion laws an easy passage for everyone concerned with right to life issues. Bill also charts a course for the future challenging us to not grow weary in defending life at every stage.

> **–Barbara Willis,** President, Crisis Pregnancy Centers of Greater Phoenix

Verdict for America offers truth and sound argument that will forge a real change if implemented. Brilliantly written and researched. Some may think the incremental approach to abortion legislature will leave out someone like myself, conceived in rape. But one should never say, "If I can't put everyone in the boat, I will rescue none." *Verdict for America* draws wisdom from America's past for creative ideas needed to overcome our tumultuous and very near future.

> **–Juda Myers**, speaker, singer songwriter, author

I can't think of a more noble, honest and passionate person to write about real solutions for America right now than Bill Ponath. I know others will speak of his experience as a lawyer and critical thinker, but I would like to speak of his integrity and character of heart and spirit. *Verdict for America* gives real answers in a world where every wind of political and religious doctrine is being thrown at Americans. He is a true genius in analyzing the facts and decimating them for the average American wanting to know the real truth, not the hype of media "sound bites". I highly recommend his book and believe he has eminent truth we desperately need for 21st century America.

> **–Pamela Carter,** founder of Ravished Heart Communications

William Ponath is a man of integrity who possesses a keen insight to the issues that most trouble our nation today. His solutions are common sense and heroic. I particularly appreciate his forthright on the chapter regarding abortion! Every Patriot should read *Verdict for America*. Thank you for your boldness Bill!

> **–Patricia Trapnell,** Founder and Director of Sofia's House

William Ponath is a man of intellect and character. He has great insight into the issues facing our nation.

> **–David Friend,** Senior Pastor, Scottsdale First Assembly

"The Common Sense Judge," Bill Ponath, has hit a home run with *Verdict for America*. Bill gives unique insight on our judicial system that could only come from someone who has been in the trenches. He has the moral compass that is necessary for our time to be able to understand what exactly is going on with our country. *Verdict for America* is a must read. Keep telling it like it is, Bill Ponath!

    –Harlon L. Picker, Senior Messianic Rabbi, Beth Yachad Messianic Synagogue

Verdict for America is a book that has been long overdue. Who better to write it than "The Common Sense Judge," Bill Ponath? Bill has exhibited exemplary moral behavior not only as a man, but as a husband, friend, colleague and person. His passion to reach America with the truth from a unique perspective is admirable. This book is a must read for those who are concerned for the plight of America. Bravo Bill Ponath!

    –Messianic Rabbi Joyce K. Picker, Co-Congregational Leader, Beth Yachad Messianic Synagogue

Verdict for America

Verdict for America

Bill Ponath

Verdict for America

Dedication

I am infinitely blessed to be married to the most wonderful woman in the world. Joan is a beautiful work of art who has stood with me through many trials. She is my coach when I need to be motivated, she is the finest gourmet chef on the planet, she will do whatever work is necessary to accomplish our goals, and she is my best friend. If every man were as blessed as I, no union would ever end. God bless this incredible woman!

Contents

Acknowledgements

My desire to live responsibly prompted me to write this book. Gathering the information is a major effort; however I learned that it truly takes a team to create a book. I am sincerely grateful for the work of Karl Schaller, Megan Rieger, Julie Kuss, and the rest of the staff at Elevation Group. Additional thanks to Brenda Josee, Mike Westphal, Jennifer Lonas and Elisabeth Hendricks. They saw what I was doing and understood that this work needs to be available to the general public.

Introduction

I called this book *Verdict for America* because we, as Americans, are the final judges and jury of America's fate. I researched long and hard into each side of every issue and am providing evidence of the critical facts that will lead us to inescapable conclusions. These final rulings are what we need to know to steer America on a prosperous path.

My purpose in *Verdict for America* is to inform readers about the most critical issues facing our nation. The first chapter concerns health care: an issue that took center stage with the evolution and enactment of the Federal Health Plan, aka Obamacare. When we look at U.S. history since 1960 we see that health care costs have soared, but that the quality, and often the availability of the care, has diminished. We have available to us a perfect solution that only needs a little bit of help from Congress. The things standing in the way are ignorance and fear that proper legislation may lose an incumbent some votes. Elected officials turn blind eyes to curing the problem in order to better the odds of re-election.

Chapter two addresses education. America is blessed with many dedicated instructors who yearn to provide a proper foundation of teaching but are handcuffed by a system that works against them. We are spending more than twice as much money on education than our government institutions are willing to admit. The perfect solution is simply to do what is proven to work well. We need to eliminate the Federal Department of Education and allow local governments to do the work. All of the good instructors will be hired; all of the bad ones will have to change careers. I show consistent evidence that students' performances will phenomenally improve in a better learning environment, and that parents are desperate for the freedom to choose their children's schools.

Thanks to the Arizona immigration law, Senate Bill 1070, chapter three about immigration is one of the hottest topics in the news and in government. I seek to clear the confusion and hype produced by the media on this issue. I provide a brief history of terrorism on U.S. soil to allow us to focus on the real issue. Namely, we need to direct our efforts at protecting our nation from attack rather than checking for admission tickets. The consensus of communities of all demographics is to allow our nation of immigrants to grow by allowing those who are not living off of our entitlement programs to stay; but to deny access to individuals simply looking for a handout. The solution is to stop providing entitlements, thereby eliminating the lure for illegal border-crossers. We can then crack down on the criminal and terrorist elements that are using border-crossers as camouflage for their operations.

Chapter four focuses on oil and explains the frustrating decline of our economy. Until 1960, the United States had a consistently positive trade balance. Since then, oil has led us to send more and more of our money overseas, and we are now feeling the crunch. The baffling reality is that the U.S. retains two-thirds of the world's oil under our feet: primarily in the Bakken and Green River Formations, not to mention the Arctic National Wildlife Refuge in Alaska. Yet we are paying premium prices for oil from Canada, Mexico, and the Middle East for what we can harvest at a much lower cost.

Many claim that the current economic environment in the U.S. is the result of the housing market collapse. Chapter five explains that this collapse has been imminent for more than thirty years due to government interference in the free market. The hard cold fact is government market control can only function in a totalitarian state—one that is purely communist or socialist. A free market economy will provide the best environment for wealth, and government interference will always impede growth. You will see that every element of our economy: jobs, housing, inflation, prices, and all investment tools depend upon each other. Any distortion of one of the elements will adversely impact the other elements. Sooner or later, citizens have to pay for government interference in the free market system.

The first five chapters address the most critical issues for our nation's survival. Chapter six has little to do with the nation's survival, but rather addresses its character. Abortion is the vicious murder of innocent children and it is perfectly legal. I discuss the legal history and describe what pro-life advocates can do to help.

Chapter seven discusses freedom of religion. The interrelationship of government and religion is a subject few understand. Our government is based upon Christian principles, but that basis must never be abused. Only by understanding our liberties and attendant limitations will we best be able to enjoy this fundamental right.

The federal budget may not be the root of all evil, but I submit that it is the trunk of the tree. This tree has never been fully trimmed because members of Congress are deathly afraid that they will be cutting off their own branches. Chapter eight addresses the federal budget and employs all of the cost reductions discussed in chapters one through five. It goes on to discuss the systematic changes in government income that have proven themselves successful in every system of

government all over the world. These very changes Congress and our executive branch are afraid to make.

America is the greatest nation in the world. We have every tool and every resource at our disposal to be feared rather than laughed at. We simply need to adjust our course and use the resources that already belong to us. Every goal and every path to that goal in this book is universally desired by every American. United we stand, divided we fall! Let us unite by understanding the facts that led us to the nation's current condition and elect brave individuals who share our knowledge and goals. Let's win!

CHAPTER 1

Health Care

On March 21, 2010, the U.S. House of Representatives voted into law the Affordable Health Care for America Act (health-care reform) to overhaul our national health-care system. During the debates and discussions over the legislation, many questions were left unanswered. Read the information presented in this chapter with an open and discerning mind. The conclusions I offer may seem pretty obvious, but those conclusions didn't keep the legislation from becoming the law of our land. We now have a duty to learn where health care used to be, where it is now, and how to improve health-care legislation in the future.

What Is Health Care Really Costing Us?

The current state of health care needs to be put in the proper perspective. The following chart graphically shows the evolution of the health-care economy from 1960 to 2008. I analyzed the data on a year-by-year basis and summarized it in five-year increments, including statistics for 2008. You can find all of the statistics at the Web site for the U.S. Department of Health and Human Services, Center for Medicare and Medicaid Services.[1] My inflation data, in general, is found at inflationdata.com.[2]

Exhibit A

Year & Population in Millions	National Health Exp. in Billions/ Per Capita	GDP in Billions/ Per Capita	Priv. Fund Exp. in Billions/ Per Capita	Consumer Payments in Billions/ Per Capita (Inc. Insurance)	Out-of-Pocket Exp. in Billions/ Per Capita	Public Funds in Billions/ Per Capita	Federal Funds in Billions/ Per Capita	State & Local Funds in Billions Per Capita	National Health Costs as % of GDP	Inflation/ Health Care Inflation
1960/ 186	27.49/ $148	526 / $2,828	20.74 / $111	18.73 / $101	12.88 / $69.25	6.743 / $36.25	2.864 / $15.40	3.879 / $20.85	5.2%	
1965/ 200	42.16 / $211	719 / $3,595	31.69 / $159	28.18 / $141	18.11 / $90.55	10.47 / $52.35	4.794 / $23.97	5.676 / $28.38	5.9%	1.59% / 9.00%
1970/ 210	74.86 / $356	1,038 / $4,943	46.76 / $223	40.41 / $192	24.92 / $118.67	28.09 / $133.76	17.74 / $84.48	10.35 / $49.29	7.2%	5.84% / 12.83%
1975/ 220	133.0 / $604	1,638 / $7,445	77.24 / $351	67.62 / $307	37.17 / $168.95	55.78 / $253.55	36.33 / $165.14	19.45 / $88.41	8.1%	9.20% / 13.97%
1980/ 230	253.4 / $1,100	2,788 / $12,122	147.0 / $638	127.0 / $552	58.14 / $252.78	106.4 / $462.61	71.56 / $311.13	34.81 / $151.35	9.1%	13.58% / 15.18%
1985/ 242	439.3 / $1,818	4,218 / $17,430	261.9 / $1,084	226.1 / $937	95.20 / $393.39	177.4 / $733.06	123.1 / $508.68	54.30 / $224.38	10.4%	3.55% / 9.41%
1990/ 254	714.2 / $2,814	5,801 / $22,839	427.4 / $1,684	369.9 / $1,456	136.1 / $535.83	286.8 / $1,129	193.9 / $763.39	92.86 / $365.59	12.3%	5.39% / 11.18%
1995/ 269	1,017 / $3,783	7,415 / $27,565	551.3 / $2,052	471.1 / $1,751	146.1 / $543.12	465.3 / $1,730	327.8 / $1,219	137.5 / $511.15	13.7%	2.81% / 5.71%
2000/ 283	1,353 / $4,789	9,952 / $35,166	756.5 / $2,678	647.4 / $2,288	192.6 / $680.57	596.4 / $2,107	417.6 / $1,476	178.8 / $631.80	13.6%	3.38% / 6.96%
2005/ 296	1,983 / $6,701	12,638 / $42,696	1,083 / $3,660	938.5 / $3,171	247.5 / $836.15	899.8 / $3,040	641.4 / $2,167	258.4 / $872.97	15.7%	3.39% / 6.90%
2008/ 305	2,339 / $7,681	14,441 / $47,348	1,232 / $4,046	1,061 / $3,478	277.8 / $910.82	1,107 / $3,630	816.9 / $2,678	289.8 / $950.16	16.2%	3.85% / 4.42%

Following is a series of facts derived from the historical data listed in the previous chart. These facts allow us to look objectively at the impact of decisions made by governmental institutions without being bombarded by opinions and statistics from Op Ed pieces and news reports. These numbers will enable us to realistically project what the future impact of health-care reform may be.

1. Health-care costs in the U.S. have increased by 5,189.86% per person since 1960.

2. Our nation's gross domestic product (GDP) has grown by 1,674.26% per person, which means that health-care costs have gone up three times faster (specifically 3.12 times faster) than our nation's productivity and individual income.

3. Consumer funding of health care, which includes all personal out-of-pocket costs and expenses paid by insurance, has gone up 3,443.56%. But out-of-pocket funding has risen by only 1,315.26%. This means that the money coming out of our pockets, purses, and credit cards has decreased when compared to inflation as represented by GDP, but insurance payment for medical expenses has grown 2.177 times faster than the rate of inflation. Is this good or bad?

4. Public funding from government sources has increased by 10,013.79%, which is almost six times (5.981) the rate of inflation.

5. State and local funding of our health care that our taxes pay for has grown by a mere 4,557.12%, and *federal funding has grown by 17,389.61%*. President Obama and his team have enacted health care reform to further burden our federal budget with the obligation to provide medical care to everyone. The fact is that our current system needs some work that will soon be discussed; but it is still better than any public health-care system that exists in any nation of the world.

In 1960, consumer funding of health care cost about $101 per person, with $69.25 representing out-of-pocket expenditures, and the remaining $31.75 for private health insurance premiums. Public funding of health care at that time cost $36.25 per person. In 2008, consumer funding cost $3,478 per person, with about $910.82 representing out-of-pocket expenditures, and public funding covering $3,630 per person. This means that what used to be about one-quarter of the responsibility of the government (federal, state, and local) is now more than half the responsibility of government. Year after year, our government has covered more and more health-care costs (just look at the numbers in the previous chart), and year after year, health care has gotten

worse but cost more. Is this the way we want to continue? Has anyone ever heard the phrase "throwing good money after bad"?

Why Did This Happen?

One may be tempted to argue that increased health costs mean we are getting better health care. We probably are, but that quality is the result of research and discovery leading to better diagnosis and treatment. This does not necessarily mean health care should cost more. In fact, one may argue that advancements in technology should lead to lower costs.

The real answer to why we are incurring higher health care costs can be found in what we are in fact paying for. We need to follow the money trail. This isn't an easy process. I found conflicting data from multiple sources and have worked to decipher the most accurate information. According to PricewaterhouseCoopers (PwC), administrative costs covering the internal operations of the insurance companies varied between 6% and 16% of their expenses from 1966 through 2006. Right now, those costs average about 13% for private insurance plans compared with approximately 5% for Medicare.[3] As a result, a little more than one out of eight dollars in medical-insurance premiums pays for processing claims. Make note of this fact; everything will become clear later as we look for a solution to curb skyrocketing health-care costs.

This 13% average for administrative costs of health care is a start, but it doesn't tell us why we're spending three times as much of our GDP now on health care as we did in 1960. Where is the money going? A study conducted by Towers Perrin—now known as Towers Watson—shows that between 1975 and 2004, medical malpractice insurance costs paid by doctors and medical facilities increased from $450 million to almost $3 billion.[4] These numbers are adjusted for inflation, so the real cost to doctors has multiplied almost seven times, as you'll see in exhibit B.

Exhibit B

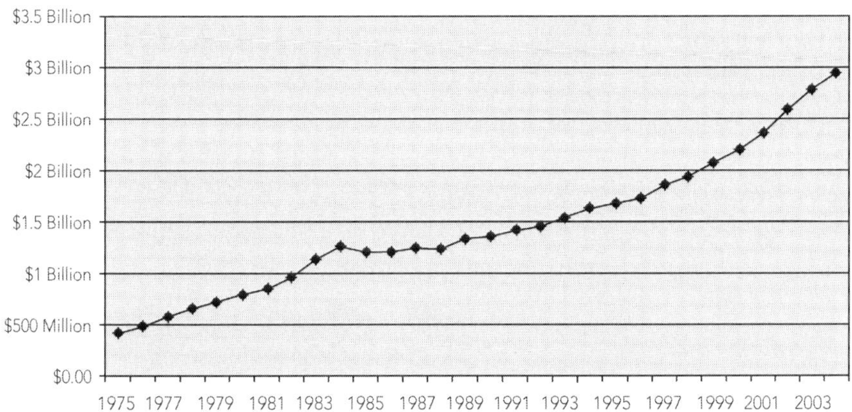

Medical Malpractice Costs 1975–2004, Adjusted for Inflation
Source: Tillinghast-Towers Perrin
http://www.towersperrin.com/tillinghast/publications/reports/2005_Tort_Cost/2005_Tort.pdf

Why in the world did doctors' malpractice insurance premiums skyrocket? According to the Congressional Budget Office, there are approximately five attorneys today for every three attorneys practicing law in 1980.[5] Medical malpractice is a popular and lucrative field of law. In addition, the total portion of our gross domestic product spent on tort litigation has almost quadrupled in a little more than fifty years.[6] Does that really have any effect on me personally? As exhibit C indicates, it most certainly does.

Exhibit C

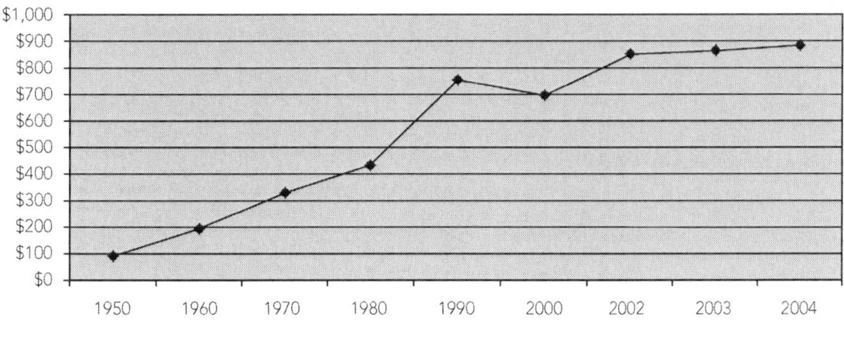

Inflation Adjusted Increase in Per Capita Tort Costs 1950–2004[7]
Source: Tillinghast-Towers Perrin
http://www.towersperrin.com:80/tillinghast/publications/reports/2005_Tort_Cost/2005_Tort.pdf

Does this mean that each and every American is shelling out nine hundred dollars or nine times as much to cover tort claims since 1950, even after adjusting for inflation? Yes! That is why one of the magic phrases we need to hear from political candidates in upcoming elections is "tort reform." We need to install a barrier in our legal system to protect doctors from frivolous lawsuits.

The data presented in the previous exhibits may lead us to assume that a doctor's costs for medical malpractice insurance and tort claims are directly proportionate to the rise in health-care costs. Nothing could be further from the truth. Malpractice premiums are a fairly small portion of most doctors' revenues, with the exception of surgeons and obstetrician-gynecologists, as shown in exhibit D.[8]

Exhibit D

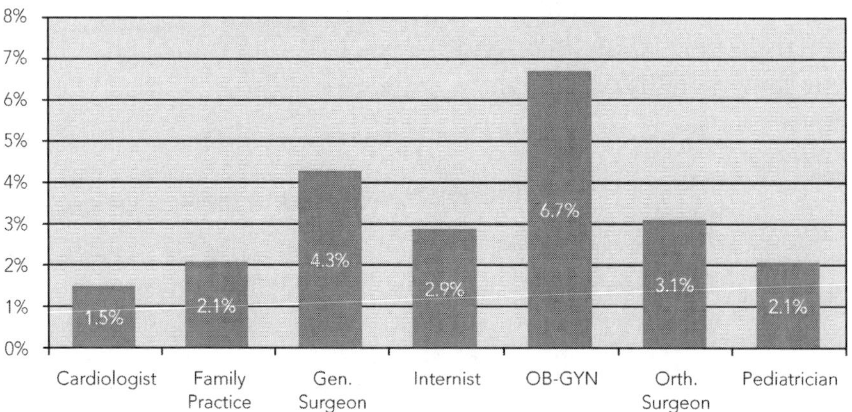

The real culprit hasn't been the higher cost of medical malpractice insurance, but the fact that MDs have now become MPs—no, not Military Police but Majorly Paranoid. As the *Washington Post* reported:

"The theory is, doctors are practicing more defensive medicine. Maybe doctors are fearful of litigation," [Dr. Jeffrey V. Spencer] added, perhaps likely to decide on a C-section at the first sign of any potential problems. The rates for malpractice rose, he said, even though both types of vaginal deliveries declined. Forceps deliveries declined from 11 percent to less than 1 percent, and vacuum deliveries went from 17.2 percent to 6.2 percent. Nationwide, C-section deliveries accounted for 30.2 percent of all deliveries in 2005, according to the U.S. Centers for Disease Control and Prevention; a record high for the nation. In 1996, in comparison, 20.7 percent of deliveries were by C-section.

"Any physician who picks up a scalpel and does major abdominal surgery, which is what a C-section is, because that doctor is afraid of litigation, is not practicing medicine but is practicing fear and greed," [Spencer] said. "The increasing C-section rate has not decreased the amount of litigation," [Dr. Marsden Wagner, a perinatologist and former director of Women's and Children's Health for the World Health Organization] said. "So their attempt to avoid litigation by doing C-section is not working." Spencer agreed. "The only thing to my knowledge that has changed or lowered malpractice rates are *states having legislation to place caps on malpractice settlements.*" (emphasis added)[9]

Further support can be found in an article published by Trial Lawyers Inc., which seems odd and may imply that these lawyers have a conscience.[10]

Trial Lawyers, Inc.'s medical-malpractice lawsuits are legion: of the 46,000 members of the American College of Obstetricians and Gynecologists, 76 percent have been sued at least once, 57 percent at least twice, and 41.4 percent three times or more.[11] And the litigation industry tends to file more cases than actually have merit: nearly half of malpractice suits—49.5 percent—are dropped, dismissed, or settled without payment. Indeed, in a study of medical-malpractice cases filed against New York hospitals, the Harvard Medical Practice Group found that in the majority of medical-malpractice claims, the plaintiff exhibited no medical injury whatsoever; *the plaintiff was injured by doctor negligence only 17 percent of the time* (emphasis added).[12]

If you're wearing a white coat, are you starting to get nervous? The article goes on:

> By 2003, medical-malpractice liability costs in the United States had reached an astounding $26 billion annually. That staggering sum represents a *2,000 percent increase* over costs in 1975. At 12 percent per year, the growth rate in medical malpractice costs since 1975 is *four times the rate of inflation and twice the rate of medical-care inflation* (emphasis added).

> In jury trials, million-dollar verdicts are now the norm. Fifty-two percent of all awards exceed $1 million while the average award now weighs in at $4.7 million.

Okay, now this looks like a little bit of bragging:

> Lawyers, Inc.'s carpet-bombing tactics helped drive average premiums up 18 percent in 2003 alone.... Doctors in plaintiff-friendly states and those in high-risk specialties like obstetrics, orthopedics, surgery, and neurology have borne the brunt of the assault. In plaintiff-friendly Cook County, Illinois, obstetricians paid $230,428 for coverage in 2004, up 67 percent from 2003 and *nearly 12 time* what they would pay in nearby Minnesota.

> Even so, these sky-high premiums have not kept pace with payouts and with the costs of defending the 70 percent of suits that are spurious. In 2003, insurers paid out $1.38 for every premium dollar they took in.

Many doctors have simply thrown in the towel:

> Palm Beach County, Florida, is one of those tort friendly locations where doctors increasingly shun risky cases. In five of the county's 13 hospitals, there are no neurologists working in the emergency room, and accident victims, stroke, and seizure patients must be transferred to hospitals in Gainesville and Tampa for treatment, over 100 miles away. Similarly, maternity patients in many parts of the country have to travel long distances because many obstetricians have stopped delivering babies. In upstate New York, seven counties

have no OB/GYNs. At Winter Park Memorial Hospital near Orlando, the number of surgeons willing to do emergency appendectomies and gall-bladder removals dropped from 14 in 2000 to zero in 2003, forcing the hospital to transfer to other facilities patients who required immediate treatment.

In a contest for plaintiff-friendly forums, Ohio is definitely in the running. In 2003, a jury in Ohio awarded $3.5 million to the family of a man who died of a heart attack, claiming that the man's doctor failed to help the man lose weight and quit smoking.

The target of a malpractice suit can also have a significant impact upon the jury:

> Trial Lawyers, Inc.'s medical-malpractice operations today include suits against not only individual doctors but also health-care facilities such as hospitals, nursing homes, and clinics. Juries tend to have less sympathy for what they perceive to be impersonal, faceless institutions. Accordingly, hospitals lose over half of malpractice cases—doctors lose only one-third—and the average compensation in suits against hospitals is over $6 million, a healthy 225 percent more than the average verdict against doctors.

Just to keep things in proper perspective, here are a few statistics[13] from research performed in 2001:

1. Fewer than one-half of 1% of the nation's doctors face any serious state sanctions each year.

2. Harvard researchers found that 1% of a representative sample of patients treated in New York State hospitals in 1984 were injured, and one-quarter of those died, because of medical negligence. Nationwide, that would have translated to 234,000 injuries and 80,000 deaths in 1988 from negligence in American hospitals.

3. A similar study conducted in California in 1974 found

that 0.8% of hospital patients had either been injured by negligence in the hospital or had been hospitalized because of negligent care.

5. An in-depth interview with 53 family physicians revealed that 47% of the doctors recalled a case in which the patient died due to physician error. Only four of the total reported errors led to malpractice suits, and none of these errors resulted in an action by a peer review organization.

12. Just 5.1 percent of doctors account for 54.2 percent of the malpractice payouts, according to data from the National Practitioner Data Bank. Of the 35,000 doctors who have had two or more malpractice payouts since 1990, only 7.6 percent of them have been disciplined. And only 13 percent of doctors with five medical malpractice payouts have been disciplined.

13. Between 44,000 and 98,000 people die in hospitals annually each year due to preventable medical errors.

14. While medical costs have increased by 113 percent since 1987, the amount spent on medical malpractice insurance has increased by just 52 percent over that time.

More recent data can be found at Wikipedia[14] :

1. No single medical condition was associated with more than five percent of all negligence claims, and one-third of all claims were the result of misdiagnosis.[15]

2. A recent study by Healthgrades found that an average of 195,000 hospital deaths in each of the years 2000, 2001 and 2002 in the U.S. were due to potentially preventable medical errors.... The Zahn and Miller study supported the Institute of Medicine's (IOM) 1999 report conclusion, which found that medical errors caused up to 98,000 deaths annually and should be considered a national epidemic.[16]

3. A 2006 follow-up to the 1999 Institute of Medicine study found that medication errors are among the most common medical mistakes, harming at least 1.5 million people every year.

4. Most (73%) settled malpractice claims involve medical error. A 2006 study published in the *New England Journal of Medicine* concluded that claims without evidence of error "are not uncommon, but most [72%] are denied compensation. The vast majority of expenditures [54%] go toward litigation over errors and payment of them. The overhead costs of malpractice litigation are exorbitant." ... Claims not associated with errors accounted for 13 to 16% of the total costs. For every dollar spent on compensation, 54 cents went to administrative expenses (including lawyers, experts, and courts). Claims involving errors accounted for 78 percent of administrative costs.

5. According to the American Medical Association, defensive medicine increases health systems costs by between $84 and $151 billion each year. Studies place the direct and indirect costs of malpractice between 5% and 10% of total U.S. medical costs.[17]

We have more than tripled our investment in health care over the past fifty years, but we cannot point to a specific cause. Insurance administrative costs have risen from 6% to 16% of your premium, malpractice insurance for doctors and medical facilities has gone up 500%, tort litigation has risen 300%, and tort costs per U.S. citizen have skyrocketed approximately 800% (all of these figures are adjusted for inflation). But those numbers make only a slight dent in the overall increase.

Regardless of our tripled and quadrupled health-care costs, we have serious issues concerning the increasing unwillingness

of the medical profession to provide care and the inefficient manner in which that care is provided. If you took your car in for an oil change and received an invoice for an engine overhaul, you wouldn't be happy. What if you are looking for someone to do an oil change, and no mechanic in the county is willing to touch your car for fear of reprisal? What did I tell you? MDs are Majorly Paranoid, and their goal now is to shield themselves from lawsuits!

Exhibit E[18]

Effect of Damage Caps and Insurance Reform on California Medical Malpractice Insurance 1975-2001

Source: The foundation for Taxpayer and Consumer Rights from National Assn. of Insurance Commissioners data

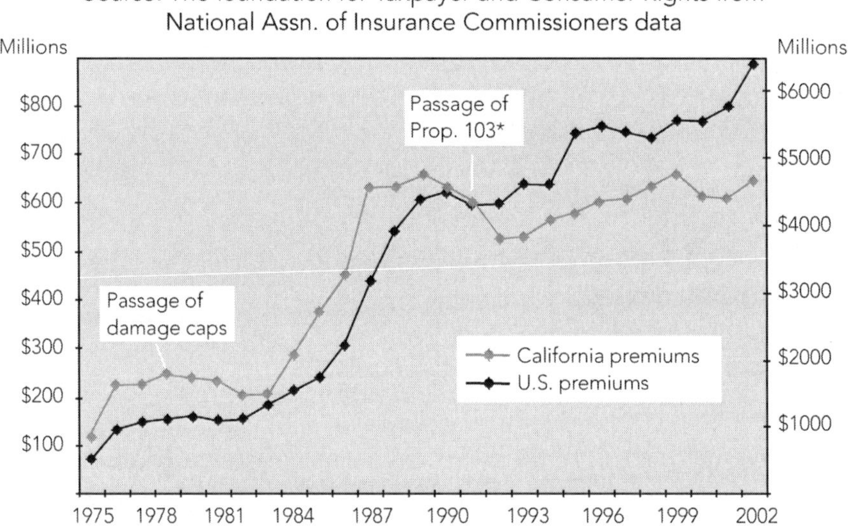

Proposition 103 was passed in 1989 by California voters to regulate insurance rates

What do you think highly skilled doctors are doing in response to this attack? I have to look to *The Beverly Hillbillies* theme song for reference: "Said Californy is the place you oughta be, so they loaded up the truck and they moved to Beverly. Hills, that is, swimmin' pools, movie stars."[19] Observe exhibit E and

see what a difference a little legislation makes in California!

Legislation that caps damages will let doctors and their insurance carriers breathe easier, and it can be an invitation for the better practitioners to move to the friendlier states.

California isn't the only state to catch on! Other legislatures have seen fit to address the dilemma by giving doctors and medical care facilities a little bit of breathing room. Just look at the maps in exhibits F and G.

Exhibit F [20]

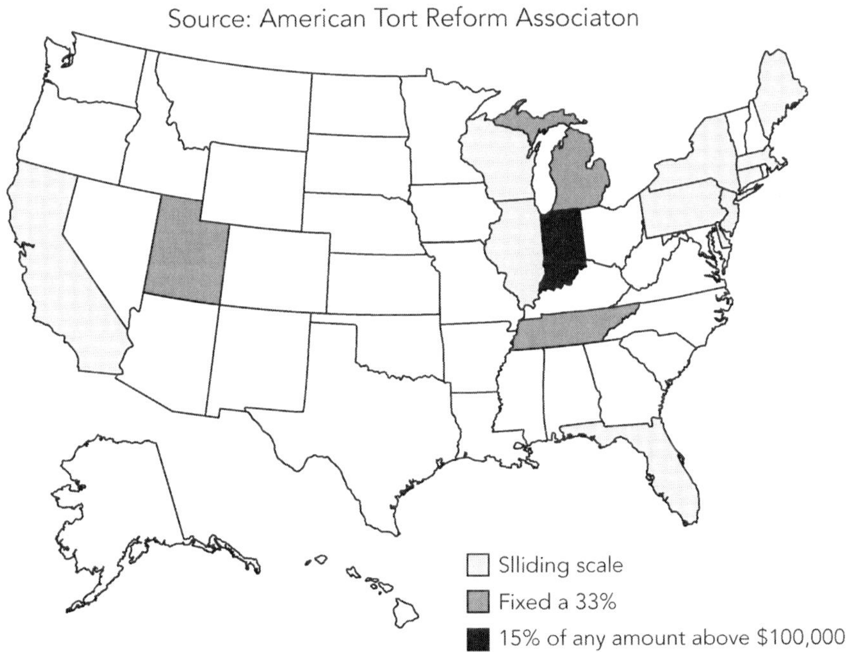

Exhibit G [21]

The real problem is that this legislation is just scratching the

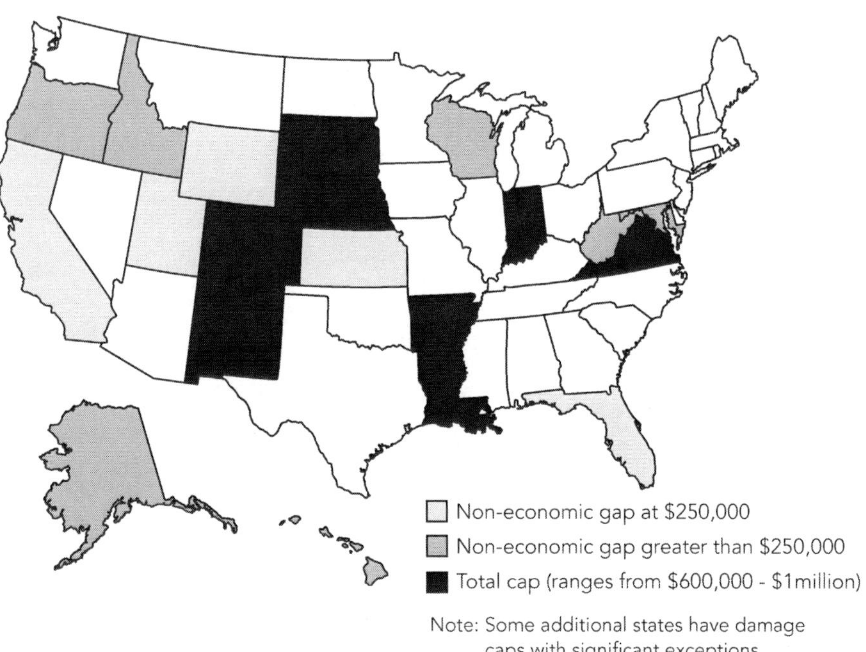

Caps on Damages for Medical Malpractice

Source: U.S. Congress, "Impact of Legal Reforms on Medical Malpractice Costs" 1993, updated with data from American Tort Reform Association

surface. I would like to make a few suggestions:

1. Plaintiffs and plaintiff's counsel have absolutely no responsibility to the courts or to our system of justice. If we were able to establish a preliminary hearing, similar to criminal litigation, as the first step in bringing a medical-malpractice lawsuit, it would have the effect of weeding out those cases that do not have a solid factual basis. If the plaintiff were not able to satisfy the required burden of proof at the hearing, that would not necessarily force dismissal of the lawsuit, but it would require that the plaintiff or plaintiff's counsel post a bond sufficient to cover the costs incurred by the defendant in defending against a frivolous claim.

2. If a doctor performs acceptably according to current medical standards but is not successful in performing a miracle, that doctor shouldn't be punished.

3. Damages for medical-malpractice cases must be limited to what is reasonable. If a person who is not otherwise insured pursues a claim against an emergency room, for example; those damages must be limited to actual damages. And the only way to pursue anything further would require proof that the doctor or medical facility has committed some specific error and is actually responsible for malpractice. But even those damages must have limitations, unless one can demonstrate malice or recklessness.

4. We are acutely aware of the exorbitant costs of emergency-room service.[22] Treating the uninsured population—a quandary that will be addressed later in this chapter—is costing us billions of dollars each year. Paying patients and taxpayers are footing the bill for Cadillac care for the uninsured. One practical way to address this issue is to establish an annex for all emergency-care facilities that will divert patients to nurse practitioners when full hospital care isn't warranted.

5. Please, don't get angry! Government health care is *not* the solution (which I will also discuss later), but we do need to make sure that everyone is covered by a program that will provide the necessary care. People with consistent need for government universal health care will be classified as "uninsured" for the purpose of pursuing malpractice claims, but they will be able to access treatment in accordance with our moral and ethical obligations. We already have Medicare, Medicaid, and the State Children's Health Insurance Program (SCHIP) available on the federal level, and many states have their own systems in place. Arizona provides the Arizona Health Care Cost Containment System

(AHCCCS). This is the only rational alternative to "Obamacare," and if we are willing to tighten our belts, we will have better care available at a much lower cost.

6. We need legislation to ensure that health insurance is uniformly available across state lines. This is another example of the free-market system and the law of supply and demand. When insurance companies compete against each other, we win with lower rates!

Who Really Is Uninsured?

This sounds like an easy question to answer, *unless* you want to use statistics to make a point. I have accessed many sources for this data, and although there is a propensity for them all to be in the same ballpark at the beginning, the consistency erodes when you try to break it all down. Health-care-reform advocates are screaming that 45.7 million Americans are uninsured to coerce us into believing that government-run health care is the only solution. Let me break that down logically.

According to the U.S. Department of Health and Human Services, the U.S. population in 2007 was estimated to be 302 million people.[23] FactCheck.org and the Business and Media Institute researched the uninsured portion of our population, whose statistics I am relying on, but I will include other supportive data sources as well. It should be noted that the government's calculation of the uninsured by the Centers for Disease Control and Prevention describes this segment in 2007 as only 43.1 million people, and 43.8 million in 2008.[24] However, I am going to use the 45.7 million figure for 2007 referenced by health-care-reform advocates because I want to use the worst possible scenario to make the point.

According to FactCheck.org, 26% of the uninsured are eligible for some form of public insurance coverage (federal, state, or local), and 21% are immigrants.[25] We have no statistics to break down the classification for immigrants into legal or illegal, but this may or may not be relevant, because Obamacare is intended to apply to all "Americans" including legal or illegal aliens.. This is a particular fault in the law that is likely to cost our government billions of dollars, but I hope that's a bridge we will never have to cross.

According to the Business and Media Institute, 19% of the uninsured (approximately 8.74 million people) have annual family incomes greater than $75,000, and another 18% (8.3 million people) have annual family incomes between $50,000 and $75,000.[26] Now let's see: This means 26% are eligible for existing public insurance coverage, 21% are immigrants, 19% have incomes greater than $75,000 per year, and 18% have incomes between $50,000 and $75,000. That adds up to 84% of the uninsured population who currently have coverage available to them or who are otherwise ineligible for Obamacare. That leaves a remainder of 16% of our population of uninsureds, or approximately 7,312,000 people. Bear in mind that this 16% includes those who are "temporarily" uninsured because of unemployment, recent graduation from school, and the young and healthy who don't believe they need insurance, which the U.S. Census Bureau estimates to be 18.3 million people.[27]

Some of the people described above can fall into more than one category. If we add some cushion to account for the overlaps, we are really looking at a maximum of about 10 million chronically uninsured people in America. Does it make any sense to enact a government health-care plan estimated to cost well over a trillion dollars in the next ten years, forcing American taxpayers to cough up at least $100,000 per uninsured person?

Almost a quarter of patients needing operations such as hip or knee replacements wait between one and two years for surgery and a small number wait more than this, new calculations of the real waiting times showed yesterday.

Across all the specialties the real waiting time from seeing a GP to treatment shows that one patient in seven waits more than a year.... By the end of 2008 the maximum waiting time should be 18 weeks.... This is the "referral to treatment" time....

Andy Burnham, the health minister, giving a first report yesterday on the drive towards the 18-week target, said that progress has been made through the year but trusts still faced a big challenge....

The figures show that most specialities treat between 30 and 50 per cent of in-patients within 18 weeks. In trauma and orthopaedics the figure is only 20 per cent.[41]

I don't want to berate England. I love and respect one of our greatest allies. One of the best times in my life was when I lived in London as part of my legal education. I pray that England's health-care system will greatly improve, but I honestly believe that Great Britain would be better off converting its system to what we have.

Daniel Hannan, a member of parliament for the European Community, appeared on the *Glenn Beck Program* on March 26, 2009. At the end of the interview—which had nothing to do with health care—Mr. Beck asked an open question: "So Daniel, what is your best advice here?"

Yeah, you should learn from our [Britain's] mistakes. I mean, the single biggest area where I could see you making this mistake is on this thing of the nationalized health care system. I mean, I hope that sanity is going to prevail. I know it's been kicked around before and it hasn't happened. I love my country even more than I love yours, you know, but ... I would love to get rid of our system

We could save hundreds of billions of dollars by just putting them all on Blue Cross and Blue Shield, Cigna, or just about any other group plan. Please remember: the "secret" to the resolution of our health-care crisis is in the data provided in exhibit A.

I believe in telling "the whole truth and nothing but the truth." Any reader who wants to conduct a more in-depth study of this subject can review a Kaiser Commission study, which states that the number of nonelderly people who were uninsured in 2005 reached 46.1 million.[28] In addition, please refer to a Dubay, Holahan, and Cook study that estimated 80% of the uninsured are currently eligible for public health-insurance coverage (Medicare, Medicaid, or SCHIP) or live in families with incomes above 300% of the federal poverty level (FPL).[29]

A Look at Government-Run Health Care

Medicare was the beginning of government dominance in any health-care market. The program was enacted in 1965, and its history provides us with an overview of what to expect with a universal health-care system. Back in 1993, *Reason* magazine published an article that we must reflect on if we're going to consider this alternative:

> At its start, in 1966, Medicare cost $3 billion. The House Ways and Means Committee estimated that Medicare would cost only about $12 billion by 1990 (a figure that included an allowance for inflation). This was a supposedly "conservative" estimate. But in 1990 Medicare actually cost $107 billion.

> The 1992 annual report of the Federal Hospital Insurance Trust Fund, which pays for the hospital-insurance portion of Medicare, warns that the Medicare program "is severely out of financial balance" and could go bust as soon as the year 2000. The report says expenditures from the hospital fund represented *1.3% of the nation's gross domestic product in 1991 and will grow to 4.7%*

by 2065. To cover the cost, the Medicare payroll-tax rate will have to more than quadruple, from the current rate of 2.9% to 13.79%. (emphasis added)[30]

Government health care advocates laughed at this article when it was published. But no one is laughing now. Let's look at the 2008 Annual Report of the Boards of Trustees of the Federal Hospital Insurance and Federal Supplementary Medical Insurance Trust Funds directed to the Honorable Nancy Pelosi and the Honorable Richard B. Cheney. Does anything look familiar?

The HI trust fund is not adequately financed over the next 10 years under the intermediate assumptions. From the beginning of 2008 to the end of 2017, the assets of the HI trust fund are projected to decrease from $326 billion to $96 billion, which would be far less than the recommended minimum level of 1 year's expenditures....

Under the intermediate assumptions the HI trust fund is *projected to be exhausted in 2019.*

The HI annual cost rate *is projected to increase from 3.11 percent of taxable payroll in 2007 to 11.40 percent in 2082*—8.02 percent of taxable payroll more than the projected income rate for 2082. Expressed in relation to the projected Gross Domestic Product (GDP), HI cost is estimated to rise from the *current level of 1.5 percent of GDP to 4.8 percent in 2082.* (emphasis added)[31]

That same annual report supplied the graph shown in exhibit H, illustrating the impending doom of the nation's Medicare account.

Exhibit H

Figure II.D1. Medicare Financial Outlook
Figure II.D1.—Medicare Expenditures as a Percentage of the Gross Domestic Product

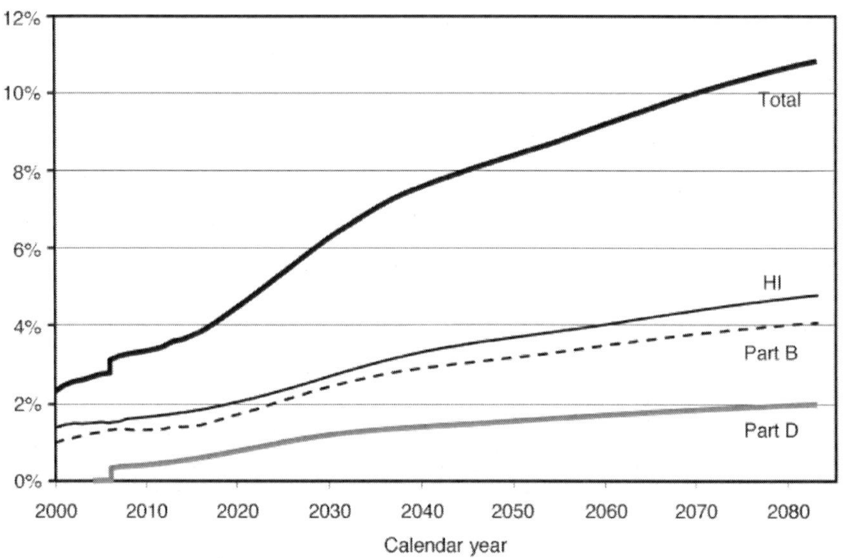

Of course, our version of universal health care, known as "Medicaid," is heralded as a technological marvel of efficiency:

> Investigators are trying to staunch a flood of Medicaid scams bleeding New York dry, including bills for unneeded prosthetic eyeballs, services for patients long dead and prenatal care—for men... . The *Post* has learned that, on the Upper West Side, unlicensed eye-care "specialist" Jeanne Prosper allegedly blindsided the Medicaid program by filing $1.2 million in fraudulent bills. Prosper, affiliated with supplier Fried & Kohler, claimed she provided hundreds of visually impaired customers with prosthetic eyes, costing $2,000 apiece. But Medicaid Inspector General James Sheehan's office said most of the customers had a good set of eyes—and didn't need or get an artificial one.

Investigators decided to take a closer look when Medicaid bills from Prosper skyrocketed from $75,000 to $600,000 over a two-year period. "Some of the customers we talked to had both of their eyes and had never heard of Prosper," said Michael Little, the deputy medical inspector based in New York City.

In Brooklyn, dentist Yuri Krainov was yanked from the Medicaid program after billing the state for patients he hadn't seen in years, the Inspector General's Office said.

Owners of nursing homes also have been caught billing the state for use of their Lexuses or Mercedes-Benzes, the office said. "It just seems to me that a pharmacist should know if his patient is dead or not," Sheehan said. "There are a lot of patients in New York who are getting treated when they're dead."[32]

Perhaps the federal government's management of Medicare and Medicaid are poor examples. Let's take a look at the universal health-care "pilot" program in Massachusetts as discussed in the *Boston Globe*:

More people are seeking care in hospital emergency rooms, and the cost of caring for ER patients has soared 17 percent over two years.... Visits to Massachusetts emergency rooms grew 7 percent between 2005 and 2007, to 2,469,295 visits. The estimated cost of treating those patients ... jumped from $826 million to $973 million.

"Just because you have insurance doesn't mean there's a [primary care] physician who can see you," said Dr. Sandra Schneider, vice president of the American College of Emergency Physicians.

[According to Dr. Peter Smulowitz, an emergency-room physician at Beth Israel Deaconess Medical Center,] "We have to pay primary care doctors what they're worth and increase the network for primary care from doctors and other providers.... It's going to take a lot of money up front to change this. But do we have any other choice?" [33]

Maybe a state's handling of universal health care isn't the best example either. Michael Moore made the movie *SiCKO*, lauding the high-quality universal health-care system in Cuba. Following is an excerpt of the interview John Stossel conducted with Moore:

> This isn't just me saying this, you know. All the world health organizations or whatever have confirmed that if there's one thing they do right in Cuba, it's health care," Moore said. "And there's very little debate about that."

> In fact, there is plenty of debate. Miami-based Cuban Human Rights activist Jose Carro says Moore's movie paints an inaccurate picture. "These films that try to portray the health care system as superior to that of the U.S. are lacking in truth," Carro said. He asserts that most hospitals for Cuban citizens are dilapidated, that conditions are filthy and that patients are so neglected that some are starving.

> George Utset, who runs the anti-Castro website called therealcuba. com, says Moore's group didn't "go to the hospital for regular Cubans. They go to the hospital for the elite and it's [a] very different condition."[34]

So far, we are not having much luck finding a national health care system to idolize. Perhaps we should take a tour of the world's national/universal health-care systems. They have national health care in England. How are they doing?

> In October, Rocky Fernandez was told he might not live to Christmas. Suffering from kidney cancer that had spread to his lungs, his doctor wanted to prescribe him Sutent, a relatively new cancer drug. But Fernandez hit a roadblock.

> The agency that tells the British government which treatments are worth paying for had decided last year that Sutent—at 3,500 pounds ($5,160) a month—was too costly to be offered free under the national health care system. ...

"Many people might not understand why we want drugs that can only give you an extra three, six or 18 months," Fernandez said. "But for some families, that can make all the difference."

Had he been in the U.S., Fernandez, 45, would likely have gotten the drug much sooner—though he might have had to pay for part of it depending on whether he had health insurance and what type of coverage.[35]

We must assume that was an isolated case:

When Bruce Hardy's kidney cancer spread to his lung, his doctor recommended an expensive new pill from Pfizer. But Mr. Hardy is British, and the British health authorities refused to buy the medicine. His wife has been distraught.

"Everybody should be allowed to have as much life as they can," Joy Hardy said in the couple's modest home outside London. If the Hardys lived in the United States or just about any European country other than Britain, Mr. Hardy would most likely get the drug, although he might have to pay part of the cost. A clinical trial showed that the pill, called Sutent, delays cancer progression for six months at an estimated cost of $54,000.

"It's hard to know that there is something out there that could help but they're saying you can't have it because of cost," said Ms. Hardy, who now speaks for her husband of 45 years. *"What price is life?"* (emphasis added)[36]

Great Britain's Health Care agency is the National Institute for Health and Clinical Excellence (NICE) and officials there decide whether to make the necessary investment for any citizen's treatment. The rule is that six months of a person's life is worth no more than £15,000, or about $22,750. Government health officials in Austria, Brazil, Columbia and Thailand are taking notice of these policies. "All the middle-income countries—in

Eastern Europe, Central and South America, the Middle East and all over Asia—are aware of NICE and are thinking about setting up something similar," said Dr. Andreas Seiter, a senior health specialist at the World Bank.[37]

Time for a Mulligan. If you've ever played golf with me you know that Mr. Mulligan and I are best of friends. If you look at these articles concerning universal health care in Great Britain and elsewhere, you will find that I'm editing out some praise and favorable comparisons to American health care. The reason for this is not to provide skewed information to readers but to avoid confusing you with conflicting information that isn't relevant to the issues. All of what I provide here is factual, at least according to the media that provides it. My purpose is to enlighten you concerning the realities of universal health care so that you can reflect upon this system as an alternative to the health-care system we currently enjoy.

I believe the best solution available to the U.S. will include all of the benefits available in any other health-care system without the burdens of rationing and long waits for necessary treatment. This solution requires some changes to our health-care system that will stimulate personal control over the costs without limiting access to the health-care facilities and medication each of us needs.

Coverage for the cost of treatment isn't the only thing you wait for in Great Britain:

> A patient with severe back pain waited nine hours 11 minutes for paramedics to show up in London. The ambulance trust blamed a lack of vehicles. Many of the slowest responses occurred over the 2007/2008 New Year period, when paramedics had to deal with thousands of drunken revellers and an upsurge in flu and breathing problems.

> There was massive variation across the country in the slowest
> response time for a category-A case. In the North West it was just
> 38 minutes, but in East Midlands, the longest response took two
> hours and 34 minutes, and in Wales, three hours and 47 minutes—
> the suspected poisoning case.
>
> Critics blamed the failures on Labour's strict four-hour waiting
> time for hospital accident and emergency units.
>
> The figures, from 2007/08, also showed that some "category-B"
> patients—those with illnesses that need urgent hospital treatment
> but are not life-threatening—are waiting as long as nine hours
> before help arrives, even though trusts are supposed to attend 95
> per cent of such calls within 19 minutes. [38]

British law requires that patients be admitted within four hours
of being dropped off at a health care facility to avoid costly
penalties. When the facility is busy—and the fact is that most
emergency facilities are like a busy airport on Christmas Eve—
patients wait in line in ambulances in the hospital driveway for
hours. The ambulance time doesn't count against the admission
clock. It also ties up the ambulance and prevents it from
attending to another person's needs.

When I was a teenager, I worked for Jack in the Box and was
on a New Year's Eve shift with a very small staff. The entire
Western world was waiting for a Jumbo Jack in our drive-
through, but we only asked if they wanted fries with the order,
not blood plasma.

You've likely heard the adage "cleanliness is next to godliness."
Isn't that a universal standard? Let's look at another example
in which hospitals in Britain are creatively cutting costs in
disturbing ways:

> Cleaners at an NHS hospital with a poor record on superbugs have
> been told to turn over dirty sheets instead of using fresh ones

between patients to save money. Housekeeping staff at Good Hope Hospital in Sutton Coldfield, have been asked to re-use sheets and pillowcases wherever possible to cut a £500,000 pound [roughly $750,000] laundry bill. Posters in the hospital's linen cupboards and on doors into the A&E department remind workers that each item costs 0.275 pence to wash. Good Hope reported a deficit of 6 million pounds last year and was subject to a report by the audit commission because of its poor financial standing…. .

Tony Field, chairman of Birmingham-based MRSA Support, said: "Is that all the safety of a patient's life is worth? 0.275 pence? It is utterly disgraceful and tantamount to murder because hygiene like changing sheets is essential to protect patients. It proves beyond all doubt that cost-cutting is directly contributing to hospital acquired infections." …

The scheme is one of many ways that cash-strapped trusts are trying to save money.[39]

Criminy! That's like pulling teeth!

People with toothaches are resorting to pulling their own teeth because they cannot find a NHS dentist, a study out today says. Almost a fifth of those questioned in the biggest patient survey of its kind said that they had missed out on dental work because of the cost. The research, involving more than 5,000 patients in England, also found that as many as six per cent had treated themselves because they could not find a dentist.

Some said they took out their own teeth or fixed broken crowns with glue. One person in Lancashire carried out 14 separate extractions with pliers. A researcher at a shopping centre in Liverpool met three separate people in one morning who had pulled out teeth themselves. Almost three fifths (58 per cent) of dentists said new contracts brought in last year had made the quality of care worse and 84 per cent thought the changes had failed to make it easier for patients to get an appointment. [40]

Time waits for no one …

and have something that puts patients in charge rather than putting doctors' unions and bureaucrats in charge. That's the single biggest thing.

More widely than that, you know, you can spend your money better than politicians can. You've got a better idea of what to do with it than governments have. You know, we have this thing for 10 years in the U.K. which is saying the current government that we've got. Of people feeling that it was kind of mean for us to think that. You know, if you said I don't want to pay any more tax, that was taken not as an intellectual critique of whether the government was better placed to spend the money than you were. It was taken as a sign that you didn't want to because you didn't care about the poor or, you know, you were greedy. And people who should have known better kind of got right along with that and talked themselves into this kind of wanting to wrap themselves in this great warm duvet of national solidarity. And, of course, the only beneficiaries of that are the state bureaucrats who take all of the money and laugh all of the way to the bank.[42]

Mr. Hannan went on to say, "You've got a great system there. Think long and hard before you toss it away."

England is certainly not the only place where the government runs a universal health-care plan. One of the most respected universal plans is in Canada, but even that system isn't perfect:

One Supreme Court decision may have done more to change health care in Canada than three major reports and a first ministers conference that ended with a $41-billion infusion into the system.

On June 9, 2005, the high court struck down a Quebec law that prohibited people from buying private health insurance to cover procedures already offered by the public system. "Access to a waiting list is not access to health care," two of the justices wrote in their decision.…

While most Canadians—80 per cent according to Statistics Canada—are satisfied with their access to the health care system,

many experience long waits to see a specialist, get diagnostic tests and undergo elective surgery. Others find themselves facing huge bills for prescription drugs they need to survive. A long wait for hip replacement surgery was what prompted the Quebec case that wound up before the Supreme Court.[43]

There is a great deal of supportive literature available for Canada's health-care system (I provide citations in the endnotes).[44] The best resource I have found to compare national health-care systems is from the Cato Institute entitled "The Grass Is Not Always Greener" by Michael Tanner:

> Critics of the U.S. health care system frequently point to other countries as models for reform. They point out that many countries spend far less on health care than the United States yet seem to enjoy better outcomes…. However, a closer look shows that nearly all health care systems worldwide are wrestling with problems of rising costs and lack of access to care. There is no single international model for national health care…. Still, overall trends from national health care systems around the world suggest the following:
>
> - Health insurance does not mean universal access to health care. In practice, many countries promise universal coverage but ration care or have long waiting lists for treatment. [See previous examples cited earlier]
>
> - Rising health care costs are not a uniquely American phenomenon. Although other countries spend considerably less than the United States on health care, both as a percentage of GDP and per capita, costs are rising almost everywhere, leading to budget deficits, tax increases, and benefit reductions.
>
> - In countries weighted heavily toward governmental control, people are most likely to face waiting lists, rationing, restrictions on physician choice, and other obstacles to care.
>
> - Countries with more effective national health care systems are successful to the degree that they incorporate market

mechanisms such as competition, cost sharing, market prices, and consumer choice, and eschew centralized government control.[45]

As I review these bullet points, they create the awful impression that the free market, capitalism, limited government involvement, and personal freedoms are good ways to foster a premium health-care environment. I recommend that readers access this article on the Web and e-mail it as an attachment to Barack Obama, Nancy Pelosi, and Harry Reid along with their pleasant (and respectful) correspondence requesting that our government officials think twice about what they're doing.

The article continues, "Health care spending is not necessarily bad. To a large degree, America spends money on health care because it is a wealthy nation and chooses to do so."[46] This fact can be clearly seen in exhibit I.

Exhibit I

Total Expenditure on Health Care as a Percentage of GDP

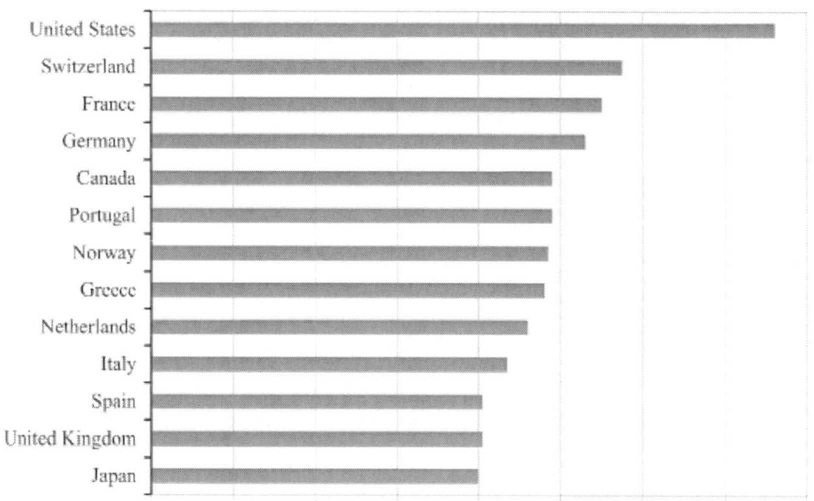

According to the Kaiser Family Foundation and Health Research and Educational Trust, average health insurance in 2007 cost $4,479 for an individual and $12,106 for a family per year.[47] Government health care programs, particularly Medicare and Medicaid, are amassing huge burdens of debt for future generations. Medicare has unfunded liabilities of more than $50 trillion. [See http://usdebtclock.org/.] At this rate, Medicaid spending will quadruple its share of federal spending over the next century.[48] The Health Care Reform Act (Obamacare) is touted to be a solution to the problem by virtue of a single-payer, national health care system.[49] Nevertheless, we have observed that countries with national health care systems have serious problems of their own, including rising costs, rationing of care, lack of access to modern medical technology, and poor health outcomes.

I again refer to the Cato Institute's "The Grass Is Not Always Greener:"[50]

> Numerous studies have attempted to compare the quality of health care systems. In most of these surveys, the United States fares poorly, finishing well behind other industrialized countries. This has led critics of the U.S. health care system to suggest that Americans pay more for health care but receive less.

> There are several reasons to be skeptical of these rankings. First, many choose areas of comparison based on the results they wish to achieve, or according to the values of the comparer. For example, *SiCKO* cites a 2000 World Health Organization study that ranks the U.S. health care system 37th in the world, "slightly better than Slovenia" (see exhibit J, "WHO Health Care Rankings").[51]

> This study bases its conclusions on such highly subjective measures as "fairness" and criteria that are not strictly related to a country's health care system, such as "tobacco control." For example, the WHO report penalizes the United States for not having a sufficiently progressive tax system, not providing all citizens with health

insurance, and having a general paucity of welfare programs. Indeed, much of the poor performance of the United States is due to its ranking of 54th in the category of fairness. The United States is actually penalized for adopting Health Savings Accounts and because, according to the WHO, patients pay too much out of pocket. Such judgments clearly reflect a particular political point of view, rather than a neutral measure of health care quality. Notably, the WHO report ranks the United States number one in the world in responsiveness to patients' needs in choice of provider, dignity, autonomy, timely care, and confidentiality.[52]

Exhibit J

Table 1
WHO Health Care Rankings

Country	Rank	Country	Rank
France	1	Switzerland	20
Italy	2	Belgium	21
San Marino	3	Colombia	22
Andorra	4	Sweden	23
Malta	5	Cyprus	24
Singapore	6	Germany	25
Spain	7	Saudi Arabia	26
Oman	8	United Arab Emirates	27
Austria	9	Israel	28
Japan	10	Morocco	29
Norway	11	Canada	30
Portugal	12	Finland	31
Monaco	13	Australia	32
Greece	14	Chile	33
Iceland	15	Denmark	34
Luxemburg	16	Dominica	35
Netherlands	17	Costa Rica	36
United Kingdom	18	United States	37
Ireland	19	Slovenia	38

Source: World Health Organization, "The World Health Report 2000" (Geneva: WHO, 2000).

The article goes on to say,

Difficulties even arise when using more neutral categories of comparison. Nearly all cross-country rankings use life expectancy as one measure. In reality though, life expectancy is a poor measure of a health care system. Life expectancies are affected by exogenous factors such as violent crime, poverty, obesity, tobacco and drug use, and other issues unrelated to health care… . Consider the nearly three-year disparity in life expectancy between Utah (78.7 years) and Nevada (75.9 years), despite the fact that the two states have essentially the same health care systems.[53] In fact, a study by Robert Ohsfeldt and John Schneider for the American Enterprise Institute found that those exogenous factors are so distorting that if you correct for homicides and accidents, the United States rises to the top of the list of life expectancy.[54]

In addition to all of this, we have the technical facilities and equipment to boot! As exhibit K indicates, in a country-by-country comparison of high-tech diagnostic equipment, the U.S. is the undisputed leader.[55]

Exhibit K
Figure 2
Number of MRI Units and CT Scanners per Million People

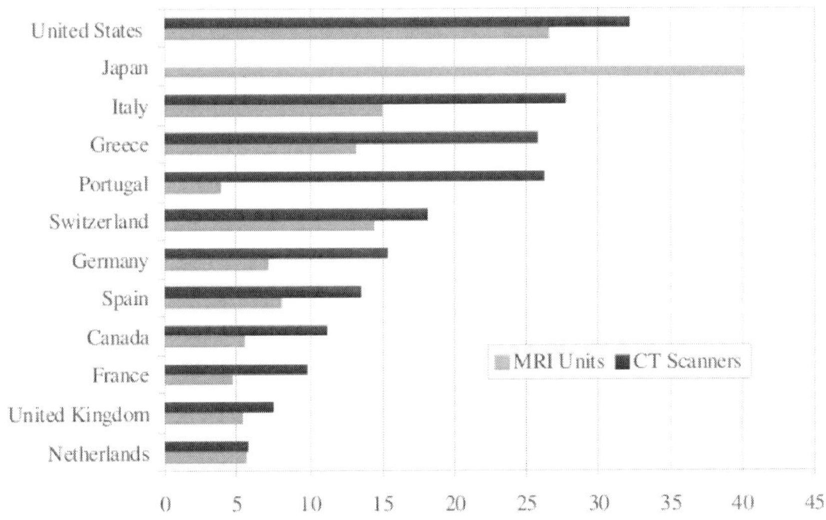

The article goes on to make several points regarding universal health-care systems in France, Canada, and many other European nations that we should take a look at, especially since many who favor governmental health care are lauding the French and Canadian systems. Let's examine the French system:

- The French health care system is the world's third most expensive, costing roughly 11 percent of GDP, behind only the United States (17 percent) and Switzerland (11.5 percent). Payroll taxes provide the largest source of funding. Employers must pay 12.8 percent of wages for every employee, while employees contribute an additional 0.75 percent of wages, for a total payroll tax of 13.55 percent. In addition, there is a 5.25 general social contribution tax on income (reduced to 3.95 percent on pension income and unemployment benefits). Thus, most French workers are effectively paying 18.8 percent of their income for health insurance.[56]

- In 2006, the [French] health care system ran a 10.3 billion euro deficit. This actually shows improvement over 2005, when the system ran an 11.6 billion euro deficit. The health care system is the largest single factor driving France's overall budget deficit.[57]

- More than 92 percent of French residents purchase complementary private insurance. In fact, private insurance now makes up roughly 12.7 percent of all health care spending in France, a percentage exceeded only by the Netherlands (15.2 percent) and the United States (35 percent) among industrialized countries.[58]

- Nongovernmental sources account for roughly 20 percent of all health care spending [in France], less than half the amount spent in the United States but still more than most countries with national health care systems.[59]

- Much of the burden for cost containment in the French system appears to have fallen on physicians. The average French doctor earns just 40,000 euros per year [$55,000] compared to $146,000 for primary care physicians and $271,000 for specialists in the United States.[60]

- More significantly, the [French] government has recently begun imposing restrictions on access to physicians.... The effect is both to lock patients into a choice of primary care physician and to establish a "gatekeeper" who limits access to specialists, tests, and some advanced treatment options.[61]

- Although the changes made so far do not amount to rationing, 62 percent of French citizens report that they "have felt the effects" of the new restrictions. Slightly less than half consider the waiting time between diagnosis and treatment to be acceptable.[62]

Wait a minute! "Slightly less than half" seems to imply that more than half find it unacceptable. The article then provides the final hint to my secret on a silver platter:

- [France's ability to hold down health care costs] is abetted by the French system's innovative response to one of the trickier problems bedeviling health-policy experts: an economic concept called "moral hazard." Moral hazard describes people's tendency to overuse goods or services that offer more marginal benefit without a proportionate marginal cost. Translated into English, you eat more at a buffet because the refills are free, and you use more health care because insurers generally make you pay up front in premiums, rather than at the point of care. The obvious solution is to shift more of the cost away from premiums and into co-pays or deductibles, thus increasing the sensitivity of consumers to the real cost of each unit of care they purchase.[63]

- The French system works in part because it has incorporated many of the characteristics that Michael Moore and other supporters of national health care dislike most about the U.S. system. France imposes substantial cost sharing on patients in order to discourage over-utilization, relies heavily on a relatively unregulated private insurance market to fill gaps in coverage, and allows consumers to pay extra for better or additional care, creating a two-tier system…. This is clearly not the commonly portrayed style of national health care.

Now let's break exhibit I ("Total Expenditure on Health Care as a percentage of GDP") down to its representative parts in exhibits L and M.[64]

Exhibit L

Figure 3
Percentage of Total Health Spending Paid by Government

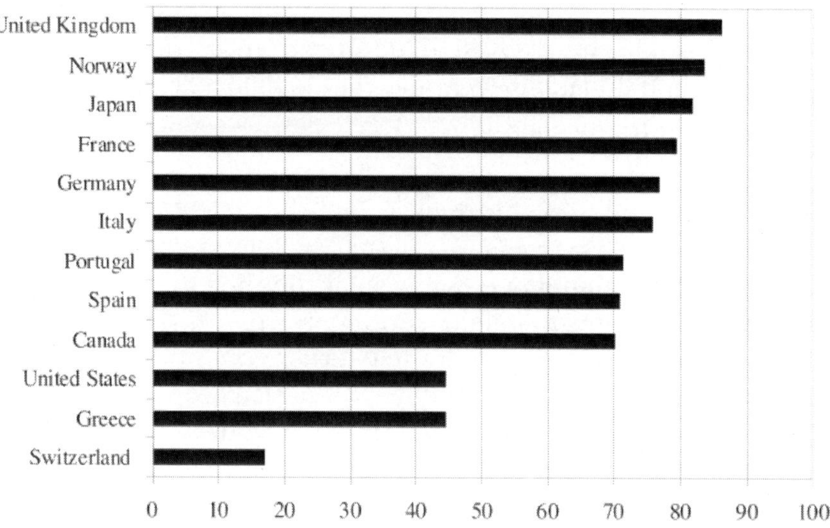

Exhibit M

Figure 4
Percentage of Total Health Spending Out of Pocket

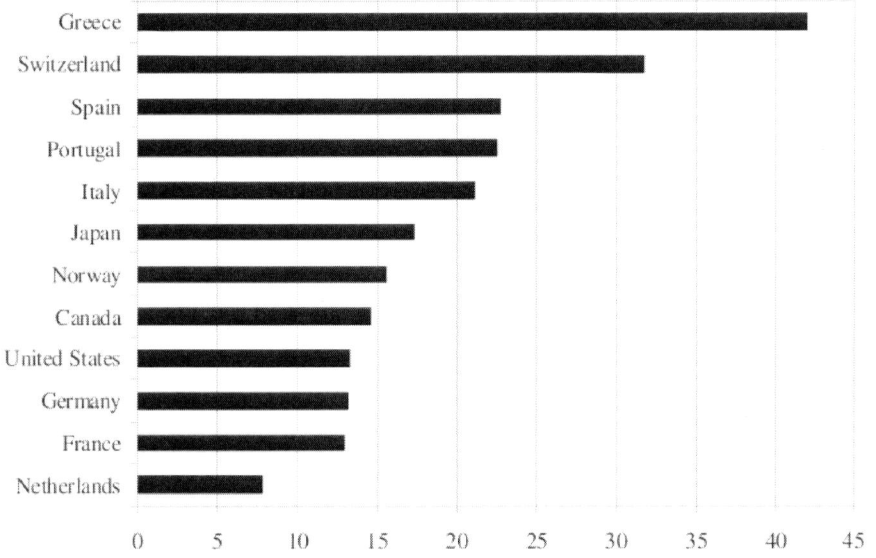

Source: OECD, "OECD Health Data 2007: Statistics and Indicators for 30 Countries."
Data for France from Simone Sandier, Valerie Paris, and Dominique Polton, *Health Care Systems in Transition: France*
(Copenhagen: European Observatory on Health Systems and Policies, 2004).
Data for Greece from the World Health Organization.

And now for the bottom line: if you break down the differences in sources of health-care spending from exhibit A and compare 1960 with 2008, you'll end up with the pie-chart results in exhibit N.

Healthcare Expenditures
1960 and 2008

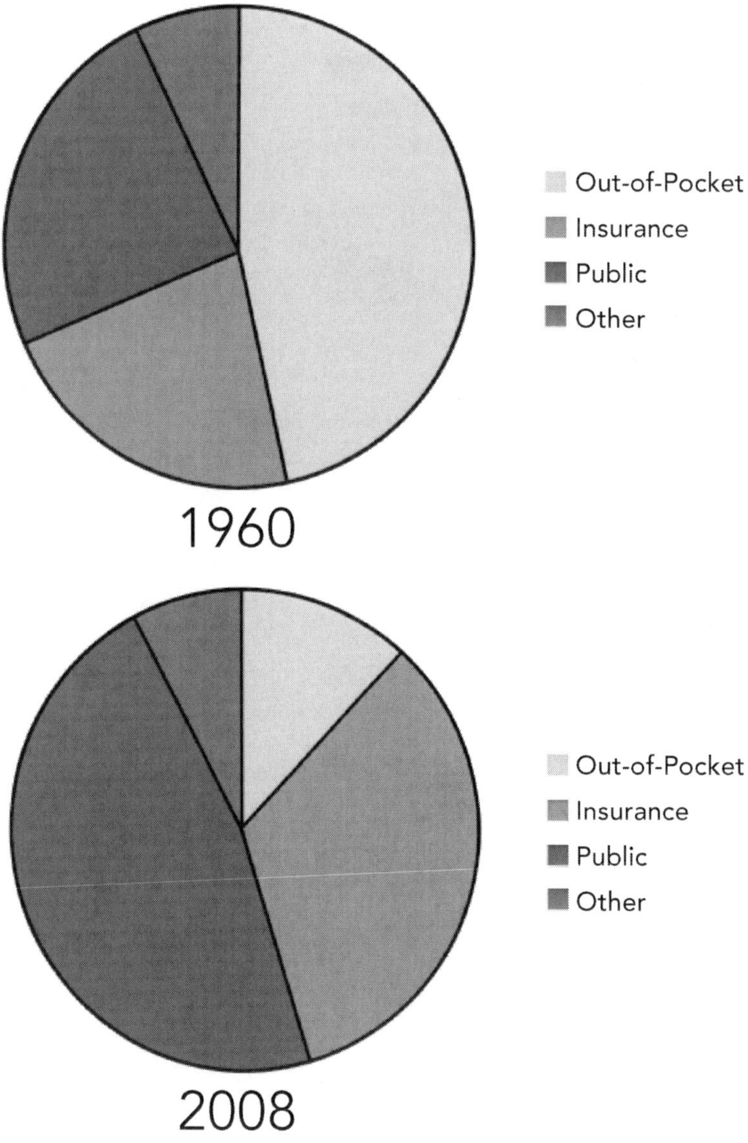

1960

2008

Out of the total per-person health-care costs of $148.00 in 1960, $69.25 (46.79%) was paid out of pocket, $31.75 (21.45%) by insurance, and $36.25 (24.49%) by the government. By 2008, health-care costs flipped so that $910.82 (11.86%) was out of pocket, $2,567 (33.42%) was paid by insurance, and $3,630 (47.26%) was paid by the government. If you have a calculator and see a gap, that is where "Other" fits in and accounts for $10.75 (7.26%) in 1960 and $573.00 (7.46%) in 2008.

We were paying almost half of our health-care costs *out of our pockets in 1960*, and now we are down to less than 12%. Insurance coverage, which we pay for up front and don't "feel the pain" of its contribution with each doctor's visit, is covering more than 150% of what it did in 1960. The administrative costs accounting for 13% of our premiums are just icing on the cake. And the government's coverage of expenses has almost doubled. Do you see a pattern?

The truth is, the United States enjoys the finest health-care system in the world, and it isn't cheap. Nevertheless, there are a number of ways we can save money *and* have better health insurance *without* any governmental entity involved. This goal is truly within our grasp if we can push the hopelessly confused ideologies out of the way. In December 2003, President Bush signed a health-care law that had two major components. The first component was the new Medicare prescription-drug benefit that has been widely labeled a disaster,[65] and the second was a new health-insurance option called Health Savings Accounts,[66] or HSAs, which became available in 2004.

Back to the Future

All right, pardon the pun, but it really fits: we need to go forward by going back to what we had fifty years ago, with or without a

DeLorean. Then, we were scrupulous and careful with the money we spent on health care *because we shelled it out of our own pockets.* We didn't call up Doc to make an appointment for a sniffly nose and then go in and slap down a $15 copay. A doctor's visit at that time meant $50 to $100, or more. From that standpoint, we are more inclined to be thrifty and not go for seconds, thirds, or fourths on the buffet line.

Let me share a personal example. My incredible wife, Joan, currently has a terrific Cigna HMO plan that costs $598 per month. That adds up to $7,176 per year, *and we have to cover copays and various percentages of this, that, and the other expense.* Guess what? She could get a plan from Cigna for $253 per month, which is $3,036 per year, and it will pay 100% of anything without a penny of co-pay or a portion of any expense. *But* she has to cover the first $5,000 of *any medical care* per year! That includes any expenses for dental care, medication, and so on. Give me a minute while I go pound my head against the nearest wall.

You see, in the long run there is a very slim chance that this plan could cost you a few more dollars, *but* the monthly premium is $345 less, medical savings go into a tax-free account, and the only way you could lose would be if your medical expenses for the year fall into a narrow wedge: the difference between $7,176 and $8,036. This could only happen if you don't see a dentist and you incur no copays or other medication expenses—which is factually impossible if you see the doctor at all. I think I need to find a new wall to pound my head against. You see, you are betting $860 of additional cost with the combined annual premium and deductible against the potential, practically guaranteed reward of the difference in annual premiums; up to $4,140. If you actually do incur significant medical expenses, that reward could be much greater because you are covered 100%!

But wait, there's more!

I alluded to it earlier, but I think I'd better pound it into your head now as well. On the high-deductible plan, you get to see *any doctor, dentist, or health-care provider.* You don't have to go by the provider's list that changes with every breath and get funneled through referrals, each of whom gets a cut of your copay. *You are in charge!* If that isn't worth the slim risk of spending an extra $860 per year to get Gucci treatment, then you can keep your HMO or PPO or whatever. My job is to help you overcome ignorance and apathy. What you do with this knowledge is up to you.

I'll be honest; there is a slight catch. *If* you incur medical expenses that cause you to tap into the 100% coverage for the rest of the year, then some policies will confine you to the doctors and/or facilities on the insurance company's list. But that may not apply if there is ongoing treatment. (I hope that's my last disclaimer for quite some time!)

Why are these numbers so skewed? Insurance companies rely on actuarial tables and use statistics to determine their rates, but they *always* have to factor in their own processing costs. If you cover the first $5,000, they have no costs. It seems to me that government-run health care would have some administrative costs too, don't you think?

The next thing we need to do is something that governmental officials rarely do. We have to think logically, objectively, intelligently, and a dozen or more adverbs that reflect well on one's mental capacity. We must look at the world of health care as something that isn't a void of mysterious nebula; we must look at it as a business. We must look for ways to accomplish things that others may not even consider. We must stand up for ourselves and *go shopping!*

You now have the ability to bargain for health care. Here are some great resources for your health care shopping: www. ehealthinsurance.com and http://healthcarebluebook.com. These Web sites will allow you to

- shop for insurance policies, and

- determine what is a reasonable fee for just about any medical procedure you may need. Insurance companies only pay certain percentages of the doctors' claims, often as low as 40%.

The National Center for Policy Analysis prepared a report packed with useful information. I will provide a condensed version here:

The market for medical care doesn't work like other markets. Providers typically do not disclose prices prior to treatment because they do not compete for patients based on price. Payments are usually not made by patients themselves but by third parties—employers, insurance companies or government. And the amounts paid are not really market-clearing prices; they are "reimbursement" rates negotiated with bureaucratic institutions and networks. Furthermore, when providers do not compete on price, they usually do not compete on quality either. In fact, in a very real sense, doctors and hospitals are not competing for patients at all—at least not in the way normal businesses compete for customers in regular markets.

This lack of competition for patients has a profound effect on the quality and cost of health care. Long before a patient enters a doctor's office, third-party bureaucracies have determined which medical services they will pay for, which ones they will not and how much they will pay. The result is a highly artificial market plagued by problems of high costs, inconsistent quality and poor access.

Can the market for medical care be different? Interestingly, in health-care markets where patients pay directly for all or most of their care, providers almost always compete on the basis of price and quality. And because they aren't trapped in a system that pays for predetermined tasks at predetermined rates, providers are free to repackage and reprice their services—just like vendors in other markets.[43]

Here are some examples:

Laboratory and diagnostic testing: Patients can order a limited range of blood tests and diagnostic procedures without a doctor's appointment and compare prices at different diagnostic testing facilities. Prices are 50 percent to 80 percent lower than identical tests performed in a hospital setting.

Price competition for drugs: Walmart became the first nationwide retailer to aggressively compete for buyers of generic drugs by charging a low, uniform price—ten dollars for a ninety-day supply.[68]

Price competition for drugs over the Internet: Rx.com was the first mail-order pharmacy to compete online in a national market for drugs.

Patient education for drugs as a product: DestinationRx. com is a pharmacy benefits-management company. In addition to operating an online mail-order drug delivery service, it also offers a Web site to help patients identify low-cost therapeutic substitutes to the drugs they currently take. In addition, the firm is partnering with Safeway supermarkets to install drug-comparison kiosks in store pharmacies.

Telephone-based practices: TelaDoc now has two million customers, paying for something that is almost impossible to get from a conventional general practitioner:

a telephone consultation. It offers patients access to a doctor at any time of day from any location. And because each on-call physician needs access to patients' medical histories (and the treatment decisions of previous physicians), personal and portable EMRs (electronic medical records) are a necessary part of the company's business model. The physicians prescribe drugs electronically, facilitating the use of safety-enhancing software that checks for harmful interactions.[69]

If we spend a little time and effort to learn what is available, we have an opportunity to have Cadillac care for the price of a 1972 Nissan B210 rusty hatchback. Rather than shelling out ever-increasing payments for our medical-insurance policy, we need to keep the money and spend it frugally. Insurance and all of its administrative expenses come in only as a last resort.

Whoa, whoa, whoa, wait a minute! What if you, a private American citizen, just so happen to be insured by your employer, like 49.76% of insureds in the U.S. in 2008, while 18.68% are insured by their government employer (which can also use this alternative and save billions!) and 31.58% are self-insured?[70] What about all of those people who aren't insured and are therefore part of our government's obligations because they work for a small company that can't afford insurance? Step into my office.

> You: Can my boss convert our group-insurance plan to one of these Health Savings Accounts, or start up a new group plan if the company doesn't have employee health insurance, and save the business money?

> Common Sense Judge (CSJ): Yes and no. Yes, it can be done, and under any circumstance it will save everyone money—with the exception that the insurance

companies' administrative costs and profits will drop like cannonballs—and the only "no" part of it is essentially in Congress's lap. Congress needs to stimulate the efficiency of group-insurance benefits for employers to be able to provide the insurance with little pain in the pocketbook.

You: How will that work?

CSJ: Your boss can negotiate a plan with just about any insurance company that will provide 100% insurance coverage after at least the first $1,150 in medical costs per person or $2,300 per family per year, with upper limits of $5,800 and $11,600, respectively.[71] The rates will be significantly lower than a full plan, and the money that would go into a full plan will be deposited into each employee's tax-free Health Savings Account, earning tax-free interest. Once each account balance reaches $3,000 for an individual or $5,950 for a family *per year*, the employer can stop putting money into the account and boost the employee's salary or include the excess as a bonus or whatever. But in the long run, your boss saves money, you save money, and you and your family are fully covered.

You: Why hasn't that been done yet?

CSJ: Insurance companies have a huge team of lobbyists that spend *portions of your premiums* to entertain legislators and contribute to their campaign funds so that they do things that will boost the companies' profit margins at your expense.

You: That doesn't sound fair.

CSJ: I agree—which is why I urge you to be well educated about the political candidates' records and intentions when you cast your ballot this November.

Now let's turn to the subject of employer-sponsored health insurance (ESI). Unfortunately, one of the best tickets to saving our system of health care is losing ground. Let's allow the Economic Policy Institute to explain:

> The share of Americans under age 65 with employment-based coverage continued to erode for the eighth year in a row from 62.9% covered in 2007 to 61.9% covered in 2008, a total fall of 6.4 percentage points since 2000... . Employer-sponsored health insurance (ESI) remains the predominant source of coverage for Americans under 65. Increasing public insurance coverage, particularly among children, is the only reason the uninsured rate did not rise one-for-one with losses in ESI... . The declines in coverage in 2008 can be attributed in part to the start of the recession. Unfortunately, these losses are likely only the tip of the iceberg for what is to come in 2009.[72]

Exhibit O illustrates the recent history of ESI.

Exhibit O

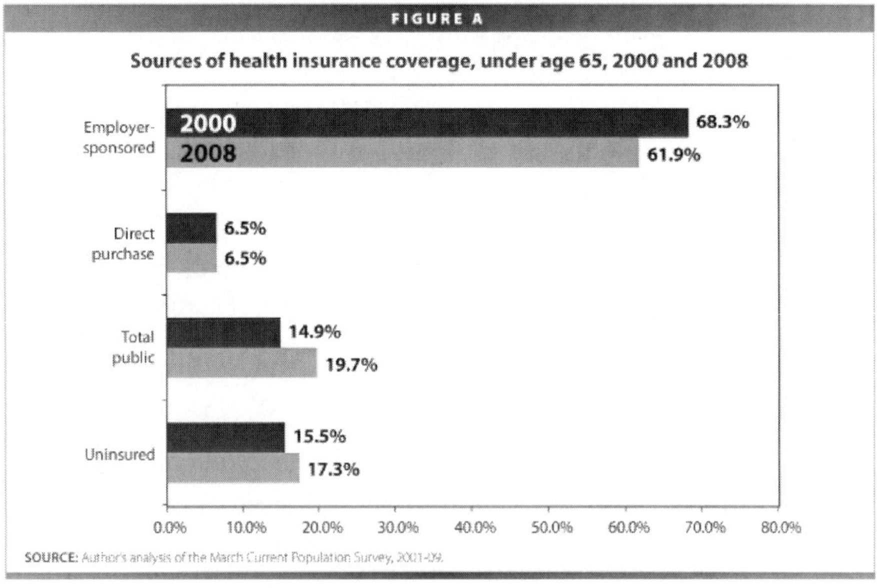

As can be seen, everything is going in the wrong direction. Even if we break it down demographically in exhibit P:

Exhibit P

TABLE 1			

Employer-sponsored health insurance coverage for entire under-65 population, 2000-08

				Percentage-point change
	2000	*2007*	*2008*	*2000-08*
Under 65 population	68.3%	62.9%	61.9%	-6.4
Age				
0-17	65.9%	59.5%	58.9%	-7.0
18-24	53.5	48.4	46.9	-6.6
25-54	72.9	66.8	65.7	-7.3
55-64	68.1	67.8	66.8	-1.3
Gender				
Male	68.2%	62.5%	61.4%	-6.9
Female	68.3	63.2	62.3	-6.0
Race				
White, non-Hispanic	75.6%	70.8%	69.8%	-5.8
Black	56.1	51.6	50.2	-5.9
Hispanic	45.8	41.4	41.4	-4.5
Other	64.3	61.7	60.8	-3.5
Nativity				
Native	70.4%	65.1%	63.9%	-6.5
Foreign born	52.2	47.4	47.1	-5.0
Education*				
Less than high school	39.0%	30.1%	29.7%	-9.3
High school	65.6	56.4	55.2	-10.5
Some college	73.3	67.0	64.8	-8.5
College	83.5	80.0	79.6	-3.9
Post-college	87.6	85.8	86.2	-1.5
Household income fifth				
Lowest	28.7%	21.9%	19.9%	-8.8
Second	61.7	53.6	50.4	-11.3
Middle	77.4	71.6	71.0	-6.3
Fourth	85.6	81.9	81.6	-4.0
Highest	88.4	86.4	86.4	-2.0

* Education reflects own education for individuals 18 and over and reflects family head's education for children under 18.

SOURCE: Author's analysis of the March Current Population Survey, 2001-09.

The final column shows that decreases are across the board for the entire under sixty-five population. What if we limit the data just to workers, as shown in exhibit Q?

Exhibit Q

TABLE 2

Employer-sponsored health insurance coverage for all workers, 2000-08

	2000	2007	2008	Percentage-point change 2000-2008
All workers	74.8%	71.0%	70.3%	-4.6
Gender				
Male	73.9%	69.4%	68.4%	-5.5
Female	75.8	72.9	72.1	-3.7
Race				
White, non-Hisp.	79.6%	76.4%	75.5%	-4.1
Black	68.3	65.6	64.4	-4.0
Hispanic	53.4	50.0	49.8	-3.6
Other	70.6	69.5	68.8	-1.8
Nativity				
Native	77.4%	74.1%	73.1%	-4.3
Foreign Born	58.7	54.0	53.9	-4.8
Education				
High school	71.8%	65.5%	64.4%	-7.4
College	85.3	82.7	82.1	-3.2
Wage quintiles*				
Lowest	49.3%	45.0%	42.7%	-6.6
Second	69.0	62.5	61.8	-7.2
Middle	80.6	77.6	76.6	-4.0
Fourth	86.9	84.6	84.3	-2.6
Highest	88.6	85.9	85.8	-2.8
Work time				
Full time	77.6%	74.3%	74.2%	-3.3
Part time	60.4	54.6	51.7	-8.8

* See technical appendix for a discussion of wage quintile analysis.

SOURCE: Author's analysis of the March Current Population Survey, 2001-09.

The Economic Policy Institute goes on to say the following:

Employer-sponsored health insurance is increasingly failing American families. If the coverage rate had not fallen 6.4 percentage points as it did from 2000 to 2008, as many as 17 million more people under 65 would have had ESI in 2008. Public insurance, primarily in the form of Medicaid and SCHIP, has been working to counteract this trend. However, many Americans are falling through the cracks each day. Given the ailing economy, it is likely that another 10 million will lose their access to ESI, and there will be well over 50 million uninsured Americans by 2010.[73]

How important is providing health insurance to employees? Small Business Majority conducted a poll[74] between December 2008 and August 2009, noting these results:

1. An average of 86% of small businesses owners who don't offer health coverage to their employees say they can't afford to provide it. Those that do offer it are struggling to afford it, say an average of 72%.

2. 83% of small business owners surveyed, on average, believe people should be able to buy insurance policies regardless of preexisting conditions.

3. Small businesses are willing to share the responsibility for making health insurance affordable along with insurers, healthcare providers, individuals and government, according to an average of 66% of respondents.

4. Respondents to the small business surveys represented a range of political points of view. 39% identified themselves as Republicans, 24% as Democrats and 27% as independents.

The O'Leary Report performed a more detailed poll[75] surveying 4,426 likely voters in September 2009 and found that

1. 55.1% of small-business owners and 55.2% of stockholders believe that "expanding the government's role in health care will do more harm than good." [All of the following information refers to small-business owners and stockholders, in that order.]

2. 69.1% and 70.9% believe that the federal government should not "require all Americans to purchase health insurance, or face a fine."

3. 64.7% and 67.0% oppose a "government-run health care system, or 'single-payer' system, where the federal government pays for and provides health care for all Americans."

4. 62.2% and 65.0% oppose the creation of an "Independent Medicare Advisory Council."

5. 81.3% and 82.5% believe that "tort reform is needed."

6. 77.2% and 77.4% oppose "taxing employer-provided health care benefits."

7. 83.9% and 80.7% favor allowing Americans to "purchase health insurance from providers in different states."

8. 78.9% and 83.8% do not favor taxation to provide health insurance for those Americans eighteen and older who can otherwise afford to purchase their own health insurance or for illegal immigrants who are uninsured.

9. 61.2% and 59.4% do not favor a 5% surtax on people who make more than one million dollars per year in order to pay for health reform."

10. 50.1% and 52.7% believe that Congress should work to "lower the deficit first before they consider a $1 trillion health care overhaul."

Although the concept of HSAs and high-deductible insurance plans is still in its infancy, I have gained details of group plans that are available from Blue Cross and Blue Shield, Health Net, and Humana, none of which include specific terms on the rates but do include those wonderful phrases "No Charge" and "100%" after the deductible is met. Some even include no charge for preventive care, as well as prenatal and postpartum care.

What does this mean? We now have insurance plans that reward you for staying healthy and give you incentives to be careful about the health costs you incur; but when you really need care, you are 100% covered. The only exception to complete coverage was a lifetime limit of $5,000,000 with Health Net.

In Your Hands

Insurance companies were working feverishly to lobby against the healthcare reform legislation. Now that it is law, we need to work with them to repeal the legislation that was crammed down our throats. The paradox is that *when* (I refuse to use the word *if*) we repeal the Affordable Health Care for America Act, we will be working against the insurance companies to promote HSAs and limit their power concerning our health care. We sincerely apologize to them for working to cut our insurance premiums to about half their current rate.

I have a dream! I believe that someday each of us will get our insurance policy through our employer or on our own, and we will each have a tax-free HSA. We will have insurance ID credit cards with encrypted access to our HSAs and our health records, and the information will be directly downloadable for preparation of our tax returns on Turbotax, Taxcut, or whatever software we prefer. Insurance companies will be minor players in our health-care decisions, and we will have 100% coverage with very little government involvement, responsibility, or cost! The population of the chronically uninsured will dwindle to a small fraction because of the affordability of the coverage, and the economic recovery based on limited government involvement will be a great stimulus for small businesses and our economy.

So far, I have made little mention of the chronically uninsured. The fact is that our current governmental health-care plans are

designed to take care of them. We desperately need to push for more incentives to self-insure. We accomplish this goal by making governmental health care less attractive. (Maybe we should produce a documentary of England's health-care system "Night of the Barely Living Dead"?) As noted earlier, we have no more than 10% of the U.S. population in this category. Rather than expand the category to include the entire U.S. population, we need to condense it. By making insurance more affordable and cutting back on the buffet mongrels, we will achieve this goal!

Feel free to challenge the authorities I've cited throughout this chapter and do your own research. Regardless of your conclusions, I encourage you to learn about the political candidates and vote according to your conscience. I believe I've provided sufficient factual data to support my conclusions. Those common-sense conclusions are as follows:

- We need to push Health Savings Accounts and avoid government involvement in health care like the plague. Individual control will stimulate frugal spending and relieve federal, state, and local governments of huge economic obligations.

- We need tort reform to protect health care providers from frivolous claims by greedy medical malpractice lawyers.

- We need a recognized standard of care that will protect doctors who are unable to perform miracles. That will save billions of dollars spent on unnecessary testing and treatment that is only proscribed to avoid frivolous malpractice claims.

- We need to enable small businesses to provide insurance to their employees rather than tax them to the point that they lay off people whose health care will then be on our dime.

- We need senators and representatives who understand this crisis and don't owe any paybacks for campaign contributions or "favors."

Conclusion

Please support the state attorneys general and governors who are arguing before the U.S. Supreme Court that this healthcare reform act violates a number of provisions of the U.S. Constitution. If that fails, please demand from any congressional candidate an absolute commitment to legislation to reverse this abuse of governmental action.

Education

Education is a valuable asset that can never be taken away. Any interference with the best possible learning environment for our children will not only harm their future aspirations, but also compromise our nation's future. In fifty years we will be completely dependent upon our next generation. We owe it to ourselves and to our children to provide the finest educational environment in the world.

Spending on Education

According to the National Center for Education Statistics, government expenditures for education, adjusted for inflation, have almost quadrupled in the last forty-five years.[1] The average investment per student in the year 1961-62 was $2,670 in 2006 dollars. By 2005-2006 this number had grown to $9,391. Unfortunately, these numbers are not accurate. You will soon see that actual government expenditures are well over twice as much as they are represented to be. The bottom line is that we are spending a lot more and getting so much less!

The most recent data concerning the economics of education is from the U.S. Census Bureau, reflecting the year 2006-07.[2] In exhibits A through D you'll find a very informative set of pie

charts describing the proportionate sources of revenue to support our schools and the applications thereof.

Exhibits A and B

Figure 1a. Percent Distribution of Total Public Elementary-Secondary School System Revenue: 2006-07

Total: $556.9 billion

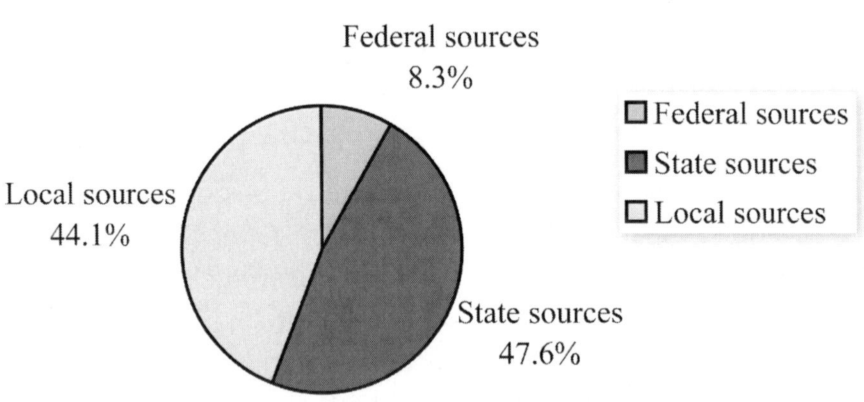

Figure 1b. Percent Distribution of Total Public Elementary-Secondary School System Local Revenue: 2006-07

Total: $245.6 billion

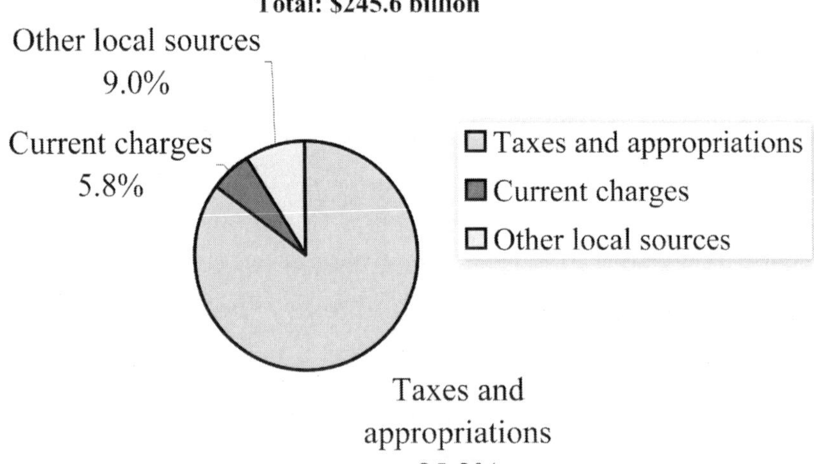

Exhibits A and B demonstrate that state, county, and city governments provide the bulk of the funding, which they gain primarily from taxes and appropriations. There were approximately 48 million students in 2006-07, which means that the federal government claimed to spend about $961 per student while all governments combined spent about $11,583 per student.

Exhibits C and D describe how the money is spent: the first including capital outlay for land, buildings, and so on, and the second reflecting the direct operating expenses.

Exhibits C and D

Figure 2. Percent Distribution of Total Public Elementary-Secondary School System Expenditure: 2006-07

Total: $559.8 billion

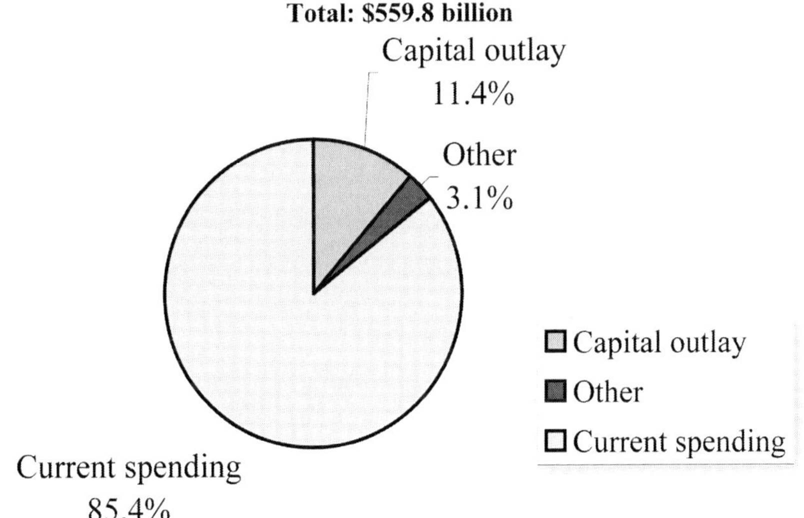

Figure 3. Percent Distribution of Public Elementary-Secondary School System Current Spending by Function
Total: $478.2 billion

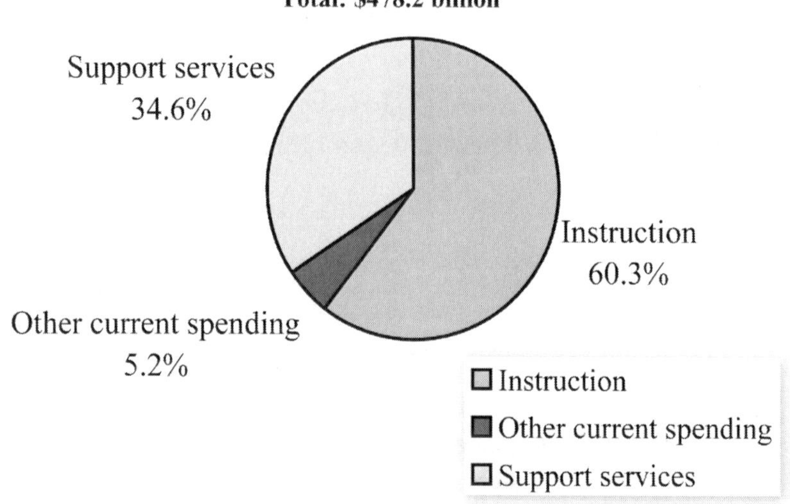

In a few pages, you'll find Exhibit E, which outlines per pupil spending for each state and the District of Columbia. It claims that the average investment is $9,666 per student with New York leading the race at $15,981, New Jersey second at $15,691, and the District of Columbia taking third with $14,324. The end of the list, or should we say best of the list, is Utah at $5,683.

This is not the only data available from the U.S. government. In fiscal 2011, The U.S. Budget Pie Chart reflects a total of $1.0998 trillion that is being spent for education.[3] $363 billion are for higher education (colleges and graduate schools) and $736 billion is spent for primary and secondary schools. There were 48,380,507 students in 2006 and 48,441,473 in 2007.[4] If we use the larger number, it means that a total of approximately $15,194 was being spent per student; which is about $3,611 in excess of what they claim to spend. Tell me this: if you buy a car that is advertised at $11,583, including tax and license, and you are then presented with an invoice for $15,194, are you going to ask questions?

Believe it or not, I am not done with the accounting, but we need to talk about the parent of this spoiled child.

Department of Education

The Department of Education (ED) was established in 1867 as an independent government agency and then transferred (1869) to the Department of the Interior as the Bureau of Education. In 1939 the bureau, by executive order, was transferred to the Federal Security Agency, which in 1953 became the Department of Health, Education and Welfare. It became an independent department when President Carter signed the Department of Education Organization Act, which began operating on May 16, 1980.

President Ronald Reagan promised to eliminate the Department of Education as a cabinet post,[5] but he was not able to do so with a democratic House of Representatives. In the 1982 State of the Union Address, he pledged: "The budget plan I submit to you on February 8 will realize major savings by dismantling the Department of Education."[6] Throughout the 1980s, the abolition of the Department of Education was a part of the Republican Party platform, but the administration of President George H. W. Bush declined to implement this idea. In 1996, the Republican Party made abolition of the department a cornerstone of their campaign promises, calling it an inappropriate federal intrusion into local, state, and family affairs. The GOP platform read:

> The Federal government has no constitutional authority to be involved in the school curricula or to control jobs in the market place. This is why we will abolish the Department of Education, end federal meddling in our schools, and promote family choice at all levels of learning.

During his 1996 presidential run, Senator Bob Dole promised, "We're going to cut out the Department of Education."[7] In 2000,

the Republican Liberty Caucus passed a resolution to abolish the Department of Education.[8]

Abolition of ED was not pursued under the George W. Bush administration, which made reform of federal education a key priority of the president's first term. In 2007 and 2008, presidential candidate Ron Paul campaigned in part in opposition to the department. ABC's John Stossel and Andrew Sullivan interviewed Mr. Paul, and they published a report:

> For example, it is a political consensus that the federal government should be involved in K-12 education and guarantee that no child is left behind, but Paul doesn't believe that government should be in control of our kids' education. He would abolish the federal Department of Education. He notes, "Since the 1950s, since the federal government's gotten involved, the quality of education has gone down, the cost has gone up." By contrast, Paul counters, if we introduce market forces into education, competition will create innovative schools that offer our kids a better education for less money.[9]

The fact of the matter is that ED assumes no real role in ensuring excellence in education. Its own discussion of "purpose" can be found at its own Web site:

> The Department carries out its mission in two major ways. First, the Secretary and the Department play a leadership role in the ongoing national dialogue over how to improve the results of our education system for all students… . Second, the Department pursues its twin goals of access and excellence through the administration of programs that cover every area of education and range from preschool education through postdoctoral research.[10]

Blah, blah, blah! I cordially invite ED to provide any nuance of evidence that it can muster to battle the evidence that you are about to see.

Back to the subject of costs: In our last episode we determined that the Fed claimed to spend $961 per student and the states

Exhibit E

State	Education Spending (millions)	Higher Education Spending (millions)	Primary & Secondary Spending (millions)	Number of Primary & Secondary Students (2007	Spending Per Student	Federal Statement Spending per student (2006-07)	Difference in Spending per Student	Total Excess Cost in millions
NY	70,000	5,304	64,696	2,754,976	23,483	15,981	7,502	20,668
NJ	33,000	1,985	31,015	1,372,748	22,593	15,691	6,902	9,475
DC	3,260	1,040	2,220	56,943	38,986	14,324	24,662	1,404
VT	2,500	88	2,411	90,970	26,503	13,471	13,032	1,186
WY	2,650	314	2,336	85,034	27,471	13,217	14,254	1,212
CT	12,300	1,002	11,298	555,996	20,320	12,979	7,341	4,082
MA	18,800	1,038	17,762	945,070	18,794	12,738	6,056	5,723
RI	3,190	162	3,028	147,861	20,479	12,612	7,867	1,163
AK	3,000	315	2,685	132,197	20,311	12,300	8,011	1,059
DE	3,000	243	2,757	114,678	24,041	11,829	12,212	1,400
MD	18,900	1,647	17,253	851,640	20,259	11,724	8,535	7,269
ME	3,400	266	3,134	193,539	16,193	11,387	4,806	930
PA	36,000	2,242	33,758	1,807,367	18,678	11,098	7,580	13,700
HI	4,100	613	3,487	180,728	19,294	11,060	8,234	1,488
NH	3,710	139	3,571	198,625	17,979	10,723	7,256	1,441
WI	16,400	1,292	15,108	870,584	17,354	10,267	7,087	6,170
VA	25,200	1,899	23,301	1,220,440	19,092	10,210	8,882	10,840
MI	34,600	2,061	32,539	1,700,665	19,133	9,912	9,221	15,682
OH	33,000	2,500	30,500	1,758,645	17,343	9,799	7,544	13,267
WV	5,110	471	4,639	281,298	16,491	9,611	6,880	1,935
IL	34,000	3,012	30,988	2,105,822	14,715	9,555	5,160	10,866
MN	15,700	1,576	14,124	816,212	17,304	9,539	7,765	6,338
CA	117,000	11,760	105,240	6,231,589	16,888	9,152	7,736	48,207
NE	5,500	633	4,867	287,135	16,950	9,141	7,809	2,242
GA	27,800	2,607	25,193	1,628,409	15,471	9,127	6,344	10,331
MT	2,680	204	2,476	144,258	17,164	9,078	8,086	1,166
ND	1,900	254	1,646	96,577	17,043	9,022	8,021	775
OR	9,900	791	9,109	561,246	16,230	9,000	7,230	4,058
KS	8,000	840	7,160	468,974	15,267	8,988	6,279	2,945
IN	17,500	1,594	15,906	1,034,685	15,373	8,938	6,435	6,658
LA	12,500	1,716	10,784	662,302	16,283	8,928	7,355	4,871
IA	9,000	935	8,065	438,122	18,408	8,769	9,639	4,223
NM	6,400	902	5,498	327,816	16,772	8,635	8,137	2,667
SC	13,400	822	12,578	701,580	17,928	8,533	9,395	6,591
MO	14,600	1,027	13,573	912,229	14,879	8,529	6,350	5,793
FL	49,000	3,344	45,656	2,656,176	17,189	8,514	8,675	23,042
AL	14,200	1,754	12,446	743,273	16,745	8,391	8,354	6,209
WA	19,700	1,877	17,823	1,026,121	17,369	8,377	8,992	9,227
KY	12,500	1,283	11,217	646,360	17,354	8,309	9,045	5,846
AR	7,600	859	6,741	474,532	14,206	8,284	5,922	2,810
CO	12,800	802	11,998	790,834	15,171	8,167	7,004	5,539
NV	7,000	628	6,372	422,782	15,072	7,993	7,079	2,993
SD	1,880	202	1,678	121,158	13,850	7,944	5,906	716
NC	26,100	3,920	22,180	1,416,028	15,664	7,883	7,781	11,018
TX	67,000	5,774	61,226	4,513,835	13,564	7,818	5,746	25,936
MS	7,500	1,071	6,429	494,135	13,010	7,473	5,537	2,736
OK	10,300	1,025	9,275	639,032	14,514	7,420	7,094	4,533
AZ	15,500	1,228	14,272	969,865	14,715	7,196	7,519	7,292
TN	12,800	1,256	11,554	978,368	11,809	7,113	4,696	4,594
ID	3,290	425	2,865	262,935	10,896	6,625	4,271	1,122
UT	7,600	826	6,774	504,079	13,438	5,683	7,755	3,909
USA	902,770	79,568	823,211	48,396,023	18,659	9,666	8,993	355,347

averaged \$9,666 for a total of \$10,627. Another version of the federal budget claimed \$11,583 in costs, but accountants will attempt to explain that the difference is due to transfers of funds from ED to the states. That excuse has nothing to do with the \$15,194 reflected above. I examined the budgets for every state in the union and the District of Columbia as reflected in exhibit E. I made sure to subtract the expenses for higher education and divided the other expenses proportionately. Almost every number used to prepare the chart is from the 2009 state and federal budgets but I had to use numbers of students and federal total estimates of spending per student from 2007. This may cause some of the numbers to be slightly off but the final tallies are directly on point.

The final tally for 48,396,023 elementary and secondary students is a little under 903 billion dollars in state spending alone, which computes to be about \$18,658.58 per student. The federal government calculates state spending to be \$9,666 per student. My calculations indicate that we are investing \$18,658.58 plus \$1,917.00 in federal funds for at least *\$20,576 per student in public education*. It therefore appears we are spending almost twice as much as we are being told.

According to the *Washington Post:*

> In the District, the spending figure cited most commonly is \$8,322 per child, but total spending is close to \$25,000 per child—on par with tuition at Sidwell Friends, the private school Chelsea Clinton attended in the 1990s. ...To calculate total spending, we have to add up all sources of funding for education from Kindergarten through 12th grade, excluding spending on charter schools and higher education. For the current school year, the local operating budget is \$831 million, including relevant expenses such as the teacher retirement fund. The capital budget is \$218 million. The District receives about \$85.5 million in federal funding. And the D.C. Council contributes an extra \$81 million. Divide all that by the 49,422 students enrolled (for the 2007-08 year) and you end up with

about $24,600 per child. … For comparison, total per pupil spending at D.C. area private schools—among the most upscale in the nation—averages about $10,000 less. For most private schools, the difference is even greater (emphasis added).[11]

According to its budget, Washington, D.C. spends an average of $38,986 per student (see exhibit E). That makes this *Washington Post* article somewhat inconsistent, but I believe we are on the same page.

Choosing the School

I will get back to the cost issue, but for now, let's address the differences between types of schools. Education Bug provides a good discussion of the differences in the institutions,[12] and I will summarize them below, with the proviso that Education Bug may hold some bias in favor of some school system and/or format:

Pro Public Schools:

- People who favor public schools usually point to the favorable tuition costs: none! Many public school districts even provide transportation in the form of busing to get students to and from the school.

- Having a common public education is one of the things that unites many Americans regardless of race, color, ethnic background, or religious beliefs. Ninety percent of children in the U.S. attend a public school.

- With the possibilities now for magnet and charter schools as part of the public school system, people may feel that some of the chief benefits of the private school system are now available without leaving the public school system.

- Public schools receiving federal funds must hire teachers who meet certification requirements, whereas private schools are not held to that standard.

- Teacher pay at public schools is overall better than at private schools.

Pro Private Schools:

- Even though there are tuition costs at private schools, there are scholarships available in many cases, and parents who select them feel that the money is well worth it.

- Private schools may have the luxury of having architecture that leads to a more inviting campus.

- Private schools may have selective admissions, whereas public schools are required to educate all students in their geographic area. Possibly for this reason, your child's class may spend less time waiting while the teacher deals with other children's behavioral issues.

- If there is a student with a behavioral issue that is disruptive, a private school is able to seek the greatest good of the greatest number, whereas public schools are as responsible to that child as to all the other children being taught.

A friend of mine teaches at a private school, but once taught in a public one. He described one instance involving a student who demanded that he be moved to a charter school to be with friends and have access to drugs. The boy wanted to be expelled so he could get his way. His tactics included yelling and doing whatever he could to be disruptive in class. My friend took him aside and explained there was no possibility of changing schools because the charter had no vacancy. The boy's only option was to do nothing and fail the class. The young man opted for failure and agreed to be quiet. The other students were finally able to learn something. Now back to the Education Bug materials:

- There's usually a good deal of investment—on the part of the parents, and often students as well—of the student being at a private school. This can mean that your child will face fewer committees mutually responsible for an assignment with only one or two children doing the work, and the others along for the ride.

- Private schools may be more welcome to parental involvement.

- Private schools have more control over class and school size.

- Parents who wish for overt teaching of morals and religion will naturally gravitate to sectarian private schools… .The public schools really don't offer a viable alternative.

- Many private schools with special missions have a much longer history and greater experience in their specialties.

- Because private schools don't have to follow the teacher certification rules of public schools, they can sometimes have diverse faculty with alternative qualifications, such as language skills and a teaching license from another country.

- Even though the pay is lower, private schools may give teachers more freedom to develop creative curriculum than public schools.

A magnet school, according to ED, refers to a public elementary or secondary school or program that has one of three goals as its focus:

- It aims to bring together students who have a variety of racial and ethnic backgrounds in order to virtually eliminate, reduce, or prevent the isolation of races.

- It aims to create an academic focus or a social focus on a chosen theme.

- A magnet school has the same governance structure as any other public school and no tuition. It follows the same laws and regulations, and its teachers, administrators, and other staff are required to have state certification.

A charter school, also according to ED, has the following characteristics:

- It has been granted a charter within the rules of the state in which it exists, usually by the state legislature, or any other designated authority.

- It is either created new or transformed from a pre-existing public or private school.

- It may be run by a regular school district, as well as by a chartering organization or a state education agency.

- Governance may be by a group or organization, including a collection of educators, a university, or a corporation.

- It is granted more authority than other schools, but has accountability standards directly related to its mission and written into its standards.

- The charter is periodically reviewed and may be revoked.

- Like magnet and private schools, charter schools can have themes, carry out particular educational philosophies, or serve particular populations.

A more detailed discussion of the population of private schools and their demographic breakdown can be found in exhibit F.[13]

Exhibit F

Private School Statistics at a Glance	
PK-12 Enrollment (2009)	**6,049,000** (11% of all Us students)
# of Schools (2007-2008)	**33,740** (25% of all Us schools)

Enrollment Source: National Center for Education Statistics
School Source: National Center for Education Statistics

Where do private school students go to school?		
	89-90	07-08
Catholic	54.4%	42.5%
Nonsectarian	13.2%	19.4%
Conservative Christian	10.9%	15.2%
Baptist	5.8%	5.5%
Lutheran	4.4%	3.7%
Jewish	3.2%	4.7%
Episcopal	1.7%	2.1%
Seventh-day Adventist	1.6%	1.1%
Calvinist	0.9%	0.6%
Friends	0.3%	0.4%

Source: National Center for Education Statistics

Analysis of Public and Private School Costs

Let's get back to the money that comes out of the taxpayer's pocket. Almost 17% of every dollar gained by government entities gets funneled into education.[14] The total 1.0998 trillion dollars represents a little more than one out of every six dollars of all government funds.

What if you were the governator of a hypothetical state named Cah-lee-foh-nee-ya that invests 26 to 31 percent of its revenue in education? What if your name is Ah-nold and you can't find enough money to spend to print IOU's as vouchers for income tax refunds?

Common Sense Judge: Good afternoon, Mr. Governor, how can I help you?

AS: I am in deep deep trahble. My bahdget says it is balanced, but who ah we keedink, we aah about funf beellion een da hole.

CSJ: Five billion in the hole? How much do you spend on education?

AS: Yah, Yah! Dat is de beegest slice uff da pie. State und local spendt aboot $126 beellion this yeah.

CSJ: Just cut it in half, drop the U.S. Department of Education, trim your state's department to an administrative role and foster private schools to pick up the slack. You can rent all of your school facilities to the private schools, and you are solvent again with about $60 billion in cash.

AS: (Pause) … . . Ees dat leegull?

CSJ: Not yet. We need to elect some people to serve us in the U.S. Congress who are willing to work for the betterment of America rather than pay back teachers' unions for campaign contributions.

We are spending $20,576 per student for public education. What is the average cost in the United States per student in private schools? Well, the first place I looked was Answers.com and (drum roll please): the answer is "about $4,700.00."[15] No, I am not kidding. The second place I checked was Freeby50.com and got the following:

According to the Department of Education the average cost of tuition for one year of private school for K-12 is $6,600. But there can be a wide variation in costs. You will generally pay more the higher the grade so high school is more than the middle which might be more than elementary school. Average cost for elementary school is $5,049 and average cost for secondary school is $8,412. As with most things the costs vary a lot depending on region. A private high school in Boise, Idaho might run you $6,500 a year while a school in Huntington Beach, California could run you $13,275.[16]

Greatschools.org offered this:

> According to the National Association of Independent Schools, the median tuition for their member private day schools in 2008-2009 in the United States was $17,441. Tuition for boarding schools was close to $37,017. Parochial schools are even more affordable. The National Catholic Educational Association reports that the mean *tuition for parish elementary schools is $2,607 and $6,906 for the freshman year of secondary school* (emphasis added).[17]

An excellent analysis and comparison of costs related both to public and private school was prepared by the Mackinac Center for Public Policy.

> A close analysis of public and private school costs shows that the commonly used measures do not accurately reflect the true costs of educating children in the two systems. Neither the prevailing "tuition" costs nor the commonly discussed "per pupil expenditures" fully take into account all costs. In the government school system, Michigan anticipates a per-pupil "guarantee" or "foundation allowance" of about $5,445 per pupil in fiscal 1998. The taxpayers also provide additional direct and indirect support of public schools. For example, taxpayer dollars help provide land and facilities for the school system, along with government services, without these facilities contributing to the local tax base. Government agencies in Michigan pay no property tax, no sales tax, and no income or single business tax; further, they borrow money at tax-exempt rates. The taxpayers indirectly pay for all these costs, and many do not appear in accounting for expenditures. Thus, the actual burden of the government school system on the taxpayers is significantly higher than the foundation allowance might imply.[18]

Privatization will not only cut the taxpayers' burden in about half, but it will create income for government entities, and where do they get most of their income? Oh yes—from taxes paid by you and me. Look at it this way: it is a two-for-one coupon for breakfast and it says that you are not the one who has to pay for the first meal! Now back to the article:

Private school tuition is about half that of the average per pupil revenue of public schools. Private school tuition in Michigan averages about $2,500, with significant variation among schools. This amount is much less than half of the expenditures of the public school system, which is consistent with the national pattern. However, just as the per-pupil expenditure of public schools is a significant underestimate of the government school costs, private school tuition also underestimates private school costs. Most religious schools receive significant contributions from their sponsoring organizations to support their operations. Many also receive volunteer time and services from parents…. *Once all private and taxpayer-funded costs are included for both systems, the ratio of total public school costs to total private school costs is less clear, but is probably about 2:1.*[19] (emphasis added)

There is that 2 to 1 ratio again. Ah-nold seemed to like it.

It should be noted, however, that the prime motivation behind the movement to parental choice in education is not efficiency or the need to save money, but the *desire to improve the education of children* (emphasis added).[20]

That is the end of my discussion concerning costs associated with education. We now need to look at how different types of schools are serving their student bodies.

Quality of Education

I open this section with a nip-it-in-the-bud presentation. In 2003, the National Center for Educational Statistics did a study entitled the "National Assessment of Educational Progress" (NAEP) to compare the quality of the education in public versus private schools and concluded as follows:

In grades 4 and 8 for both reading and mathematics, students in private schools achieved at higher levels than students in public schools. The average difference in school means ranged from almost 8 points for grade 4 mathematics, to about 18 points for grade 8 reading. The average differences were all statistically

significant. Adjusting the comparisons for student characteristics resulted in reductions in all four average differences of approximately 11 to 14 points. Based on the adjusted school means, the average for public schools was significantly higher than the average for private schools for grade 4 mathematics, while the average for private schools was significantly higher than the average for public schools for grade 8 reading. The average differences in adjusted school means for both grade 4 reading and grade 8 mathematics were not significantly different from zero.[21]

This "independent and completely unbiased study" comparing the quality of public vs. private schools was prepared by the National Center for Educational Statistics under the guise of ED.[22] If you use your search engine with a phrase like "compare public and private schools" you will be hammered by organizations that wave this "independent and completely unbiased study" as proof that private schools are no better than public ones. A good example is an article published by the National Education Association that states the following:

> The study found that when the test scores are not controlled for student background, private schools score higher than public schools. However these higher private school test scores are due to the fact that higher proportions of disadvantaged students are enrolled in public schools.
>
> "Overall, the study demonstrates that demographic differences between students in public and private schools more than account for the relatively high raw scores of private schools," the report concludes. "Indeed, after controlling for these differences, the presumably advantageous 'private school effect' disappears, and even reverses in most cases."
>
> In short, public schools are as good or better than private schools.[23]

An in-depth study into the issue performed by Paul E. Peterson and Elena Llaudet of the Kennedy School of Government at

Harvard University discredited this NCES study:

> To avoid bias, classification must be consistent for both groups under study. The NCES study repeatedly violates this rule when it infers a student's background from his or her participation in federal programs intended to serve disadvantaged students. For example, if a public school has a schoolwide Title I program, which is permitted if 40 percent of its students are eligible for free or reduced-price lunch, then every student at the school—regardless of poverty level—is said to be a recipient of Title I services. By contrast, private schools cannot directly receive Title I funds nor can they operate Title I programs. Characteristics influenced by the school the students are attending will bias estimates if they are included in statistical adjustments for student background. Three variables open to school influence were included in the NCES analysis: a) the student's absenteeism rate; b) number of books in the student's home; and c) availability of a computer in the student's home.[24]

Let me put this in layperson's terms: The factors that NCES used to assume students were disadvantaged were grossly over-emphasized and exaggerated until the numbers came out the way the testing agency wanted them to come out. The study by Peterson and Llaudet substituted three factors used by NCES with factors clearly more determinant in affecting students' test scores. Model I substituted the parents' education and the location of the school (regionally and by urban, suburban, or rural area) for the Title I and free lunch variables in the NCES study. Model II substituted programs for Limited English Proficiency with student reports of the frequency of English spoken at home. Model III replaced an Individualized Education Program with teacher reports of severe or moderate disability. These results demonstrate that private school students had advantages everywhere except Model I fourth grade math.

Time magazine, in partnership with CNN, also looked into the NCES study and concluded the following:

Combined with high-school grades, SAT scores are the best predictor of how kids will do in their freshman year of college. And the data in the new study shows that private-school students outperform public-school students on the SAT. In short, today's study shows that sending your kids to a private school—particularly one run by a holy order like the Jesuits—is still a better way to ensure that he or she will get into college. Just don't expect all education experts to agree.[25]

The Heritage Foundation looked into the study with similar results:

> According to the study, public school students are performing better than private school students in fourth grade mathematics and at the same level as private school students in fourth grade reading and eighth grade math. Policymakers and journalists need to know that the NCES findings that public schools outperform private schools employ significantly limited data. The NAEP data are not suitable for evaluating the effectiveness of private or public school attendance in raising academic achievement. In fact, the NCES authors explicitly warn against this in two sections of the report that are appropriately titled "Cautions in Interpretation."[26]

When sources relied upon the NCES study to claim public schools were just as good as private schools, if not better, I never saw one mention of the "Cautions in Interpretation." But I assume that was just a coincidence.

> In fact, the NCES study would not meet the standards of effective research set forth by the Institute of Educational Sciences—the very people responsible for releasing the study. The WWC evidence standards require research studies include either random assignment or a pretest measure for the research results to be considered effective at establishing causality.

> The NAEP data are certainly not suitable for establishing whether a specific math or reading achievement outcome is associated with attending either a private or public school. Despite this fact,

the results of the NCES study are being interpreted inappropriately to imply that voucher programs, which include private schools, are a bad idea. Voucher programs are a powerful school choice tool that results in many positive outcomes for the students who participate in them. More families should have the opportunity and flexibility to choose the most effective school for their children to achieve success.[27]

Elena Llaudet and Paul E. Peterson later contacted Commissioner Schneider, lead author of the NCES report and he offered the following:

> Asked by *Education Week* to comment on our findings, *the lead author of the NCES report freely acknowledged the problems with some of the variables used in the NCES analysis,* but asserted that our alternative models may be "underadjusting for the disadvantage in the public sector" because we do not control separately for mothers' and fathers' education.... Fortunately, the practice seems to have come to an end. *Commissioner Schneider has stated that his agency should not have initiated this study and NCES will in the future refrain from analyses of the raw data that it collects.*[28] (emphasis added)

We now know that America is spending about twice as much money on primary and secondary education as is necessary. We also know that private schools, and in some respects, charter schools are performing better than other public schools. Now that we've gained clarity on the cost and quality of education, let's discuss the question, "What is education worth?"

Value of an Education

Let's assume that children are going to attend school for different periods of time and apply their efforts in varying degrees depending on their goals. Then let us further assume that the child who drops out applies no real study time and that one who seeks to graduate from high school spends an average of ten hours per week devoted to studies, not including class

time, for the ten to twelve years of education. Lastly, we will assume that the child who aspires to a professional career requiring a college and/or a post-graduate degree averages fifteen hours per week of studies for the sixteen to twenty years of study to achieve that goal. Studying will take up thirty-six weeks per year.

The U.S. Bureau of Labor Statistics (BLS) has published data[29] that reflect average income for a wide variety of occupations. I prepared a chart that factors in the number of hours that a child spends working to gain their education, based upon the aforementioned assumptions, and calculated what each hour of study is actually worth to that child. In order to do so, I have to make a few more assumptions:

1. A person who seeks a wide assortment of service-related occupations does not need to graduate from high school. They will be assigned ten years of education and will leave school after sophomore year of high school. Assuming they will work to the age of seventy, that provides fifty-four years worth of income.

2. A high school graduate will have fifty-two years of income, the college graduate will have forty-eight years, and the doctorate or similar degree or certification will have forty-four years.

3. Wages and incomes described in the BLS study do not include retirement accounts, health insurance, and similar benefits; they will not be factored in.

Why am I doing this? Show these numbers to your children who are not motivated to do their schoolwork. These are actual numbers that prove education pays. If this information motivates one child to get off their iPod and study for school, it is worth the effort.

Job Title	Number of Hours of Study	Total Life Income	Value of Study Hour
HIGH SCHOOL DROPOUT			
Fast Food Cook		$951,480	
Lifeguards, Ski Patrol, and other Recreational		$1,311,660	
Food Preparation Worker		$1,071,900	
Dishwashers		$958,500	
Amusement and Recreation Attendants		$1,022,220	
Manicurists and Pedicurists		$1,190,160	
Shampooers		$988,200	
Farm workers		$1,237,680	
HIGH SCHOOL GRADUATE			
Loan Counselor	4,320	$2,182,440	$505.19
Computer Support Specialist	4,320	$2,411,240	$558.16
Child, Family, and School Social Worker	4,320	$2,242,240	$519.04
Law Clerk	4,320	$2,110,160	$488.46
Title Examiner	4,320	$2,188,680	$506.64
Fine Artists	4,320	$2,511,600	$581.39
Graphic Designers	4,320	$2,431,000	$562.73
Police Officer	4,320	$2,746,120	$635.68
COLLEGE GRADUATE			
General and Operation Manager	8,640	$5,182,560	$599.83
Mathematician	8,640	$4,558,080	$527.56
Aerospace Engineer	8,640	$4,511,080	$522.12
Physicist	8,640	$5,109,120	$591.33
Political Scientist	8,640	$4,767,360	$551.78
Pharmacist	8,640	$5,004,480	$579.22
Air Traffic Controller	8,640	$5,188,320	$600.50
Computer Manager	8,640	$5,698,080	$659.50
DOCTORATE/ ADVANCED DEGREE			
Chief Executive	10,800	$7,059,360	$653.61
Dentist	10,800	$6,787,880	$628.51
Orthodontist	10,800	$8,576,920	$794.16
Surgeon	10,800	$9,097,880	$842.40
Engineering Manager	10,800	$5,305,520	$491.25
Lawyer	10,800	$5,489,000	$508.24
Oral Surgeon	10,800	$8,378,480	$775.79
Psychiatrist	10,800	$6,778,200	$627.61

Comparing the Test Scores

Let's return to the subject of evaluating the quality of education available in public and private schools. There is a lot of data raving about the "superiority" of our public school system, so much so that I found it hard to believe the inconsistent authorities and data regarding private schools. I had to search for something to clear the fog. I finally found it in Florida, but if you look to that part of this chapter ahead of time you are cheating!

The first authority is from Rancho Solano in Phoenix, Arizona. In exhibit G, you'll see the comparisons of scoring for public school students and Rancho Solano students on the Stanford Achievement Tests (SATs) in Arizona:[30]

Exhibit G

Rancho Solano Private Schools Vs. AZ State Reading Statistics

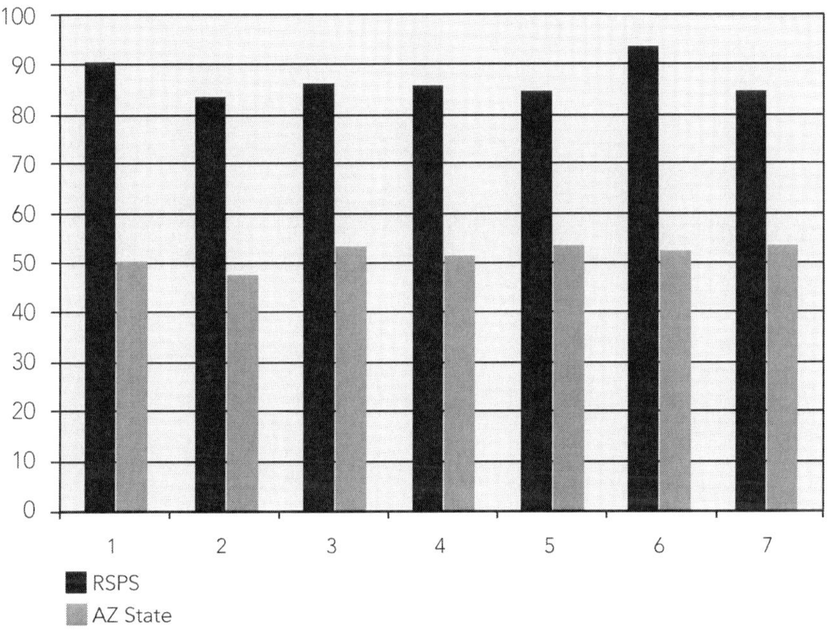

Rancho Solano Private Schools Vs. AZ State Math Statistics

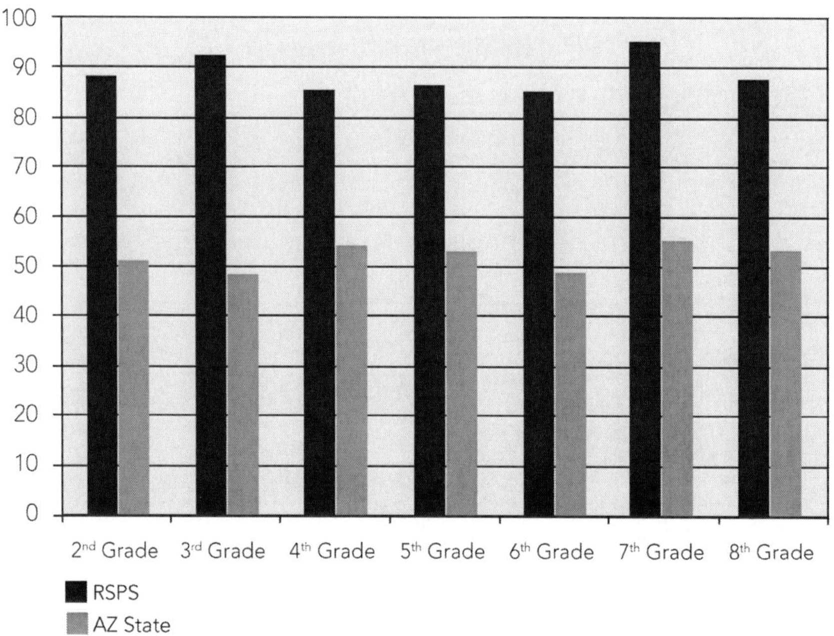

Rancho Solano Private Schools Vs. AZ State Language Statistics

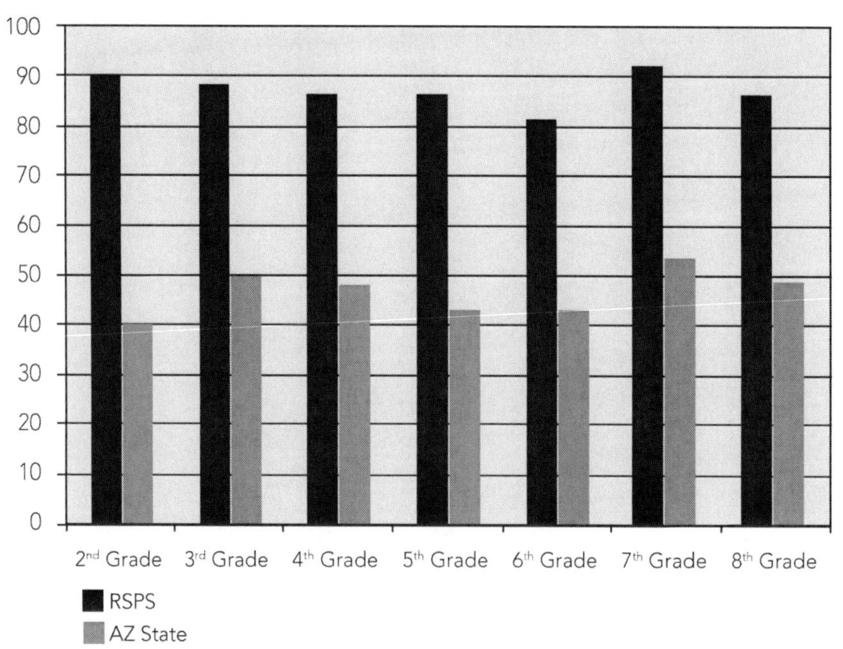

Now, if you are a parent, would you rather have your child's test results in gray or black? … No, this is not a trick question… . Thank you, black is the correct answer.

Hold the phone! This is one of those fancy-schmancy schools that only the elite kids with rich parents can attend!

Well, the fact of the matter is that the tuition at this school is a little over $13,000 and we know that your tax dollars are paying about $14,715 per student in Arizona. Not only that, but Rancho Solano has open enrollment; everyone is welcome. Nevertheless, this is a common objection concerning the demographics of the student population. I assure you that we will get to Florida very soon.

ED itself did a comparison of public and private schools in 2003 and came up with the following:

> 191,400 Grade 4 public school students and 7,500 Grade 4 private school students took NAEP reading assessments and gained average scores as follows: Public 216; Private 235. 191,400 Grade 4 public school students and 4,700 Grade 4 private school students took NAEP mathematics assessments and scored: Public 234; Private 244. The same comparison was done for grade 8 Reading with 155,000 public school students and 8,300 private school students with these average scores: Public 261; Private 282. Finally; 153,500 public eighth-graders and 5,100 private eighth-graders averaged 276 and 292; respectively, for math.[31]

The Council for American Private Education,[32] also known as "CAPE," compared 2005 SAT scores among different types of schools. Exhibit H specifically discusses the demographic differences that need no explanation.

Exhibit H

SAT Test Scores Class of 2005		
	VERBAL	MATH
National	508	520
Public	505	515
Religious	539	534
Independent	553	577

Percentage Increase in Standardized Test Scores of 12th Grade Religious School Students Compared to Public School Students, After Controlling for SES and Gender		
SUBJECT	BLACK AND LATINO	WHITE
Reading	4.6%	3.4%
Matematics	4.2%	3.0%
Social Studies	5.2%	3.4%
Science	2.0%	1.2%
Total Composite	4.8%	3.7%

The average test scores for students are remarkably higher for graduates of private schools. What is more impressive is the fact that those who may otherwise appear to be challenged demographically are the ones who gain the greatest benefit from the private school environment.

Now if I were working hard to champion the equality of civil rights and access to government services for the betterment of the less privileged citizens of this nation, I would be very interested in pleading the benefits that a transformation of our system of education would provide to disadvantaged children.

The SAT is not the only uniform national examination that is reviewed by colleges for admission; there is also the ACT. Nicole C. Focareto, B.A. prepared a Master's thesis entitled "Private vs. Non-Private: A Correlational Study Between ACT and GPA":

> The purpose of this study was to examine the correlation between ACT scores and GPA's of private and non-private or public high-school seniors that applied for admission to Marietta College. The researcher used data from all applicants for the Fall 2005 semester.… The researcher compared the ACT scores and grade point averages of 80 private high school students and 80 non-private or public high school students in the effort to conclude that private high school students would have a high test score and a low grade point average while public school students would have a high GPA and lower test score.[33]

The study revealed the following. The GPA and ACT scores effectively flip-flopped. The ACT score compares apples to apples, while the GPA for each set of students is highly subjective, meaning that a public high school student with the average ACT score of 22.0 will have a GPA well below 3.00 at the private school and the private school student with a 22.95 ACT score will be pretty close to a 4.00 GPA at a public school. See exhibit I.

Exhibit I

FIGURE 1. Average GPA for Public HS and Private HS Applicants

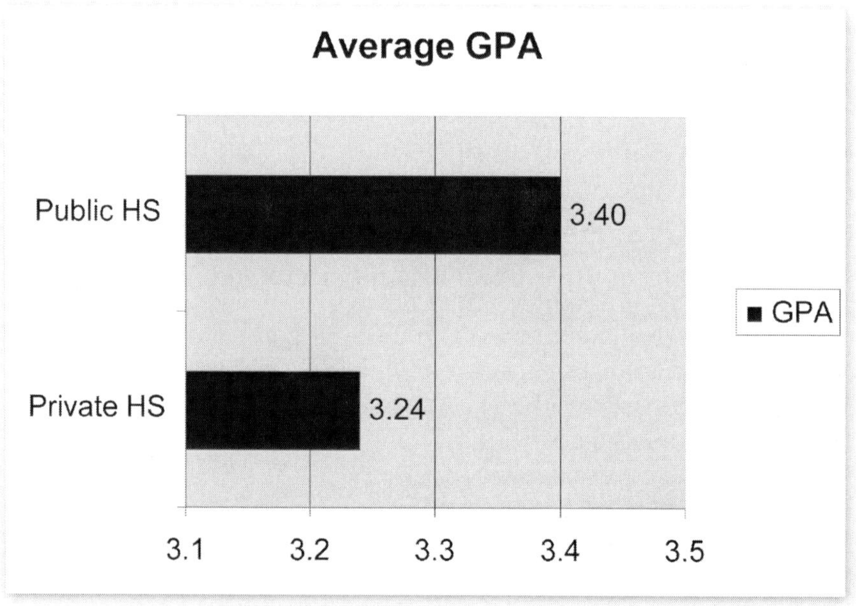

FIGURE 2. Average ACT score for Public HS and Private HS Applicants

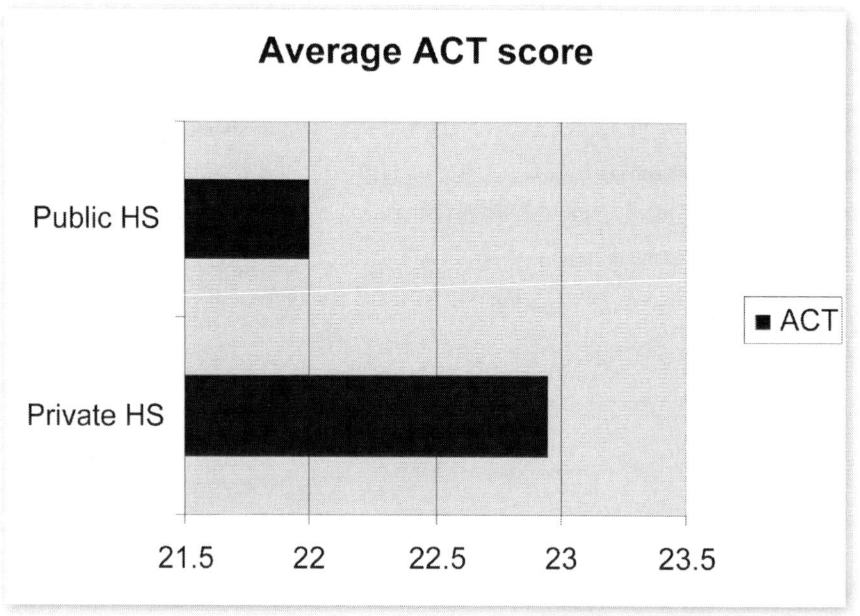

It is virtually impossible to find the perfect example of what a private school environment can do for a demographically challenged student. But then I found this article in *San Diego Magazine*:

> We found eight San Diego public schools that made our "800 club." All meet the following criteria: they serve grades nine through 12; have a minimum of 1,000 students; are accredited by the Western Association of Schools and Colleges; and have an Academic Performance Index (API) base score of at least 800 (out of 1,000) and a statewide rank of 10, the maximum.[34]

Let me explain what I find to be interesting: All of these schools are in the nicest parts of the San Diego area. I will name each school along with its Academic Performance Index score:

Coronado	838	La Jolla	834	Rancho Bernardo	832
Poway	829	Mount Carmel	824	Torrey Pines	821
San Dieguito Acad.	816	Westview	809	Preuss School UCSD	861
River Valley Charter	866				

OK, River Valley Charter got the highest score of 866, but what do you know about Preuss, the school that got the close second with 861? Here are the rules: To be eligible for enrollment at Preuss School, students must come from low-income families, and neither parent may be a college or university graduate. Small class size, an extended school year, and a longer school day help students succeed. Students are chosen for admission by lottery.

Now let's see, these are some of the most extremely disadvantaged students in the area, and they are excelling well beyond more than 99% of the remainder of the area because they are in an educationally stimulating environment! There must be a catch. *You can't tell me that they can achieve that much success on a large scale!* **Welcome to Florida.**

Florida has the fourth highest student population in the United States, behind California, Texas, and New York. Jeb Bush campaigned for governor in 1998 on a clear and bracing set of education reforms. The Goldwater Institute prepared a detailed discussion concerning this:

> In 1999, when these reforms were enacted, nearly half of Florida fourth-graders scored "below basic" on the NAEP reading test, meaning that they could not read at a basic level. But by 2007, less than a decade after the reforms took effect, 70 percent of Florida's fourth-graders scored basic or above. *Florida's Hispanic students now have the second-highest statewide reading scores in the nation, and African-Americans score fourth highest, when compared with their peers.... In fact, the average Florida Hispanic student's score is higher than the overall score for all students in Alabama, Alaska, Arizona, Arkansas, California, Hawaii, Louisiana, Mississippi, Nevada, New Mexico, Oklahoma, Oregon, South Carolina, Tennessee, and West Virginia.*
>
> In education reform, no state has been a more ambitious laboratory of democracy than Florida. Florida has implemented reforms designed to foster accountability and improvement, including establishing high academic standards, implementing innovative student-centered testing policies, ending "social promotion" and increasing early intervention, creating new pathways for hiring and compensating quality teachers, and offering parents greater school choice options.[35] (emphasis added)

For those who are not in the know: "social promotion" effectively allows a student to advance to the next grade without any evidence that they have learned anything. "No child left behind" is a great mantra, except when it means that all of the other children are dragged down by those without the incentive to learn or that there is no effective standard for progress. By the way, educational policy scholars argue No Child Left Behind created an incentive for states to lower standards to make tests easier to pass to avoid federal sanctions.

The gains of Florida's fourth- and eighth-grade students on the National Assessment of Educational Progress (NAEP) examinations far exceed the progress of students across the nation. Importantly, the "achievement gap" is narrowing in Florida since *African-American and Hispanic children are making even greater progress than their white peers on the NAEP examination.*

Policymakers across the nation should look to Florida as a model of education reforms that can improve student learning among all students.[36]

Pictures tell a thousand words and so I am now going to import a lot of pretty pictures from the Goldwater Institute policy report. If you are an educator from another state, please take notice of exhibit J and try to envision what a little bit of effort will do for the children in your care.

Exhibit J

Figure 1: Percentage of Students Scoring Basic or Better on 4th Grade NAEP Reading, 1998 and 2007

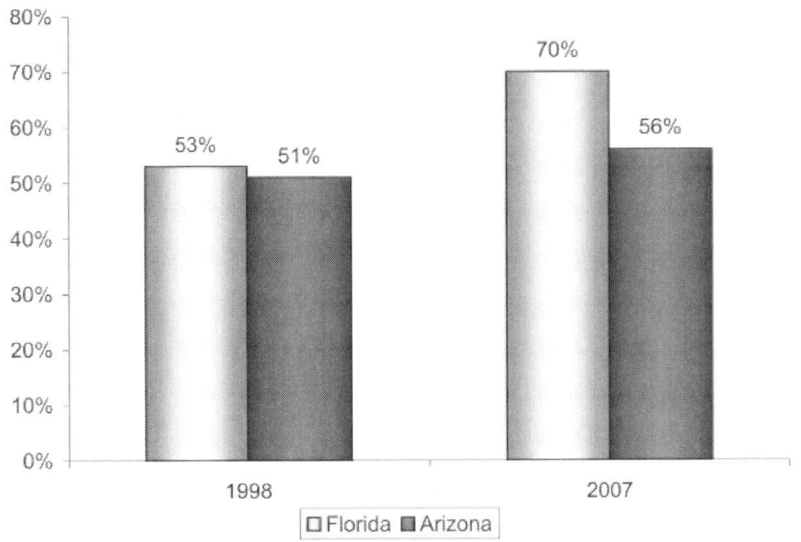

Figure 2: Florida 4th Grade NAEP Reading Scores, 1998 and 2007

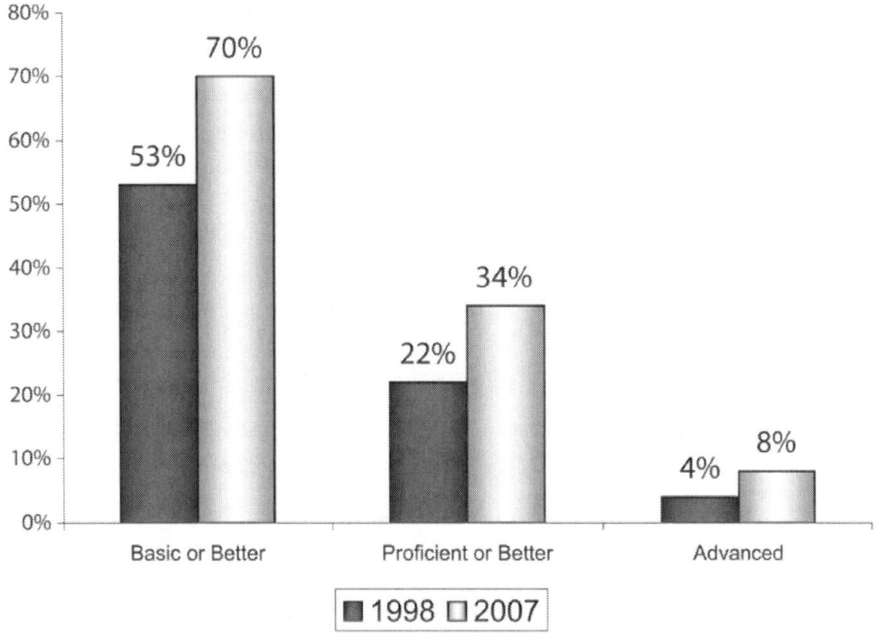

Figure 3: 4th Grade Reading NAEP Scores, All California Students, Florida's Low-Income Hispanics and African Americans, 1998-2007

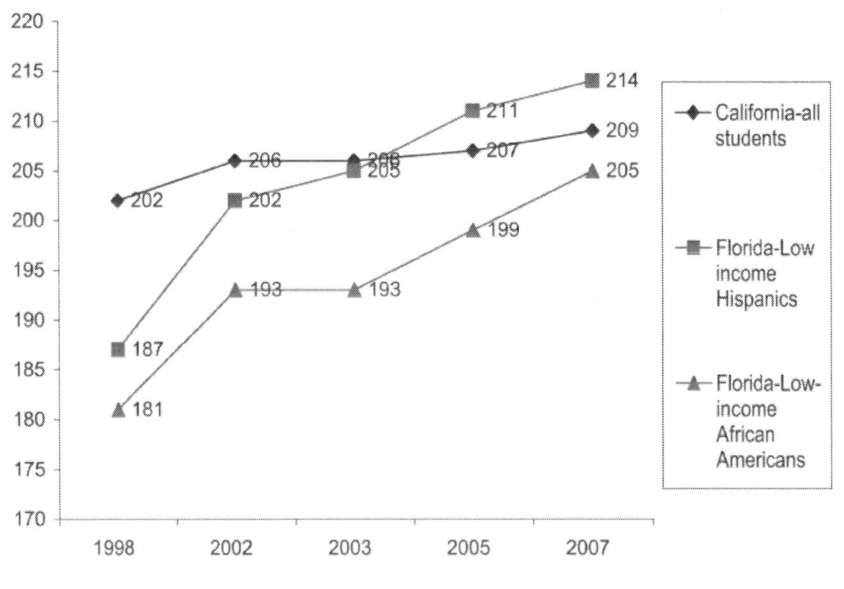

Figure 4: 4th Grade Reading NAEP, Low-income Florida Children and All Arizona Students

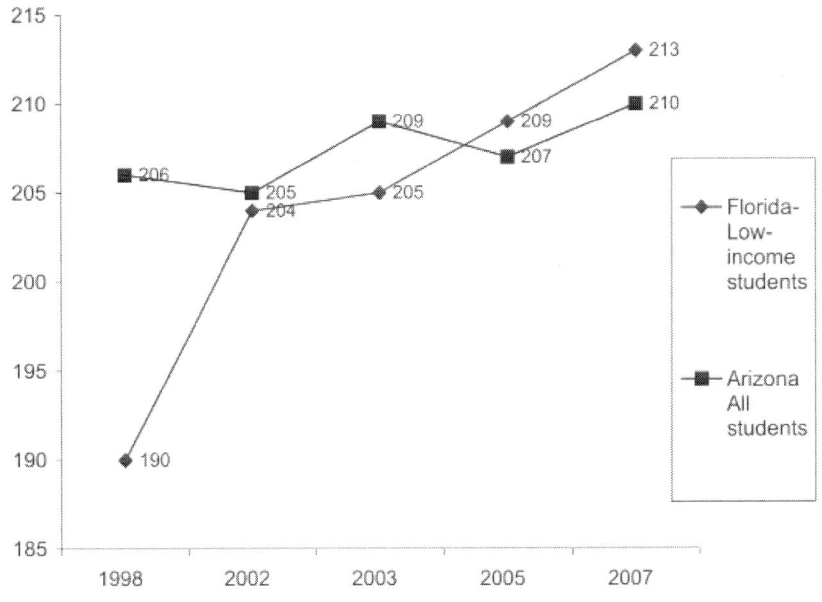

Figure 5: Inner City Florida Students Eligible for a Free or Reduced Price Lunch and All Arizona Students, NAEP 4th Grade Reading, 1998-2005

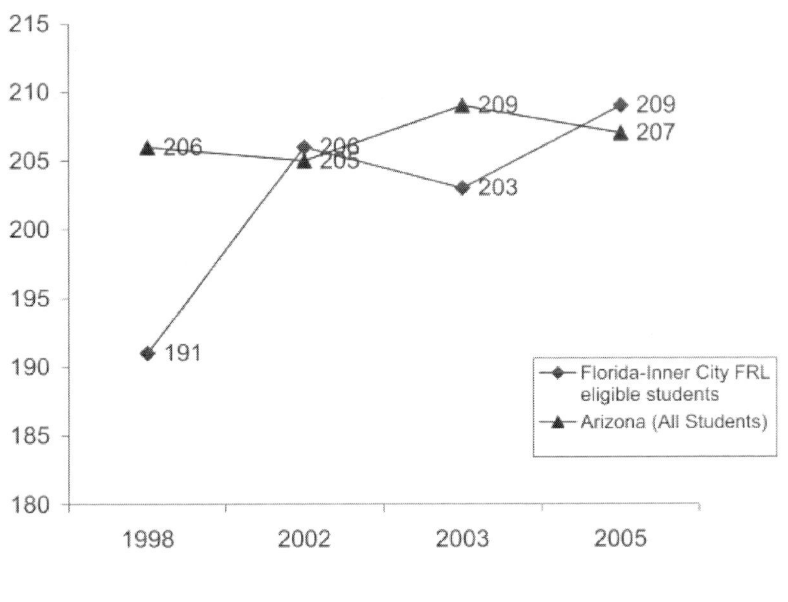

Figures 3, 4, and 5 display the fact that Florida is, in no uncertain terms, hammering my home state of Arizona and the state of California. This is somewhat embarrassing, but it gives us a picture of what can be done if we simply grab the bull by the horns and address the issue. We are patently aware that our public school system deserves an F-, and we know that it is an illness that can be healed. Florida proves that this healing can be done on a massive scale, and that the greatest beneficiaries are the demographically challenged students. My point is that these figures should be posted in the teachers' lounges of every school in Arizona and California. Fear is a strong motivator.

Table 3: Percentage of Students at or above Grade Level on FCAT (Reading)

Grade Level	2001	2002	2003	2004	2005	2006	2007
3	N/A	60	63	66	67	75	69
4	53	55	60	70	71	66	68
5	N/A	53	58	59	66	67	72
6	N/A	51	53	54	56	64	62
7	N/A	50	52	53	53	61	63
8	43	45	49	45	44	46	49
9	N/A	29	31	32	36	40	41
10	37	36	36	34	32	32	34

Table 4: Percentage of Students at or above Grade Level on FCAT (Math)

Grade Level	2001	2002	2003	2004	2005	2006	2007
3	N/A	59	63	64	68	72	74
4	N/A	51	54	64	64	67	69
5	48	48	52	52	57	57	59
6	N/A	43	47	46	47	53	50
7	N/A	47	47	50	53	55	59
8	55	53	56	56	59	60	63
9	N/A	47	51	55	59	59	60
10	59	60	60	63	63	65	65

Tables 3 and 4 are also from Florida. Just look at the progress; 60 to 69, 53 to 72, 59 to 74, 47 to 60. This is what one state in the union did. Some people started looking for excuses to try to explain this radical progress by examining possible changes in the demographic characteristics based on the presumption that students from low-income families have lower achievement levels. Yet the U.S. Census Bureau reported that the population percentage of families living in poverty from 2000 to 2005 increased in Florida but decreased in Arizona.

What Florida Did

In 1999 Governor Jeb Bush delivered his first "State-of-the-State" speech and outlined broad categories of education reform. These included annual testing for grades three through ten and schools being ranked based on achievement. Social promotion was no longer an option, *and funding was tied to performance.* Parents had the ability to transfer their children to better schools, and students receiving two F grades in any four-year period could get vouchers to attend another public or private school.

The state enacted new policies to attract and reward high-quality teachers. These included alternative certification of otherwise-qualified professionals by attendance at Educator Preparation Institutes. Almost half of Florida's teachers now come through these programs.

Florida also offers bonuses of up to 10% of a teacher's salary based on performance. That may sound expensive, but the National Center for Education Statistics reported that Florida's per pupil expenditures, adjusted for inflation, grew by 7% between 1998 and 2004 while the U.S. average grew by 14.7%.[37]

Jay Green and Marcus Winters of the University of Arkansas evaluated the results of the social promotion policy after two years and found that the academic benefit increased after the second year:

> "That is, students lacking in basic skills who are socially promoted appear to fall behind over time, whereas retained students appear to be able to catch up on the skills they are lacking." … Beyond the

> likely benefit of increased remediation, the threat of being retained
> also creates a strong incentive for children to improve their studies
> to proceed to the next grade with their peers.[38] (emphasis added)

Fear is a useful motivational tool. A 2003 Manhattan Institute study evaluated the effect of school choice and found that competition was leading to significant improvements in public schools: "Public schools currently facing voucher competition or the prospect of competition made exceptional gains on both the FCAT and the Stanford-9 test compared to all other Florida public schools and other subgroups in our analysis."[39] They also learned that reforms undertaken by the low-performing public schools contributed to their improvement: "When faced with *increased accountability pressure*, schools appear to focus on low-performing students, lengthen the amount of time devoted to instruction, adopt different ways of organizing the day and learning environment of the students and teachers, increase resources available to teachers, and decrease principal control."[40]

Before vouchers were made available, the A+ program spurred modest improvement in public schools. *But the program produced dramatic gains in threatened public schools once vouchers were incorporated:* "In 2002-03, public schools whose students were offered vouchers outperformed other Florida public schools by 69 points."[41] Moreover, additional evaluations have found that increasing competition through school choice options (both private school choice and charter schools) leads to improvement in traditional public schools facing competition.

> Education scholars such as Harvard political scientist Paul
> Peterson and Stanford economist Carolyn Hoxby have argued
> that incentive- and instruction-based reforms are not mutually
> exclusive, but rather mutually reinforcing. Florida in fact
> represents the perfect test case for this thesis. Governor Bush's
> reforms, as presented above, encompass both incentive reforms
> (parental choice, the ranking of schools, merit pay), instruction-

based reforms (statewide testing, efforts to improve teacher quality), and others that fit into both categories (ending social promotion).

Compared with Massachusetts, Florida faces greater challenges improving public school performance. The percentage of low-income students stands at 45.8 percent in Florida, but only 28.2 percent in Massachusetts. Reflective of this higher wealth, Massachusetts spends 57 percent more per pupil than Florida—$11,584 versus $7,359.[42] Florida's K-12 population has crossed the threshold into being "majority minority," with whites constituting 49.6 percent of the K-12 population. Massachusetts, meanwhile, has a K-12 population that is 63.5 percent white.[43]

The significance of these demographics makes exhibit K more compelling.

Exhibit K

Figure 6: African American 4th Grade NAEP, Massachusetts and Florida, 1992-2007

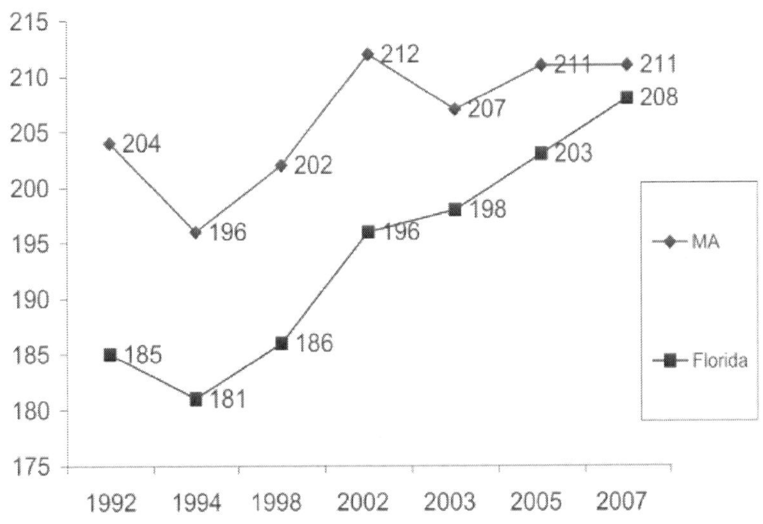

Figure 7: Hispanic 4th Grade NAEP, Massachusetts and Florida, 1992-2007

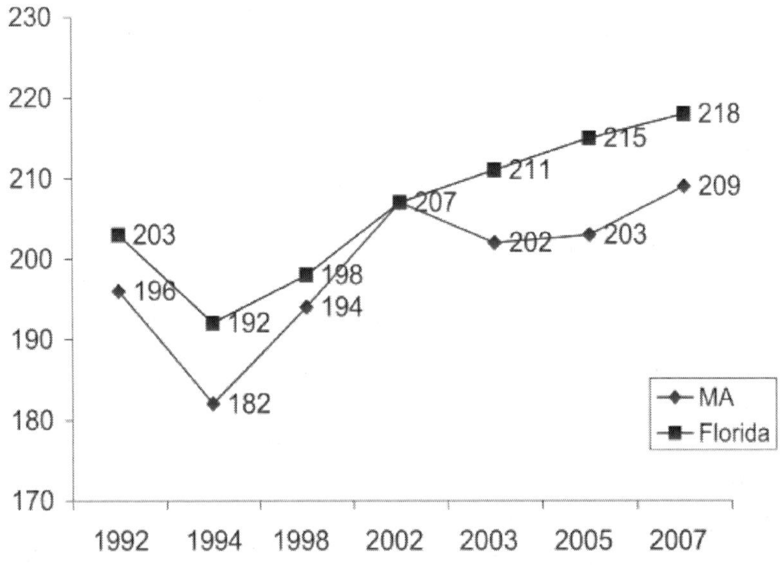

Figure 8: 4th Grade Reading NAEP, Low-income Florida and Massachusetts Students

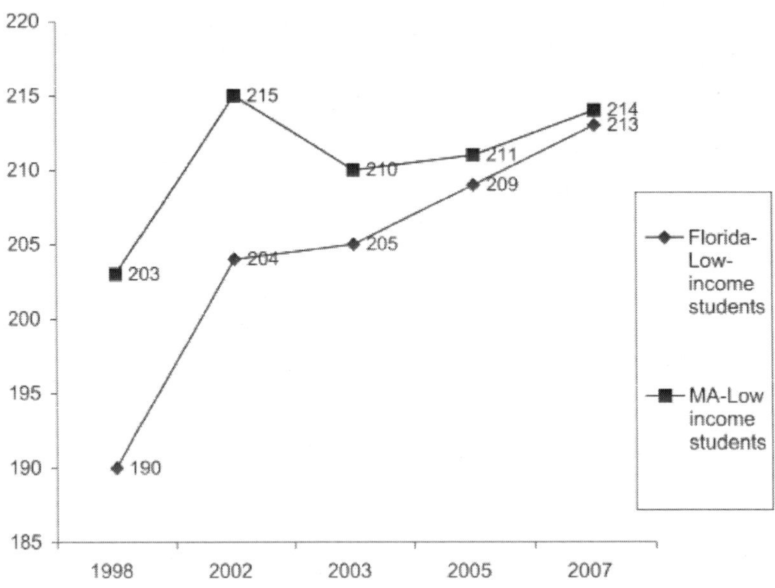

Figures 3, 4, and 5 compare Florida's demographically challenged students to ALL students in Arizona and California, demonstrating remarkable progress. Figures 6 and 8 also show incredible progress in a few short years. Figure 7 shows great progress that spiked in 2002 and then leveled off a year later.

Florida students are improving academically at a higher rate than are students across the country. Importantly, children from minority populations are making the greatest improvements—proof that Florida is making progress in reducing the achievement gap.

An old saying holds that the difference between a condition and a problem lies in whether or not you have given up. A problem is something you are still trying to solve; a condition is something that one has grown to accept as unalterable. The improved academic achievement of Florida's minority and economically disadvantaged students shows that demographic disadvantages are a problem to be solved, not a condition to be accepted. Florida's reforms have greatly improved education in that state, but they are still far from achieving true international competitiveness when compared with our Asian and European counterparts.

I am ecstatic about what Florida is accomplishing, but I am not satisfied. This information proves common sense logic: our children are not born stupid; they grow into it. Preuss School and the state of Florida reveal that every child born in America can and will do great things if given a chance. Today's class of students is GIGO. No it is not Geico; I have all of the insurance I need. GIGO means "Garbage In; Garbage Out." ABC News did a show entitled *"John Stossel's 'Stupid in America'—How Lack of Choice Cheats Our Kids Out of a Good Education"* that I would not classify as in-depth because he didn't have to work hard to find the material. It is in virtually every public classroom in America:

"Stupid in America" is a nasty title for a program about public education, but some nasty things are going on in America's public schools and it's about time we face up to it.

Kids at New York's Abraham Lincoln High School told me their teachers are so dull students fall asleep in class. One student said, "You see kids all the time walking in the school smoking weed, you know. It's a normal thing here."

We tried to bring *20/20* cameras into New York City schools to see for ourselves and show you what's going on in the schools, but officials wouldn't allow it. Washington, D.C., officials steered us to the best classrooms in their district. We wanted to tape typical classrooms but were turned down in state after state.[44]

Just a little observation: Your children are in their room with the door locked and all of a sudden you knock on the door. You hear scrambling around with the comment "Give us a minute!" Are you curious? Try this: let a public school know that you want to come by and give a "parental inspection" of the grounds while school is in session. You will get a super writer's cramp halfway through filling out the forms for a controlled and chaperoned visit to limited areas. Now try that at a private school. They will be glad to proudly show off everything they have. You will think you are at a lawyers' convention in a wheelchair after yelling "I just got rear-ended by Donald Trump!" Do you get the picture?

Back to Mr. Stossel's report:

Finally, school officials in Washington, D.C., allowed *20/20* to give cameras to a few students who were handpicked at two schools they'd handpicked. One was Woodrow Wilson High. *Newsweek says it's one of the best schools in America.* Yet what the students taped didn't inspire confidence.

One teacher didn't have control over the kids. Another *20/20* student cameraman videotaped a boy dancing wildly with his shirt off in front of his teacher.[45] (emphasis added)

I assume he got extra credit.

Here's an idea—competition. Private schools are trying to get your business. You compare uniform test scores and reputations as you shop for a school you want your children to attend—does that sound like a good plan?

> Ben Chavis is a former public school principal who now runs an alternative charter school in Oakland, California, that *spends thousands of dollars less per student* than the surrounding public schools. He laughs at the public schools' complaints about money…."That is the biggest lie in America. They waste money," he said…. *Even though he spends less money per student than the public schools do, Chavis pays his teachers more than what public school teachers earn…* . Since he took over four years ago, his school has gone from being among the worst in Oakland to being the best. His middle school has the highest test scores in the city.
>
> To give you an idea of how competitive American schools are and how U.S. students performed compared with their European counterparts, we gave parts of an international test to some high school students in Belgium and New Jersey… . .Belgian kids cleaned the American kids' clocks, and called them "stupid." … . The Belgian students didn't perform better because they're smarter than American students. They performed better because their schools are better… . American schools don't teach as well as schools in other countries because they are government monopolies, and monopolies don't have much incentive to compete. *In Belgium, by contrast, the money is attached to the kids—it's a kind of voucher system. Government funds education—at many levels—but if a school can't attract students, it goes out of business.*[46] (emphasis added)

Every casino in Las Vegas greets you with a huge $1 million dollar slot machine at the door. *Somebody* is going to win that prize! Yet we are throwing more and more money into ED and we have not had a child win in fifty years. Our alternative is to convert to private schools and we have a guaranteed winner every time for half the cost!

Citizenship Education

Strategic Vision, LLC conducted a poll on November 21-23, 2008 concerning general civil knowledge of 1,134 public, 136 charter, and 1,350 private high school students in the state of Arizona.[47] This poll is discussed in a Goldwater Institute study. Applicants for U.S. citizenship must take a test provided by U.S. Citizenship and Immigration Services. These students took one of these exams and I offer it to you as well. You need six correct answers to pass.

Questions

1. What is the supreme law of the land?

2. What do we call the first ten amendments to the Constitution?

3. What are the two parts of the U.S. Congress?

4. How many justices are on the Supreme Court?

5. Who wrote the Declaration of Independence?

6. What ocean is on the east coast of the United States?

7. What are the two major political parties in the United States?

8. We elect a U.S. senator for how many years?

9. Who was the first president?

10. Who is in charge of the executive branch?

Exhibit L

Arizona High School Students attending Public Schools
Number of Citizenship Questions Answered Correctly (N=1,134)

NUMBER OF ANSWERS CORRECT	NUMBER OF STUDENTS	PERCENT OF THE TOTAL
0	26	2.3%
1	146	12.9%
2	295	26%
3	331	29.2%
4	199	17.5%
5	97	8.6%
6	31	2.7%
7	9	0.8%
8	0	0.0%
9	0	0.0%
10	0	0.0%

Arizona High School Students attending Charter Schools
Number of Citizenship Questions Answered Correctly (N=136)

NUMBER OF ANSWERS CORRECT	NUMBER OF STUDENTS	PERCENT OF THE TOTAL
0	2	1.5%
1	16	11.8%
2	32	23.5%
3	37	27.2%
4	27	19.9%
5	12	8.8%
6	9	6.6%
7	1	0.7%
8	0	0.0%
9	0	0.0%
10	0	0.0%

| Arizona High School Students attending Private Schools | | |
| Number of Citizenship Questions Answered Correctly (N=1,350) | | |
NUMBER OF ANSWERS CORRECT	NUMBER OF STUDENTS	PERCENT OF THE TOTAL
0	16	1.2%
1	115	8.5%
2	237	17.6%
3	303	22.4%
4	283	21%
5	211	15.6%
6	129	9.6%
7	48	3.6%
8	7	0.5%
9	1	0.1%
10	0	0.0%

Answers to questions on page 96

1. The Constitution.

2. The Bill of Rights.

3. The Senate and the House of Representatives.

4. Nine.

5. Thomas Jefferson.

6. Atlantic.

7. Democratic and Republican.

8. Six.

9. Washington.

10. The president.

How did you fare? In exhibit L, you will see how the students who get the most conservative estimate of $223,908 of your tax dollars spent on their education have done on the same test.

To put this in proper perspective: the people who take the exam in order to gain U.S. citizenship know that the subject matter of the test is imperative to their gaining the citizenship they yearn for. They have a reason to concentrate on the specific subject matter. Elsewhere in the study, the researchers found, only 26.5% can identify George Washington as the first president and less than half know that the two major political parties are Democrat and Republican.

A very thin silver lining is the demonstrated superiority of a private school education. Public school students had a 3.1% pass rate; Charter students had 7.3%; and private school students had 13.2%; more than four times the pass rate at public schools.

Students Grade Their Schools

If you enjoy your work, you look forward to doing the job. The same is true of students in school. If we create a pleasant environment, students will be more motivated to spend greater effort in their work.

The Goldwater Institute took a poll of 1,350 Arizona public and private high school students and published a report in 2009 evaluating how students rate their public and private schools.[48] This is an excellent example of "pictures speak louder than words" so I will offer the results with a slight caution: many will argue that these are subjective polls based upon the students' dissimilar demographic backgrounds. The demographic characteristics could distort the outcome in either direction—you be the judge. Take a look at exhibit M.

Exhibit M

FIGURE 1: Arizona Public and Private High School Students Grade their Schools

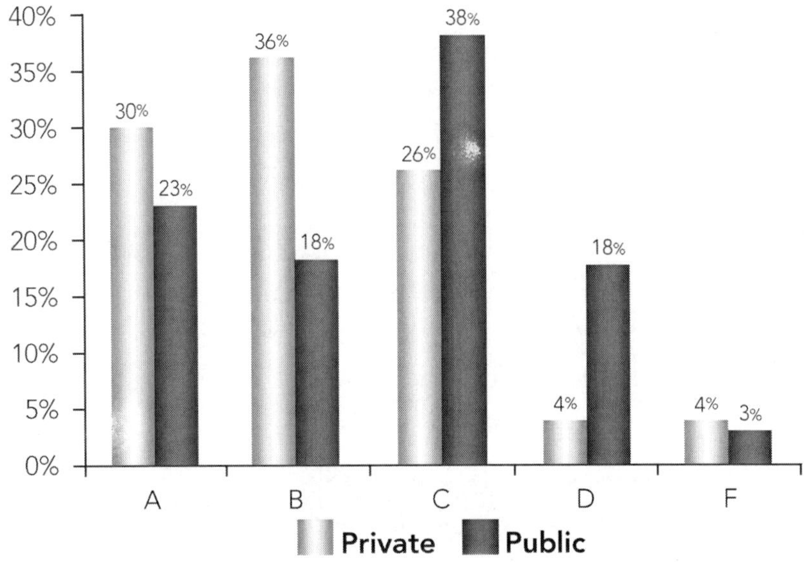

FIGURE 2: Students respond to "Staff at my school care about the students."

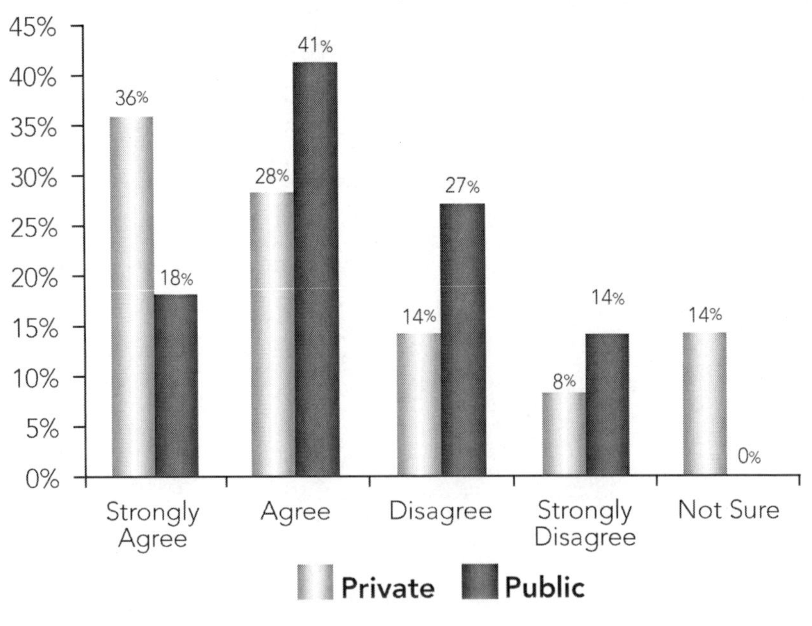

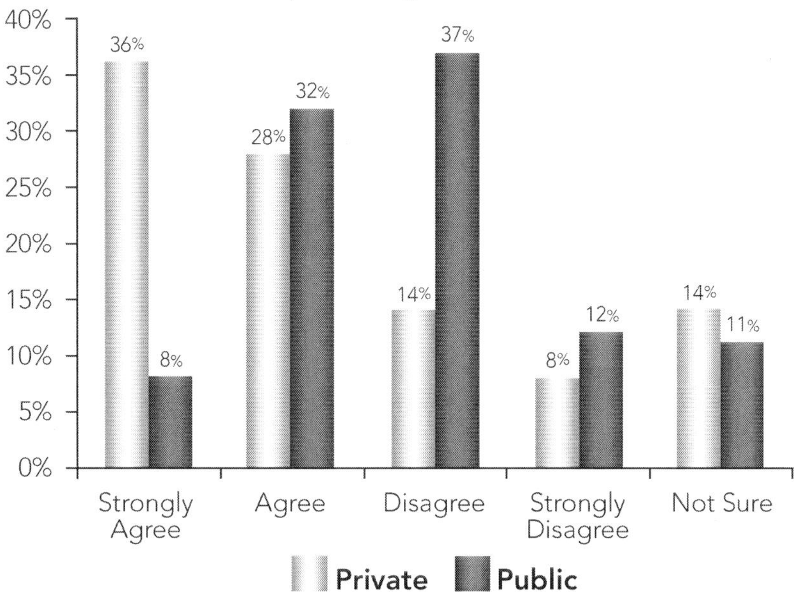

FIGURE 3: "My school treats all students with respect regardless of race."

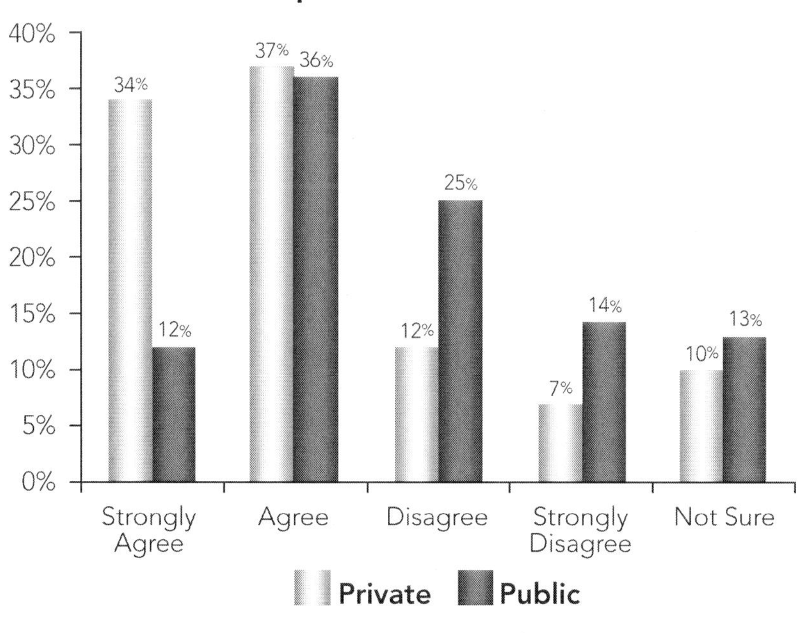

FIGURE 4: "My school has high expectations of me."

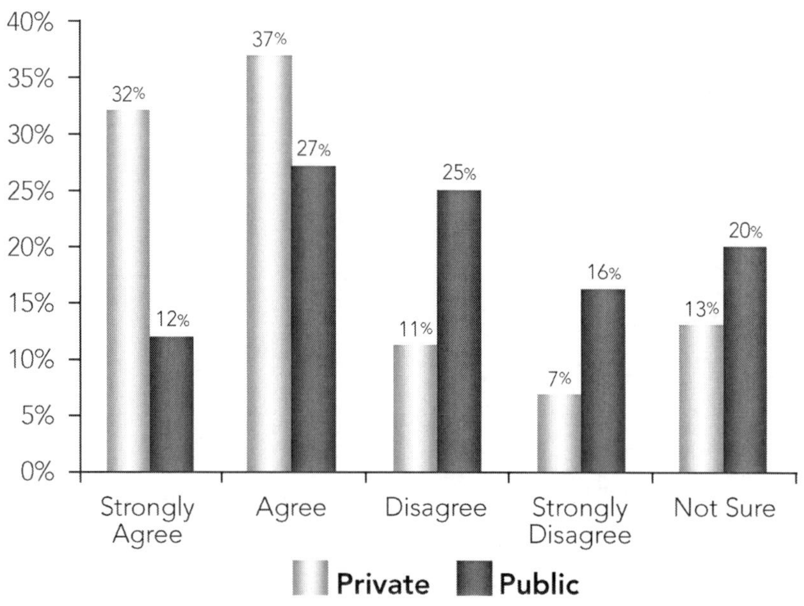

FIGURE 5: "Students at my school focus on learning."

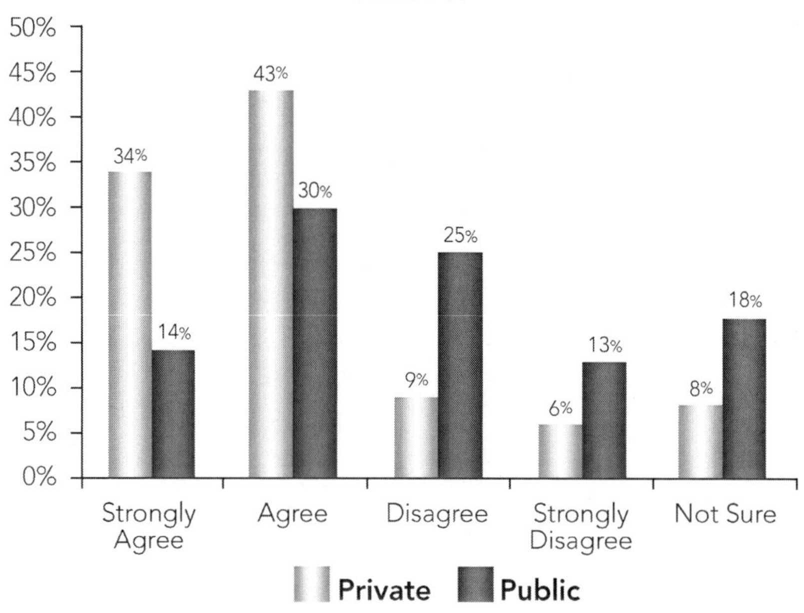

FIGURE 6: "My school offers challenging classes."

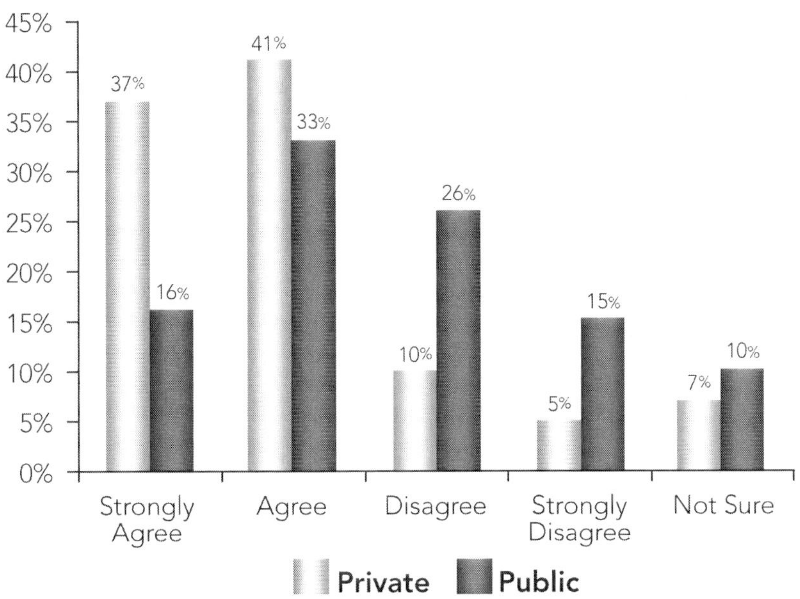

FIGURE 7: "My teachers give me challenging work."

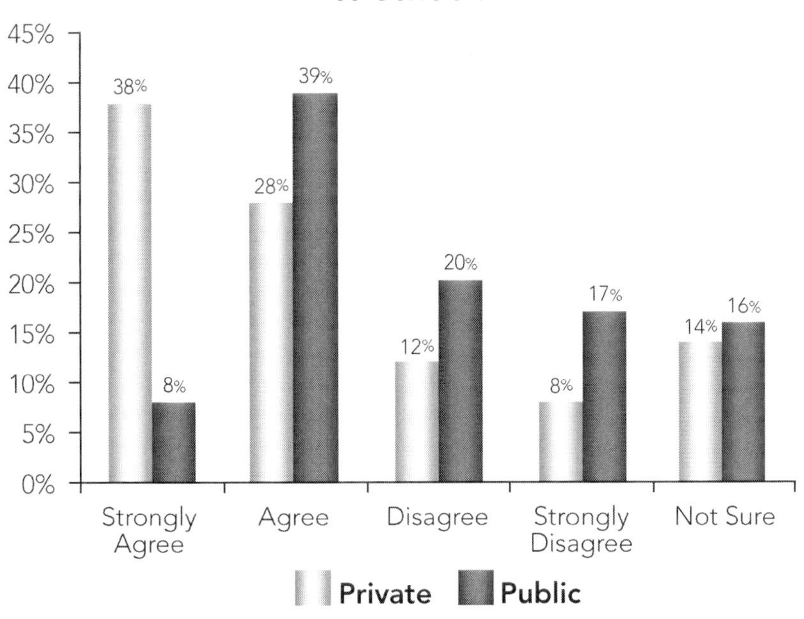

FIGURE 8: "I look forward to going to school."

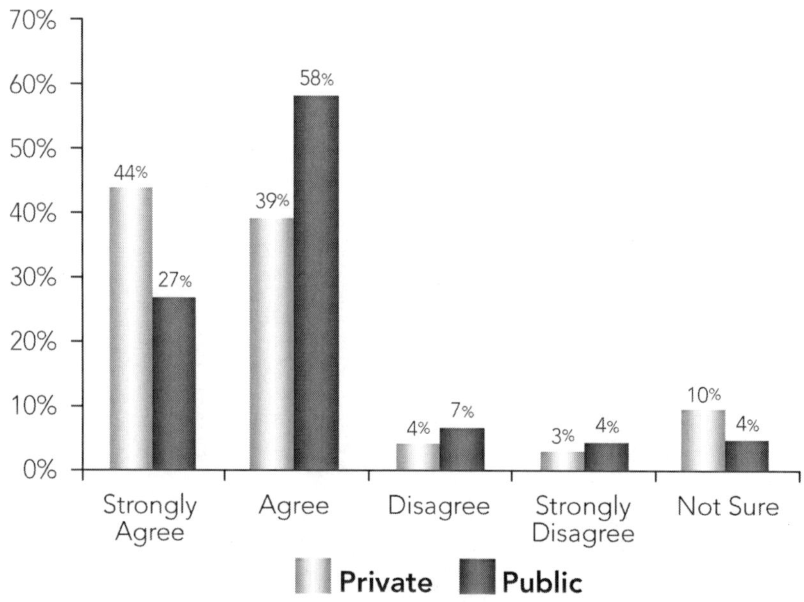

FIGURE 9: "My school promotes a drugfree environment."

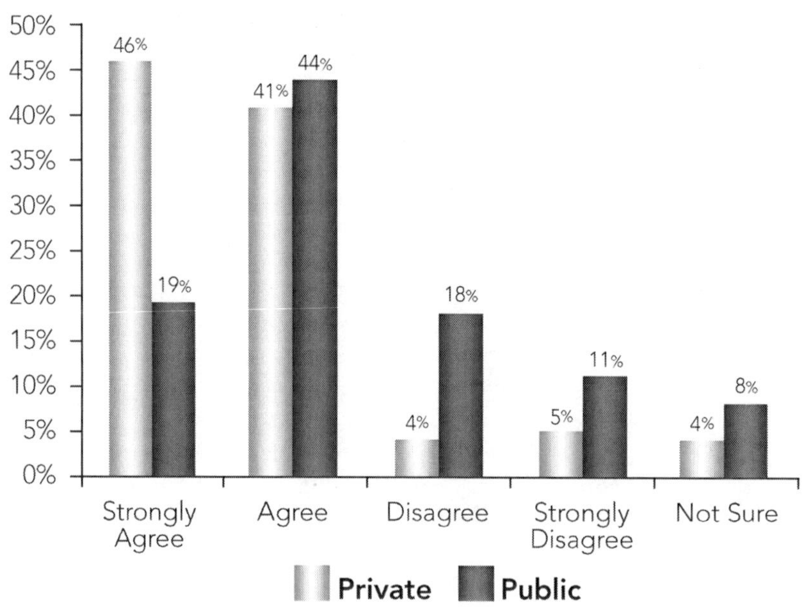

FIGURE 10: "My school makes sure classrooms are safe and orderly."

Seriously, if you are a parent, don't you want your child in a school that has the left-column scores?

Lessons to Apply

We must never forget the lessons of our past; our present challenges are products of where we have been. Only the future provides us flexibility. Very little is cast in stone about tomorrow and practically none of us know where we will be in a year. Our children are the future. What we are doing to them with the educational system is practically criminal.

The other issues addressed in this book: health care, immigration, oil, housing, freedom of religion, and even abortion are matters that can be corrected with proper government action. All we need to do is reverse the trends by electing qualified individuals to Congress. Education is different. Correcting the system today does not help yesterday's graduates.

Take this opportunity to act. Look carefully at the voting records of your elected officials and hold them accountable for what is right. The State of Florida and Preuss School in San Diego are telling us that we can win. We know disadvantaged students are not bound by demographics but by the foolish and false presumptions hammered into the public mind. Be brave! Demand that the U.S. Department of Education be dismantled and that State Departments of Education be completely transformed.

No student should be chained to a specific school because they reside in a particular block or neighborhood. Teachers have the responsibility to provide the most valuable gift any person outside of the immediate family can share. Caring parents are aching for the proper school environment for their children, but they are lost and bewildered based upon pure ignorance. You are no longer ignorant. You know how bad it is and how good it can be. You

will speak to your government on November 2. Tell the candidates what needs to be done for the sake of the children by demanding to know what their plans are before you cast your vote! If enough cry out for reform it will happen; their jobs depend on it!

Immigration and Border Control

Immigration and border control have merged as the hottest and most polarized issue facing our nation today. I reach that conclusion based upon the arguments, rallies, and marches upon government buildings reported by news media every day. The problem is that these arguments are based upon confused misinterpretations of the facts and the law. According to recent polls, the great majority of each demographic group is looking to achieve a similar end, but we have trouble deciding how to get there.

I am going to approach this subject by discussing the bases for my analyses and conclusions before I open the discussion. I will then discuss the criminal gang activity that has exploded in recent years. We need to understand the friction immigration policies can create in relation to our national security. That will help us see the proper path that serves the United States, its citizens, and all aliens, both legal and illegal, who reside in and out of this country.

Any reference to "illegal immigrants" or "illegal aliens" in this chapter is benign and makes no reference to those from a specific nation or classification of countries.

Citizenship for Illegal Aliens

The plea for citizenship of illegal aliens is entirely out of place. The United States is the melting pot of the world. With the exceptions of Native Americans and many Hispanics, practically everyone who resides in the U.S.A is an immigrant or an immigrant's descendant. To enable those who have broken the law to establish residency to then gain citizenship would deny those who have honorably applied for legal immigration the benefits they seek. We would be punishing the people who have played by the rules and rewarding those who have abused the compassion and charity this great nation offers.

Babies Born to Illegal Aliens

Children born to illegal aliens should not be granted citizenship. This is a reward for breaking the law. Federal law denies citizenship to the child of a diplomat who is born in the U.S.[1] This law may also be applied to illegal aliens' births based upon the premise that the mother's and child's presence in the U.S. is a product of international diplomacy. Another alternative is to amend the U.S. Constitution to deny citizenship to children of those who entered illegally. Many more will be served by charitable work in their native countries than by entitlements claimed by the illegal border-crossers. One thousand dollars provided to a family in America may provide for its needs for a week or two, but $1,000 forwarded to a needy community in central Mexico would provide for ten families for over a month. A humanitarian health center in an impoverished Mexican community will provide medical care for thousands, while the delivery of an anchor baby in a U.S. hospital gives an illegal immigrant access to hundreds of thousands of dollars in entitlements.

Incentives for Illegals

The influx of illegal aliens is caused by the fact that the United States has many incentives to draw people across the border, often causing them to risk their lives to gain these privileges. Congress must work to amend our laws and cease to provide direct financial benefits to illegal aliens. This legislation would unfortunately burden many who have already established residence in the U.S.

Congress may contemplate a sort of "severance pay" to those currently receiving financial assistance who agree to return to their native countries, thereby accelerating the move(s). An incentive to return will cost the U.S. less and emigrants will benefit from the much lower cost of living in their native countries. We simply cannot afford to continue to provide financial support to those who have illegally immigrated. Doing so acts as an advertisement to their countrymen.

Rethink Deportations

The institution of a program of this nature is not intended to apply to all. There are many who do not represent burdens upon our nation or economy. I am saddened that many illegal alien deportations have been applied to productive members of our communities. We need to establish standards to separate them from those who are abusing the system.

Terrorism

U.S. soil has been the victim of terrorist attacks since 1865. That was the beginning of work by the Ku Klux Klan to overthrow the reconstructionist governments in the American South and reestablish segregation. On September 16, 1920, a TNT bomb killed thirty-five people in New York City. Since then, there have been thirty-two more terrorist acts. These include Timothy McVeigh's bombing of a federal office building in Oklahoma City, two separate attacks on the World Trade Center, and most recently, Joseph Stack piloting a one-engine plane into an office building in Austin, Texas on February 18, 2010, and Faisal Shahzad's attempt to set off a bomb in Times Square on May 1, 2010.

Terrorism will never disappear. We must always be on guard. Proper management of immigration and our borders is a critical step in finding those who seek to cause harm and thwarting their efforts.

Organized Crime and Illegals

The Ladders employment search agency created an advertisement involving two people playing tennis.[2] In the commercial, all of a sudden the tennis court is swarmed by hundreds of people swinging their rackets. The southern borders of the United States are just like that tennis court. How would you like to be in charge of U.S. Immigration and Customs Enforcement, the Department of Homeland Security, the border patrol, or any other law enforcement agency working to protect our borders? They not only have the burden of protecting us against terrorists, but they also must discern which border-crossers are hardened criminals and which are simple immigrants.

The inevitable evolution of our nation's wealth and government entitlements lure illegal immigrants and nurture an influx of criminal gangs who view the United States as ripe for picking. Government agencies must look for these hardened criminals in the parade of traffic that makes a Los Angeles freeway look like a side street. According to border patrol figures from 2005, an estimated one in five illegal crossers was apprehended.[3] They caught over 1.2 million trespassers that year, which means that there were 6 million who attempted to cross and almost 5 million were successful.

The Center for Immigration Studies (CIS) conducted an elaborate study of immigrant gangs.[4] "Since 2005, the Bureau of Immigration and Customs Enforcement (ICE) has arrested more than 8,000 gangsters from more than 700 different gangs as part of a special initiative known as Operation Community Shield" (OCS). Many of the immigrant gangsters in the most notorious gangs are illegal aliens. This report describes the exceptional public safety problems posed by immigrant gangs and looks at how one jurisdiction, Virginia, has used immigration law enforcement

tools successfully to check their further proliferation. Among the findings:

- The growth of transnational gangs has been a dangerous side effect of our failure to control the U.S.-Mexico border and our tolerance for high levels of illegal immigration.

- ICE gang arrests have occurred nationwide, with the largest numbers made by the offices in San Diego, Atlanta, San Francisco, and Dallas. Some jurisdictions with serious gang problems had just a few OCS arrests, such as Phoenix, with only 81 arrests, and Houston, with 84 arrests. Los Angeles, the gang capital of the nation, had fewer than 300 arrests. These same jurisdictions also had controversial "sanctuary" or "don't ask, don't tell" policies on immigration status in place over the time period studied.

- Nearly half (3,080) of the aliens arrested over the two-and-a-half-year period studied, were affiliated with MS-13 and Surenos-13 two of the most notorious gangs with largely Hispanic immigrant memberships.

- Nearly 60% of alien gangsters arrested by ICE were Mexican citizens; 17% were from El Salvador, and 5% were from Honduras.

The Justice Department's National Youth Gang Center also reported rapid growth of gangs in the U.S. It estimated that in 1980 there were approximately 2,000 gangs with almost 10,000 members in 286 jurisdictions. By 2002, the estimated number of youth gangs grew to 21,500 (975% increase), with 731,500 members (7,215% increase).[5] The Federal Bureau of Investigation (FBI) today estimates that there are 30,000 violent street, motorcycle, and prison gangs, with about 800,000 members.[6] Much of the growth has been in suburban and rural parts of the country, where criminal activity is still relatively new. According to the FBI, "gangs are more violent, more organized, and more widespread than ever before. They pose one of the greatest threats to the safety and security of all Americans."[7]

A recent Drug Enforcement Administration report concludes that gangs are responsible for most of the serious violent crimes in major U.S. cities.[8] Gang members in the U.S. come from fifty-three different nationalities, but 75% of them are from Mexico and El Salvador. In fact, Honduras, El Salvador, and Guatemala are considered to be the center of the gang crisis. In comparison: 2004 murder rates per 100,000 people in the U.S. were 5.7; Guatemala 34.7; El Salvador 41.2; and Honduras 45.9. Salvadoran police estimate that at least 50% of the 2,756 murders were gang-related.[9]

The Case of MS-13

There are hundreds of immigrant gangs and thousands of immigrant gangsters, but only a few gangs have a significant interstate and international membership. Just ten gangs account for 63% of the ICE arrests during the period studied. (See exhibit A). The most notorious is MS-13. By some accounts, MS-13 has "mushroomed into the size of a small army." The FBI estimated in 2005 that there were approximately 10,000 "hardcore" members of MS-13 in the United States.[10] Estimates of the number of gang members in Central America and Mexico range from 50,000 up to 300,000 members. A significant percentage is part of MS-13.[11]

Exhibit A

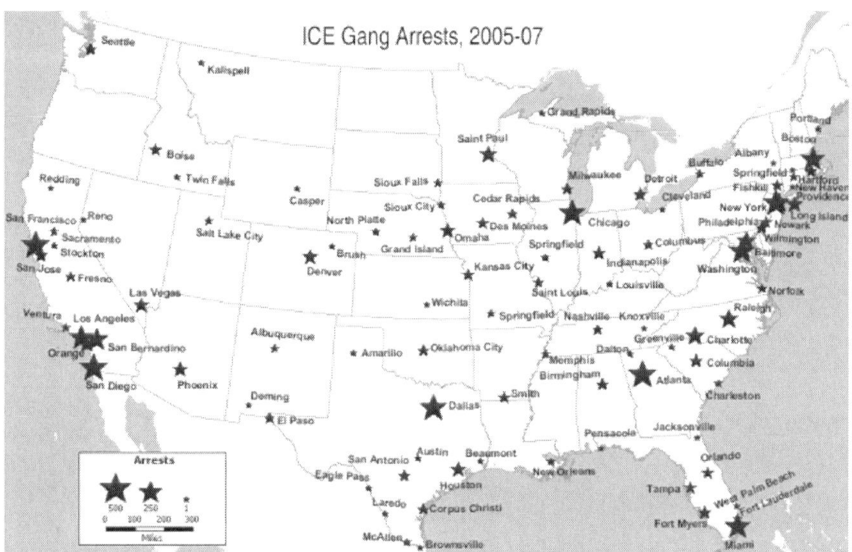

According to Jon Freere and Jessica Vaughan in their report "Taking Back the Streets: ICE and Local Law Enforcement Target Immigrant Gangs":

> A variety of factors have enabled the MS-13 to flourish within the United States. *Gaps in security along the U.S.-Mexico border have permitted large numbers of MS-13 members to enter and re-enter the country without major difficulty in recent years.*[12] (emphasis added)

> The gangs also benefited from shifts in law enforcement priorities. Following years of success in the 1990s, many law enforcement agencies shifted focus away from gang suppression, a trend that was accelerated after 9/11, when preventing terrorist attacks became the top priority. For example, the number of agents dedicated to gang investigations in the Washington, D.C. Field office of the FBI reportedly declined by 50% after 9/11.

> Exact numbers are impossible to obtain, but a variety of law enforcement and outside observers maintain that the majority of MS-13 gang members are in the country illegally, with national estimates ranging from 60 to 90%.[13]

MS-13 wants the reputation of being the most violent and feared gang in the world. Smugglers have hired them to kill Border Patrol agents who block common smuggling routes, according to a confidential Department of Homeland Security memo. MS-13 gangs frequently work extortion schemes. "In Central America, hundreds of bus drivers have been killed for refusing to pay 'tolls' to MS-13 gang members; store owners have been executed by the gang for refusing to pay a 'tax' levied by the gang; and reportedly the gang has demanded payment from the parents of young girls to insure that the girls will not be raped by gang members."[14]

This discussion of violent crime gives us a vision of hardened and experienced criminals. Exhibit B demonstrates that is not the case. Both the perpetrators and the nameless, faceless victims are the youths who are caught in the legislative disregard of immigration management and border control.

Exhibit B

Figure 4. Age Distribution of OCS Arrests, 2005-2007

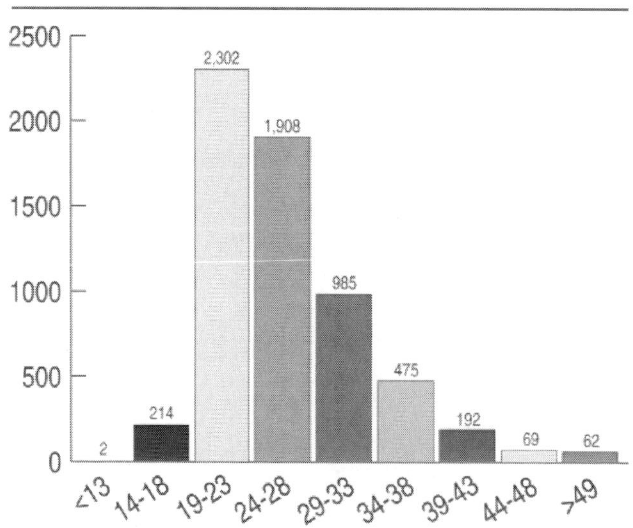

Source: U.S. Immigration and Customs Enforcement.

Operation Community Shield

As gangs expand their criminal activities, U.S. Immigration and Customs Enforcement (ICE) is responding with Operation Community Shield (OCS). Its purpose is to complement federal and local gang suppression initiatives by separating immigration benefit and enforcement functions in the Department of Homeland Security. As a result, ICE has arrested more than 8,000 immigrant gangsters from 2005 to 2007. The Dallas Police Department attributes a 20% reduction in the city's murder rate to OCS.[15] This cooperation between ICE and the Northern Virginia Regional Gang Task Force (NVGTF) in Fairfax County, Virginia, led to a 32% drop in gang-related crime in 2006 and continued decline in 2007.[16] A large majority of the gangsters arrested—at least 70%—entered the United States illegally. Only 99 had green cards or had otherwise been granted asylum. More than one out of six (16.73%) had already been formally deported at least once.

ICE agents often use administrative charges to arrest dangerous individuals wanted for crimes in other countries. Jesus Ruben Moncada is a Mexican gangster who was wanted for the murder of nineteen people, including eight children, in Baja California in 1998. In August, 2008 he was arrested in Los Angeles on administrative investigation charges.[17] He was then expedited to Mexico to face criminal prosecution, thereby saving the U.S. the complicated, time-consuming expense of its own criminal prosecution. The end result is the same: the alien was removed.

ICE-conducted searches are so valuable for gang and other criminal investigations because the subject often believes that the ICE agents are there simply to look into immigration status. The agents often walk out the door with major intelligence and, in some cases, evidence of criminal activity that was copied from a cell phone or computer hard drive.

Immigration special agents can often spur cooperation of informants or witnesses that might otherwise be difficult to obtain. Not only does cooperation mean reduced time behind bars, but the alternative of deportation for a gang member who aided in an investigation; even unwillingly, is a sure death sentence soon after leaving the plane in El Salvador. In the gang world, no "snitch" goes unpunished.

Border Control

We have established that border control, in and of itself, should not be primarily directed at keeping out illegal aliens who are simply yearning to gain access to a superior environment. A wiser solution is to eliminate entitlement lures. This will enable our law enforcement authorities to concentrate on national security interests. As a practical matter, based upon the data referenced above that approximately 4.8 million of the 6 million attempts to enter this country illegally in 2005 were successful, what do we really know about border control?

The borders of the United States include four distinct segments. The first three, airports, ports, and guarded land points, are recognized as "official." The fourth, the unguarded borders and shoreline, is unofficial, and it is the access almost exclusively used by migrants, smugglers, traffickers, and terrorists. Obviously, the fourth segment creates the complexities that face us.[18]

One might assume that everyone caught by the U.S. Border Patrol is treated equally. Nothing could be further from the truth. Approximately 57% of the illegal immigrants are from Mexico and 24% are from other Latin American countries.[19] Those from Mexico are deported back to their home country, but non-Mexicans are shortly detained and given a "notice to appear" at

an immigration hearing weeks later.[20] Most "Other-Than-Mexicans," or "OTMs" never appear. As a matter of fact, they pretty much all know the rules and procedures, so they make a beeline to the nearest Border Patrol agent so they can "surrender" and then be released with nary a future care. According to *Voice Of America:*

> Brazilians are now the largest category of Other Than Mexicans who cross illegally into the United States. In the first half of 2005, more than 12,000 undocumented Brazilians have been caught and released by the U.S. Border Patrol, exceeding the total count from 2004…. Border Patrol statistics show 39,000 non-Mexican crossers were caught in all of 2003. That number has already reached 85,000 this year. [21]

That article was dated June 30, 2005. The OTM illegal immigration went from about 3,250 per month in 2003 to 14,167 per month a year and a half later—an increase of 335.9%. These statistics are five years old, and we can only speculate on the current numbers. We also need to acknowledge that not every illegal OTM immigrant goes to the nearest Border Patrol agent. Some may not want to be bothered by the inconvenience. The recorded illegal entry of 170,000 for the year 2005 is a very conservative estimate of the total. These numbers will continue to rise unless we change our laws and treatment of illegal aliens.

Border Fencing

One of the hottest topics representing a number of pros and cons for everybody on either side of the fence—er, border—is the border fence itself. The border fence primarily impacts common immigrants while the criminals and terrorists are more sophisticated and less likely to be deterred. The fence's import will greatly improve when we take away the lures of government entitlements and allow our effort to be directed at the ultimate goal: protecting our nation.

According to Fox News on April 08, 2009:

> Illegal immigrant deaths along the U.S.-Mexico border have risen in the past six months despite a nearly 25 percent drop in arrests by the Border Patrol, according to patrol statistics. … The rise in deaths was "the direct result of more agents, more fencing and more equipment" the Rev. Robin Hoover, founder of the Tucson-based Humane Borders, which provides water stations for migrants crossing the southern Arizona desert, said Tuesday. "The migrants are walking in more treacherous terrain for longer periods of time, and you should expect more deaths." … Hoover said locations where bodies had been found were farther away from roads than in previous years, indicating the migrants were taking greater risks to avoid capture… . "So they're going around the fences, the technology and where the agents are," he said. "And the further you walk from a safe place, the more likely a broken ankle becomes a death sentence." [22]

The Congressional Reporting Service has painfully examined border security and published a series of reports I will outline herein.

> In 1990 the United States Border Patrol (USBP) began erecting a physical barrier to deter illegal entries and drug smuggling in the San Diego sector… . It soon became apparent to immigration officials and lawmakers that the USBP needed, among other things, a "rigid" enforcement system that could integrate infrastructure (i.e., a multi-tiered fence and roads), manpower, and new technologies to further control the border region. [23]

> During the last decade, the USBP has seen its budget and manpower more than triple [see illustrations below]. This expansion was the direct result of Congressional concerns about illegal immigration and the agency's adoption of "Prevention Through Deterrence" as its chief operational strategy in 1994.

The strategy called for placing USBP resources and manpower directly at the areas of greatest illegal immigration. Post 9/11, the USBP refocused its strategy on preventing the entry of terrorists and weapons of mass destruction, as laid out in its recently released National Strategy. In addition to a workforce of over 17,000 agents, the USBP deploys vehicles, aircraft, watercraft, and many different technologies to defend the border.[24]

Exhibit C

Figure 1. Border Patrol Appropriations

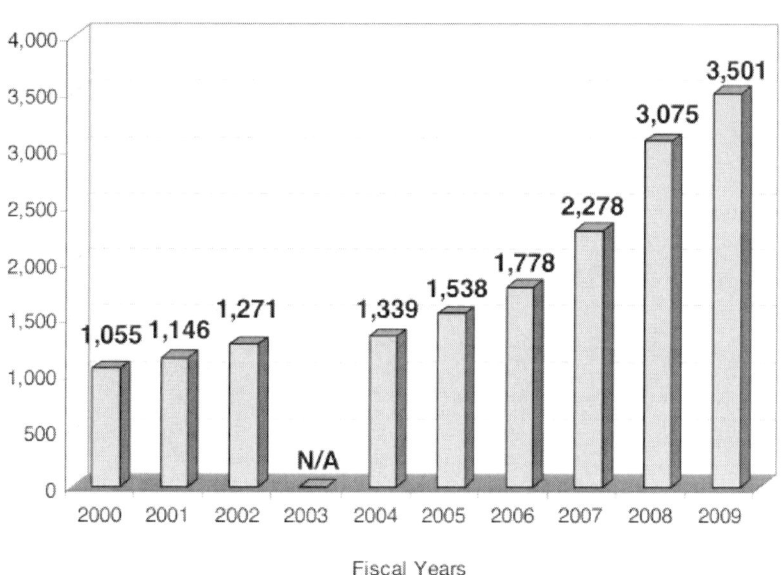

As can be seen in exhibit C, the amount of money spent on the border patrol went up 3.32 times in nine years. This has enabled a significant increase in manpower as well (see exhibit D).

Paradoxically, as spending and manpower increased, the number of arrests decreased. This can hardly be recognized as progress. We are now investing a lot more time, energy, and money into chasing down the common immigrants (see figure 3).

Exhibit D

Figure 2. Southwest Border Agent Manpower

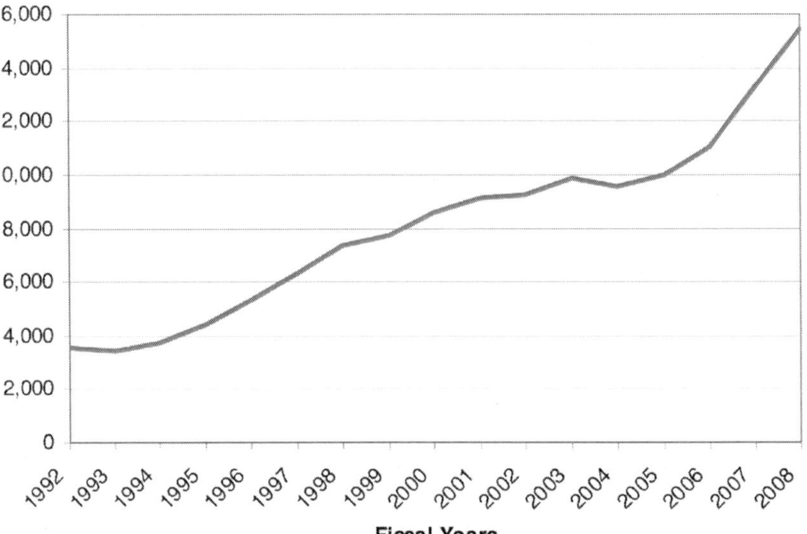

Source: CBP Congressional Affairs.

Figure 3. SW Border Apprehensions

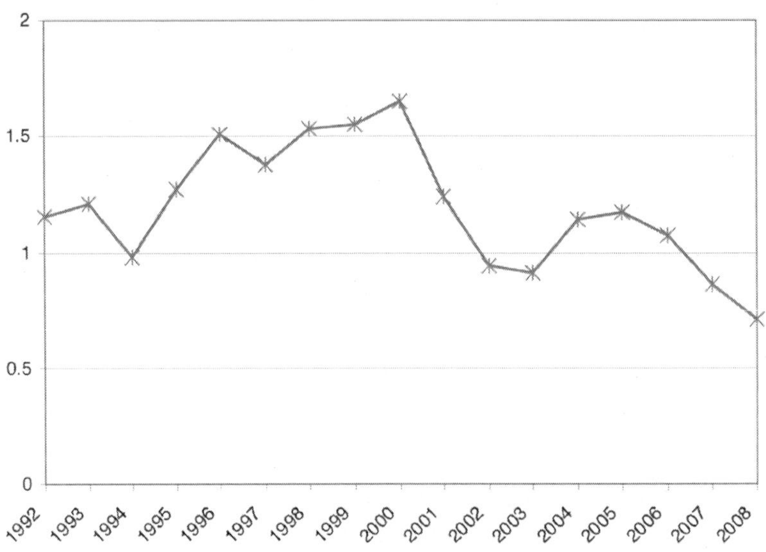

Source: CRS Presentation of CBP Data.

There is a logical explanation. Illegal aliens have moved away from the more populated areas and into more desolate terrain. As mentioned before, this is making the immigration more difficult and dangerous, but not really making a big dent in the number of people who make the crossover.

Another detail yet to be addressed concerns our northern border with Canada that is more than 4,000 miles long, not including the 1,500-mile border with Alaska. Exhibit E shows that we increased the manpower at the northern border by almost six times, but that apprehensions there have in fact decreased.

Exhibit E

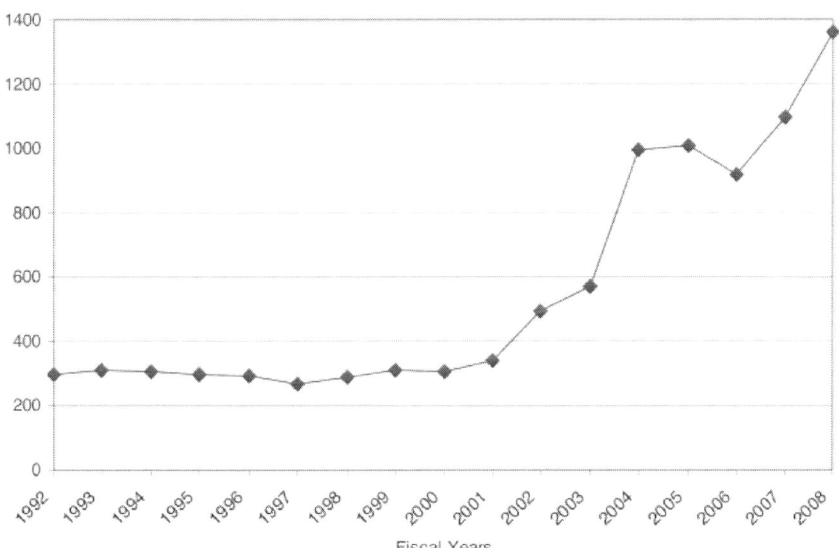

Figure 6. Border Patrol Agents at the Northern Border

Source: CRS Presentation of CBP Data.

Figure 7. Northern Border Apprehensions

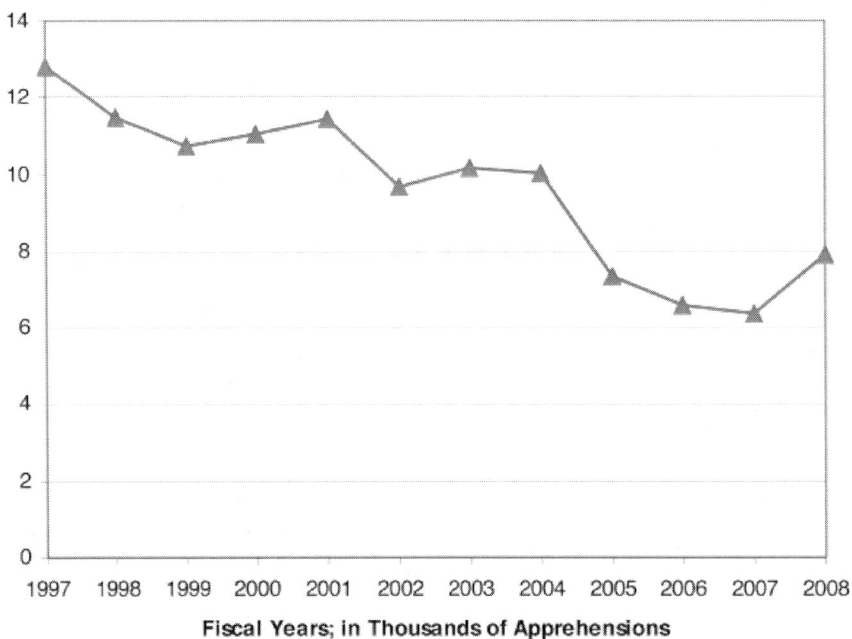

Source: CRS Presentation of CBP Data.

Our northern border is logistically an entirely different animal. It is not the place we need to concern ourselves with the garden-variety illegal aliens, but it is where we need to protect ourselves from terrorists and the more sophisticated criminal element. Border fencing would be entirely wasted because there are very few significantly populated areas that act as a catalyst for border-crossers of any nature. We have the advantage of significant cooperation by the Canadian government, enabling us to use more sophisticated technology rather than sending thousands of border patrol agents to monitor the line.

Despite its limitations, the fence is beneficial in controlling our border and preventing unwanted aliens from entering our land. Despite the fact that it represents a nuisance to many of our citizens,[25] it is here to stay. It will be more useful when we are able to employ its deterrent nature against terrorists and criminals, thereby supporting the efforts of our law enforcement agencies. As stated before, we are spending way too much time and effort dealing with everyday illegal aliens, and it is hindering our attention to the national security risks.

Costs of Illegal Immigration

Robert Rector and Christine Kim of the Heritage Foundation prepared an excellent study entitled *The Fiscal Cost of Low-Skill Immigrants to the U.S. Taxpayer.*[26] This study addresses the fiscal impact of households headed by immigrants without a high school diploma. In fiscal year 2004, approximately 5% of the U.S. population, about 15.9 million people, was in this category. Forty percent were illegal. The problem is that this is *just an estimate.* Many excellent and reliable sources of data[27] include estimates ranging from about 11.5 million to 20 million and beyond; the proportions of legal and illegal immigrants also vary. We can't come up with exact numbers because many of this segment of the population prefer to maintain their secrecy. The Urban Institute prepared the pie chart and map in exhibit F based on population data from the years 2000 and 2002.[28] These numbers are conservative in comparison to 2010, but they provide valuable information.

Exhibit F

FIGURE 2. SHARE UNDOCUMENTED OF FOREIGN-BORN POPULATION, BY STATE, 2000

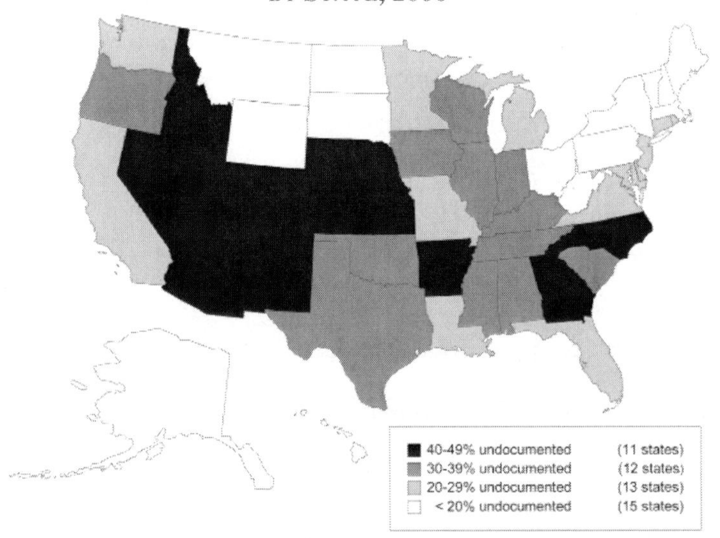

SOURCE: Urban Institute estimates based on Census 2000.

FIGURE 1. LEGAL STATUS OF THE FOREIGN-BORN POPULATION, 2002

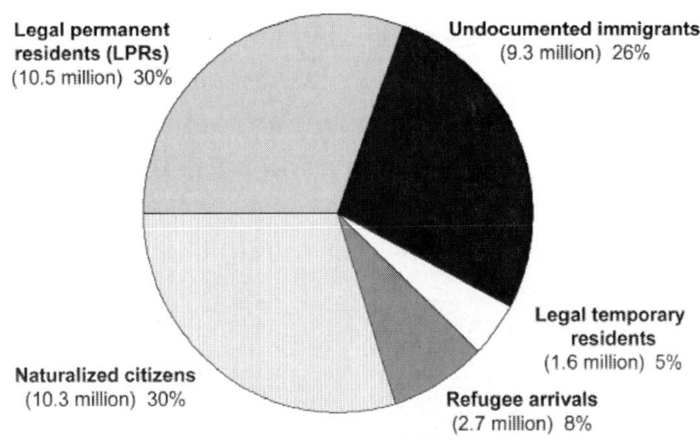

SOURCE: Urban Institute estimates based on March 2002 Current Population Survey.

Now back to the Heritage Foundation article:

In [fiscal year] 2004, federal, state, and local expenditures combined amounted to $3.75 trillion. Government expenditures can be divided into six categories:

- **Direct benefits**, which include Social Security, Medicare, and a few smaller transfer programs;

- **Means-tested benefits**, including cash, food, housing, social services, and medical care for poor and near-poor individuals;

- **Public educational services**, which include the governmental cost of primary, secondary, vocational, and post-secondary education;

- **Population-based services**, which are governmental services made available to a general community, including police and fire protection, highways, sewers, food safety inspection, and parks.

These first four categories can be termed "immediate benefits and services." Entry of legal or illegal immigrants into the U.S. will generally cause expenditures in these categories to rise. Two additional spending categories are:

- **Interest and financial obligations resulting from prior government activity,** including interest payments on government debt and other expenditures relating to the cost of government services provided in earlier years; and

- **Pure public goods,** which include national defense, international affairs and scientific research, and some environmental expenditures.

Entry of immigrants into the U.S. will generally not cause expenditures in the last two categories to increase, at least in the short term. Therefore, these categories are not included in the calculations on the fiscal burden imposed by low-skill immigrant households in this paper.

In FY 2004, low-skill immigrant households received $30,160 per household in immediate benefits and services (direct benefits, means-tested benefits, education, and population-based services) (emphasis added). In general, low-skill immigrant households received about $10,000 more in government benefits than did the average U.S. household, largely because of the higher level of means-tested welfare benefits received by low-skill immigrant households. In contrast, low-skill immigrant households pay less in taxes than do other households. On average, low-skill immigrant households paid only $10,573 in taxes in FY 2004 (emphasis added). Thus, low-skill immigrant households received nearly three dollars in immediate benefits and services for each dollar in taxes paid. …The average low-skill household had a fiscal deficit of $19,588[29] (expenditures of $30,160 minus $10,573 in taxes.)

Hold on a minute! The United States had a work force of 138,530,696 on January 22, 2010.[30] Factor in the population of 4.5 million low-skill immigrant households in the U.S. Now let's see: 4.5 million times $19,588 equals $88.149 billion. Now, you divide $88.149 billion by 138 million and *gasp! Every taxpayer in the U.S. is paying $636.31 per year in taxes to provide for low-skill immigrants.*

Unfortunately that is not the end of the story. The concept of $636.31 per year per taxpayer *implies* that we all pay the same amount of taxes, which is patently untrue. In dollars and cents from your perspective, just look at all the taxes that you paid (income tax, sales tax, property tax, etc.) and know that 2.35% of the expenses incurred by all of the government institutions went directly to low-skill immigrant households.[31] Also, whatever taxes you pay are only a little over half of what the current government is obligating you for, so that means that *a little more than 4% of what you pay in taxes covers the low-skilled immigrant population*. Now, let's return to the Heritage Special Report:

> American families often are net tax payers during working age and net tax takers (benefits exceeding taxes) during retirement. This is not the case for low-skill immigrant households; in these households benefits substantially exceed taxes at every age level. Consequently, low-skill immigrant households impose substantial long-term costs on the U.S. taxpayer. Assuming an average adult life span of 60 years for each head of household, the average lifetime cost to the taxpayer will be nearly $1.2 million for each low-skill household for immediate benefits received minus all taxes paid.… Over the next ten years, the net cost (benefits minus taxes) to the taxpayer for low-skill immigrant households will approach $1 trillion.

> At least 50 percent and perhaps 60 percent of illegal immigrant adults lack a high school degree.[32] … By contrast, only 9 percent of non-immigrant adults lack a high school degree.[33]

I have my thinking cap on; which is rare enough that I should make some use of it. In Mexico, the source of more than half of our immigrants, both legal and illegal, the cost of living is about $685.11 per month, or about $8,221.33 per year.[34] Hopefully this question is obvious to you. *Is there any rational basis for incurring a $19,588 annual fiscal deficit for someone whose cost of living in his or her home country is $8,221?*

Cost of living in this article is described this way: "The cost of living ranges are set within the costs *for a middle to upper class family lifestyle*, which considers a $1,300 to $17,400 USD monthly income."[35] This means that the average cost of living for the whole population of Mexico may in fact be lower, but I think I made my point.

The majority of immigrants in America are not simply looking to leech off of our charitable nature. According to the Urban Institute: "Virtually all undocumented men are in the labor force. Their labor-force participation rate (96%) exceeds that of men who are legal immigrants or who are U.S. citizens because undocumented men are younger and less likely to be disabled, retired, or in school."[36] This does impede low-skill Americans from the same jobs and puts them on the public dole. The moral of the story is that our current system of providing government subsidies and assistance to illegal immigrants is not solving a problem; it is distorting reality and making things worse. We will be able to provide much more for illegal aliens by sending them back home to a much more affordable economy and environment.

Further supportive documentation can be found by examining the State of California's costs associated with illegal immigration. According to Robert Longley of about.com:

> A new study from the Federation for American Immigration Reform (FAIR) examines the costs of education, health care and incarceration of illegal aliens, and concludes that the costs to Californians is $10.5 billion per year…. the state's already struggling K-12 education system spends approximately $7.7 billion a year to school the children of illegal aliens who now constitute 15 percent of the student body. Another $1.4 billion of the taxpayers' money goes toward providing health care to illegal aliens and their families, the same amount that is spent incarcerating illegal alien criminals… ."A small number of powerful interests in the state reap the benefits, while the average native-born family in California gets handed a nearly $1,200 a year bill," [stated Dan Stein, President of FAIR].[37]

Newsmax.com also talks about the Golden State:

> According to the Department of Homeland Security, in 2000 the population of California had the highest percentage of illegal immigrants in the country. The estimate by the Immigration and

Naturalization Service was that 2,209,000 aliens resided illegally within the state. That was 31.6 percent of the estimated national total. Current 2005 illegal estimates vary between 14 million and 22 million nationwide.... Total uncompensated educational, health care and incarceration costs were estimated to be 10.5 billion.[38]

National Public Radio interviewed Bruce Chernoff, County Health Chief for Los Angeles County on April 27, 2006 and got the following:

> We did a study that showed that about $340 million of our overall budget was spent on healthcare for individuals who may be undocumented, but that's only an estimate.... An industry group estimates illegal immigrants cost California hospitals $800 million a year. But Ira Mehlman of FAIR, the Federation for American Immigration Reform, says it's really almost twice that. Add in Texas and Arizona and you get 2.6 billion.... FAIR says it's also worried about illegal immigrants spreading TB, tapeworm and even leprosy among the general population.[39]

Another reference to the personal costs we, as Americans, bear is made by *Slate* reporter Timothy Noah:

> According to a May 2009 study by Families USA, a nonprofit consumer group, the annual cost of uncompensated care is about $73 billion, of which $30 billion is paid by government and charity. The remaining $43 billion is passed onto health insurers, thereby raising the average family insurance premium by $1,017 annually, about 8 percent of the average family premium. Families USA calls this a "hidden health tax." An August 2008 study by the Kaiser Family Foundation crunched the numbers a bit differently, Kaiser also found that the cost to government of uncompensated care was $43 billion, as against the $30 billion that Families USA calculated for both government and charity. According to Kaiser, fully 75 percent of the cost of uncompensated care gets billed to taxpayers. Spread equally among the roughly 138 million taxpayers in the United States, the uninsured cost the average taxpayer about $312 annually. Through some combination of higher taxes and higher

premiums, the rest of us end up paying for the uninsured—either $43 billion in higher premiums or $43 billion in higher taxes.[40]

What this tells me is that the $88.149 billion in government benefits at $19,588 or $22,449 per year per immigrant family, depending on the study, is not all-inclusive. The costs that individual Americans incur to subsidize immigrants through our insurance policies can be as high as $1,017 per year, and that has nothing to do with our taxes. We all know this: somebody has to pay for everything, and the money is eventually going to come out of every American's pocket. The estimate of $636.29 per year in taxes has nothing to do with our increased insurance costs.

Illegals in Prison

Illegal immigrants are flooding the correction system.[41] U.S. prisons are overwhelmed with 147,000 illegal aliens in local jails, 74,000 in state prisons, and 46,000 in federal prisons. About 28% of all federal prisoners are illegal immigrants, mostly from Mexico, and U.S. taxpayers pay about $5.4 billion a year to accommodate them. That is "only" about $39.13 per taxpayer, but the cost of incarceration is only a fraction of the costs that we have incurred regarding whatever put them in prison in the first place. Many prisoners are repeat offenders and are simply released back into communities rather than deported.

Early in 2010, the *Los Angeles Times* reported that it costs the State of California about $1 billion each year to jail illegal immigrants. There are 19,000 illegals in California's prisons.[42] In 2010, the state is expected to receive roughly $90 million in federal money, about 9% of its costs.

Thank goodness the state of California is so overwhelmingly wealthy it can afford to do whatever is asked. It can keep its

entire staff of employees and give them big raises each year, and of course no taxpayer will ever dream of getting an IOU signed by the Governator as their tax refund. California will welcome with open arms the proposal for amnesty of about three to six million illegal aliens who will gain full access to all of the financial benefits that may not otherwise be available to them. *Do you love this country or what?*

Arizona State Senate Bill (SB) 1070

Unless you have been in a coma since April 19, 2010, you are aware that Governor Jan Brewer of the State of Arizona signed SB 1070 into law on April 23. The intent of the statutes encompassed in that legislation is summarized in Section One as follows:

> The legislature finds that there is a compelling interest in the cooperative enforcement of federal immigration laws throughout all of Arizona. The legislature declares that the intent of this act is to make attrition through enforcement the public policy of all state and local government agencies in Arizona. The provisions of this act are intended to work together to discourage and deter the unlawful entry and presence of aliens and economic activity by persons unlawfully present in the United States.[43]

Before I go into the details of this legislation, let's be perfectly clear: These statutes are *both perfectly right and perfectly wrong.* They are perfectly right because they address a national crisis as discussed in this chapter. They are perfectly wrong because they are closing the barn door after the chickens have left the coop; the illegal aliens are already here where they shouldn't be in the first place. More importantly, these statutes are perfectly wrong because they are not the responsibility of the State of Arizona; they are the responsibility of the federal government. Complaints of racial profiling are factually correct simply because the state is overrun by illegal aliens of Hispanic descent rather than Norwegian descent. Nevertheless, the wording of the statute makes it clear that a law officer has the exact same concerns whether the driver is brown-skinned and answers to "Manuel" or if he is blonde-haired, blue-eyed, and hails from Oslo, Norway. But what are the odds of stopping "Lars" on I-8?

A review of the federal[44] and Arizona statutes is in order. The federal work is much more voluminous, seventy-nine pages, whereas the Arizona laws discussed in the act only occupy nine single-spaced pages. Title 8 of the U.S. Code, Section 1373 includes the following:

> (a) In General
> Notwithstanding any other provision of Federal, State, or local law, a Federal, State, or local government entity or official may not prohibit, or in any way restrict, any government entity or official from sending to, or receiving from, the Immigration and Naturalization Service information regarding the citizenship or immigration status, lawful or unlawful, of any individual.

All right, this tells us that there is federal law that provides for open communication between the Immigration and Naturalization Service and all government agencies. Section 1644 of Title 8 goes on to say:

> Notwithstanding any other provision of Federal, State, or local law, no State or local government entity may be prohibited, or in any way restricted, from sending to or receiving from the Immigration and Naturalization Service information regarding the immigration status, lawful or unlawful, of an alien in the United States.[45]

Yes, this looks redundant at first glance, which is a shocking revelation concerning any governmental action, but the net effect is that no government individual or entity can (1) restrict the exchange of information or (2) be restricted from exchanging information regarding any individual and/or any alien. OK, nobody can tell you, if you are a government employee, not to release information, and even if they tell you not to, you have to release the information anyway.

U.S. Code Title 8, Section 1324 makes it a crime to bring in or attempt to bring in and/or harbor or transport ANY alien, legal or illegal, other than at a designated port of entry through proper channels. The penalties range from imprisonment of up to one, five, ten, twenty years or life, depending on the seriousness of the offense. Anyone convicted can also be fined in varying amounts. It goes on to address penalties of up to ten years in prison for hiring illegal aliens.

Section 1324a goes into much more detail regarding the hiring and employment of unauthorized aliens and requires that any employer retain all verification documentation concerning the hire of any employee for the longer of at least three years or one year from the date that individual's employment is terminated.

Moving back to the new Arizona laws, Title 11, Chapter 7, Article 8 is entitled "Enforcement of Immigration Laws." Section 11-1051 adds the following (By the way. it is published in all caps, but I will use lowercase where proper):

A. No official or agency of this State or a County, City, Town, or other political subdivision of this State may limit or restrict the enforcement of Federal Immigration laws to less than the full extent permitted by Federal law.

B. For any lawful contact made by a law enforcement official or a law enforcement agency of this State or a law enforcement official or a law enforcement agency of a County, City, Town or other political subdivision of this State where reasonable suspicion exists that the person is an alien who is unlawfully present in the United States, a reasonable attempt shall be made, when practicable, to determine the immigration status of the person, except if the determination may hinder or obstruct an investigation, any person who is arrested shall have the person's immigration status determined before the person is released. The person's immigration status shall be verified with the Federal government pursuant to 8 United States Code Section 1373(c). A law enforcement official or agency of this State or a County, City, Town, or other political subdivision of this State *may not solely consider race, color or national origin in implementing the requirements of this subsection except to the extent permitted by the United States or Arizona Constitution* (emphasis added). A person is presumed to not be an alien who is unlawfully present in the United States if the person provides the law enforcement officer or agency any of the following:

1. A valid Arizona Driver's License.

2. A valid Arizona Nonoperating Identification License.

3. A valid Tribal Enrollment card or other form of Tribal identification.

4. If the entity requires proof of legal presence in the United States before issuance, any valid United States Federal, State or local government issued identification.[46]

Sections C and D go on to address the proper administration and handling of an illegal alien. Section E provides for open communication similar to 8 U.S. Code Sections 1373 and 1644 as noted above.

Section G provides standing to any legal resident of the State of Arizona to bring action against any government official or agency subject to Arizona law that "adopts or implements a policy or practice that limits or restricts the enforcement of Federal immigration laws to less than the full extent permitted by federal law."

Section J indemnifies any law enforcement officer or agency that enforces these laws unless it is adjudged that the officer or agency acted in bad faith.

The remainder of the Act discusses primarily the enactment of criminal statutes to deal with illegal aliens. These include a number of supplements to Title 13, which is where most crimes are; Title 23, which discusses employment of illegal aliens; Title 28 regarding impoundment of vehicles; and Title 41, Section 1724, which describes a "Gang and immigration intelligence team enforcement mission fund."

The fact is, the new Arizona laws merely enable enforcement of the already existing federal laws that the States have the responsibility to enforce. There is absolutely nothing new in the laws, with the exception that they create misdemeanors for crimes that are already felonies under federal statutes. For the most part, they are instructions to law enforcement to do what they are supposed to do anyway. U.S. Code Title 8, Section 1324(c) provides "No officer or person shall have authority to make any arrests for a violation of any provision of this section except officers and employees of the Service designated by the Attorney General, either individually or as a member of a class, *and all other officers whose duty it is to enforce criminal laws*"[47] (emphasis added). The "sanctuary" cities that refuse to enforce the federal laws are effectively violating this federal statute. The only reason mayors and/or governors of these sanctuaries are avoiding criminal prosecution is due to the fact the Federal statute *limits* the enforcement of the laws to "all other officers" rather than to *order* all other officers to enforce it. This is magnified because the federal government is lax in enforcing immigration laws. You ask, why? (Take a wild guess.) It is not a very popular road for political aspirants to travel.

Look to the language in Section 11-1051 "may not solely consider race, color, or national origin ..."[48] This language is entirely unnecessary because no law enforcement officer or agency in their right mind would dream of using race, color, or national origin as a determinative factor. Any epithet of evidence down that road would lead someone to a slew of lawsuits by the ACLU, Chicanos Por La Causa, NAACP, and a long list of similar organizations. Do you remember the "Beer Summit" involving President Barack Obama, Harvard Professor Henry Louis Gates, and Cambridge police Sergeant James Crowley? Mr. Crowley is highly skilled in interracial contact and handled the incident with perfect decorum, yet he was hammered by the media. I think Governor Brewer and Sergeant Gates should have their own beer summit to compare notes.

The most disturbing aspect of all of this is that a great portion of the news media is amplifying the misconception of the basis for this law to effectively, for lack of a better term, incite a riot. The crowds of protestors, many of whom have become violent, are angry based upon two possibilities: (1) They misconstrue the Act as a legalization of racial profiling; (2) They are afraid of being caught and subsequently deported. As for the first issue, the officers must have a valid reason to initiate contact, and that reason cannot have anything to do with race. As for the second, sadly there are way too many illegal aliens here exhausting our resources. I don't want any productive member of our society to leave; I do want to relieve us of the population that is abusing our spirit of compassion and charity.

A number of recent polls have been taken concerning the impact of SB 1070. The results of a poll of 400 Hispanic people found:

1. 75% believe that anti-immigrant sentiment against Hispanics – not just illegal immigrants – is growing.

2. 59% said immigration is a very important issue to them and their families.

3. 69% know undocumented immigrants as friends, relatives, neighbors, or co-workers.

4. 87% will not vote for any congressional candidate who is in favor of forcing illegal immigrants to leave the country.[49]

The answers to questions 1 and 4 are, in no uncertain terms, the products of media coercion. Question 4 implies that the Arizona legislature has authorized a witch-hunt. Hey, if you ask a question just the right way you don't have to wait for an answer, you already know what it will be. If you find that hard to believe, take a look at this poll: the National Latino Survey of 1,000 Hispanic adults from December, 2005.[50] (Note that they included some other poll results from different sources).

1. 52.4% support (38.2% do not support) legislation stating that any person living in this country illegally cannot become a United States citizen unless they reapply for citizenship legally from their country of origin.

2. 49.6% support (41% do not support) increasing the number of U.S. Border Patrol agents on the border between U.S. and Mexico.

3. 49.9% support (41.2% do not) new laws to make sure that employers can only hire workers who are in the U.S. legally.

4. 81.9% (to 14%) support immigration reform " … to create a temporary worker program for illegal immigrants that would legalize their status …"

5. 42% of Hispanics consider U.S. immigration "too open." (*Wall Street Journal*, March 2000)

6. 75% of California Latinos think that illegal immigration from Mexico to California has been a "big problem" or "somewhat of a problem." (Public Policy Institute of California, Jan. 1999)

7. Two-thirds of likely Latino voters in California support the governor's veto of a bill that would have allowed illegal aliens to get driver's licenses. (*Los Angeles Times*, Oct. 2002)

8. 89% of Hispanics strongly support an immediate moratorium on immigration. (Hispanic USA Research Group, June 1993)

9. 75% of Mexican-Americans, 79% of Puerto Ricans, and 65% of Cuban-Americans agree that there are too many immigrants in this country. (Latino National Political Survey, Dec. 1992)

10. 61% of Hispanics favor increasing money spent on patrolling the border. (The Tarrance Group, August 1983)

The *New York Times* and CBS News conducted a poll April 28 through May 2, 2010 of 1,079 adults and got the following results:

1. 78% believe that the United States could be doing more along its border to keep illegal immigrants out.

2. 57% said the federal government should determine the laws addressing illegal immigration. But 51% said the

Arizona law was "about right" in its approach to the problem. 36% said it went too far and 9% said it didn't go far enough.

3. Just 8% of Americans said the immigration system needed only minor changes. The vast majority said it needed reworking, including 44% who said it needed to be completely rebuilt and 45% who said it needed fundamental changes.

4. Three quarters said that, over all, illegal immigrants were a drain on the economy because they did not all pay taxes but used public services like hospitals and schools.[51]

Rasmussen Reports also looked into the new Arizona laws and surveyed Arizona voters.[52] Here is what they learned:

1. Like voters across the nation, *most Arizona voters (57%) favor an immigration policy that welcomes all immigrants except "national security threats, criminals and those who would come here to live off our welfare system."* ... 27% oppose such a welcoming policy (emphasis added).

2. 76% say it is more important to gain control of the border than it is to legalize the status of undocumented workers. Only 19% believe it is more important to legalize the status of undocumented workers already in the country.

3. 64% of Arizona voters favor the new immigration law signed last week by Governor Jan Brewer. 30% are opposed.

4. 36% of Arizona voters are angry about the immigration situation. Another 25% say they're frustrated, and 37% say immigration is just one of many issues they have an opinion on.

5. 85% say they're angry at the federal government, while 10% express anger at immigrants. This is also similar to views held nationwide.

6. 87% say the new legislation will be important in determining how they vote. That includes 65% who say it will be very important. Among those who consider the legislation very important in their voting decision, 67% favor the law, and 31% are opposed.

7. By a 47% to 39% margin, Arizona voters believe that the new law has had a negative impact on the state's image. However, by a 44% to 37% margin, they believe it will be good for the state's economy.

8. 55% say they favor "authorizing local police to stop and check the immigration status of anyone they suspect of being in the country illegally." That's down from 70% two weeks ago.

I believe that these polls demonstrate a significant consensus in America that we don't want to round up all of the illegal aliens and deport them, but that we want to retain the productive members of our communities with or without a green card. We simply need to end the entitlement programs that draw the illegals.

I propose that Gallup, Rasmussen, Zogby, or any other reputable polling agency asks the following questions to 10,000 people. I will offer what I believe the responses will be:

1. Do you believe that all aliens, legal and illegal, who are gainfully employed, pay their taxes, and are otherwise responsible individuals should be permitted to stay in the United States?

    Yes   99.9%

    No   How did you get my phone number?

2. Do you believe that all aliens, legal and illegal, who are simply siphoning off of our government entitlement programs for more than a year should be deported?

    Yes   99.9%

    No   Is this a trick question?

3. Do you believe that the U.S. Congress should become more active and directly address immigration reform by denying entitlements to illegal aliens?

    Yes   Can we deport members of Congress?

    No   Yeah, let's deport members of Congress.

The Future of Immigration

We, as a nation, are burdened by our humanitarian and charitable character. This is not in any way bad, but we are going about it all wrong.

We have a responsibility to do all that we can to provide the greatest benefit in the most efficient manner. We can no longer harbor those who are draining the resources of tax-paying citizens. We can do many things to ensure greater prosperity for the aliens by sending them back to their native land. These are some of the options available:

1. Health care in third world countries is hampered by unavailability and/or unaffordability. A very valid solution to this dilemma would be to impose a

responsibility on aliens who attend medical schools in the United States to go back to their native country to provide free care during their internships. We may even be able to use it as a payback for student loan debts because medical schools are not cheap! Remember, the investment we make into an anchor baby born to an illegal alien is equivalent to needed medical care for hundreds, if not thousands, of people in an impoverished environment.

2. A national worker ID[53] that cannot be copied or forged will prevent illegal aliens from gaining employment and thereby protect jobs for American citizens. Illegal aliens who are gainfully employed should be provided with an opportunity to plead for a green card, depending on the facts and circumstances of each case. This does not mean everyone who is employed will be able to stay, but we want the United States to remain a nation of immigrants and their descendants, with the only limitation being the capacity to accommodate deserving applicants.

3. Denial of government support with food stamps, welfare, and medical services will remove some of the fundamental lures for illegal immigration and serve us in many ways. We can be more selective of deserving applicants for legal immigration and no longer be burdened by six million people per year treating the Sonoran desert like a Los Angeles freeway. We will no longer be saddened by those who have attempted to cross the border and died trying. Our law enforcement and national security agencies will be able to focus on the much more daunting task of avoiding a repeat of 9-11.

Immigration is truly critical for our nation's future. Yet there may soon be legislation proposing amnesty for the population of illegal aliens currently living in the U.S. The burden on this nation would be too much to bear. We can recover from the current crises, but only if we make no further critical mistakes.

Any individual that seeks election to this nation's Congress must commit to doing what may be unpopular in some circles, but is absolutely necessary for this nation to continue as we know it. Immigration reform must not be posting fences and beefing up border patrol to keep people out, but rather a cessation of the lures that attract people and entice them to break the laws. We will accomplish so much more at far less cost if we can just get the proper legislation through Congress.

Oil

Crude oil is the life-blood of any industrialized nation. Limiting access to this natural resource will effectively strangle a nation's productivity and force almost every industry to a halt. In the 1970s we experienced a series of energy crises[1] that began with the 1973 Arab Oil Embargo employed by OAPEC (Organization of the Arab Petroleum Exporting Countries). The word "Arab" was removed as OPEC grew to include oil producers outside of the Middle East as a tool to drive the price of oil much higher. It was a very successful venture that caused the price to effectively triple. Did the United States take a look at this and say, "We need to make sure this doesn't happen again?" No.

A Sequence of Crises

The second major crisis occurred in 1979 as a result of the Iranian revolution that shut down Iran's oil production for a number of months. The price of oil doubled and there was a drastic shortage, but the price then settled back to a slightly lower level than where it had been at the end of 1978. Did the United States do anything to be prepared for pending future crises? No.

The latest oil crisis began on April 20, 2010 when a BP well in the Gulf of Mexico, near the Mississippi River Delta, exploded due to a surge of methane gas.[2] This caused the death of eleven people and injured seventeen. The estimates as of June 28, 2010 were 35,000 to 60,000 barrels per day leaking into the gulf, which equals 1.5 to 2.5 million gallons per day. President Obama issued an executive order to stop any further drilling in the gulf because of the dangers of deep-water drilling, but he also chose to invest 2 billion U.S. dollars into a plan to drill in much deeper water off of the coast of Brazil. The executive order to stop drilling was found to be illegal by U.S. District Judge Martin Feldman.

Each of these oil crises was based upon gross mismanagement of the oil market in the United States. In order for us to understand why we had to endure these setbacks and what needs to be done to prepare for the future, we need to examine oil from every perspective. We will look at questions concerning the oil reserves of each nation, the different types of reserves, and the individual costs associated with their production. We will then examine the histories of production, consumption, and most importantly, the economic impact upon each nation, especially the United States, concerning the imports and exports of this valued commodity.

A great source of my oil information is the U.S. Energy Information Administration, or the EIA.[3] If you have questions concerning the content of this chapter, their website will provide answers and links to hundreds of resources and data.

OPEC Formation

The fact that oil is such a critical commodity makes its possession a unilateral basis for wealth. Those who formed OPEC at a conference in Baghdad in September 1960 set forth the objective "to coordinate and unify petroleum policies among

member countries, in order to secure fair and stable prices for petroleum producers; and a fair return on capital to those investing in the industry."[4] The actual goal of OPEC was and continues to be to gain as much wealth as possible with significant control over the supply of the most necessary marketable good for any industrialized nation. OPEC's original members were Iran, Iraq, Kuwait, Saudi Arabia, and Venezuela.

They were later joined by Qatar, Indonesia (suspended its membership in January 2009), Libya, United Arab Emirates, Algeria, Nigeria, Ecuador (suspended its membership from December 1992 to October 2007), Angola, and Gabon. OPEC's goal of wealth is accomplished by monitoring its release of oil and thereby controlling the worldwide price for the same. We must understand that this price control is not perfect. The existence of other suppliers makes management of the oil market a complicated chess game for OPEC. Nevertheless, they seem to have the hang of it.

Reserves

There is no way to put specific numbers on the quantities of oil reserves owned by various nations or principalities. The numbers themselves are constantly changing because new oil formations are being found on a random but regular basis. An example of this is contained in one of the most pessimistic resources that I found, "Global Oil Production and Consumption" by Marc Wieczorek.[5] This article lists Saudi Arabia as owning 25.5% of the world's oil, Iraq having 11.1%, and the U.S. owning 2.2%. Other numbers attributable to members of OPEC give that organization a total of more than 75% of the world's oil. Nevertheless, a footnote in this article notes a newly discovered oil field near Alberta, Canada. This oil field increases that nation's share from only a fraction of 1% to the equivalent of

more than two-thirds of Saudi Arabia's reserve (approximately 175 billion barrels compared to Saudi Arabia's 261.7 billion barrels) equivalent to almost 15% of the world's known reserves.

Exhibit A

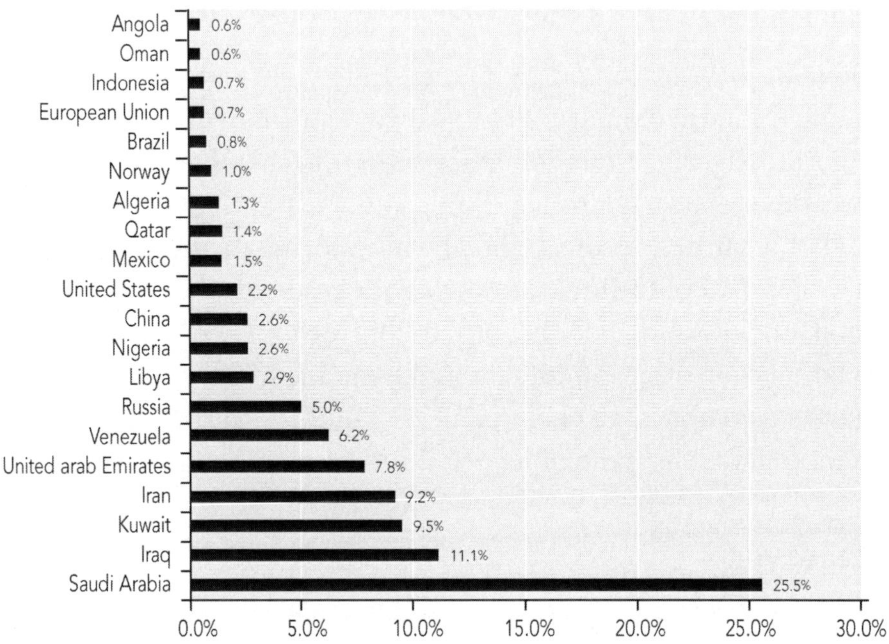

This is good news for the U.S. to have a friendly nation to buy oil from, however, we must remember that not all massive oil discoveries are made in North America. In 2006, Bernard A. Gelb prepared a report for Congress discussing much larger oil reserves than had previously been accounted for in the Caspian Sea area of central Asia.[6] The bottom line is that we need to take advantage of what we have before it is too late. Waiting for other suppliers to flood the market will inhibit the gain available to us as a nation.

Wikipedia references confirm Canada has "the world's second largest oil reserves" and addresses the otherwise conservative estimate of the United States' holdings. Prospective resources include an estimated 90 billion barrels of oil and 44 billion barrels of natural gas liquid in the Arctic. A great portion of this is under Alaska, and it is estimated that 84% is located offshore.[7]

Arctic National Wildlife Refuge

The most heated debate in the past twenty years regarding oil reserves in the U. S. concerns the Arctic National Wildlife Refuge (ANWR) —one of Alaska's largest stocks.[8] If we accessed the estimated 16 billion barrels of high-quality oil that is recoverable there, we would have enough to support the entire United States' need for about eight years, based upon our current rate of consumption. That would mean relying on only one source, which is not practical. The better solution would be to make full use of all our current known resources, which would supply all our needs for well over a thousand years. Unfortunately, getting a go ahead for oil drilling is a daunting task on any of our "sacred" ground.

The U.S. House approved drilling at ANWR as part of an energy bill on April 21, 2005, but the House-Senate conference committee removed this portion from the bill. The Senate also passed a bill for Arctic Refuge drilling on March 16, 2005 as part of the federal budget resolution for 2006, but it was removed in similar fashion. The last bill that made it out of Congress was 1996 House Bill H.R. 2909, an amendment to the Silvio O. Conte National Fish and Wildlife Refuge Act. It would have permitted drilling at ANWR but was vetoed by President Clinton on October 2, 1996.[9] Most recently, President Barack Obama answered a questionnaire from League of Conservation Voters

by stating "I strongly reject drilling in the Arctic National Wildlife Refuge because it would irreversibly damage a protected national wildlife refuge without creating sufficient oil supplies to meaningfully affect the global market price or have a discernible impact on US energy security."[10]

Many argue that drilling at ANWR would have opened the door for drilling and excavation of oil in many other known reserves, especially based on the fact that ANWR is only a piece of the puzzle. We can only speculate, but if you look ahead to exhibit M you will see that we could have saved well over a trillion dollars in our accumulated trade deficit had we begun to drill there. The volatile nature of the oil market means that the existence of a new source of supply would also have affected OPEC's marketing power and pushed the prices lower.

Additional Reserves

The published estimates of oil reserves can vary in numbers based upon new discoveries and newly evaluated discoveries. The estimations of U.S. oil reserves at 2.2% or 2.1% are the most conservative estimates available. Two massive recent discoveries of oil deposits almost entirely within the United States are: the Bakken Formation primarily in Montana, North Dakota, and surrounding states with some in Canada; and the Green River formation found primarily under Colorado, Utah, and Wyoming. Bakken is conservatively estimated to have 3 to 3.4 billion barrels of top-grade oil,[11] but it may have more than 500 billion barrels.[12] Green River is estimated to have 1.5 to 1.8 trillion barrels of oil under the Rocky Mountains.[13] If we were to conservatively add up all of the oil we have rights to in the U.S., they total 2.3 trillion barrels.[14]

We have almost ten times as much oil as Saudi Arabia has in all its fields and more than triple the reserves of all of OPEC.

All of the known oil reserves in the world outside of the United States add up to less than half of what we have under our feet. At the current rate of oil usage and consumption we can take care of the entire world for more than 300 years. This does not include the reserves that we have not yet found or confirmed and I am applying only the most conservative estimates.

We have Green River and Bakken but we are not extracting the oil, why? There are essentially two reasons. The first is the cost of extracting shale oil. According to Rand Corporation, reclamation of shale oil is not going to be profitable unless real crude oil prices are at least $70 to $95 per barrel.[15] Shell Oil Company is working to develop a process for shale oil to make it profitable in the mid-$20s per barrel price range. That would mean a current profit of about $50 per barrel—more than a dollar per gallon of gas! The second reason we are not extracting from these U.S. reserves is the environmental impact. It is painfully obvious that any oil development project will affect the land and impact the environment, but the reward for doing so is the U.S. will be energy independent. We have a choice to make: do we want to develop our energy supply under the watchful eye of government agencies that work to protect our environment, or do we want third-world countries to do all of the oil excavation with complete disregard for environmental protection? We have the ability to excavate all that is necessary to allow our nation to survive and thereby impede third world production affecting the global environment.

Production

The Energy Information Administration provides an excellent discussion of how oil is formed, how it is produced, and what affects the costs of production.[16] In summary, oil is based upon the remains of animals and plants that lived millions of years

ago. The production is the most critical factor because its cost can vary widely depending on the form and grade of the oil that one is trying to excavate.

Exhibit B

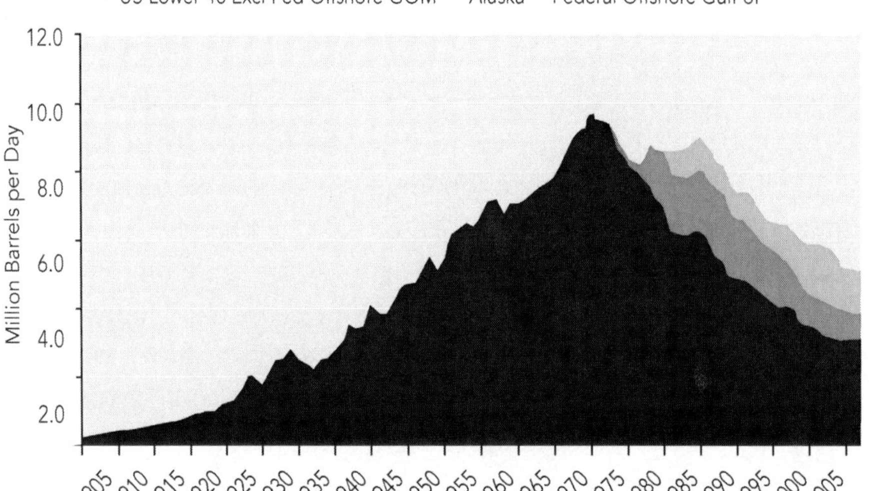

Production Costs

Exhibit C

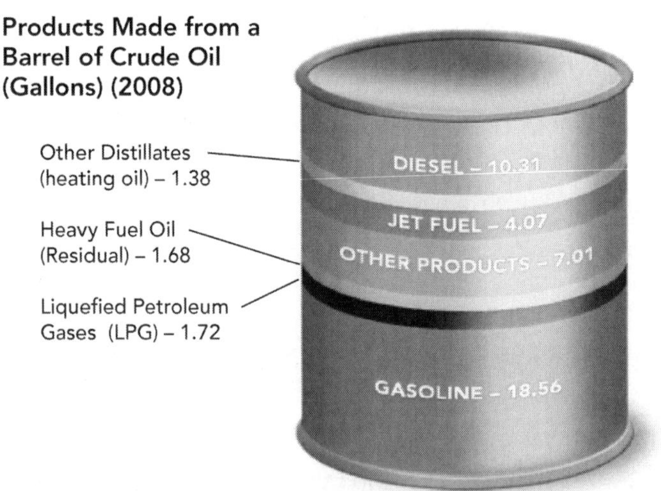

In order to properly evaluate the production costs for oil, we must understand that a barrel of oil equals 42 gallons, but that after processing it will produce approximately 44 gallons of the finished product: fuel, motor oil, and other distillates[17] (see exhibit C). What are the costs? The answer is a bit tricky. Kanabona has accessed data from the Energy Information Administration and prepared a chart (exhibit D) depicting total production costs by region for FRS (Financial Reporting System) companies for the years 2003-2005 and 2004-2006.[18]

Exhibit D

Finding Costs by Region for FRS Companies, 2003-2005 and 2004-2006
(2006 Dollars per Barrel of Oil Equivalent)

Region	2003-2005	2004-2006	% Change
United States: Onshore	7.05	11.34	60.9
United States: Offshore	45.76	63.71	39.2
Total United States	10.40	15.62	50.2
Canada	17.43	19.39	11.2
Europe	10.26	22.79	122.1
Former Soviet Union	13.74	NM	NM
Africa	16.19	25.66	58.5
Middle East	4.95	5.26	6.3
Other Eastern Hemisphere	9.50	12.59	32.6
Other Western Hemisphere	26.56	42.59	60.4
Total Foreign	12.46	19.51	56.6
Worldwide	11.38	17.23	51.3

Notes: NM = Not meaningful. The above figures are 3-year weighted averages of exploration and development expenditures, excluding expenditures for proven acreage, divided by reserve additions, excluding net purchases of reserves. Natural gas is converted to equivalent barrels of oil at 0.178 barrels per thousand cubic feet. Sum of components may not add to total due to independent rounding.

Exhibit D shows Middle Eastern production costs during this period were $4.95 and $5.26 per barrel, while offshore costs for the United States were $45.76 and $63.71 per barrel. Why should we consider spending that much money for domestic oil? Because if we don't produce our own, that will give OPEC the right to charge whatever they want. Any alternative source of oil will impact OPEC's power and cause the equilibrium price per barrel to be lower. Producing our oil at a high cost will allow us to pay less for what we import and, in the long run, may reduce our overall average cost per barrel.

The logical conclusion is that we should continue to produce our oil in the most efficient but ever-increasing manner available to us. Unfortunately, our government does not necessarily think logically. The Energy Information Administration has published a series of graphs and data which show that U.S. oil production peaked in 1970 at 3.5 trillion barrels (see exhibit B), but since then it has steadily dropped to 1.8 trillion barrels in 2008, which is roughly equivalent to our total production in 1947.[19]

Why are we being led like lambs to the slaughter?

OPEC is a reasonably well-managed organization. The market conditions and rate of inflation in 2010 led OPEC to do its best to maintain the global price of a barrel of oil at about $75.00.[20] A lower price leads to a loss in profit. A higher price stimulates competition and urges our government to allow drilling, which would impact market control and drive the price eventually lower. OPEC could boost income in the short run, but the long run costs would be staggering. An excellent article discussing the history of OPEC's control of the oil market is published by James Williams of West Texas Research Group Economics.[21] It includes a series of graphs and illustrations (exhibits E and F) that show the history of the U.S. has been almost completely inconsistent with the rest of the world in oil production.

Exhibit E

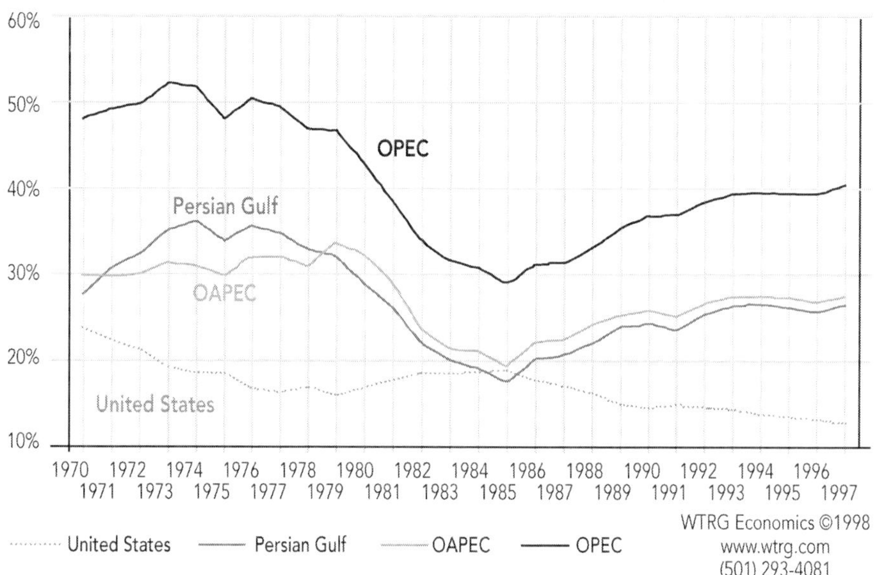

Exhibit F

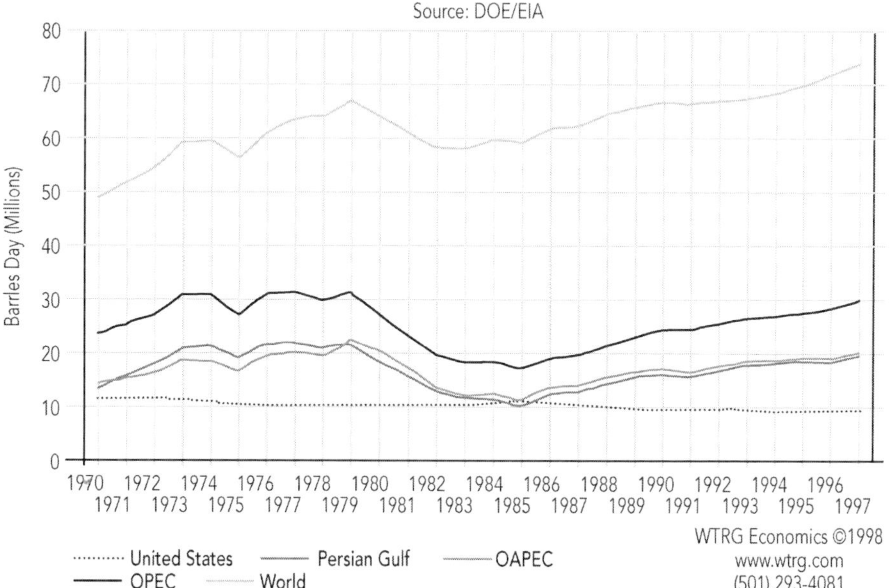

Exhibit G

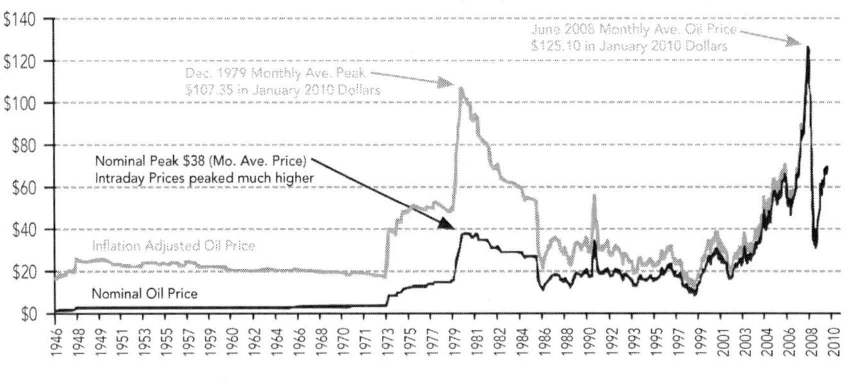

©www.inflationData.com • Updatd 3/11/10
Source: Oil Prices - www.ioga.com/Special/crudeoil_Hist.thm
CPI-U Inflation index - www.bis.gov

Notice the peculiarities in these graphs. Which lines don't seem to follow along with the rest of the crowd? They would be the dotted lines associated with the United States. Exhibit E appears to show that we boosted our oil production from about 1979 to 1984. That would be a sad misinterpretation. The fact is that we have consistently reduced our oil production, as is confirmed in exhibit F. What appears to be a rise in U.S. crude oil production in exhibit E is based on OPEC's reducing its supply in order to create a need for its oil and thereby control the market price. Exhibit G demonstrates that, with the exception of the two oil crises in the '70s, OPEC gained almost complete control of the market by stabilizing prices in the $20 to $25 range and then steadily increasing the price to what it considers to be the best profit margin that the economy will allow.[22]

Although OPEC was organized in 1960, it didn't really begin to play its hand until 1979, resulting in the monthly average price going from about $18 to a peak of $38, which when adjusted for

inflation, equaled more than \$100 in 2010. After gaining control of the market, OPEC worked out a strategy to maintain continued control within a certain price range, thus avoiding any stimulation of competition.

The leader of industry in the world is the United States, and that makes us the largest consumer of crude oil. In 1980, the U.S. consumed 794.1 million tonnes (mt) of oil, or approximately 27% of all of the oil used in the world.[23] At the same time China used 85.4 mt, or 2.87% of the world's consumption. In 1990, the U.S. used 781.8 mt (24.79%) and China used 112.8 mt (3.58%) of oil. In 2000, the U.S. used 897.6 mt (25.24%) and China 223.6 (6.23%). In 2006, the U.S. used 938.8 of 3,889.8 mt (24.13%) and China 349.8 (8.99%). I make note of China based upon the fact that it is populated by more than 2 billion people and is considered to be the heart of the current industrial revolution. China's need for oil will continue to grow at an alarming rate, and that fact is one of the tools that we need to use to enable our nation to recover. Other significant users of oil in 2006 were: Japan 6.04%, Russian Federation 3.30%, Germany 3.17%, India 3.09%, South Korea 2.71%, Canada 2.54 %, France 2.39%, and Saudi Arabia 2.38%. We need to use the significant demands for oil in China, Japan, and the European Union as tools for our recovery. If we can produce enough to manage our needs and sell the excess to these desperate nations, we win on all counts.

One could assume that oil production statistics would significantly parallel oil consumption statistics, at least in those nations with access to their own oil reserves. Exhibit H is derived from information provided by the U.S. Department of Energy.[24] The columns indicate millions of barrels of daily productivity of oil with percentages of the global productivity below. The rows show the years from which these statistics were derived.

Exhibit H

World Crude Oil Production
millions of barrels daily/percentage of global production

Year	World	OPEC	U.S.	Canada	China	Mexico	USSR/Russia
1960	20.99	8.27 39.40%	7.04 33.54%	33.54% 2.48%	.52 .0048%	2.48% 1.23%	.10 13.86%
1970	45.89	22.56 49.16%	9.64 21.00%	1.26 2.75%	.60 1.31%	.49 1.07%	6.99 15.23
1980	59.56	25.38 42.61%	8.60 14.43%	1.44 2.42%	2.11 3.54%	1.94 3.26%	11.71 19.66%
1990	60.49	22.49 37.18%	7.36 12.17%	1.55 2.56%	2.77 4.58%	2.55 4.22%	10.98 18.15%
2000	68.49	28.98 42.31%	5.82 8.50%	1.98 2.89%	3.25 4.75%	3.01 4.39%	6.48 9.46%
2008	73.78	32.47 44.01%	4.96 6.72%	2.59 3.51%	3.79 5.14%	2.79 3.78%	9.36 12.69%

With few exceptions, every significant supplier and user of oil has increased its production on a consistent basis. The only great exception is the United States, which has consistently reduced its production since 1970.

Consumption

As noted before, the United States has always been the largest consumer of oil in the world. In 2006, we used 24.13% of the world's oil compared to second-place China's (which has about seven times our population) 8.99%. During the period 1990 to 2006 our consumption has increased 22% while our production has decreased 15%. In comparison, China's consumption has increased 215% while its production has increased only 17%.[25] Careful review of these statistics shows that only Italy (-8%), Russia (-36%), and Japan (-2%) reduced their consumption of oil during this period. As for Italy, we can only assume they are working very hard to make more efficient use of their oil based upon its considerable cost in Europe. Russia is somewhat of a misnomer due to the break-up of the Eastern Block; there is a much lower population and access to the oil reserves was pretty much cut in half. Japan is experiencing a slow decline in population and therefore demand for oil is decreasing.

When we look at the production statistics, we see that only the U.S., Venezuela, and Norway have been significant producers with declines in production. Venezuela was forced to reduce its production in order to comply with OPEC's quotas (this has given OPEC much better price control) and Norway's costs of production simply outweigh OPEC's pricing. Russia's production increased by 60%, which is even more significant based upon the loss of land area and oil reserves in the Eastern Block. Mr. Wieczorek prepared two charts to illustrate the diversities of production and consumption, which you'll find in exhibits I and J.

Exhibit I

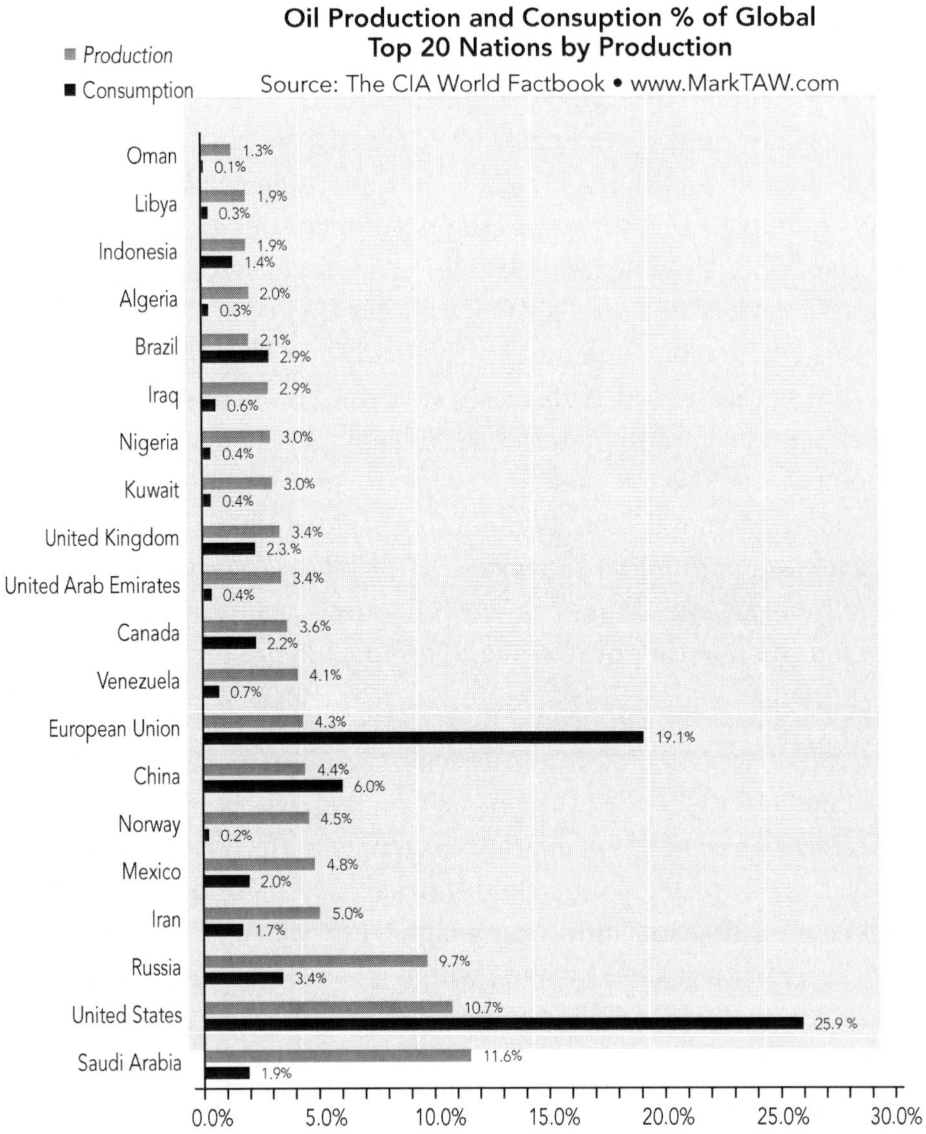
Oil Production and Consuption % of Global
Top 20 Nations by Production
Source: The CIA World Factbook • www.MarkTAW.com
Production
Consumption
Oman 1.3% 0.1%
Libya 1.9% 0.3%
Indonesia 1.9% 1.4%
Algeria 2.0% 0.3%
Brazil 2.1% 2.9%
Iraq 2.9% 0.6%
Nigeria 3.0% 0.4%
Kuwait 3.0% 0.4%
United Kingdom 3.4% 2.3.%
United Arab Emirates 3.4% 0.4%
Canada 3.6% 2.2%
Venezuela 4.1% 0.7%
European Union 4.3% 19.1%
China 4.4% 6.0%
Norway 4.5% 0.2%
Mexico 4.8% 2.0%
Iran 5.0% 1.7%
Russia 9.7% 3.4%
United States 10.7% 25.9 %
Saudi Arabia 11.6% 1.9%
0.0% 5.0% 10.0% 15.0% 20.0% 25.0% 30.0%

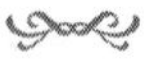

Exhibit J

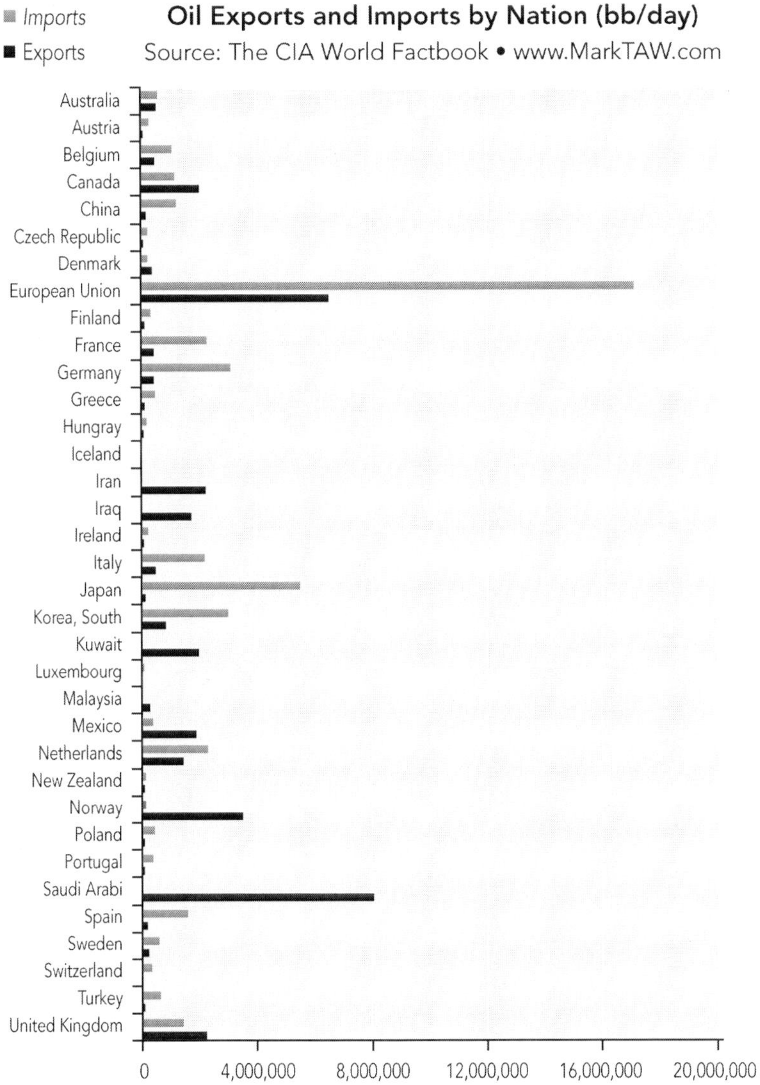
Imports
Exports
Oil Exports and Imports by Nation (bb/day)
Source: The CIA World Factbook • www.MarkTAW.com
Australia
Austria
Belgium
Canada
China
Czech Republic
Denmark
European Union
Finland
France
Germany
Greece
Hungray
Iceland
Iran
Iraq
Ireland
Italy
Japan
Korea, South
Kuwait
Luxembourg
Malaysia
Mexico
Netherlands
New Zealand
Norway
Poland
Portugal
Saudi Arabi
Spain
Sweden
Switzerland
Turkey
United Kingdom
0
4,000,000
8,000,000
12,000,000
16,000,000
20,000,000

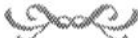

As can be seen in exhibit I; only four out of the twenty entries consume more than they produce: Brazil uses 2.9% and produces 2.1%, China 6.0% and 4.4% (Note that these statistics are from 2003), European Union 19.1% and 4.3%, and the United States uses 25.9% but produces only 10.7%. Every one of these nations is using all of the oil that is reasonably within its grasp except one: the United States.

Imports

The Energy Information Administration provides a detailed record of U.S. oil imports (see exhibit K) in statistical graphs showing that we have been importing oil since 1910.[26] Those imports were reasonably nominal until 1960, the first year that our imports exceeded our exports. That deficit began at 1,015 barrels per day and peaked at 10,126 barrels per day in 2005. Since then it has decreased to 9,783 barrels per day for 2008, but we must attribute some of this to the economic recession we currently face.

Exhibit K

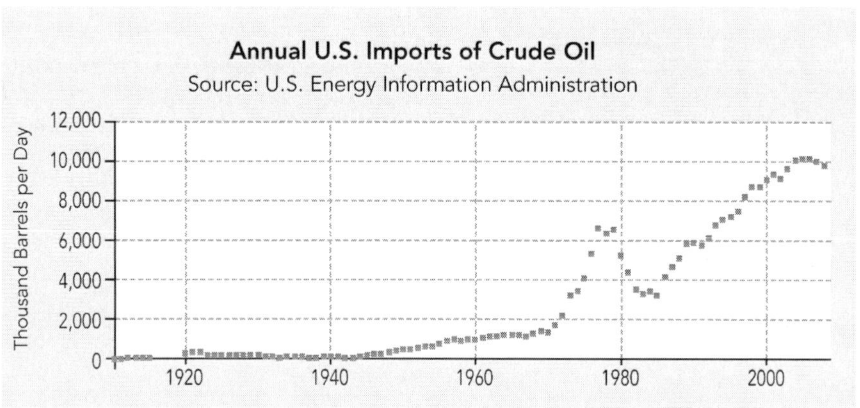

Exhibit L

U.S. Imports of Crude Oil (Thousand Barrels per Day)

Decade	Year-0	Year-1	Year-2	Year-3	Year-4	Year-5	Year-6	Year-7	Year-8	Year-9
1910's	2	5	20	49	46	50	NA	NA	NA	NA
1920's	290	343	349	225	213	169	165	160	218	216
1930's	170	129	122	87	97	88	88	75	72	91
1940's	117	139	34	38	122	204	236	267	353	421
1950's	487	491	573	648	656	782	934	1,023	953	965
1960's	1,015	1,045	1,126	1,131	1,198	1,238	1,225	1,128	1,291	1,409
1970's	1,324	1,681	2,216	3,244	3,477	4,105	5,287	6,615	6,356	6,519
1980's	5,263	4,396	3,488	3,329	3,426	3,201	4,178	4,674	5,107	5,843
1990's	5,894	5,782	6,083	6,787	7,063	7,230	7,508	8,225	8,706	8,731
2000's	9,071	9,328	9,140	9,665	10,088	10,126	10,118	10,031	9,783	9,013

The primary sources for our total petroleum imports in 2009 are, in order of decreasing quantities: Canada, Mexico, Saudi Arabia, Venezuela, and Nigeria. In order to be fair, the U.S. also has a history of exporting crude oil, and that quantity must be subtracted from the import totals in order to show reliable data.[27] I prepared a table (exhibit M) to analyze the imports and exports along with the prices paid for each barrel of oil.[28] This will allow us to properly evaluate the current economic impact. The final column is the cost paid by our nation in today's dollars for failing to produce our supply of oil. The entry for 2009 is a conservative estimate based upon the limited information that is presently available.

Exhibit M

Year(s)	Imports (in 1000's of Barrels)	Exports (in 1000's of Barrels)	Net Imports (in 1000"s)	Price per Barrel	Inflation Adjusted Price 2009	Cost for Year's Net Import 2009 dollars
1960-64	2,012,975	11,165	2,001,810	$2.90 avg.	$20.70 avg.	$41,437,467,000 ($8.3 billion avg.)
1965-69	2,296,215	32,353	2,263,862 avg.	$3.15 avg.	$20.12	$45,548,903,440 ($9.1 billion avg.)
1970	483,260	4,991	478,269	$3.39	$18.84	$9,010,587,960
1971	613,565	503	613,062	$3.60	$19.18	$11,758,529,160
1972	808,840	187	808,653	$3.60	$20.57	$16,339,922,100
1973	1,184,060	697	1,183,363	$4.75	$22.89	$27,087,179,070
1974	1,269,105	1,074	1,268,031	$9.35	$40.84	$51,786,386,040
1975	1,498,325	2,146	1,496,179	$12.21	$48.91	$73,178,114,890
1976	1,929,755	2,941	1,926,814	13.10	$49.66	$95,685,583,240
1977	2,414,475	18,255	2,396,220	$14.40	$51.22	$122,734,388,400
1978	2,319,940	57,728	2,262,212	$14.95	$49.47	$111,911,627,600
1979	2,379,435	85,707	2,293,728	$25.10	$73.89	$169,483,561,900
1980	1,920,995	104,935	1,816,060	$37.42	$98.07	$178,101,004,200
1981	1,604,540	83,166	1,521,374	$35.75	$84.93	$129,210,293,800
1982	1,273,120	86,279	1,186,841	$31.83	$71.20	$84,503,079,200
1983	1,215,085	59,948	1,155,137	$29.08	$63.00	$72,773,631,000
1984	1,250,490	66,234	1,184,256	$28.75	$59.71	$70,711,925,760
1985	1,168,365	74,513	1,093,852	$26.92	$53.98	$59,046,130,960
1986	1,524,970	56,205	1,468,765	$14.44	$28.41	$41,727,613,650
1987	1,706,010	54,964	1,651,046	$17.75	$33.69	$55,623,739,740
1988	1,864,055	56,714	1,807,341	$14.87	$27.16	$49,087,381,560
1989	2,132,695	51,683	2,081,012	$18.33	$31.88	$66,342,662,560
1990	2,151,310	39,654	2,111,656	$23.19	$38.17	$80,601,909,520
1991	2,110,430	42,384	2,068,046	$20.20	$31.99	$66,156,791,540
1992	2,220,295	32,474	2,187,821	$19.25	$29.59	$64,737,623,390
1993	2,477,255	35,873	2,441,382	$16.75	$25.02	$61,083,377,640
1994	2,577,995	36,020	2,541,975	$15.66	$22.78	$57,906,190,500
1995	2,638,950	34,509	2,604,441	$16.75	$23.71	$61,751,296,110
1996	2,740,420	40,211	2,700,209	$20.46	$28.12	$75,929,877,080
1997	3,002,125	39,308	2,962,817	$18.64	$25.05	$74,218,565,850
1998	3,177,690	40,102	3,137,588	$11.91	$15.77	$49,479,762,760
1999	3,186,815	43,032	3,143,783	$16.56	$21.39	$67,245,518,370
2000	3,310,915	18,352	3,292,563	$27.39	$34.29	$112,901,985,300
2001	3,404,720	7,386	3,397,334	$23.00	$28.03	$95,227,272,020
2002	3,336,100	3,295	3,332,805	$22.81	$27.33	$91,085,560,650
2003	3,527,725	4,537	3,523,188	$27.69	$32.47	$114,397,914,400
2004	3,682,120	9,781	3,672,339	$37.66	$42.97	$157,800,406,800
2005	3,695,990	11,620	3,684,370	$50.04	$55.21	$203,414,067,700
2006	3,693,070	8,999	3,684,071	$58.30	$62.36	$229,738,667,600
2007	3,661,315	10,007	3,651,308	$64.20	$66.66	$243,396,191,300
2008	3,570,795	10,462	3,560,333	$91.48	$91.35	$325,236,419,600
2009	n/a	15,984	n/a	$43.11	$43.56	$150,000,000,000

This adds up to approximately $3,964,399,211,460, or almost 4 trillion dollars that was sent to foreign distributors for oil. This averages to about $13,214 per person living in the United States today. This is money that each of us had in our possession but is now in the hands of a foreign oil entrepreneur.

Our Trade Deficit

These numbers can be looked at in a number of ways. If we look at the entire trade deficit for the United States since 1960, it totals a little over 7 trillion dollars through the year 2008.[29] The fact that the deficit has been in the neighborhood of 700 billion dollars each year for 2005 through 2008 implies that we are currently sitting near an 8 trillion dollar deficit. It should be noted, however, that we had a trade surplus for many of the years prior to 1978. Therefore, during the past thirty-two years we have sent 8 trillion dollars overseas. Bear in mind that the U.S. population was under 190 million in 1960.[30] Yet even when we divide that total by 300 million people (today's estimated population) we come up with about $26,667 per person in trade deficit, and oil is responsible for the largest slice of the pie.

If we have 2.5 trillion dollars in oil trade deficit (that's the number without adjustment for inflation) and 8 trillion dollars deficit overall (also without adjustment), that must be good, right? No, the oil is a consistent and steadily increasing drag on the economy while the trade deficit overall has exploded. The first year that the trade deficit broke 100 billion dollars was 1984, which was also the second year that the trade deficit (see exhibit N, column 5) exceeded the oil deficit (column 2), with the exception of 1972. In other words, as foolish as we were buying our oil overseas, we were consistently getting money back from sales of other commodities, goods, and services until 1983. Since then, our oil import has gradually risen while our

overall trade deficit has shot through the roof. The bottom line is that we must stop the bleeding everywhere, but oil is an excellent place to start.

I will reformulate exhibit M to more accurately compare oil to total imports and exports. Note that the trade numbers include services as well as goods and that our export of services has grown consistently since 1970 with a surplus of $144,315,000,000 for the year 2008. That is good news except for the fact that the cumulative total services surplus is subtracted from the total trade deficit, thus masking our trade deficit debacle by more than 1.5 trillion dollars ($1,542,969,000,000). If we weren't doing so well in services we would be more than 9.5 trillion dollars in the hole rather than the paltry sum of 8 trillion dollars. How much is 8 trillion dollars? If you laid one dollar bills end to end, you could go from earth to the sun for about four-and-a-half round trips. If you stacked the bills on top of one another, you would get to the moon and halfway back. If you spend one million dollars *per day* it will take you a little over 21,902 years to blow that much cash, and yes, I factored in leap years.

Exhibit N

Year(s)	Costs for Year's net oil import w/out adjustment for inflation	Trade Imports (millions)	Trade Exports (millions)	Balance in Trade Deficit (millions)	Balance in Trade Deficit Excl. oil (millions)	Accumulated Total Trade Deficit from 1960 (millions)
1960-64	$5,805,249,000	$121,721	$143,026	$21,305 surplus	$27,110 surplus	$21,305 surplus
1965-69	$7,131,165,300	$199,759	$210,307	$10,548 surplus	$17,679 surplus	$31,853 surplus
1970	$1,621,331,910	$54,386	$56,640	$2,254 surplus	$3,875 surplus	$34,107 surplus
1971	$2,207,023,200	$60,979	$59,677	$1,302 surplus	$905 surplus	$32,805 surplus
1972	$2,911,150,800	$72,665	$67,222	$5,443 surplus	$2,532 surplus	$27,362 surplus
1973	$5,620,974,250	$89,342	$91,242	$1,900 surplus	$7,521 surplus	$29,262 surplus
1974	$11,856,089,850	$125,190	$120,897	$4,293 surplus	$7,563 surplus	$24,969 surplus
1975	$18,268,345,590	$120,180	$132,585	$12,405 surplus	$30,673 surplus	$37,374 surplus
1976	$25,241,263,400	$140,798	$142,716	$1,918 surplus	$27,159 surplus	$39,292 surplus
1977	$34,505,568,000	$179,547	$152,301	$27,246 surplus	$7,260 surplus	$12,046 surplus
1978	$33,820,069,400	$208,191	$178,428	$29,763 surplus	$4,057 surplus	$17,717 surplus
1979	$57,572,572,800	$248,696	$224,131	$24,565 surplus	$33,008 surplus	$42,282 surplus
1980	$67,956,965,200	$291,241	$271,834	$19,407 surplus	$48,550 surplus	$61,689 surplus
1981	$54,389,120,500	$310,570	$294,398	$16,172 surplus	$38,217 surplus	$77,861 surplus
1982	$37,777,149,030	$299,391	$275,236	$24,155 surplus	$13,622 surplus	$102,016 surplus
1983	$33,591,383,960	$323,874	$266,106	$57,768	$24,177	$159,784
1984	$34,047,360,000	$400,166	$291,094	$109,072	$75,025	$268,856
1985	$29,446,495,840	$410,950	$289,070	$121,880	$92,434	$390,736
1986	$21,208,966,600	$448,572	$310,033	$138,539	$117,331	$529,275
1987	$29,306,066,500	$500,552	$348,869	$151,683	$122,377	$680,958
1988	$26,875,160,670	$545,715	$431,149	$114,566	$87,691	$795,524
1989	$38,144,949,960	$580,144	$487,003	$93,141	$54,997	$888,665
1990	$48,969,302,640	$616,097	$535,233	$80,864	$31,895	$969,529
1991	$41,774,529,200	$609,479	$578,344	$31,135 surplus	$10,639 surplus	$1,000,664 surplus
1992	$42,115,554,250	$656,094	$616,882	$39,212 surplus	$2,904 surplus	$1,039,876 surplus
1993	$40,893,148,500	$713,174	$642,863	$70,311	$29,418	$1,110,187
1994	$39,807,328,500	$801,747	$703,254	$98,493	$58,686	$1,208,680
1995	$43,624,386,750	$890,771	$794,387	$96,384	$52,760	$1,305,064
1996	$55,246,276,140	$955,667	$851,602	$104,065	$48,819	$1,409,129
1997	$55,226,908,880	$1,042,726	$934,453	$108,273	$53,046	$1,517,402
1998	$37,368,673,080	$1,099,314	$933,174	$166,140	$128,771	$1,683,542
1999	$52,061,046,480	$1,230,974	$965,884	$265,090	$213,029	$1,948,632
2000	$90,183,300,570	$1,450,432	$1,070,597	$379,835	$289,652	$2,328,467
2001	$78,138,682,000	$1,370,400	$1,004,896	$365,504	$287,365	$2,693,971
2002	$76,021,282,050	$1,399,071	$977,470	$421,601	$345,580	$3,115,572
2003	$97,557,075,720	$1,515,225	$1,020,190	$495,035	$397,478	$3,610,607
2004	$138,300,286,700	$1,769,220	$1,159,233	$609,987	$471,687	$4,220,594
2005	$184,365,874,800	$1,996,728	$1,281,459	$715,269	$530,903	$4,935,863
2006	$214,781,339,300	$2,212,044	$1,451,685	$760,359	$545,578	$5,696,222
2007	$234,413,973,600	$2,344,590	$1,643,168	$701,422	$467,008	$6,397,644
2008	$325,699,262,800	$2,522,532	$1,826,596	$695,936	$370,237	$7,093,580
2009	$150,000,000,000					

These are lots of pretty numbers, but what do they tell us? Columns 2, 6, and 7 show that since 1960, we were throwing money away hand over fist on oil but we were able to balance it pretty well by exporting other commodities (goods and services) until 1976. Had it not been for oil we would have been ahead until 1982, and we did well in 1991 and 1992. Oil imports didn't really hurt us for about twenty years because we were able to compensate. Look now at the accumulated total for 1985 and see that it is four times the total for 1982. 1990 was twice 1985 and 1999 was twice 1990's total. It doubled in 2004 and again in 2009. The deficit was *quadrupled* in the first decade of the new millennium.

Now compare columns 2, 5, and 6. Oil imports started out as the mammoth drag on our economy but in 1983 other products did a little bit of a takeover. Then in about 2000, oil regained its momentum and we now have two massive burdens, not including the federal deficit. The $325 billion dollar oil deficit for 2008, which is almost half of the total trade deficit that averaged almost $700 billion for 2004 through 2008, simply cannot be maintained. Each and every American sent about $1,080 overseas each year just to keep their tank full in 2008 and another $1,200 for Gucci, Louis Vuitton, Mercedes, and imported wines.

Here are the facts that can be found at usdebtclock:[31]

1. The U.S. national debt is just over 12.3 trillion dollars, which is about $41,000 per citizen or $113,000 per taxpayer. (I use taxpayer because that is a fairly constant proportion of our population, meaning that we will always have a significant number of persons who are too young to be part of the workforce or are retired or otherwise unable to work.) The recent

increase passed by our legislature allows it to be more than 14 trillion dollars, but I will be conservative for this illustration and just leave it at the actual debt owed.

2. The gross domestic product (GDP) for 2009 is estimated at 14.19 trillion dollars by usdebtclock and it is reported as 14.4634 trillion by the Bureau of Economic Analysis.[32]

3. The GDP per citizen is $45,990 and the GDP per worker is $102,421.

Let me make clear that this debt is what is actually owed and payable. It does not include the government's future obligations to currently eligible citizens for Social Security, Medicare, and Medicaid. The usdebtclock estimates that these obligations increase our real debt to be $54.8 trillion dollars, which is about $503,447 per taxpayer, or a little over half a million. The total U.S. unfunded liabilities are actually more than 107 trillion dollars, but I will stick with the more conservative numbers to represent our obligations. What would happen if you (being the USA) telephoned a bankruptcy attorney with these numbers?

Atty: Hello, how can I help you?

You: Hi there. My name is USA. I have been looking at my finances and may need some help.

Atty: Well, tell me this: what is your monthly income and how much do you owe?

You: I bring home $102,421 per year and I owe more than $500,000. [*Numbers based on gross domestic product and U.S. total debt divided by number of wage earners.*]

Atty: Wow! Is any of your debt secured by any real property?

You: No. As a matter of fact, a great portion of the money I owe is to the same entity [*China*] where I spend most of my money.

Atty: I guess they saw you fall off the turnip truck. So they sell you everything that they make and turn around and lend you money so you can buy more?

You: Yeah.

Atty: Oh brother! Well, here's the scoop. Any person in their right mind would want to file a Chapter 7 bankruptcy and discharge all of the debt. You, being USA, can't really do that. Sooner or later it all has to be paid back. Now a Chapter 13 bankruptcy allows you to set up a structured payment plan based upon your income minus your expenses. But federal law limits you to only $250,000 in unsecured debt to be eligible.[33] *[Please understand that this means that EVERY wage-earner in the U.S. owes more than twice as much as they can owe to be otherwise eligible for this relief.]* Chapter 11 also lets you make monthly payments, but the court watches over everything you do. So how much is your income and expenses?

You: Revenue last year was about $15,674 *[per member of work force of a total Federal Tax Income of 2.115 trillion dollars]* and my spending was $26,601*[per member of work force with a total Federal Expense Schedule of 3.685 trillion dollars]*.

Atty: Wait a minute! You spent almost two times (about 175%) your income and are borrowing money to support your spending habits from the same person [*China*] who is making money hand-over-fist by selling their goods to you.

❧

You: Not only that, but my budgets for this year and next year are even worse![34]

Atty: I would love to help you out, but you are going to have to learn how to act a little, no, a *lot* more sensibly. Is there anyone in your family who you trust that may be able to help you control your spending habits?

You: Well, we have elections this November and I believe there will be people available who will understand the situation and lead us on the right path.

Atty: Give me a call when you have things under control. There is nothing that anyone can do to help until you are able to get a proper focus and control your spending habits.

Alternative Energy

A smorgasbord of alternative energies has made a run at the automobile market. Natural gas was a useful tool for a number of years, but its practicality of application never really caught on. Biofuels made from corn and other crops are functional but expensive to produce. Nevertheless, we have electricity, which is the basis for many new automobile designs, including the hydrogen-fueled vehicle manufactured by Honda.

Electricity is an abundant source of power and it can be made available from turbines, dams, windmills, coal, solar batteries, and nuclear power plants. Electric motors are practically foolproof. I have two personal examples: I own a Sears Craftsman 3/8" electric drill that I bought in 1969. The motor started to fail about twenty years ago. I opened it and oiled the shaft and it has run like a top ever since. The second example is the Black and Decker GrassHog I use to trim the edge of my lawn. It ran fine for a few years and then started to shake. I

pulled it apart and found that the axle sleeve had worn down. I wrapped it with electrical tape and it has run perfectly for many years since. My point is electric motors are inexpensive and will run virtually forever with very little maintenance. The real issue concerns the batteries, the recharge time, and recharge sources away from home.

I will compare two electric cars, the 2010 Tesla Roadster and the 2011 Nissan Leaf. The Tesla power pack contains 6,831 individual lithium ion battery cells and a full charge, which takes about 3.5 hours at 240 volts/70 amps, will give a 244-mile range. The Leaf has 192 lithium-manganese cells. These take about eight hours for a full recharge (but an 80% charge can be done in thirty minutes), the cost of which is estimated to be about 4 cents per mile. If you get 30 miles per gallon, how would you like gas to cost $1.20? Nissan is working with gas stations to provide convenient recharge stations as well. The Tesla Model S is a family sedan that will be available in 2011 with room for five adults, two kids, and plenty of luggage, along with battery storage for up to 300 miles that will recharge in 45 minutes. Its current base price is $57,400 and the Nissan Leaf is priced at $32,780. Both vehicles enable a tax credit of $7,500; thereby making final costs $49,900 and $25,280.

Recharging the batteries is the next big hurdle. Even 45 minutes is quite an inconvenience. Nevertheless, the electric automobile is in its infancy and there are many new developments concerning battery mass, charge-time, and reliability. One of my favorite breakthroughs concerns carbon fiber. It is used to manufacture many high performance products instead of steel, aluminum, or other metals. If you are a cycling enthusiast you know that virtually all bike frames (and many parts) used by professionals in the Tour de France are composed of carbon fiber. Auto racing fans know that the body of every Indy car is similarly made.

Tru Group and Angstrom Materials LLC are working independently on carbon fiber infused with a chemical compound to make the material itself a rechargeable battery.[35] The product is much lighter than Lithium Ion batteries and does not overheat. It is cheaper to produce and has a much longer life span; conceivably indefinite! Imagine the frame and body of your car also being the battery for the engine! That will clear up plenty of storage space and still give you power for many hundreds, if not thousands of miles of driving.

Recharging the battery is also going to happen in a much shorter time span. ABC News ran an article entitled "Battery breakthrough could make electric cars practical" discussing a new lithium ion battery that could charge in 20 seconds, as opposed to 6 minutes, and is light enough to give extended range.[36] Ars Technica confirms the lithium ion developments and *Technology Review* discusses a metal-air battery with even more capacity and less weight.[37]

As of publication, there are at least thirty electric vehicles that you can buy[38] and the big automakers will soon have theirs available, including all-electrics and electric hybrids.[39] There are a number of conversion kits and converted versions available for existing vehicles.[40]

Why am I spending so much time talking about electric cars under the subject heading of oil? These developments will soon lessen the enormous value of oil. As alternative supply increases, the demand decreases. Not only that, but out of the thirty electric vehicles already for sale, the Fly Bo and the Miles are from China and the Reva is from India. If we don't harvest and use the advantageously abundant natural resource of oil that is currently under our feet, we may never have an opportunity to do so. What if you were running a computer store and stocked

up on Windows Vista as soon as it was available, assuming that its value would continue to rise? Right now you can't give it away! We have to prepare for the future by selling this valuable resource now. Oil's value is based upon the law of supply and demand. Once we have properly harvested the alternative energy resources, oil will be an also-ran. We have it now and we better sell it now!

The Future of Energy

Even if we give a carte blanche to oil companies to drill for oil in the U.S., it might take about ten years to produce enough for our use. That is far too long. We have a duty to accelerate this to the point that we are energy independent within five years and exporting just as much as we use by 2020. Exporting is not a problem; we have many allies and trade partners who are desperate for oil. If we can produce half of the world's oil, we will have happy buyers in Europe who are tired of paying the equivalent of almost $8.00 per gallon of gas. Remember, Europe uses approximately 18 to 20% of the world's oil![41] China and Japan have similar needs and these nations hold more than $3 trillion of the U.S. national debt. Selling them oil will kill two birds with one stone.

Another advantage to selling our oil is that it will be produced *and taxed* here in the U.S. If we treat the oil as OPEC is treating it, we will be able to tax the difference between their $75.00 per barrel price and the actual cost of extraction. We have grown accustomed to paying $2.60 per gallon for regular gas and $2.80 for premium. We can now use a great deal of that money to cover the massive national debt and to replace a significant portion of our income.

According to the Energy Information Administration, in June, 2010 approximately 65.6% of the money you pay for gasoline

covers the cost of crude oil.[42] This means that $2.73 for a gallon of gas pays about $1.79 for the crude. If we begin to harvest our oil in the Bakken and Green River reserves at $25 per barrel, which is about 51 cents per gallon of gas, the U.S. government will be able to tax fuel consumption at $1.00 per gallon and you will pay less at the pump. The U.S. consumption of oil for 2008 was approximately 19,498,000 barrels per day and about half of that was for gasoline (8,989,000 barrels/378 million gallons).[43] This means that the one dollar per gallon tax on gasoline alone will give the U.S. almost $138 billion. A dollar per gallon of oil altogether would mean $281 billion. That number alone would cover 7.39% of the current federal budget of almost $3.8 trillion or a little over 2% of the entire federal deficit estimated at $14 trillion.[44] That may not seem like much but it would be the first step in the right direction. If we combine our internal taxation with exports of oil to China and Japan, we will be able to pay off the $3 trillion national debt owed to those countries in about seven years.

The moral of the story is we are sitting on top of a huge advantage we are not using. It has already cost us about $2.5 (four with inflation) trillion and the billions are flying out of our doors every day. *We need to stop the bleeding!* Will it fix everything? No! But it is the big first step we need to make to get back on track. Oil production will give us jobs, stimulate the economy, and protect us from foreign abuse of power. Even if our production causes OPEC to lower its prices, who cares? We will be keeping our money, getting our money back, and that will enable our economy to recover and expand.

The bottom line: Every candidate for Congress must pledge an absolute commitment to oil drilling and production. We have a lot of other work to do, but this is a necessity and we must begin somewhere.

Housing And The U.S. Economy

Many people believe that our economic recession is the product of the housing-market collapse. But that's putting the cart before the horse. The recession was waiting to happen; the market collapse was simply the shot from a loaded pistol. Once the trigger was pulled, the results were inevitable. The housing-market collapse was simply the last of a sequence of events that caused our economy to fall.

More than thirty years ago, in 1977, President Carter and Congress enacted the Community Reinvestment Act (CRA). This legislation was intended to ease the administrative transfer of funds to mortgage homes and therefore enable lower-income people to obtain home-mortgage loans.[1] The goals were noble, but in order to accomplish them, the money had to come from somewhere.

This is just one example of our federal government putting its hand into the free-market system. This interference invariably distorts an otherwise smooth-running system and creates an imbalance. At the time the CRA came into being, I was attending an economics course at Arizona State University. The class concluded that the housing market was going to collapse, but we weren't able to predict a date. We understood that if the government was overly aggressive, the collapse would come sooner. If the government wasn't as aggressive, the market might eventually recover. In a nutshell, understanding the dynamics of the collapse requires looking at the system of supply and demand.

Before the CRA, the housing market was reasonably balanced. The supply was approximately equal to the demand. The price of any residence was based upon free trade. After the CRA was enacted, there was a significant increase in the demand for homes because many more people were able to afford them, not based on an increase in income, but on government distortion of the market. The government then had to step in to enable lower-income buyers to purchase homes at falsely inflated prices. Eventually the market recovered, and home values stabilized, at least until the next government stimulus legislation or the next booming economy. Once again, home values went up until the market came to another balance point. The problem was, this "balance" consistently moved to a thinner and more precarious tightrope that eventually snapped.

The CRA wasn't the only government-stimulus program, but it was a major step. Government involvement in the housing market began in 1908 with Teddy Roosevelt's Country Life Commission, and altogether; as many as 106 actions by the federal government have directly impacted the housing market. The Department of Housing and Urban Development (HUD) specifically acknowledges 25 of these beginning with the Emergency Relief and Construction Act of 1932.[2] Many of these were Acts of Congress, and the only restraint was exercised during the Reagan administration. The most significant of these federal actions[2] were as follows:

- The National Housing Act of 1934, which set up the Federal Housing Administration

- The 1954 Housing Act that restructured the Federal National Mortgage Association (FNMA or Fannie Mae)

- The 1965 Housing and Urban Development Act that created the Department of Housing and Urban Development (HUD)

- The 1968 Fair Housing Act that created Government National Mortgage Association (GNMA or Ginnie Mae) and transferred Fannie Mae to private ownership

- The Community Reinvestment Act of 1977 (described earlier) was accompanied by seven other programs

- The 1986 Low-Income Housing Tax Credit

- The Low-Income Housing Preservation and Resident Homeownership Act of 1990

- The aggressive promotion of the Community Reinvestment Act by the Clinton administration in 1992

Who Is Paying the Bill?

The free-market balance of supply and demand continued to grow out of balance. More and more people owned homes worth much more than they could afford. Try to imagine a Jenga puzzle. Every housing act was like pulling one or two of the wooden blocks out of the housing-market tower. It eventually had to collapse. Who is paying for the collapse? Tax-paying American citizens! You are footing the bill for actions by Congress and other government officials who were pleading for your vote by claiming that they were instrumental in putting you into a home. But they neglected to tell you that they knew their actions would eventually force the housing market to fall apart and that you would at least be in danger of losing your home.

How did we come to bear this economic burden? The U.S. government insures almost all home loans, and the U.S. government effectively blackmailed all lending institutions to lend to otherwise unqualified buyers. This created the gap of so many people living in homes they cannot afford.

How much is a home really worth? The actual value is practically a constant, especially when you factor inflation into the equation. Yale economist Robert Shiller performed a study of home values that demonstrates how sale prices of existing homes have had many rises and falls over the years. But they always come back to almost the same value when you adjust for inflation, as seen in exhibit A.

Exhibit A

A History of Home Values

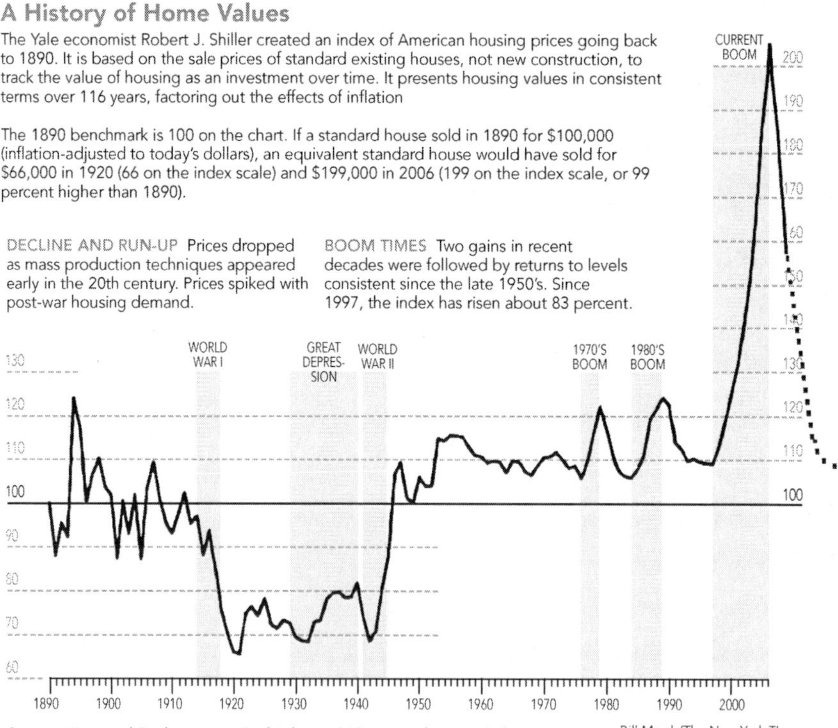

Source: "Irrational Exuberance." 2nd Edition, 2006. By Robert J. Shiller   Bill Marsh/The New York Times

The baseline, or 1890 benchmark, in this graph is 100 points, allowing the percentage of change each year to be based upon a constant. There was a sharp rise above 120 in 1895, which meant the economy was good, and home values increased in market value more than 20%. The price index dropped to the mid-60s during World War I because the stagnant economy caused homes to lose almost half of their immediate market values. They were actually still worth about 100 points, but there weren't many buyers. That market lasted through the Great Depression. Home values then rose to a little over 110 during and after World War II, and the market was reasonably stable until the 1970's economic boom when values went above 120. Prices then fell below 110 until the eightie's boom, when values again broke the 120 mark. These adjustments were generally based on the condition of our economy and had nothing to do with actual home values.

In 1997, prices started to shoot from about 110 to more than 200. Every piece of real estate almost doubled in value! The problem was that it was a *false value* produced by governmental interference with the free market. Our government created a demand by enabling a much bigger supply of demanding customers. Once the economic realities caught up with this imaginary demand, the housing market had to settle back to reality. The only way the crash could have been avoided was by further distortion of the market, which would have led to an even deeper fall.

All right, hindsight is always a perfect twenty-twenty. As we look at this history of home values, we're able to see that the value of a home is virtually constant *unless* something significant happens to greatly affect the value. In today's market, nothing significant has caused the rise in home values to be permanent. Now, if we had a massive earthquake and California slid into the ocean, Yuma, Arizona, would become beachfront property, and there would be a valid reason for real estate in that area to skyrocket in value. Nevertheless, during the years preceding the housing boom, no significant event occurred to disrupt the market. It was in no uncertain terms a mirage, and virtually everyone fell for it.

Economics and Finance

We need to understand the worlds of economics and finance to gain a clearer picture of the housing-market crash and what caused it. You can take as many graduate courses as you like, but here is what it all boils down to: the quantity of money *must be equal* to the commodities that can be purchased with that money. Other economic factors will push the numbers around, but the increase in value of one thing causes other things to lose their worth.

Imagine the world as a game of Monopoly. What if you decide to tack a "0" onto the end of every bill in the cash drawer? As you play, you'll discover that the properties will be too cheap for the game to go on. Eventually the property values will have to increase tenfold to regain a balance. If the property values were the first to increase, you wouldn't have enough money to do business, and you would be forced to demand more income (raise your prices) and provide your employees with raises to compensate for the increase in their cost of living; ergo, inflation.

Everyone wants to make money. You would like your IRA, your 401(k), or your mutual fund to appreciate at a higher rate than inflation. If inflation is 3% and your accounts are getting 10%, you're happy because you are wealthier as time passes. Here's the catch: in order for you to have more, *someone* has to have less. Where do the aggressive accounts get their money? From

the moneys invested at a lower rate of return, and from high-risk investments that fail. Conservative accounts, such as money market funds, protect equity but provide a small return. Checking accounts contain money but rarely gain interest and therefore decrease in actual value every day. Your investment accounts may have gone from $100 to $110, but after inflation, it's really worth $107. A money-market account at 2% may have increased from $100 to $102, but after inflation, it's really worth $99. A checking account after a year may still have $100, but it's actually worth only $97 of the prior year's dollars.

Does Gold Make a Good Investment?

Most people believe that gold is the ultimate investment and that it always goes up in value. This statement is basically true unless you factor inflation into the equation. Gold, just like the housing market, has its ups and downs, but when all is said and done, it will eventually settle to an average value that increases almost parallel to inflation, as you can see in exhibit B.

Exhibit B

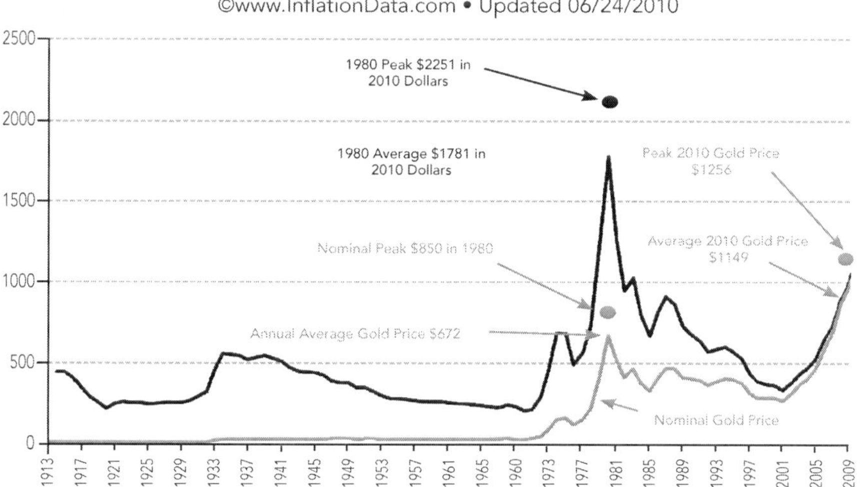

On August 6, 2010, gold closed at \$1,206.04 per ounce, which, in dollars, is almost its highest value. But in 1980 it peaked at \$850, which is equal to \$2,189 in 2009 dollars, adjusted for inflation. Why was gold worth almost twice as much in that year as it is now? 1980 marked the end of President Carter's term in office, when we had skyrocketing inflation. Investors were looking for a safe place to put their money, which made gold an attractive investment. Since then, gold's value has plummeted, because during President Reagan's term, we got the economy back on track, and President Clinton maintained prosperity during his term in office. Gold was a relatively poor investment because its value gradually dropped. Then the September 11, 2001, terrorist attacks caused people to look for a safe place to invest their money, because the world economy was chaotic. The actual low for gold in 2001 was \$255.95 on April 2.[4] On September 11, it sold for \$287.00 per ounce, and the price has consistently increased to its current level.

What Does All This Mean?

All commodities and investment properties will have their nominal values. They must balance because the amount of money in the world's economy is equal to the total value of the available commodities (goods and services.) If you compare the histories of all regularly traded goods or commodities, you will see a pattern. When one investment resource increases in value, other resources will generally decrease. Balance will always be reestablished because in the laws of economics, all opposing values must cancel each other out. The only "exception" is that there really is more money changing hands in booming economic times because there are more commodities to be gained. But there is always a balance!

Still not satisfied? To bring the picture into a little clearer focus, I prepared a table (exhibit C) that compares the average inflation rate, the average (mean) household income, the average price of houses sold in the U.S., the average Dow Jones Industrial Average at the close of the year, and the average gold price for the year.[5] Numbers beating inflation are in *italics*, and those that don't keep up with inflation appear in regular (unitalicized) text style. I analyzed data for gold dating back to 1833, for the Dow dating back to 1928, and for inflation dating back to 1925. However, this illustration begins with 1973 because gold was near an equilibrium at that time.

Exhibit C

Year(s)	Average Inflation Rate	Average Mean Household Income		Average Price Houses Sold in the U.S.		Dow Jones Industrial Average for Year		Gold Price Averaged for year	
1973	6.16%	$12,157	7.72%	$35,100	16.71%	$917.53	-3.84%	$97.32	67.33%
1974	11.03%	$13,094	7.71%	$38,725	10.33%	$745.70	-18.73%	$159.26	63.65%
1975	9.20%	$13,779	5.23%	$42,525	9.81%	$812.78	9.00%	$161.02	1.11%
1976	5.75%	$14,922	8.29%	$48,050	12.99%	$982.30	20.86%	$124.84	-22.47%
1977	6.50%	$16,100	7.89%	$54,350	13.11%	$885.81	-9.82%	$147.71	18.32%
1978	7.62%	$17,730	10.12%	$62,700	15.36%	$813.97	-8.11%	$193.22	30.81%
1979	11.22%	$19,554	10.29%	$71,450	13.96%	$843.24	3.60%	$306.68	58.72%
1980	13.58%	$21,063	7.72%	$76,375	6.89%	$895.23	6.17%	$612.56	99.74%
1981	10.35%	$22,787	8.18%	$83,175	8.90%	$932.70	4.19%	$460.03	-24.90%
1982	6.16%	$24,309	6.68%	$83,850	0.81%	$890.15	-4.56%	$375.67	-18.34%
1983	3.22%	$25,401	4.49%	$89,775	7.07%	$1,197.87	34.57%	$424.35	12.96%
1984	4.30%	$27,464	8.12%	$97,550	8.66%	$1,175.20	-1.89%	$360.48	-15.05%
1985	3.55%	$29,066	5.83%	$100,825	3.36%	$1,345.81	14.52%	$317.26	-11.99%
1986	1.91%	$30,759	5.82%	$112,075	11.16%	$1,815.10	34.87%	$367.66	15.89%
1987	3.66%	$32,410	5.37%	$127,575	13.83%	$2,273.37	25.25%	$446.46	21.43%
1988	4.08%	$34,017	4.96%	$138,650	8.68%	$2,077.34	8.62%	$436.94	-2.13%
1989	4.83%	$36,520	7.36%	$148,125	6.83%	$2,535.72	22.07%	$381.44	-12.70%
1990	5.39%	$37,403	2.42%	$149,075	0.64%	$2,662.23	4.99%	$383.51	0.54%
1991	4.25%	$37,922	1.39%	$147,275	-1.21%	$2,964.36	11.35%	$362.11	-5.58%
1992	3.03%	$38,840	2.42%	$144,675	-1.76%	$3,296.37	11.20%	$343.82	-5.05%
1993	2.96%	$41,428	6.66%	$147,475	1.94%	$3,571.79	8.36%	$359.77	4.64%
1994	2.61%	$43,133	4.12%	$154,175	4.54%	$3,792.86	6.19%	$384.00	6.73%
1995	2.81%	$44,938	4.18%	$157,750	2.32%	$4,534.19	19.55%	$384.17	0.04%
1996	2.93%	$47,123	4.86%	$165,525	4.93%	$5,780.13	27.48%	$387.77	0.94%
1997	2.34%	$49,692	5.45%	$174,875	5.65%	$7,437.57	28.67%	$330.98	-14.65%
1998	1.55%	$51,855	4.35%	$181,150	3.59%	$8,610.20	15.77%	$294.24	-11.10%
1999	2.19%	$54,737	5.56%	$194,675	7.47%	$10,474.78	21.66%	$278.88	-5.22%
2000	3.38%	$57,135	4.38%	$205,375	5.50%	$10,688.04	2.04%	$279.11	0.0008%
2001	2.83%	$58,208	1.87%	$211,050	2.76%	$10,139.93	-5.13%	$271.04	2.89%
2002	1.59%	$57,852	-0.06%	$226,700	7.42%	$8,548.55	-15.69%	$309.73	14.27%
2003	2.27%	$59,067	2.10%	$244,550	7.87%	$9,017.92	5.49%	$363.38	17.32%
2004	2.68%	$60,466	2.37%	$272,125	11.28%	$10,325.97	14.51%	$409.72	12.75%
2005	3.39%	$63,344	4.76%	$291,275	7.04%	$10,529.13	1.97%	$444.74	8.55%
2006	3.24%	$66,570	5.09%	$303,900	4.33%	$11,472.08	8.59%	$603.46	35.69%
2007	2.85%	$67,609	1.56%	$309,800	1.94%	$13,197.98	15.04%	$695.39	15.23%
2008	3.85%	Data not available		$289,075	-6.69%	$11,224.23	-14.95%	$871.96	25.39%
2009	-0.34%	Data not available		$266,533	-7.80%	$8,887.83	-20.82%	$972.35	11.51%

There is a tendency for investments to flow in one direction, causing certain commodities to be above or below their equilibrium. If you compare Dow Jones and gold, you'll see that they were in opposition on a fairly consistent basis.

I prepared exhibit D to illustrate the balance based on exhibit C data. I assigned a value of 1 for each of the five elements as of January 1 of 1973, similar to the use of 100 as the starting point in exhibit A. The change in each value is computed as a multiple of that value for each year. For example; the average price of a house actually sold in 1973 was $35,100 and the average home sale price in 1974 was $38,725. The home sales price line starts at 1 and a year later it is $38,725 divided by $35,100; or 1.103. 1975's entry is at 42,525 divided by 35,100; or 1.216. Exhibit D shows that inflation and average income are fairly consistent, and our standard of living has gradually improved over time. This conclusion is supported by the U.S. Census Bureau, which found that real median household income based on 2007 dollars increased from $38,771 in 1965 to $50,233 in 2007.[6] This also shows that housing values have fared well, with the exception of the housing boom that began in 1997 and the crash beginning in December 2006. This demonstrates the balance between gold and stocks as investment tools—when one rises, the other tends to fall.

Exhibit D

Black Line:	Inflation
Dark Gray Line:	Average Mean Income
Light Gray Line:	Average Home Price
Dashed Black Line:	Dow Jones Industrial Average
Dashed Gray Line:	Gold

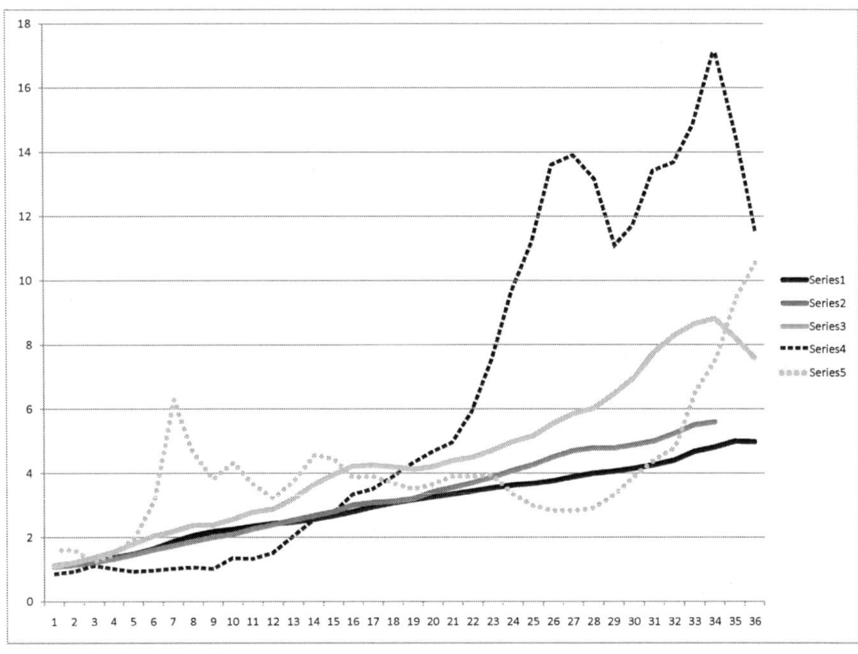

By comparing these lines, it is fairly easy to understand my point. Gold and the Dow Jones were consistently running in opposite directions. Home values were steady, except for the spike from 1997 to 2006. This only demonstrates the trends and the interplay between all of these elements. What appears to soon be a crossing of the lines for Gold and the Dow may indicate that the market is recovering, but this graph is only one of the pieces of the puzzle. Perhaps gold is reaching the end of its run, but that will depend on the rate of our economic recovery.

A Confused Market

As I stated at the beginning of this chapter, government involvement in housing finance has confused the market, and we're all paying for it in one way or another. The distortion of home values is only one of the primary causes of the current recession. This crisis makes it important for us to learn from our errors and prepare for the future. The only way for the housing market and our economy to stabilize and recover will be to limit government involvement to only what is necessary for administrative purposes.

Allowing the financial world and the free-market system to freely function will stimulate the economy, produce jobs, and put more people in homes that will not be taken from them because of a massive market collapse. Under Presidents Harding, Coolidge, Kennedy and Reagan, tax rates were reduced and tax revenues increased. The alternative of allowing our government to contort the system with mismanaged coercion of financial institutions will only lead us down the path to another fall. Anyone with aspirations to serve the legislature of this nation must commit to cutting back on federal interference and allow the banks and lending institutions to fight for our business! A free-market economy will provide the greatest prosperity, and we will no longer need to stimulate the housing market because wage earners will be able to afford a home.

A Final Look

If you look again at exhibits B and C, you will see that gold and the Dow both appear to be above their equilibrium levels. That's because the real-estate market is in a recovery process, the prime rate is set far below its market equilibrium, and stocks are fluctuating based on many uncertainties. Does that mean you need to sell your gold today because everything else is about to go up? I have no idea. The only thing I can say with confidence is that gold will decline in value when *and if* our economy recovers. A good showing at the polls in November will work to save our economy, and I believe at that point, everything will begin to fall into place. Homes will appreciate, stocks will appreciate, and gold will be disposed of to free capital. But that's just an opinion based on over 100 years of history and an optimistic outlook.

When Will Economic Recovery Happen?

If I knew these things ahead of time, I would already be the richest person in the world. Buy low and sell high is the codified rule of investment. The problem is that we never know in advance when a commodity reaches its absolute high or absolute low. We must leave that to the experienced financial advisors. I believe it is prudent to understand that buying something on its way up and already above its equilibrium means that you need to be ready to sell at an unforeseen time. Odds are, you're going to lose, because once the bottom falls out, everybody is looking to sell.

Making good decisions on every purchase is more important today than ever. Becoming aware of how you can impact the national economy will equip you to be a better manager of your personal resources.

Freedom of Religion

"Congress shall make no law respecting an establishment of religion, or prohibiting the free exercise thereof."[1] Those are the first words of the First Amendment to the United States Constitution. They appear to express a plain and simple mandate regarding the U.S. government, so why are we still arguing thousands of cases before courts of every venue looking for the interpretation of sixteen simple words? The answer lies in two words: *respecting* and *prohibiting*. Those terms are consistently fighting with each other. Any government action involving religion will have one individual or group arguing that a government institution is promoting or denigrating some form of religion. The other side will argue that it is well within the means of government prudence to so act.

Lemon Test Rulings

I am providing a brief history of the relationship between federal, state, and local governments and religion. I will also discuss the evolution of our courts' rulings concerning this relationship. We will use this as a guide to analyze the interplay of government and religion as drafted by Chief Justice Warren Earl Burger in *Lemon v. Kurtzman* in 1971.[2] This ruling resulted in the affectionately termed "*Lemon* Law" or "*Lemon* test." Chief Justice Burger explained the *Lemon* test as follows:

1. The statute must have a secular legislative purpose.

2. Its principal or primary effect must be one that neither advances nor inhibits religion.

3. The statute must not foster "an excessive government entanglement with religion."

The *Lemon* test is a very useful tool, but it is not perfect. Supreme Court Justice Antonin Scalia had this comment about the *Lemon* test in his concurring opinion in *Lamb's Chapel v. Center Moriches Union Free School District* (1993):

> As to the Court's invocation of the Lemon test: like some ghoul in a late-night horror movie that repeatedly sits up in its grave and shuffles abroad after being repeatedly killed and buried, Lemon stalks our Establishment Clause jurisprudence once again, frightening the little children and school attorneys of Center Moriches Union Free School District. Its most recent burial, only last Term, was, to be sure, not fully six feet under: Our decision in *Lee v. Weisman*, 505 U.S. 577, 586–587 (1992), conspicuously avoided using the supposed "test," but also declined the invitation to repudiate it. Over the years, however, no fewer than five of the currently sitting Justices have, in their own opinions, personally driven pencils through the creature's heart (the author of today's opinion repeatedly), and a sixth has joined an opinion doing so.
>
> The secret of the Lemon test's survival, I think, is that it is so easy to kill. It is there to scare us (and our audience) when we wish it to do so, but we can command it to return to the tomb at will.[1]

Ouch! If I were the *Lemon* test, I would have packed my bags in 1993. Nevertheless, it is still with us and was most recently referenced in *Ken L. Salazar, Secretary of the Interior, et al. v. Frank Buono*, decided April 28, 2010. This case concerned the Latin cross in the Mojave National Preserve. Justice Anthony Kennedy described it in *Salazar v. Buono* as follows:

> A government religious practice or symbol will survive an Establishment Clause challenge when it (1) has a secular purpose, (2) has a primary effect that neither advances nor inhibits religion, and (3) does not foster excessive state entanglement with religion. *Buono I*, supra, at 1214–1215 (citing *Lemon v. Kurtzman* 403 U. S. 602, 612–613 (1971)[2]

Do you see any difference? Even though the *Lemon* test is maligned by Justice Scalia, its power has grown beyond actions by Congress (referred to by Burger as a "statute" or an "act") to any action by any governmental entity. The *Lemon* test is now the all-encompassing "ghoul in a late-night horror movie."

It may appear that I've revealed the final scene in the movie at the beginning of the show, but I hope that this vision of the current state of affairs will interest the reader to look at the past with greater enthusiasm.

Religion and Government Throughout History

Government's interrelationship with religion dates back long before the birth of America. I think we should reflect on our roots in order to gain the proper perspective. I am going to briefly address excerpts from important documents that influenced the U.S. Constitution. Let's begin with the First Virginia Charter drafted on April 10, 1606:

> James, by the grace of *God* [King of England, Scotland, France, and Ireland, Defender of the Faith], etc. Whereas our loving and weldisposed subjects, Sir Thomas Gates and Sir George Somers, Knightes, … and divers others of our loving subjects, have been humble sutors unto us that wee woulde vouchsafe unto them our licence to make habitacion, plantacion, and to deduce a colonie of sondrie of our people into that parte of America commonly called Virginia, and other parts and territories in America either appartaining unto us or which are not nowe actuallie possessed by anie *Christian* prince or people …

Wee, greatly commending and graciously accepting of theire desires to the furtherance of soe noble a worke which may, by the providence of *Almightie God*, hereafter tende to the glorie of *His Divine Majestie* in propagating of *Christian* religion to suche people as yet live in darkenesse and miserable ignorance of the true knoweledge and worshippe of *God* and may in tyme bring the infidels and salvages living in those parts to humane civilitie and to a setled and quiet governmente, doe by theise our lettres patents graciously accepte of and agree to theire humble and well intended desires;

Provided alwaies, and our will and pleasure is and wee do hereby declare to all *Christian* kinges, princes and estates ... [5] (emphasis added)

A word to the wise: if you run spell-check on documents from the 1600s, have a fire extinguisher handy for your CPU. No, wait! I have an even better idea: All school children reading this should quote some of the text in schoolwork and hand it in. When your teacher gives you a D-minus for your spelling errors, just give your teacher a copy of the authority and ask where he or she went to school ... but be gentle.

The Second Virginia Charter and the Third Virginia Charter[3] were issued, respectively, on May 23, 1609, and March 12, 1612. Each contained similar references to God and Christianity.

The Mayflower Compact was signed November 11, 1620:

IN THE NAME OF *GOD*, *AMEN*. We, whose names are underwritten, the Loyal Subjects of our dread Sovereign Lord King James, by the *Grace of God*, of Great Britain, France, and Ireland, King, *Defender of the Faith*, &c. Having undertaken for the *Glory of God*, and *Advancement of the Christian Faith*, and the Honour of our King and Country, a Voyage to plant the first Colony in the northern Parts of Virginia; Do by these Presents, solemnly and mutually, in the Presence of *God* and one another, covenant and combine ourselves together into a civil Body Politick, for our better Ordering and Preservation, and Furtherance of the Ends aforesaid: And by Virtue hereof do enact, constitute, and frame, such just and equal Laws, Ordinances, Acts, Constitutions, and Officers, from time to time, as shall be thought most meet and convenient for the general Good of the Colony; unto which we promise all due Submission and Obedience. IN WITNESS whereof we have hereunto subscribed our names at Cape-Cod the eleventh of November, in the Reign of our Sovereign Lord King James, of England, France, and Ireland, the eighteenth, and of Scotland the fifty-fourth, *Anno Domini*; 1620.[4] (emphasis added)

The 1629 Charter of Massachusetts Bay includes the following:

Whereby our said People, Inhabitants there, may be soe religiously, peaceablie, and civilly governed, as their good Life and orderlie Conversation, maie wynn and incite the Natives of Country, to the Knowledg and Obedience of the onlie true *God* and *Savior of Mankinde*, and the *Christian Fayth*, which in our Royall Intention, and the Adventurers free Profession, is the principall Ende of this Plantation.[5] (emphasis added)

Similar references to God, Jesus, Christianity, and their relationship to government are contained in each of the following documents:

1. The Fundamental Orders of Connecticut, dated January 14, 1639[6]

2. The Connecticut Colony Charter of 1662[7]

3. Excerpts from Frame of Government of Pennsylvania by William Penn, 1682[8]

4. Pennsylvania Charter of Privileges, dated October 28, 1701[9]

5. Resolutions of the Stamp Act, dated October 19, 1765[10]

The first "official" proclamation of a day of thanksgiving by a government entity was made by the governing council of Charlestown, Massachusetts, on June 20, 1676.[11] This proclamation also includes many references to God and Jesus Christ. I use the word *official* because the actual evolution of the Thanksgiving holiday is somewhat complicated. The first actual Thanksgiving in America happened in Plymouth, Massachusetts, in 1621 after the Mayflower settlers had a bountiful harvest and celebrated a three-day feast with the local Indians.[12] Had it not been for the Indians' assistance during the winter of 1621, it is not likely the Pilgrims would have survived.

In October 1774, the First Continental Congress prepared The Declaration of Rights and Grievances for the king of England and Parliament. This declaration included the following:

> Also the act passed the same session for establishing the *Roman Catholic Religion* in the province of Quebec, abolishing the equitable system of English laws, and erecting a tyranny there, to the great danger, from so great a dissimilarity of *Religion*, law, and government, of the neighboring British colonies by the assistance of whose blood and treasure the said country was conquered from France.[13] (emphasis added)

On July 6, 1775, the Continental Congress issued the Declaration of the Causes and Necessity of Taking Up Arms:

> A declaration by the representatives of the united colonies of North America, now met in Congress at Philadelphia, setting forth the causes and necessity of their taking up arms. If it was possible for men, who exercise their reason to believe, that *the divine Author* of our existence intended a part of the human race to hold an absolute property in, and an unbounded power over others … But a reverence for our *Creator*, principles of humanity, and the dictates of common sense … Our forefathers, inhabitants of the island of Great Britain, left their native land, to seek on these shores a residence for civil and *religious freedom.*

Our cause is just. Our union is perfect. Our internal resources are great, and, if necessary, foreign assistance is undoubtedly attainable—We gratefully acknowledge, as signal instances of the *Divine favour towards us, that his Providence* would not permit us to be called into this severe controversy, until we were grown up to our present strength, had been previously exercised in warlike operation, and possessed of the means of defending ourselves. With hearts fortified with these animating reflections, we must solemnly, *before God and the world*, declare, that, exerting the utmost energy of those powers, which *our beneficient Creator hath graciously bestowed upon us*, the arms have been compelled by our enemies to assume, we will, in defiance of every hazard, with unabating firmness and perseverence [sic], employ for the preservation of our liberties; being with one mind resolved to die freemen rather than to live slaves.

With a humble confidence in the mercies of t*he supreme and impartial Judge and Ruler of the Universe, we most devoutly implore his divine goodness* to protect us happily through this great conflict, to dispose our adversaries to reconciliation on reasonable terms, and thereby to relieve the empire from the calamities of civil war.[14] (emphasis added)

On June 12, 1776, three weeks and a day before the Continental Congress formally accepted the Declaration of Independence, the State of Virginia issued the Virginia Declaration of Rights.[15] George Mason and James Madison drafted this document, which was used as a model for the Bill of Rights. That Virginia Declaration of Rights included the following:

I. That all men are by nature equally free and independent, and have certain inherent rights, of which, when they enter into a state of society, they cannot, by any compact, deprive or divest their posterity; namely, the enjoyment of life and liberty, with the means of acquiring and possessing property, and pursuing and obtaining happiness and safety.

> XVI. That religion, or the duty which we owe to our *Creator*, and
> the manner of discharging it, can be directed by reason and
> conviction, not by force or violence; and therefore, *all men
> are equally entitled to the free exercise of religion, according
> to the dictates of conscience; and that it is the mutual duty
> of all to practice Christian forbearance, love, and charity
> towards each other.* (emphasis added)

The Declaration of Independence is; in no uncertain terms, the birth certificate of the United States of America. It was signed by fifty-six of our founding fathers[16] including fifteen Episcopalians, eleven Congregationalists, eleven Presbyterians, three deists, two Anglicans, one Quaker, one Roman Catholic, one Unitarian, and thirteen unaffiliated signers. With George Clymer listed as both a Quaker and Episcopalian and James Wilson classified as both an Episcopalian and Deist. This means that forty-three of the fifty-six signers had clear religious affiliations. The document includes the following:

> When, in the course of human events, it becomes necessary for one people to dissolve the Political Bands which have connected them with another, and to assume among the Powers of the Earth, the separate and equal Station to which the *Laws of Nature and of Nature's God entitle them*, a decent Respect to the Opinions of Mankind requires that they should declare the causes which impel them to the Separation.

> We hold these Truths to be self-evident, that all *Men are created equal, that they are endowed by their Creator with certain unalienable Rights*, that among these are Life, Liberty, and the Pursuit of Happiness.[17] (emphasis added)

The Articles of Confederation were a rough draft or blueprint for the U.S. Constitution. Congress agreed to the articles on November 15, 1777, and forty-eight delegates signed them, only sixteen of whom had also signed the Declaration of

Independence.[18] The signers' religious affiliations were proportionately similar to signers of the Declaration, but thirty-three had no known affiliation with any religion.[19] The articles were then circulated and became effective after Maryland's ratification on March 1, 1781. They included the following words:

> And Whereas it hath pleased the *Great Governor of the World* to incline the hearts of the legislatures we respectively represent in Congress …

Thomas Jefferson was the primary author of the Declaration of Independence and also a signer, but he had little to do with the Articles of Confederation. He was also the primary author of the Virginia Act for Establishing Religious Freedom written in 1777, slightly edited in 1779 and renamed the Virginia Statute for Religious Freedom, and finally adopted into law in 1786.[20] This statute is often called "the precursor to the Religion Clauses of the First Amendment" to the Constitution and is credited with "erecting a wall of separation between church and government," thereby providing for the common phrase that Mr. Jefferson coined in his letter to the Danbury Baptist Association in 1802.[21] The Virginia law read:

> No man shall be compelled to frequent or support any *religious worship, place, or ministry* whatsoever, nor shall be enforced, restrained, molested, or burdened in his body or goods, nor shall otherwise suffer, on account of his *religious opinions or belief;* but that all men shall be free to profess, and by argument to maintain, their opinions in *matters of religion*, and that the same shall in no wise diminish, enlarge, or affect their civil capacities. (emphasis added)

Jefferson's letter stated:

> Believing with you that religion is a matter which lies solely between man & his god, that he owes account to non other for his faith or his worship, that the legitimate powers of government reach actions

only, and not opinions, I contemplate with sovereign reverence that act of the whole American people which declared that their legislature should make no law respecting an establishment of religion, or prohibiting the free exercise thereof, *thus building a wall of separation between church and state.* (emphasis added)

The first Constitutional Convention met a little more than a year after the Virginia statute was passed, on May 14, 1787. Mr. Jefferson was a minister to France and not a member of this convention. When he saw the draft of the proposed Constitution, he expressed his disappointment in a letter to James Madison:

> I will now add what I do not like. First the omission of a bill of rights providing clearly & without the aid of sophisms for *freedom of religion*, freedom of the press, protection against standing armies, restriction against monopolies, the eternal & unremitting force of the habeas corpus laws, and trials by jury in all matters of fact triable by the laws of the land & not by the law of nations. To say, as Mr. Wilson does that a bill of rights was not necessary because all is reserved in the case of the general government which is not given, while in the particular ones all is given which is not reserved, might do for the audience to whom it was addressed, but it is surely a gratis dictum, opposed by strong inferences from the body of the instrument, as well as from the omission of the clause of our present confederation which had declared that in express terms … The election of a President of America some years hence will be much more interesting to certain nations of Europe than ever the election of a king of Poland was. Reflect on all the instances in history ancient & modern, of elective monarchies, and say if they do not give foundation for my fears…. But experience shews that the only way to prevent disorder is to render them uninteresting by frequent changes.[22] (emphasis added)

Was Thomas Jefferson a wise man? He not only drafted the Declaration of Independence, but he was adamant about each of the terms of the Bill of Rights long before their adoption. John Adams argued vehemently in Philadelphia for Jefferson's declaration, and many believed it was the only issue that these two friends were in total agreement about. Both of them died on the fiftieth anniversary of the birth of our nation: July 4, 1826. Adams survived Jefferson by a little more than two hours, and horsemen carrying notice of their deaths passed each other between their homes. John Adams was seven years older than Jefferson, but he regularly proclaimed that he would outlive his friend. On Adams's deathbed, his last words were "Thomas Jefferson survives," because he was not yet aware of Jefferson's death.[23]

The United States Constitution was drafted by fifty-five men, all of whom were members of a church, and six of whom subscribed to two different denominations.[24] There were seven Congregationalists, three deists, two Dutch Reformed, twenty-nine Episcopalians, two Lutherans, two Methodists, eleven Presbyterians, three Quakers, and two Roman Catholics. Thirty-nine of these men signed the Constitution, but there were no religious references anywhere in the document. Why was this document entirely secular? These leaders endured great trials working to establish a government that provided religious freedom without repression. They knew that this instrument was the blueprint for what they believed to be the perfect union. They also knew that their relationship with the Almighty was a personal matter not within the realm of government control.

All of these documents reflect both the history and growth of our nation's conscience. The Declaration of Independence was our birth certificate; the Constitution and its amendments are our doctoral degree.

Freedom of Religion in the Law

I begin the legal discussion of freedom of religion with *Lemon v. Kurtzman*[25] because it is recognized as a ruling in which the

Supreme Court effectively said, "We are tired of nitpicking at all of these obscure details; let's see if we can put together an iron-clad rule that can be relied on everywhere." Needless to say, the making of the rule did little to stop the number of Establishment Clause/freedom of religion cases, but it did give us the beginning of what may be referred to as a "Blue Book" to evaluate a dispute. It narrows the issues and allows us to avoid immaterial collateral matters.

In *Lemon*, the State of Rhode Island enacted a statute to provide for a 15 percent salary supplement to be paid to teachers in nonpublic schools *if* the average expenditure on secular education for each student was below the average expenditure in public schools. Pennsylvania had previously enacted similar legislation. It turned out that, with very few exceptions, the only teachers benefitting from the acts in both Rhode Island and Pennsylvania were those at Roman Catholic schools.

David H. Kurtzman, the Superintendent of Public Instruction in Pennsylvania, argued that the salary boosts were only applied to classes that were also taught in public schools, and therefore no government funds were paid for religious education in a religious institution. The Supreme Court found as follows:

> In the absence of precisely stated constitutional prohibitions, we must draw lines with reference to the three main evils against which the Establishment Clause was intended to afford protection: "sponsorship, financial support, and active involvement of the sovereign in religious activity." See *Walz v. Tax Commission*.[26]

> Three such tests may be gleaned from our cases. First, the statute must have a secular purpose; second, its principal or primary effect must be one that neither advances nor inhibits religion;[27] finally, the statute must not foster "an excessive entanglement with religion." *Walz*, supra at 674, 1414.

We conclude that the cumulative impact of the entire relationship arising under the statutes in each state involves excessive entanglement between government and religion.

Our prior holdings do not call for total separation between church and state; total separation is not possible in an absolute sense. Some relationship between government and religious organizations is inevitable.[28]… Judicial caveats against entanglement must recognize [that] the line of separation, far from being a "wall," is a blurred, indistinct, and variable barrier depending on all of the circumstances of a particular relationship.

In order to determine whether the government entanglement with religion is excessive, we must examine the character and purposes of the institutions that are benefited [sic], the nature of the aid that the State provides, and the resulting relationship between the government and the religious authority.[29]

This ruling supports the premise that there are two sides to every story, and it guides us in balancing the facts. The "wall of separation" is not made of brick but is more of a hedge of oleanders that you can squeeze through when there is a valid reason to be on the other side, and no one is really harmed as a result.

In weighing each of the three elements of the test, a court has discretion to apportion their significance. In *Lemon*, the court discussed the secular purpose by reflecting on two prior cases—*Everso*[30] and *Allen:*[31]

Our decisions from Everson and Allen have permitted the States to provide church-related schools with secular, neutral, or nonideological services, facilities, or materials. Bus transportation, school lunches, public health services, and secular textbooks supplied in common to all students were not thought to offend the Establishment Clause.

The court recognized that each of these elements was sufficiently benign, and there was little danger of government sponsorship of a religious enterprise, but salary supplements to teachers in religious schools were too direct. The court went on to note that government sponsorship of busing, lunches, and so on, were effectively state aid for the students (and parents) rather than the schools. The difference in *Lemon* was that the government was paying money directly to the teachers who provided religious education. The court concluded that this type of support simply didn't have a secular purpose.

The second element of the test concerned whether the effect of the legislation was to have the primary effect of either advancing or inhibiting religion. A conclusion on advancement was easy to determine based upon the same set of facts: direct financial support to the teachers in any religiously affiliated schools had the effect of advancing religion.

The third element of the test was to determine whether government was entangled with religion. The court found that the State's need to monitor the schools' records in order to determine which teachers were eligible for assistance was simply too much, and therefore these laws were struck down.

In 1980, the Supreme Court heard *Thomas v. Review Board of the Indiana Employment Security Division*. Eddie C. Thomas was a Jehovah's Witness and was initially hired to work in his employer's roll foundry, which fabricated sheet steel for a variety of industrial uses. When the foundry closed, Mr. Thomas was transferred to a department that fabricated turrets for military tanks. He learned that all of the remaining departments in the company engaged directly in the production of weapons and asked to be laid off. That request was denied, and he quit, asserting that his religious beliefs prevented him from participating in the manufacture of weapons. He then applied for unemployment-compensation benefits, but they were denied. The hearing referee found that Thomas had terminated his employment because of his religious convictions, but the referee held that he was not entitled to unemployment benefits because his voluntary termination was not based upon a "good cause [arising] in connection with [his] work," as required by Indiana statute.[32]

The Supreme Court held that the "State's denial of unemployment compensation benefits violated [Thomas's] First Amendment right to free exercise of religion."

It should be noted that the Supreme Court did not apply the *Lemon* test to this case, much to Justice William Rehnquist's dismay, as you will soon see. The Court instead took a look at the facts and found the following:

> The State's denial of unemployment compensation to petitioner violated his First Amendment right to free exercise of religion under *Sherbet v. Verner*.[33] ... A person must not be compelled to choose between the exercise of a First Amendment right and participation in an otherwise available public program.... . Where the [S]tate conditions receipt of an important benefit upon conduct proscribed by a religious faith, or where it denies such a benefit because of conduct mandated by a religious belief, thereby putting substantial pressure on an adherent to modify his behavior and to violate his beliefs, a burden upon religion exists.

Justice Rehnquist presented this dissenting view:

> In recent years the Court has moved away from the mechanistic "no-aid-to-religion" approach to the Establishment Clause and has stated a three-part test to determine the constitutionality of governmental aid to religion. See *Lemon v. Kurtzman* ... .
>
> It is not surprising that the Court today makes no attempt to apply those principles to the facts of this case. If Indiana were to legislate

what the Court today requires—an unemployment compensation law which permitted benefits to be granted to those persons who quit their jobs for religious reasons–the statute would "plainly" violate the Establishment Clause as interpreted in such cases as Lemon and Nyquist…. The proviso would clearly serve only a religious purpose…. Second, there can be little doubt that the primary effect of the proviso would be to "advance" religion by facilitating the exercise of a religious belief. Third, any statute including such a proviso would surely "entangle" the State in religion far more than the mere grant of tax exemptions.

The reason I provide both of these opinions is that they are both 100 percent correct. The difference between the opinions is a matter of perspective, something you need to understand if you ever have a dispute concerning freedom of religion.

Justice Burger and the majority embraced the perspective that the unforeseen closure of the sheet-steel department forced Mr. Thomas into a role he could not conscientiously accept. Justice Rehnquist looked at the Indiana Unemployment Compensation law on its face and found that it had no religious implication or involvement. The problem was that the facts confronting Mr. Thomas had not been contemplated when the law was drafted. An easier solution may have been to conclude that the job Thomas was hired to do no longer existed and that he was effectively "fired" as if the company had gone out of business.

The Supreme Court had a different perspective when it heard *Marsh v. Chambers*.[34] In that case; Ernest Chambers was a member of the Nebraska State Legislature. The legislature opened every session with a State-hired chaplain offering prayer, as had been done for almost two hundred years. This offended Mr. Chambers, and he brought the action. The district court held that the Establishment Clause had been breached not by the prayer but by paying the chaplain with public funds. The court of appeals held that the entire chaplaincy practice was in violation of the Establishment Clause and prohibited the State from engaging in any aspect thereof. Supreme Court Chief Justice Burger delivered the opinion that reversed this judgment:

> The Establishment Clause does not always bar a state from regulating conduct simply because it "harmonizes with religious canons." … Here the individual claiming injury by the practice is an adult, presumably not readily susceptible to "religious indoctrination." …
>
> In light of the unambiguous and unbroken history of more than 200 years, there can be no doubt that the practice of opening legislative sessions with prayer has become the fabric of our society. To invoke Divine guidance on a public body entrusted with making the laws is not, in these circumstances, an "establishment" of religion or a step toward establishment; it is simply a tolerable acknowledgment of beliefs widely held among the people of this country. As Justice Douglas observed, "[We] are a religious people whose institutions presuppose a Supreme Being."[35]
>
> The Court of Appeals was concerned that Palmer's long tenure has the effect of giving preference to his religious views. We cannot, any more than Members of Congress of this century, perceive any suggestion that choosing a clergyman of one denomination advances the beliefs of a particular church. Absent proof that the chaplain's reappointment stemmed from an impermissible motive, we conclude that his long tenure does not in itself conflict with the Establishment Clause.
>
> Nor is the compensation of the chaplain from public funds a reason to invalidate the Nebraska Legislature's chaplaincy; remuneration is grounded in historic practice initiated, as we noted earlier, supra, at 788, by the same Congress that drafted the Establishment Clause of the First Amendment. Currently, many state legislatures and the United States Congress provide compensation for their chaplains. The content of the prayer is not of concern to judges where, as here,

there is no indication that the prayer opportunity has been exploited to proselytize or advance any one, or to disparage any other faith or belief.[36]

If you are a zealous Christian, this authority may give you cause to wave the flag of victory concerning the interplay of government and religion. Nevertheless, the ruling is limited to a certain context. Traditions of prayer do not imply endorsement of any specific religion to the detriment of any other, including the practice of atheism. They merely acknowledge traditional and social formalities that are not to be perceived as rites of religion but rather as symbolic social practices intended to dignify government administration.

In 1984 Justice Sandra Day O'Connor observed that the direction of the Court in Establishment Clause cases was hard to manage. She took the opportunity to discuss the confusion in a concurring opinion in *Lynch v. Donnelly*.[37] That case involved the display of a crèche—a nativity scene—during the holiday season in Pawtucket, Rhode Island. The Court found that the display did not violate the Establishment Clause, and Justice O'Connor wanted to clarify the Court's evaluation processes whenever it is faced with a dispute of this nature. I will offer a significant portion of that opinion because it is very enlightening:

I

I concur in the opinion of the Court. I write separately to suggest a clarification of our Establishment Clause doctrine. The suggested approach leads to the same result in this case as that taken by the Court, and the Court's opinion, as I read it, is consistent with my analysis.

The Establishment Clause prohibits government from making adherence to a religion relevant in any way to a person's standing in the political community. Government can run afoul of that prohibition in two principal ways. One is excessive entanglement with religious institutions, which may interfere with the independence of the institutions, give the institutions access to governmental powers not fully shared by nonadherents of the religion, and foster the creation of political constituencies defined along religious lines. The second and more direct infringement is government endorsement or disapproval of religion. Endorsement sends a message to nonadherents that they are outsiders, not full members of the political community, and an accompanying message to adherents that they are insiders, favored members of the political community. Disapproval sends the opposite message.

Our prior cases have used the three-part test articulated in *Lemon v. Kurtzman*[38] as a guide to detecting these two forms of unconstitutional governmental action. It has never been entirely clear, however, how the three parts of the test relate to the principles enshrined in the Establishment Clause. Focusing on institutional entanglement and on endorsement or disapproval of religion clarifies the *Lemon* test as an analytical device.

II

In this case, as even the District Court found, there is no institutional entanglement. Nevertheless, the respondents contend that the political divisiveness caused by Pawtucket's display of its crèche violates the excessive entanglement prong of the *Lemon* test.... In my view, political divisiveness along religious lines should not be an independent test of constitutionality.

Although several of our cases have discussed political divisiveness under the entanglement prong of *Lemon*, ... we have never relied on divisiveness as an independent ground for holding a government practice unconstitutional. Guessing the potential for political divisiveness inherent in a government practice is simply too speculative an enterprise.... The entanglement prong of the *Lemon* test is properly limited to institutional entanglement.

III

The central issue in this case is whether Pawtucket has endorsed Christianity by its display of the crèche. To answer that question, we must examine both what Pawtucket intended to communicate in displaying the crèche and what message the city's display actually conveyed. The purpose and effect prongs of the *Lemon* test represent these two aspects of the meaning of the city's action.

As addressed earlier, the first prong of the test is that the action "must have a secular legislative purpose." This is the only area of law where the question "Why did you do it?" is a determinative factor in reaching a conclusion. Keep in mind that this is not the same as "Did you intend to do it?" but rather the question is "Why?"

The city would not have won this case if evidence had appeared to demonstrate that the person most responsible for the display actually intended to promote Christianity or any other form of religion. In other words, even if no person looking at the display were affected in a manner that advanced or inhibited any element of religion (part two of the *Lemon* test) and there was no appreciable entanglement in any form of religion (part three), it still could have been found to be an unconstitutional display if it was intended to have that effect. This is what Justice O'Connor meant by the "purpose" prong of *Lemon*:

> The meaning of a statement to its audience depends both on the intention of the speaker and on the "objective" meaning of the statement in the community.... If the audience is large, as it always is when government "speaks" by word or deed, some portion of the audience will inevitably receive a message determined by the "objective" content of the statement, and some portion will inevitably receive the intended message. Examination of both the subjective [part one of the test] and the objective [part two] components of the message communicated by a governmental

action is therefore necessary to determine whether the action carries a forbidden meaning.

The purpose prong of the *Lemon* test asks whether government's actual purpose is to endorse or disapprove of religion. The effect prong asks whether, irrespective of government's actual purpose, the practice under review in fact conveys a message of endorsement or disapproval. An affirmative answer to either question should render the challenged practice invalid.

A

The purpose prong of the *Lemon* test requires that a government activity have a secular purpose. That requirement is not satisfied, however, by the mere existence of some secular purpose, however dominated by religious purposes. In Stone v. Graham,[39] for example, the Court held that posting the Ten Commandments in schools violated the purpose prong of the *Lemon* test, yet the State plainly had secular objectives, such as instilling most of the values of the Ten Commandments and illustrating their connection to our legal system... . The proper inquiry under the purpose prong of *Lemon*, I submit, is whether the government intends to convey a message of endorsement or disapproval of religion.

Justice O'Connor explains here the balancing that must be done when weighing conflicting purposes and effects emanating from the same governmental source. We will soon see that the emphasis on the message will be very persuasive in determining the constitutionality of a display or any other sort of communication. The end result is that exposing public school children to the Ten Commandments is a valuable tool of education, but overemphasis of the source and amplification of its significance will push the message past its secular purpose and create an image of a religious context that does not fall within the First Amendment's parameters. Justice O'Connor continues the clarification:

∽

The evident purpose of including the crèche in the larger display was not promotion of the religious content of the crèche but celebration of the public holiday through its traditional symbols. Celebration of holidays, which have cultural significance even if they also have religious aspects, is a legitimate secular purpose.

B

Focusing on the evil of government endorsement or disapproval of religion makes clear that the effect prong of the *Lemon* test is properly interpreted not to require invalidation of a government practice merely because it in fact causes, even as a primary effect, advancement or inhibition of religion.... What is crucial is that a government practice not have the effect of communicating a message of government endorsement or disapproval of religion. It is only practices having that effect, whether intentionally or unintentionally, that make religion relevant, in reality or public perception, to status in the political community.... The crèche is a traditional symbol of the holiday that is very commonly displayed along with purely secular symbols, as it was in Pawtucket.... It cannot fairly be understood to convey a message of government endorsement of religion.

IV

Every government practice must be judged in its unique circumstances to determine whether it constitutes an endorsement or disapproval of religion. In making that determination, courts must keep in mind both the fundamental place held by the Establishment Clause in our constitutional scheme and the myriad, subtle ways in which Establishment Clause values can be eroded. Government practices that purport to celebrate or acknowledge events with religious significance must be subjected to careful judicial scrutiny.

As noted earlier, this opinion from Justice O'Connor was a concurring opinion. This means that it was not the "official" ruling by the Court but rather an addendum she attached to the ruling. Nevertheless, Justice O'Connor's opinion was referenced and relied upon by almost every case I am going to address in the rest of this chapter. The majority opinion in Lynch concluded as follows:

(a) The concept of a "wall" of separation between church and state is a useful metaphor but is not an accurate description of the practical aspects of the relationship that in fact exists. The Constitution does not require complete separation of church and state; it affirmatively mandates accommodation, not merely tolerance, of all religions, and forbids hostility toward any. Anything less would require the "callous indifference," *Zorach v. Clauson*,[40] that was never intended by the Establishment Clause.

(c) Our history is pervaded by official acknowledgment of the role of religion in American life, and equally pervasive is evidence of accommodation of all faiths and all forms of religious expression and hostility towards none.

(d) Rather than taking an absolutist approach in applying the Establishment Clause and mechanically invalidating all government conduct or statutes that confer benefits or give special recognition to religion in general or to one faith, this Court has scrutinized challenged conduct or legislation to determine whether, in reality, it establishes a religion or religious faith or tends to do so. In the line-drawing process called for in each case, it has often been found useful to inquire whether the challenged law or conduct has a secular purpose, whether its principle or primary effect is to advance or inhibit religion, and whether it creates an excessive entanglement of government with religion. But this Court has been unwilling to be confined to a single test or criterion in this sensitive area.

(f)   Based on the record in this case, the city has a secular purpose for including the crèche in its Christmas display and has not impermissibly advanced religion or created an excessive entanglement between religion and government. The display is sponsored by the city to celebrate the Holiday recognized by Congress and national tradition and to depict the origins of that Holiday; these are legitimate secular purposes. Whatever benefit to one faith or religion or to all religions inclusion of the crèche in the display effects, is indirect, remote, and incidental, and is no more an advancement or endorsement of religion than the congressional and executive recognition of the origins of Christmas, or the exhibition of religious paintings in governmentally supported museums.

(g) It would be ironic if the inclusion of the crèche in the display, as part of a celebration of an event acknowledged in the Western World for 20 centuries, and in this country by the people, the Executive Branch, Congress, and the courts for 2 centuries, would so "taint" the exhibition as to render it violative of the Establishment Clause.

With that concluding statement, law school is no longer in session. We are now aware that institutions of government are free to display what may otherwise be considered expressions of religion according to the simple rules of the *Lemon* test. Before you celebrate, however, I have more news. Lynch v. Donnelly was decided in a 5 to 4 split. This means that if any of the five justices were to have changed his or her mind, there would have been no further displays of anything related to the birth of Christ at any government institution, period. The justices in the majority were Burger, White, Powell, Rehnquist, and O'Connor. The minority consisted of Brennan, Marshall, Blackmun, and John Paul Stevens, who announced his retirement on April 9, 2010. Elena Kagan's appointment gives us a whole new team. This leads us to understand that the next appointment to the Supreme Court may very well change the character of our judiciary for many years to come. President Obama or his successor will likely make a decision that we must live with for many years. We must therefore be wise at the voting booths.

A good example of the *Lemon* "purpose" test can be found in *Edwards v. Aguillard.*[41] In 1982, the State of Louisiana enacted the Balanced Treatment for Creation-Science and Evolution-Science in Public School Instruction Act (Creationism Act). That act forbade the teaching of the theory of evolution in public schools unless accompanied by instruction in "creation science." The Supreme Court analyzed the creation of the law and the character of its language and found that it was the *purpose* of the Louisiana State Legislature to promote religious teaching, but it was disguised in an act that appeared to say that creationism only had to be taught *if* evolution was taught. In 1987 Justice Brennan delivered the opinion:

> Families entrust public schools with the education of their children, but condition their trust on the understanding that the classroom will not purposefully be used to advance religious views that may conflict with the private beliefs of the student and his or her family. Students in such institutions are impressionable and their attendance is voluntary.

> True, the Act's stated purpose is to protect academic freedom.[42] This phrase might, in common parlance, be understood as referring to enhancing the freedom of teachers to teach what they will. The Court of Appeals, however, correctly concluded that the Act was not designed to further that goal.... . The goal of providing a more comprehensive science curriculum is not furthered either by outlawing the teaching of evolution or by requiring the teaching of creation science.

> Furthermore, the goal of basic "fairness" is hardly furthered by the Act's discriminatory preference for the teaching of creation science and against the teaching of evolution. While requiring that curriculum guides be developed for creation science, the Act says nothing of comparable guides for evolution.

> We do not imply that a legislature could never require that scientific critiques of prevailing scientific theories be taught.

Indeed, the Court acknowledged in *Stone*[43] that its decision forbidding the posting of the Ten Commandments did not mean that no use could ever be made of the Ten Commandments, or that the Ten Commandments played an exclusively religious role in the history of Western Civilization. In a similar way, teaching a variety of scientific theories about the origins of humankind to schoolchildren might be validly done with the clear secular intent of enhancing the effectiveness of science instruction. But because the primary purpose of the Creationism Act is to endorse a particular religious doctrine, the Act furthers religion in violation of the Establishment Clause.

The plain meaning of the statute's words, enlightened by their context and the contemporaneous legislative history, can control the determination of legislative purpose.

Are you beginning to see the light? "Purpose" is literally within the mind of the person or persons who perform an act that is under review by any court that hears Establishment Clause disputes. The fact that judges don't use brain scans or truth serum (not yet anyway) means that they are going to examine all of the surrounding facts, the history of the litigants, and anything else that they can get their hands on to decipher the purpose for the action that is before the court. Sometimes that purpose is easy to spot; sometimes it takes a little digging. As you will soon see, once the improper purpose is perceived, it doesn't matter what the litigant tries to do to clean it up. An improper purpose will taint a person's actions, and he or she may be "branded" for the rest of life as a zealot, a radical, or some other unsavory character. If you want to put up any kind of display or take any action in a government work environment, make sure that you have a crystal-clear record, or the ACLU will have damaging evidence against you.

Holiday Displays

Where does the Supreme Court draw the line? A good example of "You can do this, but you can't do that" is *County of Allegheny et al. v. American Civil Liberties Union, Greater Pittsburgh Chapter*.[44] It concerned the constitutionality of two recurring holiday displays on public property in Pittsburgh, Pennsylvania. The first was a crèche depicting the nativity scene, which was placed on the Grand Staircase of the Allegheny County Courthouse. The crèche had been donated by the Holy Name Society, a Roman Catholic group, and bore a sign to that effect.

The second display was an eighteen-foot Chanukah menorah or candelabrum placed just outside the city-county building next to the city's forty-five-foot decorated Christmas tree. A Jewish group; Chabad, owned the menorah but it was stored, erected, and removed by the city each year. The district court held that neither display violated the Establishment Clause, but the court of appeals held the opposite; that they were both violations. The final ruling by the Supreme Court was divided into seven parts because Justices Blackmun, O'Connor, White. Kennedy, and Scalia agreed with the final result, but couldn't agree with how they got there. Justice Blackmun wrote the following opinion:

> 2. When viewed in its overall context, the crèche display violates the Establishment C'ause. The crèche angel's words endorse a patently Christian message: Glory to God for the birth of Jesus Christ... . Although the government may acknowledge Christmas as a cultural phenomenon, it may not observe it as a Christian holy day by suggesting that people praise God for the birth of Jesus.

> 3. (a) History cannot legitimate practices like the crèche display that demonstrate the government's alliance to a particular sect or creed.

3. (c) The Constitution mandates that the government remain
    secular, rather than affiliating itself with religious beliefs or
    institutions, precisely in order to avoid discriminating against
    citizens on the basis of their religious faiths.

… The menorah display does not have the prohibitive effect of
endorsing religion, given its "particular physical setting." Its
combined display with a Christmas tree and a sign saluting liberty
does not impermissibly endorse both the Christian and Jewish
faiths, but simply recognizes that both Christmas and Chanukah
are part of the same winter-holiday season, which has attained a
secular status in our society.… The tree, moreover, by virtue of its
size and central position in the display, is clearly the predominant
element, and the placement of the menorah beside it is readily
understood as simply a recognition that Christmas is not the only
traditional way of celebrating the season.

Justice O'Connor also concluded that the city's display of a
menorah, together with a Christmas tree and a sign saluting
liberty, does not violate the Establishment Clause. By
including the menorah with the tree, however, and with the
sign saluting liberty, the city conveyed a message of
pluralism and freedom of belief during the holiday season,
which, in this particular physical setting, could not be
interpreted by a reasonable observer as an endorsement of
Judaism or Christianity or disapproval of beliefs.

Justices Kennedy, White, and Scalia concluded that both the
menorah display and the crèche display are permissible under
the Establishment Clause.

In the final analysis, this ruling demonstrates that any
expression or display by a government entity of anything that
relates to religion needs to have some subtlety. The crèche that
is perfectly legal in many displays can be illegal if it is over-

emphasized, if it is alone or separated from other displays, if it is too big, and so on. It all depends on the facts of each particular display. Despite this conclusion, we see that three of the justices didn't have a problem with any of the displays. If you are associated with a government entity, listen to Clint Eastwood: "A good man always knows his limitations."[45] I advise you to learn ahead of time what is within reason and has passed the purview of our system of justice. If you have something that is overboard, try to fix it with subtleties: a Christmas tree, a menorah, Santa and his reindeer. Move it to the side or give some alternatives. If you try to put something up and it is removed by the court, then it is officially branded as a violation of the Establishment Clause and you won't be able to hang it in a government closet!

If, on the other hand, you are offended by a display on government property, you need to look at these authorities to learn what the threshold of acquiescence is on your part. If you regularly complain about displays deemed to be reasonable, you can also be branded, and that may impede your credibility in any court of law. You may become the person that Jay Sekulow[46] peers at and says "Go ahead, make my day."[47]

Religion in Public Schools

In January 1985, Bridget C. Mergens was attending Westside High School and requested permission from her principal, Dr. Findley, to form a Christian club at the school. Findley denied the request, as did Associate Superintendent Tangdell. They informed her that school policy required all student clubs to have a faculty sponsor. The district court found for the school board and the court of appeals reversed. It was argued before the Supreme Court on January 9, 1990,[48] and Justice O'Connor

delivered the opinion, except as to Part III, confirming the decision by the court of appeals:

> This case requires us to decide whether the Equal Access Act, 98 Stat. 1302, U.S.C. §§ 4071–4074, prohibits Westside High School from denying a student religious group permission to meet on school premises during noninstructional time, and if so, whether the Act, so construed, violates the Establishment Clause of the First Amendment.

I should point out here that the Christian club was already meeting after school. The issue arose when Ms. Mergens requested that the club have official recognition so that it would have equal access to the school newspaper, bulletin boards, public address system, and the annual club fair.

> In *Widmar v. Vincent*,[49] we invalidated, on free speech grounds, a state university regulation that prohibited student use of school facilities "for purposes of religious worship or religious teaching." In doing so, we held that an "equal access" policy would not violate the Establishment Clause under our decision in *Lemon v. Kurtzman*.[50] In particular, we held that such a policy would have a secular purpose, would not have the primary effect of advancing religion, and would not result in excessive entanglement between government and religion.

> In 1984, Congress extended the reasoning of *Widmar* to public secondary schools. Under the Equal Access Act, a public secondary school with a "limited open forum" is prohibited from discriminating against students who wish to conduct a meeting within that forum on the basis of the "religious, political, philosophical, or other content of the speech at such meetings."[55]

> If a [S]tate refused to let religious groups use facilities open to others, then it would demonstrate not neutrality but hostility toward religion. "The Establishment Clause does not license government to treat religion and those who teach or practice it, simply by virtue of their status as such, as subversive of American ideals and therefore subject to unique disabilities." *McDaniel v. Paty*[56.]

> There is a crucial difference between *government* speech endorsing religion, which the Establishment Clause forbids, and *private* speech endorsing religion, which the Free Speech and Free Exercise Clauses protect. We think that secondary school students are mature enough and are likely to understand that a school does not endorse or support student speech that it merely permits on a nondiscriminatory basis.

> To be sure, the possibility of *student* peer pressure remains, but there is little if any risk of official state endorsement or coercion where no formal classroom activities are involved and no school officials actively participate.

This ruling provides you with a different perspective regarding freedom of religion. Most of the other cases involve government sponsorship of a display, whereas here, we are examining equal rights between religion and other common interests. From the *Lemon* test perspective:

(1) The purpose of the Christian club was overtly to promote religion, similar to the objective of the Chess Club to promote participation in the game or the Scuba Club to promote participation in diving. The difference is that the school, an institution of government, had nothing to do with promoting any expression of religion. It was simply providing an open forum to speak.

(2) The effect of the students' club may have actually caused more children to learn about Christianity, but again this was a derivative of free speech that cannot be impeded by a government institution or representative that disagrees with the content of the message. The school did not promote or foster Christianity; it simply provided an equal and open forum to enable the students to do so in the exact same fashion as the other clubs.

(3) The entanglement of the government with the club was completely benign and had no effect on the content of its activity. The rules were uniformly applied to each club and there was no advantage or disadvantage to any person or group.

Now, let's take a look at *Lamb's Chapel v. Center Moriches Union Free School District,*[57] referenced earlier to show Justice Scalia's frustration over the continued use and application of the *Lemon* test. In this case, New York law authorized local school boards to adopt reasonable regulations permitting after-hours use of school property for ten specified purposes, not including meetings for religious purposes. Lamb's Chapel made two separate requests to use the school's auditorium for a religious-oriented film series on family values and child-rearing. Both requests were denied and the church filed suit. The district court found for the school district and the court of appeals confirmed the ruling. Justice White delivered the unanimous decision to reverse:

> [There is no question that the District, like the private owner of property, may legally preserve the property under its control for the use to which it was dedicated.].[58] It is also common ground that the District need not have permitted after-hours use of its property for any of the uses permitted by N.Y. Educ. Law §414. The District, however, did open its property for 2 of the 10 uses permitted by §414. The Church argued below that … the District had opened its property for such a wide variety of communicative purposes that restrictions on communicative uses of the property were subject to the same constitutional limitations as restrictions in traditional public forums such as parks and sidewalks…. The argument has considerable force, for the District's property is heavily used by a wide variety of private organizations, including some that presented a "close question," which the Court of Appeals resolved in the District's favor, as to whether the District had in fact already opened its property for religious uses.[59]

This ruling follows the same pattern as *Mergens*; once a government institution opens itself as a forum of communication or expression, it has opened its door to freedom of speech. The content of the message, whether it be for or against religion or any other subject of controversy, cannot be controlled or edited by any governmental institution, entity, or individual unless there is a valid and proper independent cause that will overcome the freedom guaranteed by the U.S. Constitution.

It is tempting to believe that all of these decisions by the Supreme Court and its inferior venues would have answered all of the questions concerning the interplay of freedom of religion, freedom of speech, and government participation or interference with same. Nevertheless, as soon as you close the book another question arises.

In 1992, the University of Virginia established a Student Activities Fund (SAF) that required a donation of fourteen dollars from each student to then be disbursed to outside contractors for printing costs of a variety of publications issued by student groups called Contracted Independent Organizations (CIOs). Wide Awake Productions (WAP) was a student group that had already qualified as a CIO. WAP published *Wide Awake*, a newspaper with a Christian perspective discussing both personal and community issues relevant to students at the university. By June 1992, WAP had distributed 5,000 copies of *Wide Awake* to university students, free of charge. WAP requested that SAF pay its printer $5,862 for the cost of printing. That request was denied by the university for the sole reason that their student paper "primarily promotes or manifests a particular belie[f] in or about a deity or an ultimate reality." Justice Kennedy drafted the opinion of the court in a 5 to 4 ruling:[60]

WAP had acquired CIO status soon after it was organized. This is an important consideration in this case, for had it been a "religious organization," WAP would not have been accorded CIO status. As defined by the Guidelines, a "religious organization" is "an organization whose purpose is to practice a devotion to an acknowledged ultimate reality or deity." App. To Pet. For Cert. 66a. At no stage in this controversy has the University contended that WAP is such an organization.

It is axiomatic that the government may not regulate speech based on its substantive content or the message it conveys.[61] Discrimination against speech because of its message is presumed to be unconstitutional.[62] Once it has opened a limited forum, however, the State must respect the lawful boundaries it has itself set. The State may not exclude speech where its distinction is not "reasonable in light of the purpose served by the forum."[63]

The SAF cannot be used for unlimited purposes, much like the illegitimate purpose of supporting one religion. Much like the arrangement in Widmar,[64] the money goes to a special fund from which any group of students with CIO status can draw for purposes consistent with the University's educational mission; and to the extent the student is interested in speech, whether it manifests a religious view, an antireligious view, or neither. Here, disbursements from the fund go to private contractors for the cost of printing that which is protected under the Speech Clause of the First Amendment. This is a far cry from a general public assessment designed and effected to provide financial support for a church.

We must put this ruling in proper perspective. We, as citizens of the United States, pay our taxes for the purpose of funding the common good as represented by legitimate expenses incurred by our government entities. We have no independent control regarding the proportionate expenses that these governments incur. Independent control over our funding would create a chaotic accounting nightmare. We are very much aware that an infinitesimal fraction of the taxes that we pay do effectively support nuances of religion, i.e.: holiday decorations that are maintained and displayed by government entities.

Even crèche displays may have subtle religious influences on a limited portion of the audience. In comparison, these funds for the printing costs incurred by WAP crossed an entirely different threshold. The student population of the University of Virginia includes a wide variety of religious viewpoints and there can be no doubt that many of the students will avow to atheism. Fourteen dollars per year in "taxation" demanded by the university from each student may appear to be slight, but a significant portion of same is used to fund a publication openly devoted to religion. This creates a friction that cannot be overlooked. Nevertheless, the Court has reasoned, by a 5 to 4 margin, that the facts and circumstances have sufficiently removed the expenditure of community resources from any appearance of direct investment in a religious enterprise. In my opinion, WAP won the battle by the skin of its teeth. Justice O'Connor issued a concurring opinion that properly defines the thinness of the margin of victory:

> "We have time and again held that the government generally may not treat people differently based on the God or gods they worship, or don't worship."[65] This insistence on government neutrality toward religion explains why we have held that schools may not discriminate against religious groups by denying them equal access to the facilities that the schools make available to all. See *Lamb's Chapel* …; *Widmar v. Vincent* …

> This case lies at the intersection of the principle of government neutrality and the prohibition on state funding of religious activities. It is clear that the University has established a generally acceptable program to encourage the free exchange of ideas by its students, an expressive marketplace that includes some 15 student publications with predictably divergent viewpoints. It is equally clear that petitioners' viewpoint is religious and that publication

of Wide Awake is a religious activity, under both the University's regulation and a fair reading of our precedents. Not to finance Wide Awake, according to petitioners, violates the principle of neutrality by sending a message of hostility toward religion. To finance Wide Awake, argues the University, violates the prohibition on direct state funding of religious activities.

When two bedrock principles so conflict, understandably neither can provide the definitive answer. Reliance on categorical platitudes is unavailing. Resolution instead depends on the hard task of judging - sifting through the details and determining whether the challenged program offends the Establishment Clause. Such judgment requires courts to draw lines, sometimes quite fine, based on the particular facts of each case.

… In Witters v. Washington Dept. of Services for Blind[66], for example, we unanimously held that the State may, through a generally applicable financial aid program, pay a blind student's tuition at a sectarian theological institution. The Court so held, however, only after emphasizing that "vocational assistance provided under the Washington program is paid directly to the student, who transmits it to the educational institution of her choice." Id., at 487. The benefit to religion under the program, therefore, is akin to a public servant contributing her government paycheck to the church.… . "The aid to religion at issue here is the result of petitioner's private choice. No reasonable observer is likely to draw from the facts before us an inference that the State itself is endorsing a religious practice or belief."

The need for careful judgment and fine distinctions presents itself even in extreme cases. *Everson* (supra) provided perhaps the strongest exposition of the no-funding principle: "No tax in any amount, large or small, can be levied to support any religious activities or institutions, whatever they may be called, or whatever form they may adopt to teach or practice religion." Id., at 16. Yet the Court approved the use of public funds, in a general program, to reimburse parents for their children's bus fares to attend Catholic schools.… . ("the most fitting precedent is that of Julia who, according to Byron's reports, 'whispering "I will ne'er consent,"—consented'"), the decision reflected the need to rely on careful judgment—not simple categories—when two principles, of equal historical and jurisprudential pedigree, come into unavoidable conflict.

So it is in this case. The nature of the dispute does not admit of categorical answers, nor should any be inferred from the Court's decision today, see ante, at 18. Instead, certain considerations specific to the program lead me to conclude that by providing the same assistance to Wide Awake that it does to other publications, the University would not be endorsing the magazine's religious perspective.

First, the student organizations, at the University's insistence, remain strictly independent of the University.... Any reader of Wide Awake would be on notice of the publication's independence from the University.

Second, financial assistance is distributed in a manner that ensures its use only for permissible purposes.... the funds are paid directly to the third-party vendor and do not pass through the organization's coffers.

Third, assistance is provided to the religious publication in a context that makes improbable any perception of government endorsement of the religious message. Wide Awake does not exist in a vacuum. It competes with 15 other magazines and newspapers for advertising and readership.... Besides the general news publications, for example, the University has provided support to The Yellow Journal, a humor magazine that has targeted Christianity as a subject of satire, and Al-Salam, a publication to "promote a better understanding of Islam to the University Community," App. 92. Given this wide array of non-religious, anti-religious and competing religious viewpoints in the forum supported by the University, endorsing one particular viewpoint would be illogical.

Finally, although the question is not presented here, I note the possibility that the student fee is susceptible to a Free Speech

challenge by an objecting student that she should not be compelled to pay for speech with which she disagrees.

The significance of the subtleties in the facts presented before the Court cannot be readily gleaned from this opinion. We are plainly ignorant of what, if anything, tipped the scale in the petitioner's favor. What if there were fewer publications financed by SAF? What if there were more publications but they did not include *The Yellow Journal* or *Al-Salam*? What if *Wide Awake* had published a particular article that appeared to be too aggressive? What if the system of funding had one less detail, one more detail? What if, as Justice O'Connor suggested, an independent student in the university had interpled as an interested third party and objected to the Christian publication?

To put this ruling in proper perspective, think back to Super Bowl XXXIV at the Georgia Dome in Atlanta.[67] On the final play of the game, with St. Louis leading Tennessee 23-16, Kevin Dyson of the Titans caught a pass within the five-yard line and dragged Mike Jones of the Rams as far as he could but was tackled on the one-yard line with his hand stretching the ball to the end zone as time expired. Had that play been *Rosenberger v. University of Virginia*, they would still be looking at where the ball ended up, deciding whether it was a touchdown. A gnat's wing could not fit between the ball and the goal line.

Ten Commandments Displays

In November 2000, the Honorable Roy S. Moore was elected as chief justice of the Alabama Supreme Court. Prior to his election, Justice Moore had a history of openly displaying his Christian faith by hanging a hand-carved wooden plaque depicting the Ten Commandments behind his bench in the courtroom. He routinely invited clergy to lead prayer at jury organizing sessions. Both of these actions spurned high-profile lawsuits; each of which was dismissed on justiciability grounds. His campaign committee capitalized on his name recognition and referred to him as "The Ten Commandments Judge."

During his campaign, Justice Moore promised he would install a Ten Commandments monument in the rotunda of the Alabama State Judicial Building that houses the Alabama Supreme Court, the Court of Criminal Appeals, the Court of Civil Appeals, the State Law Library, and the state's Administrative Office of the Courts. He installed the monument at his expense after the close of business on July 31, 2001. It is a 5,280-pound granite monument approximately three feet wide, three feet deep, and four feet tall. The monument featured excerpts from Exodus 20:2-17 of the King James Version of the Holy Bible with the Ten Commandments chiseled into the tablets.

Three attorneys who did not consider the monument appropriate brought two separate lawsuits to remove the monument. The district court agreed that it violated the Establishment Clause of the First Amendment and ordered it to be removed.[68] Chief Justice Moore appealed the ruling to the U.S. Court of Appeals for the Eleventh Circuit:

During the trial the Chief Justice testified candidly about why Moore had placed the monument in the rotunda. The following exchanges between him and one of the plaintiffs' attorneys establish that purpose:

> Q: [W]as your purpose in putting the Ten Commandments monument in the Supreme Court rotunda to acknowledge God's law and God's sovereignty? …
>
> A: Yes.

Q: Do you agree that the monument, the Ten Commandments monument, reflects the sovereignty of God over the affairs of men?

A: Yes.

Q: And the monument is also intended to acknowledge God's overruling power over the affairs of men, would that be correct?

A: Yes.

Q: [W]hen you say "God" you mean God of Holy Scripture?

A: Yes. 69

Moore also denied an atheist group's request to display a symbol of atheism in the rotunda. The chief justice did add two smaller displays to the rotunda after the Ten Commandments monument was installed. The first, a plaque entitled "Moral Foundation of Law," contains a quotation from the Rev. Dr. Martin Luther King Jr.'s letter from the Birmingham jail speaking of just laws and "the moral law or law of God," and a quotation from Frederick Douglass speaking of slavery as hiding man "from the laws of God." The second display is a brass plaque showing the Bill of Rights. The two plaques are inconspicuous compared to the Ten Commandments monument. Each is not only much smaller than the monument, but also is located seventy-five feet from it.

Needless to say, the court of appeals determined that the Ten Commandments display violated the Establishment Clause on all three counts: (1) Chief Justice Moore admitted during his testimony that his purpose in displaying the monument was to promote religion; (2) The principal effect of the monument upon all visitors to the courthouse was an appearance that the

government of the State of Alabama specifically supported Christianity; (3) The grandiose appearance of the monument in the rotunda was a gross entanglement of government and religion that could not be ignored by any visitor to the Alabama State Judicial Building.

Why did Justice Moore construct the monument and display it in that fashion? We are only able to surmise that he did so based upon his campaign promise. We can conjecture Moore was so elated regarding his election victory that his emotions overcame his judgment. I hope that the monument is now in a benign environment that may serve the community in a manner consistent with our constitutional standards.

A proper question now would be: can that massive granite monument be re-installed in the Alabama State Judicial Building Rotunda? For Justice Moore, I would have to give an emphatic No! He already has the massive burden of losing the *Lemon* purpose test to overcome. Let us speculate, however, that the next elected chief justice of the Alabama Supreme Court has an impeccable record that demonstrates no history of work to proselytize a fly. Let us assume they prepare a series of displays designed to educate the layperson concerning the evolution of our legal system in America. Let us imagine these displays can readily be perceived as a history lesson rather than a sermon. We will have to wait and see, but if I may borrow Justice Scalia's tone in *Lamb's Chapel,* I would conclude that this ghoul of a monument may in the future rise from the ashes like a phoenix, like another sequel to *Friday the 13th,* like James Bond in *Never Say Never Again.*

When faced with a First Amendment question, the court is bound to pull the scales of justice out of the drawer and perform a precision balancing test. Whenever the objective is large, like a granite monument, the balance must have equal weight plus an extra milligram. *Rosenberger* is a perfect example. The larger the goal, the more significant are the details.

Final Analysis

I trust I have provided sufficient analysis and explanation of the first sixteen words of our Bill of Rights. I pray every citizen of the United States will have the capacity to grasp the thinness of the ice under our feet. Each of the 5 to 4 rulings discussed may have had a minor physical effect on the character of this nation, but if those rulings had gone the other way, our nation's soul would have been compromised. We are all patently aware that justices of the Supreme Court are nominated by the sitting president and that their confirmation to take office is in the hands of our senators.[70] Do not sit passively, assuming that whoever is elected to office will take care of you. Stand up for your rights and invest your time in preparing for the future by learning who will best serve the entire community as opposed to a select few.

C H A P T E R   7

Abortion

When Is a Baby a Person?

A woman's claimed right to rid her person of the responsibility to carry a fetus to term faces the counterclaim that the unborn child has the individual right to grow, mature, and be delivered into the world. That child's claimed right is perceived from many perspectives. Under current law, the infant has very little standing until the point of viability—meaning the point at which the child is considered to have the capacity to survive outside the womb.

At that critical level of development certain legal privileges begin to attach to the infant, but even these are tentative and subject to many interpretations. Morally the debate goes on and will never end. The legal debate in courts of law wages as a literal battle to the death, but the only soldiers who die are the subject of the battle itself. No matter which side wins, the fight only moves the battleground to a new venue and a new subject for debate. These conflicting claims have waged fierce wars that always find a new battleground when the last skirmish has been put to bed. Judge Jon Newman of the U.S. Second Court of Appeals made this observation in *National Abortion Federation v. Gonzales:*

Abortion is the killing of a fetus prior to birth. For centuries abortion has been a matter of intense controversy. Some consider abortion the illegitimate killing of a person. Others consider abortion a legitimate medical procedure used by a pregnant woman, in consultation with her doctor, to terminate a pregnancy prior to birth. Those on both sides of the controversy acknowledge that the fetus is a living organism, starting as a collection of cells just after conception and developing into a recognizable human form as the time for birth approaches. The destruction of a fetus is a distressing event, whether one views abortion as the killing of a person or a pregnant woman's personal choice concerning her body.[1]

On November 8, 2006, the U.S. Supreme Court heard Gonzales v. Carhart.[2] Dr. Leroy Carhart and Planned Parenthood of America had claimed that the Partial-Birth Abortion Ban Act of 2003 as enacted by the U.S. Congress was unconstitutional because it criminalized all D&X (dilation and extraction) abortions, but permitted D&E (dilation and evacuation) abortions when the doctor saw fit to employ that procedure. The plaintiffs claimed that the two techniques were so similar that an abortion practitioner was in danger of violating the act and committing a crime without any intention to do so.

The 2003 act was the result of repeated attempts by Congress to enact legislation concerning the D&X method of abortion. Congress passed similar acts in 1996 and 1997 but both were vetoed by President Clinton. The basis for the interest in enacting a ban on this type of abortion was gleaned from testimony by Dr. Martin Haskell's nurse Brenda Pratt Shafer in 1995 before a Senate Judiciary Committee.[3] She observed the abortion of a 26 ½-week-old fetus:

Dr. Haskell went in with forceps and grabbed the baby's legs and pulled them down into the birth canal. Then he delivered the baby's body and the arms—everything but the head. The doctor kept the head right inside the uterus. The baby's fingers were clasping and unclasping, and his little feet were kicking. Then the doctor stuck the scissors in the back of his head, and the baby's arms jerked out, like a startled reaction, like a flinch, like a baby does when he thinks he is going to fall.

The doctor opened up the scissors, stuck a high-powered suction tube into the opening, and sucked the baby's brains out. Now the baby went completely limp. He cut the umbilical cord and delivered the placenta. He threw the baby in a pan, along with the placenta and the instruments he had just used.

Dr. Haskell claimed that banning these D&X abortions interfered with his ability to perform legal abortions because they both began the same way. The difference was that in a D&E abortion the doctor would effectively dismember the baby and pull him or her out piece by piece. The head was normally the last to go, and its brains would also be sucked out to allow it to pass more freely. Some attempted D&E abortions didn't go according to plans because the baby would not easily dismember into separate parts, which was more and more common for older fetuses. The end result of any failure to dismember a fetus was that the doctor was performing an "intact D&E" which was exactly the same as a D&X. The doctor therefore feared he could be criminally prosecuted.

This testimony caused not only the U.S. Congress to respond with limiting legislation, but many states also enacted statutes banning the D&X procedure. You will see a long series of rulings by the Supreme Court and many courts of appeals that found these laws to be unconstitutional. Nevertheless, these legislatures continued to press the issue looking for something that would pass judicial muster. The first victory came in 2003 when the Sixth Circuit Court of Appeals[4] ruled for Governor Taft against the above-referenced Doctor Haskell regarding an Ohio statute that limited D&X abortions because it did allow

that method of abortion "whenever the procedure is necessary to protect the mother from significant health risks."

The second victory came in *Ayotte v. Planned Parenthood of Northern New England*,[5] where the Supreme Court let stand a New Hampshire Parental Notification Prior to Abortion Act even though it lacked sufficient latitude for medical emergencies. The Court found that they could let the act stand because "lower courts may be able to render narrower declaratory and injunctive relief." This ruling did not concern D&E versus D&X abortions, but it was important because it opened the door for the courts to validate laws that had some invalid but separable portions. This gives Congress and state legislatures the ability to act and make progress against abortion when only a portion of their work is found to be invalid. They are then able to reword the rejected pieces of legislation and see what the courts will allow.

The final blow to Partial Birth Abortions was *Gonzales v. Carhart*,[6] in which Justice Kennedy delivered the opinion of the Court providing that Congress has the ability to forbid the D&X abortion procedure with the exception of a medical emergency or a "health exception."

The Legal Environment of Abortion

The purpose of this chapter is to enlighten the reader concerning the legal environment regarding abortion. There are four adjectives for voters in this regard:

- Pro-life
- Pro-choice
- Well-informed
- Uninformed

I will provide a brief history of abortion leading up to the *Roe v. Wade*[7] and *Doe v. Bolton*[8] decisions. I will then discuss these rulings and their progeny so that we will be able to follow along in the development of the laws. It will be very useful for the reader to understand the frustration of many courts and legislatures who have worked to interpret their responsibilities to mothers, unborn infants, other interested persons, and the general public. The repeated failure of state and federal legislatures to enact statutes that protect an unborn fetus, followed by the recent progress, raises the following three questions:

(1) Did the legislatures finally figure out what the courts were looking for?

(2) Did the courts get sick and tired of hearing the same old arguments?

(3) Are the courts giving any deference to the growing public sentiment that disapproves of the carefree attitude toward the destruction of life?

I submit that the end result is a combination of all three factors.

The recent limitation of D&X abortions is a very small victory because D&E procedures yield the same result and cause suffering to the infant that may be even more severe. I believe state and federal legislative bodies have the continued responsibility to chip away at this privilege to end life by drafting statutes that will pass constitutional muster. *Roe v. Wade* acknowledges that states have an interest in protecting an unborn fetus and that interest can overcome a woman's desire to abort when the fetus becomes viable. Medical technology is pushing viability to an earlier threshold.

I am asking Congress and the legislature of each state to stop compromising this interest and work to establish a date that preservation of the infant's life preempts the expectant mother's desire to abort. Codification of a 16-week gestation period to protect the fetus is reasonable. We need legislatures to enact codification of this time-frame and await the court challenges. Even if the law is voided, it will provide insight for the next try. If we keep plugging away we will give the infant fetus standing and rights that are consistent with our moral obligations to new and existing life. The legal right that a woman holds to rid herself of this burden must be tempered by our compassion for the unborn.

History Highlights the Issue

Exodus 21:22-25 provides: "If men who are fighting hit a pregnant woman and she gives birth prematurely but there is no serious injury, the offender must be fined whatever the woman's husband demands and the court allows. But if there is serious injury, you are to take life for life, eye for eye, tooth for tooth, hand for hand, foot for foot, burn for burn, wound for wound, bruise for bruise."[9]

Ancient Greece recognized that life begins upon conception but progresses in certain stages. The Greeks said the first state is literally a vegetative soul, it later becomes an animal soul, and finally a human soul. A human male was formed forty days after conception and a female 90 days after conception. Killing a fetus after it had become human was homicide punishable by death.

In 1400 BC Antigenes prosecuted his own wife for the murder of their unborn son. Had he personally approved of the abortion there could be no prosecution due to the fact that there was no community police power. Any charge of a crime had to be prosecuted by the victim.

In 66 BC Marcus Tullius Cicero represented a client who had been charged with assaulting another man. The alleged victim of the assault was the same man who had been convicted of killing a fetus by causing a woman's abortion in order to gain rights to her deceased husband's estate. That alleged victim was now suing Cicero's client as a form of revenge because he had lost his right to share in the estate. Cicero won dismissal of that complaint.

The first codified legislation concerning abortion is found in a counsel held at Elvira, Spain in 305 AD.

Ancient Rome adopted Cornelian law that criminalized the act of abortion. In his *Roe v. Wade* ruling, Justice Blackmun stated that the Roman Catholic Church had adopted the Aristotelian theory applied in ancient Greece concerning mediate or immediate animation, but the church's only conclusion is that a human gains a soul before birth.

Roman law held a well-known legal axiom: "conceptius pro iam nato habetur," which means, "whenever some benefit to the fetus is at stake it is to be treated as a person already born." Nevertheless, in ancient Rome the father had the right to let a newborn baby die if he so chose.

U.S. law is based primarily on English common law which almost mirrors Roman law concerning abortion. From 1200 to 1600 abortion matters were heard by ecclesiastical courts, which regulated secular law. Abortion at that time meant a violent attack to the mother's abdomen in order to kill the baby. The only records of anyone found guilty of the crime of abortion depended on the mother's dying as well. If she died that was sufficient evidence. If she lived there was no way to prove that a child had been aborted.

From 1601 to 1803, the common law courts took over the duties of the ecclesiastical courts, but there was no change in law regarding abortions. In 1803, Lord Ellenborough's Act codified abortion as a crime and provided a death penalty if the woman was "quick with child." By 1861 all abortions in England and in 70% of the United States (which included 85% of the population) by any means were criminal. At that time embryology began to develop and we recognized that human life began at the point of conception.

Any surgery on a human during the 1800s was a very dangerous proposition; approximately one out of every three patients died as a result of the operation. At that time abortion was the only form of surgery considered to be illegal.

The U.S. Supreme Court has decided the meaning of the word "person" only twice. In 1886 the Court heard *County of Santa Clara v. Southern Pacific Railroad*[10] and found that Southern Pacific Railroad Company was a person consistent with the 14th Amendment to the U.S. Constitution and therefore subject to taxation. In 1973 the Supreme Court determined in *Roe v. Wade* and *Doe v. Bolton* that an unborn fetus is not a person.

Strategic Court Decisions—*Wade and Bolton*

Wade and *Bolton* were not accidents. Supreme Court Justice Thurgood Marshall had previously worked as counsel for the NAACP. Organizations working to establish what they perceive to be "individual rights" look for a perfect "victim" for which to champion the cause. Thurgood Marshall, before his appointment as Justice of the Supreme Court, argued *Sweatt v. Painter*[11] before that Court in 1950. Mr. Sweatt was an African-American who had applied to the University of Texas School of Law and was denied admission "solely because he is a Negro and state law forbids the admission of Negroes to that Law School."

Mr. Sweatt was fifty years old and had a family. The NAACP chose him as their "perfect victim" to avoid the appearance of championing integration for ulterior motives. Had he been a young man, the organization may have had to confront a claim of access to Caucasian female students. He was chosen because he had no "excess baggage." By choosing a perfect victim the NAACP was able to overcome a system of segregation.

Norma McCorvey was the chosen "victim" in *Roe v. Wade* and Sandra Cano was the "victim" for *Doe v. Bolton*. Both these women are now active pro-life advocates, pleading before federal courts that their victories in 1973 be overturned. These pleas were not successful because their victories were not personal, but rather represented what the Supreme Court determined to be universal rights held by women to be free from the undesired burden of carrying a child to term.

Ms. McCorvey was unmarried and pregnant and represented to the court that she was financially unable to assume the responsibility of caring for an infant. She stated that she could not afford the cost of travel to another jurisdiction outside her home state of Texas to have the abortion where it was legally available. She was joined by Doctor James Hubert Hallford, who had two charges of aborting a fetus pending against him, and John and Mary Doe, who claimed Mary was suffering from a "neural-chemical disorder" such that a pregnancy would have threatened her health.

Justice Blackmun delivered the opinion of the Court. He began with a discussion of the history of abortion that is fairly consistent with what I provide above, but there are some differences. He came to the conclusion that American law is based primarily on English common law, but noted that state legislatures have begun to chip away at the absolute

criminality of abortion unless necessary to save the life of the expectant mother.

The Court noted that "The Constitution does not explicitly mention any right of privacy." Justice Blackmun went on to find an implied right of privacy in either the Fourteenth Amendment's concept of personal liberty, or the Ninth Amendment's reservation of rights to the people " broad enough to encompass a woman's decision whether or not to terminate her pregnancy." He went on to balance the interest of the State with the interest of the expectant mother:

> With respect to the State's important and legitimate interest in the health of the mother, the "compelling" point, in the light of present medical knowledge, is at approximately the end of the first trimester. This is so because of the now-established medical fact, referred to above at 149, that until the end of the first trimester mortality in abortion may be less than mortality in normal childbirth. It follows that, from and after this point, a State may regulate the abortion procedure to the extent that the regulation reasonably relates to the preservation and protection of maternal health.

This is the first time that a specific time period is discussed by the court, but it only relates to the health of the expectant mother. He soon discusses the State's interest in the fetus:

> With respect to the State's important and legitimate interest in potential life, the "compelling" point is at viability. This is so because the fetus then presumably has the capability of meaningful life outside the mother's womb. State regulation protective of fetal life after viability thus has both logical and biological justifications. If the State is interested in protecting fetal life after viability, it may go so far as to proscribe abortion during that period, except when it is necessary to preserve the life or health of the mother.

Doe v. Bolton provided the Court with an opportunity to confirm its conclusions in *Roe v. Wade* and to discuss the rights and duties of medical facilities along with their freedom to refuse to perform abortions if they so chose. The net result of both these rulings was the establishment of an unprecedented set of guidelines concerning the rights and privileges of all persons or entities concerning abortion. Those guidelines have evolved to the following standards:

1. A woman has the absolute right to abort a child at any time until that child is viable. Justice Blackmun took judicial notice of viability "at about seven months (28 weeks) but may occur earlier, even at 24 weeks." This was in 1973. Since that date medical science has been pushing viability to a confirmed 22 weeks and 6 days[12]. In September of 2009, Sarah Capewell of England gave birth to a premature baby after 21 weeks and 5 days of gestation,[13] but the hospital refused to admit him to a special care facility because it had no legal obligation to care for a baby before the 22-week threshold. Jayden Capewell lived for almost two hours without any medical support.

2. The State's interest in regulating abortion facilities is in the interest of the mother. That interest does not give rise to the ability to regulate these facilities until the end of the first trimester. Justice Blackmun took judicial notice of an average gestation period of 266 days, thereby implying that the first trimester ended after 87 days.

3. The State's legitimate interest in potential life begins at viability, which the above-referenced authorities establish to be no later than 152 days, thus providing the State with the ability to proscribe abortion "except when it is necessary to preserve the life or health of the mother."

These simple guidelines are the basis for the ensuing evolution of abortion laws, court battles, and inconsistent standards that have confounded our nation. The following brief discussion of the series of court battles and their results gives a proper perspective concerning the challenges that we face.

Court Battles After *Wade*

Diamond v. Charles:[14] The State of Illinois enacted the "Illinois Abortion Law of 1975" that required doctors who performed abortions to provide women with abortion-related information and to provide medical care to both viable fetuses and possibly viable fetuses. A number of doctors successfully challenged the constitutionality of the act, and Doctor Eugene F. Diamond, a pediatrician, appealed the ruling. Doctor Diamond claimed that the statutes would have provided the mothers with knowledge about their prospective children that may have led them to change their minds and carry them. He claimed an interest in the litigation based upon the likelihood of gaining more business due to more births.

The Supreme Court found that Doctor Diamond did not have standing to contest the lower court's ruling that the Illinois statutes were unconstitutional.

Catholic League v. Women's Health Center:[15] Approximately 16,000 aborted fetuses were discovered by a container company on the premises of a defunct pathology laboratory, and were turned over to the Los Angeles County District Attorney. The Southern California Chapter of the Catholic League asked that the bodies be turned over to them for proper burial and the District Attorney announced publicly his plan to do so. A private cemetery offered space to the State free of charge. The Feminist Women's Health Center objected based upon the Establishment Clause of the U.S. Constitution.

The California Court of Appeals found that turning the bodies over to the Catholic League would have violated the Establishment Clause and ordered the District Attorney not to do so. The Supreme Court confirmed that ruling.

These first two opinions provide notice of the character of both public and judicial opinion concerning the subject. In *Diamond* the Court gave no deference to the potential of saving an aborted fetus nor to properly informing the potential mother of the consequences of such a procedure. In *Catholic League* we can easily infer that the Court was concerned regarding the appearance of cooperating with a church-based group.

The first ruling recognized as "landmark" is *Thornburgh v. American Coll. Of Obst. & Gyn.*[16] The State of Pennsylvania had enacted the "Pennsylvania Abortion Control Act of 1982" that required:

(1) A woman must provide "informed consent" to an abortion;

(2) She must be provided the name of the doctor;

(3) She must be advised of the medical risks of the procedure being used;

(4) She must be advised of the likely psychological effects upon her; and

(5) She must be advised of the availability of assistance for her if she chose to go through with the birth, including healthcare for herself and the baby, along with assistance in gaining support from the father.

The act also required that a second physician be available to care for the child if he or she were born alive and that the doctor performing the abortion must use best efforts of care for the fetus. The Supreme Court ruled:

3. The States are not free, under the guise of protecting maternal health or potential life, to intimidate women into continuing pregnancies.

(a) The printed materials required by 3205 and 3208 are nothing less than an attempt to wedge the State's message discouraging abortion into the privacy of the informed-consent dialogue between the woman and her physician.

The Court essentially assumed that the doctor performing the abortion would provide all of the necessary information to the woman and that the State had no interest in interfering with or supplementing that relationship.

In *FEC v. Massachusetts Citizens For Life, Inc.*[17] the defendant was a non-profit, nonstock corporation that spent its money advertising political candidates' records concerning abortion. Section 316 of the Federal Election Campaign Act prohibited corporations from using treasury funds to make an expenditure "in connection with" any federal election. The Court confirmed the statute was unconstitutional and interfered with the First Amendment's Freedom of Speech.

In April 1988, a child was conceived by the girlfriend of a man who was separated from his wife. Soon thereafter the man reunited with his wife, but learned that the girlfriend was pregnant with his child. He also learned that she intended to have the child aborted, so he pled for an injunction. Justice John Paul Stevens heard the claim as Circuit Justice on June 15, 1988: *Doe v. Smith.*[18] Justice Stevens found "that although the Plaintiff expressed a legitimate and apparently sincere interest in the unborn fetus, his interest would not be sufficient to outweigh the constitutionally protected right of the Defendant to abort her child." He went on to hold that although the father of any fetus does carry a protected interest, "in this particular case the balancing would be in the mother's favor."

The rulings thus far have been consistently pro-choice. The pro-life perspective finally got a breakthrough in *Webster v. Reproductive Health Services.*[19] The State of Missouri had enacted a statute regulating abortions that included in its preamble that "[t]he life of each human being begins at conception," and that "unborn children have protectable interests in life, health, and well-being," and provided that all state laws be interpreted to provide unborn children with the same rights enjoyed by other persons, subject to the Federal Constitution and "this Court's precedents." It required that any physician, prior to performing an abortion on a woman whom he has reason to believe is 20 or more weeks pregnant, must ascertain whether the fetus is viable by performing "such medical examinations and tests as are necessary to make the finding of [the fetus'] gestational age, weight, and lung maturity." The statute went on to make it illegal to provide public funding for any abortion not necessary to save the mother's life.

The district court struck down all of these provisions and enjoined their enforcement. The Supreme Court reversed the ruling on all counts and held the statute entirely enforceable. Chief Justice Rehnquist delivered the opinion and found that each of the elements was derived from the ruling in *Roe v. Wade*. He confirmed that the State had a valid interest in each of the elements addressed in the statute and that it was drafted to narrowly fit within the confines of *Wade*:

> Section 188.029 of the statute—which specifies, in its first sentence, that a physician, shall first determine if the unborn child is viable by using the degree of care, skill, and proficiency that is commonly used by practitioners in the field … is constitutional, since it permissibly furthers the State's interest in protecting human life.

As stated above, it would be reasonable and prudent to assign a status of viability to a fetus with 16 weeks of gestation. The fact that Jayden Capewell, born at 21 weeks and 5 days, lived for almost two hours without medical assistance gives foundation for that plea.

While the district court found that uncontradicted medical evidence established that a 20-week fetus is not viable, and that

23½ to 24 weeks' gestation is the earliest point at which a reasonable possibility of viability exists, it also found that there may be a 4-week error in estimating gestational age, which supports testing at 20 weeks.

This ruling provides judicial precedent that supports a 4-week grace period that we can now apply to 21 weeks, thereby giving us authority to argue that viability has legal grounds to begin at 17 weeks. It doesn't take that much work to push it to 16 weeks, especially with current medical technology. Justice Rehnquist offered two more powerful points:

> While Roe recognized the State's interest in protecting human life as "important and legitimate," it also limited state involvement in second-trimester abortions to protecting maternal health. Roe's rigid trimester analysis has proved to be unsound in principle and unworkable in practice. There is also no reason why the State's compelling interest in protecting human life should not extend throughout pregnancy rather than coming into existence at the point of viability. Thus, the Roe trimester framework should be abandoned.

> Justice Scalia would reconsider and explicitly overrule Roe v. Wade.

Webster is a perfect example of what a State legislature can do with carefully drafted legislation that fits within the guidelines established by the Supreme Court. *Hodgson v. Minnesota*[20] is another example of using all of the space that is available. The Minnesota legislature enacted a statute providing that no abortion could be performed on a woman under eighteen years of age until at least forty-eight hours after both of her parents had been notified, with the exception of a case of parental abuse or neglect.

The district court found the Minnesota statute unconstitutional. The Eighth Circuit Court of Appeals reversed the ruling based primarily on the bypass procedure. The Supreme Court acknowledged the unusual need to notify both parents but held:

> The state statute's 48-hour waiting period is necessary to enable notified parents to consult with their daughter or her physician, if they so wish, results in little or no delay, and is therefore constitutional. Subdivision 6 of the statute—which requires two-parent notification unless the pregnant minor obtains a judicial bypass—is constitutional. By creating a judicial mechanism to identify, and exempt from the strictures of the law, those cases in which the minor is mature or in which parental notification is not in her best interest, subdivision 6 precisely addresses the concern underlying the [District] Court's invalidation of subdivision 2 [which references two-parent notification].

Hodgson and *Akron Center* (see note 20) represent state statutes that passed the Supreme Court's review, but they are not active in every state. We still see examples in the news of children being taken to abortion clinics from their school nurse's office without notice to a parent or a judicial bypass. These travesties are the fault of acquiescent voters who don't demand that their state legislatures address these issues. A wave of communications from voters will cause candidates for state legislatures to take notice. Their jobs depend on satisfying their constituents!

In 1988 the Secretary of Health and Human Services issued new regulations that prohibit Title X projects advocating abortion as a method of family planning. A number of Title X grantees and doctors filed suits that were consolidated in *Rust v. Sullivan*.[21] The Court found that the State (in this case the federal government) could choose not to fund abortions and held "The regulations do not violate a woman's Fifth Amendment right to choose whether to terminate her pregnancy. The Government has no constitutional duty to subsidize an activity merely because it is constitutionally protected, and may validly

choose to allocate public funds for medical services relating to childbirth but not to abortion." This decision to permit the State not to fund abortions was 5 to 4. Of those nine justices only three are still on the Court: Kennedy and Scalia voted with the majority and Stevens voted against.

Do you remember *Thornburgh*? The Supreme Court struck down the Pennsylvania Abortion Control Act of 1982. The Keystone State tried again because the ruling appeared to be too extreme. It turned out they were right! The newer version of the Pennsylvania Abortion Control Act of 1982 was challenged in *Planned Parenthood of Southeastern Pa. v. Casey*:[22]

> An examination of Roe v. Wade[23] and subsequent cases, reveals a number of guiding principles that should control the assessment of the Pennsylvania statute:
>
> (a) To protect the central right recognized by Roe while at the same time accommodating the State's profound interest in potential life … the undue burden standard should be employed. An undue burden exists, and therefore a provision of a law is invalid, if its purpose or effect is to place substantial obstacles in the path of a woman seeking an abortion before the fetus attains viability.
>
> (b) Roe's rigid trimester framework is rejected. To promote the State's interest in potential life throughout pregnancy, the State may take measures to ensure that the woman's choice is informed. Measures designed to advance this interest should not be invalidated if their purpose is to persuade the woman to choose childbirth over abortion. These measures must not be an undue burden on the right.

The Court went on to hold that the State can impose reasonable regulations to further the woman's health or safety as long as they weren't a substantial obstacle to the abortion. It reaffirmed the State's interest in the life of the fetus except where the woman's life or health is in jeopardy.

Section 3205's informed consent provision is not an undue burden on a woman's constitutional right to decide to terminate her pregnancy. To the extent Akron I[24] and Thornburgh find a constitutional violation when the government requires the giving of truthful, nonmisleading information about the nature of the abortion procedure, those cases are inconsistent with Roe's acknowledgment of an important interest in potential life, and are *overruled.* Requiring that a woman be informed of the availability of information relating to the consequences to the fetus does not interfere with a constitutional right of privacy between a pregnant woman and her physician. The premise behind Akron I's invalidation of a waiting period between the provision of the information deemed necessary to informed consent and the performance of the abortion is also wrong. (emphasis added)

Casey not only confirms pro-life advocates must keep fighting for every inch, but also establishes that the judicial climate is growing to give deference to protection of the unborn. The sad point is that these favorable rulings often reflect upon only one jurisdiction, meaning a particular state. That provides other jurisdictions with the authority to ignore these protections of the fetus until comparative legislation is in place.

Protests Protected

An association of pro-life advocates was regularly coordinating anti-abortion demonstrations in the Washington, D.C. area. Alexandria Women's Health Clinic sued to enjoin these people from conducting these demonstrations by claiming that they conspired to deprive "any person or class of persons of the equal protection of the laws, or of equal privileges or immunities under the laws" pursuant to U.S. Code Title 42, Section 1985(3). The district court found for the Clinic and the court of appeals confirmed the ruling by concluding that the demonstrations were specifically directed against women as a class. The

Supreme Court[25] reversed the ruling and found that opposition to abortion is not class-based nor can it be presumed to be a sex-based intent. It held "there are common and reasonable reasons for opposing abortion other than a derogatory view of women as a class."

The Supreme Court later heard *National Organization for Women, Inc. v. Scheidler*,[26] which effectively took approximately twenty years to resolve. N.O.W. claimed that Joseph Scheidler and his organization, the Pro-Life Action Network (PLAN), had violated the Hobbs Act by engaging in racketeering and extortion in an effort to effectively shut down the plaintiff's abortion clinics. Mr. Scheidler himself testified before the Senate[27] and stated that the aim was "to shut down the clinics and persuade women not to have abortions." The district court and the court of appeals found that the plaintiff did not have a proper claim because the extortion and racketeering claims depended on an economic motive. The Supreme Court reversed and held that the defendant's actions may not have been to get money, but they could have the effect of harming the plaintiff's businesses and costing it money. The case then went back and forth to the Supreme, appeals, and district courts with findings of liability that were then overturned. The Supreme Court finally ruled for Mr. Scheidler in 2006:

> We conclude that Congress did not intend to create a freestanding physical violence offense in the Hobbs Act. It did intend to forbid acts or threats of physical violence in furtherance of a plan or purpose to engage in what the statute refers to as robbery or extortion (and related attempts or conspiracies).[28]

In the case of *Madsen v. Women's Health Center, Inc.*[29] concerned protestors loudly demonstrated around an abortion clinic. The court effectively held that they could be there based on freedom of speech and assembly, but they must not abuse their presence to interfere with the operation of the clinic. This included loud bullhorns or speakers that interrupted a doctor's concentration. Nevertheless, they were free to hold up posters containing graphic images because the clinic could just go ahead and shut its drapes or blinds.

Arkansas had enacted an amendment to the state's constitution that limited the state's funding of abortions "except to save the mother's life." Little Rock Family Planning Services[30] claimed that the amendment violated Title XIX of the Social Security Act. The Supreme Court held that the state had the ability to limit funding for abortions, even in cases of rape or incest, where no federal funding was involved. If the facility received any federal funding, the Hyde amendment to the act would have required that the state fund abortions, but the state did not use any federal funds and therefore was immune.

Jodene Santana worked for Zilog, Inc. Her job in computer chip fabrication involved exposure to dangerous chemicals. She suffered six miscarriages; the longest period of gestation had been seventeen weeks. She sued Zilog pursuant to an Idaho wrongful death statute.[31] The Ninth Circuit Court of Appeals held that the statute did not support a cause of action for nonviable fetuses. It noted that most states allow recovery for prenatal injury of a viable fetus, but only six states: Georgia, Louisiana, Illinois, Missouri, West Virginia, and South Dakota have extended tort liability to encompass the wrongful death of a nonviable fetus.

This is an opportunity for people in forty-four states to plead before their legislators for laws to protect nonviable fetuses. If we can get every state to enact such a statute, which can be done because these six states provide precedent, we will give these children a foot in the door to establish more rights and push protection to an earlier time. Despite Justice Scalia's open

plea to overturn *Roe v. Wade*, we have to chip away at the existing laws until that opportunity appears. The *Thornburgh* reversal is evidence that my previous reference to:

(1) legislatures' maturity and persistence,

(2) courts' frustration of hearing abortion pleas, and

(3) most particularly the courts' deference to a growing public sentiment is directly on point. The squeaky wheel gets the grease.

Minors and Abortion

A minor child's ability to get an abortion was revisited in *Causeway Medical Suite v. Ieyoub*.[32] The Fifth Circuit Court of Appeals found that the Louisiana statute providing for judicial determination to bypass parental notice had no time limit for a judge's decision. It therefore did not protect the minor's right to a swift determination of that question and interfered with her right to an abortion. The real issue concerned an amendment to the statute that previously provided that if the court finds that the child is mature enough to decide to have an abortion, then the court "shall" order the abortion. The amended statute used "may" instead of "shall".

On August 16, 1995, the Ohio General Assembly enacted House Bill 135. That act included (1) a ban on the use of the D&X abortion procedure, (2) a ban on the performance of post-viability abortions, and (3) a viability testing requirement. This was a bold effort to protect the unborn but the district court found all three major elements unconstitutional in *Voinovich*[33] and the Sixth Circuit Court of Appeals confirmed the ruling.

The most important element is that all three of these objectives were obtainable and since then they have each become parts of enforceable law. The difference was that the legislature was reaching too far and that caused the effort to be wasted. First, the language of the statute made it hard to differentiate between pre- and post-viability abortions, thereby failing to advise doctors of their duties. Second, its exception for a medical emergency "must be objectively reasonable to other physicians" which denied a doctor independent authority to determine what is and is not an emergency.

Strong Anti-Abortion Statute

In 1995 the State of Utah enacted a strong anti-abortion statute that specified only five circumstances in which an abortion could be performed before 20 weeks of gestation. After 20 weeks the law limited abortion to only two of the five circumstances:

> (d) in the professional judgment of the pregnant woman's attending physician, to prevent grave damage to the pregnant woman's medical health; or

> (e) in the professional judgment of the pregnant woman's attending physician, to prevent the birth of a child that would be born with grave defects.[34]

In 1992, Jane L. objected to the severity of the law and the Tenth Circuit Court of Appeals found the statute restrictions too extreme concerning the first 20 weeks of gestation and that the provisions for after 20 weeks could not be severed from the invalid portions of the law. The Supreme Court agreed that the statute could not be enforced for the first 20-week period because it interfered with a woman's right to choose to get an abortion. Nevertheless, it found that the statute was separable and enforceable after the 20 weeks.[35]

This Utah case gave state legislatures the ability to draft strong anti-abortion legislation as long as the language allowed a court to carve it into pieces to determine what could and could not be enforced.

A Father's Rights

In 1998 the Seventh Circuit Court of Appeals ruled that a potential father has no right to interfere with a mother's decision to abort.[36] It entertained the possibility that a medical facility may have an obligation to inform the father of the pending abortion, but noted that it would be up to the legislature to decide.

Partial Birth Abortions

Earlier in the chapter, I included a portion of nurse Brenda Pratt Shafer's testimony in 1995 before a Senate Judiciary Committee regarding partial birth abortions. Those graphic details caused many state legislatures to enact laws intended to ban this procedure. But the legislators were careless and failed to provide the necessary deference to doctors' professionalism and women's rights. Here is a brief synopsis of the partial birth abortion case-law history:

Planned Parenthood of Wisconsin v. Doyle:[37] Wisconsin enacted a criminal statute that decreed life imprisonment for anyone who performs a partial birth abortion. The U.S. Seventh Circuit Court of Appeals noted the graphic description of the procedure and that the U.S. Congress had passed two bans that President Clinton had vetoed. It then stated, "It is true that Casey permits the state to trade off a de minimus risk to the mother's health against an interest in fetal life. But here there is no interest in fetal life. This case involves merely the method of abortion."[38] It then held that the threat of life imprisonment is bound to induce doctors to make decisions that may not be in the best interest of the pregnant woman. This would interfere with the doctor's best medical judgment. For this reason the statute was struck down.

Carhart v. Stenberg:[39] A Nebraska statute banning D&X abortions was too vague in differentiating them from D&E procedures. It also lacked the "health of the mother" exception to allow a D&X abortion when it was deemed necessary. *Planned Parenthood v. Farmer*[40] and *Richmond Medical Center For Women v. Gilmore*[41] produced the exact same results for New Jersey and Virginia statutes, respectively.

The first wedge in the D&X procedure came from *Women's Medical Professional Corporation v. Taft,*[42] a case that involved Dr. Martin Haskell, whose nurse Brenda Pratt Shafer, effectively started the war with her testimony. Ohio had enacted new statutes attacking partial birth abortions, similar to laws that had been struck down in *Voinovich,* but they now include a maternal health exception and a narrow and reliable definition of the D&X procedure. The district court had declared the laws unconstitutional, but the appeals court reversed the ruling on all counts.

The victory was short-lived. Virginia was beaten twice,[43] and a federal statute was defeated in Nebraska.[44] Each defeat was based on the lack of an exception to the rule when it was necessary for the woman's health. The final victory for pro-choice came in *National Abortion Federation v. Alberto Gonzales.*[45] The court of appeals had a serious struggle with this issue, as described at the beginning of this chapter. Judge Newman went on to say:

> I can think of no other field of law that has been subject to such sweeping constitutionalization as the field of abortion. Under the Supreme Court's current jurisprudence, the legislature is all but foreclosed from setting policy regulating the practice; instead,

federal courts must give their blessing to nearly every increment of social regulation that touches upon abortion.

In the end, I cannot escape the conclusion that, in these abortion cases, the federal courts have been transformed into a sort of super regulatory agency—a role for which courts are institutionally ill-suited and one that is divorced from accepted norms of constitutional adjudication. In today's case, we are compelled by a precedent to invalidate a statute that bans a morally repugnant practice, not because it poses as significant health risk, but because its application might deny some unproven number of women a marginal health benefit. Is it too much to hope for a better approach to the law of abortion —one that accommodates the reasonable policy judgments of Congress and the state legislatures without departing from established, generally applicable, tenets of constitutional law?[46]

This dissertation of exhaustion and frustration by Judge Newman was the last straw for pro-choice advocates. It is a prime example of one of the tenets that leads us to keep fighting for the children. The courts are getting very tired of legislative efforts to restrict the vicious mutilation and murder of the unborn. Legislatures have now become more sophisticated and detail-oriented in drafting statutes that correspond with the avenues available under *Roe v. Wade*. While I give great deference to Judge Newman's agony of serving our nation as a "regulatory agency," I am grateful that the tide has now turned pursuant to those three tenets outlined at the beginning of the chapter:

(1) Legislative persistence and maturity
(2) Exhausted courts
(3) Public Sentiment

The Supreme Court Reaction

The Supreme Court threw in the towel in *Gonzales v. Carhart*.

The U.S. Congress had enacted the Partial-Birth Abortion Ban Act of 2003 which specifically banned D&X abortions but provided doctors with an exception when the procedure was an unintentional result of a D&E.[47] The court also acknowledged that a D&E may be "in some respects as brutal, if not more, than the intact D&E, so that the legislation accomplishes little." In the final analysis:

> Considerations of marginal safety, including the balance of risks, are within the legislative competence when the regulation is rational and in pursuit of legitimate ends. When standard medical options are available, mere convenience does not suffice to displace them; and if some procedures have different risks than others, it does not follow that the State is altogether barred from imposing reasonable regulations. The Act is not invalid on its face where there is uncertainty over whether the barred procedure is ever necessary to preserve a woman's health, given the availability of other abortion procedures that are considered to be safe alternatives.

The Federal Partial-Birth Abortion Ban Act of 2003 stimulated state legislatures to enact conforming statutes with some personal attention to details not completely addressed in the Federal Act. I believe it is prudent to continue to throw these limitations at the federal court wall to see what will stick. The State of Virginia enacted its own "Partial Birth Infanticide" Act in April, 2003, which was to become effective July 1, 2003, but it was successfully challenged several times by Richmond Medical Center for Women (see above). Persistence was a virtue because Richmond Center challenged it again and obtained the opposite result:

> The complaint alleged that the Act (1) impermissibly failed to include an exception for the preservation of the mother's health, and (2) defined the term "partial birth infanticide" so broadly as to

ban the safest and most common second trimester method of abortion, the [standard] dilation and evacuation ("D & E") method, and thus [to] impose an undue burden on the woman's ability to choose abortion."(sic)

We now conclude that insofar as Dr. Fitzhugh mounts a facial challenge against the Virginia Act, the challenge fails because (1) Dr. Fitzhugh's posited circumstance does not present a sufficiently frequent circumstance to render the Virginia Act wholly unconstitutional for all circumstances; (2) the Virginia Act's scienter language, although different from the Federal Act, nonetheless provides sufficient notice to a reasonable doctor of what conduct is prohibited by the statute; and (3) the provisions for a safe harbor and affirmative defenses, as well as the requirement of "an overt act," ensure that the Virginia Act will not create a barrier to, or have a chilling effect on, a woman's right to have a standard D & E or her physician's ability to undertake that procedure without fear of criminal liability.[48]

The Significance to State Legislatures

The significance of this is that it invites state legislatures to push the envelope. It also gives notice to the medical profession that the momentum has shifted. The general rule was that if an exception to reasonable application of an abortion law existed, that would void the entire statute. The new rule allows exceptions to exist but assumes that those exceptions will be tended to as they arise. This puts doctors on notice. They now have responsibilities to the unborn child and these responsibilities must be weighed as they contemplate an abortion procedure.

We now have our foot in the door, but we must be careful not to barge in. That may cause momentum to change direction. We must consistently work to chip away at these abortion laws by giving the unborn child standing to be awarded compassion and dignity. Even in instances where we are not yet able to stop this horrible procedure, we have a vehicle enabling us to promote a more peaceful and less painful act that causes death. Our courts of law and legislatures have heard many arguments concerning humane ways to cause the death of those who sit on death row. It is time to provide equal dignity to innocent infants.

Personal Liability

In 1997 the State of Louisiana legislature took a new approach and enacted a personal liability statute entitled "Liability for termination of a pregnancy."[49] This included potential unlimited liability for damage to the mother *and to the unborn child.* Ifeanyi Charles Anthony Okpalobi, a doctor who managed Gentilly Medical Clinic for Women, sued the State of Louisiana and its governor, Mike Foster, claiming that the law was unconstitutional.[50] The case was dismissed for lack of federal jurisdiction according to the Eleventh Amendment to the Constitution that immunizes state governments from suit with few exceptions. That law still stands in Louisiana, and I urge all other state legislatures to use the law as an example.

In January 1995, the American Coalition of Life Activists released a poster listing the names and addresses of the "Deadly Dozen," a group of doctors who performed abortions. Later that year the group released a second poster that targeted Dr. Robert Crist and included his business and home addresses and featured his photograph. In January, 1996 the group unveiled a series of dossiers it had compiled on all of the doctors, clinic employees, politicians, judges and other abortion rights supporters. It also included the names of six members of the U.S. Supreme Court, Bill Clinton, Al Gore, Janet Reno, Jack Kevorkian, C. Everett Koop, Mary Tyler Moore, Whoopi

Goldberg, and for unknown reasons retired Supreme Court Justice Byron White, who had dissented with Justice Rehnquist in both Wade and Bolton. ACLA dubbed these the "Nuremberg Files," and announced that it had collected the pictures, addresses, and other information so that war crimes trials could be conducted in "perfectly legal courts once the tide of this nation's opinion turns against the wanton slaughter of God's children."

A number of doctors and health care centers sued the organization and a number of activists. The district court instructed the jury that the defendants could only be held liable if ACLA's statements were "true threats" and thereby unprotected under the First Amendment. The jury found for the doctors and health facilities and awarded $107 million. The Ninth Circuit Court of Appeals reversed the ruling and held, "we deem it highly significant that all the statements were made in the context of public discourse, not in direct personal communication."[51]

Sandra Cano, the "victim" used in *Doe v. Bolton* has become an active pro-lifer and pled before the Eleventh Circuit Court of Appeals to have her victory overturned. The court issued its ruling on January 11, 2006, simply stating that neither the district court nor the court of appeals has authority to overturn the Supreme Court's ruling.[52]

Norma McCorvey, the *"Roe"* in *Roe v. Wade*, tried in similar fashion to reverse her victory and the Fifth Circuit Court of Appeals was much more kind, but was also powerless to grant her wish.[53] The Hon. Edith H. Jones delivered her concurring opinion that evinces our frustration:

> McCorvey presented evidence that goes to the heart of the balance
> *Roe* struck between the choice of a mother and the life of her unborn

child. First, there are about a thousand affidavits of women who have had abortions and claim to have suffered long-term emotional damage and impaired relationships from their decision. Studies by scientists, offered by McCorvey, suggest that women may be affected emotionally and physically for years afterward and may be more prone to engage in self-destructive conduct as a result of having had abortions. Second, *Roe's* assumption that the decision to abort a baby will be made in close consultation with a woman's private physician is called into question by affidavits from workers at abortion clinics, where most abortions are now performed. According to the affidavits, women are often herded through their procedures with little or no medical or emotional counseling. Third, McCorvey contends that the sociological landscape surrounding unwed motherhood has changed dramatically since Roe was decided.... Finally, neonatal and medical science, summarized by McCorvey, now graphically portrays, as science was unable to do 31 years ago, *how a baby develops sensitivity to external stimuli and to pain much earlier than we then believed* (emphasis added). In sum, if courts were to delve into the facts underlying *Roe's* balancing scheme with present-day knowledge, they might conclude that the woman's "choice" is far more risky and less beneficial, and the child's sentience far more advanced, than the *Roe* court knew.

The perverse result of the Court's having determined through constitutional adjudication this fundamental social policy, which affects over a million women and unborn babies each year, is that the facts no longer matter. This is a peculiar outcome for a Court so committed to "life" that it struggles with the particular facts of dozens of death penalty cases each year.

Hard and social science will of course progress even though the Supreme Court averts its eyes. It takes no expert prognosticator to know that research on women's mental and physical health following abortion will yield an eventual medical consensus, and neonatal science will push the frontiers of fetal "viability" ever closer to the date of conception (emphasis added). One may fervently hope that the Court will someday acknowledge such developments and re-evaluate Roe and Casey accordingly. That the Court's constitutional decisionmaking (sic) leaves our nation in a position of willful blindness to evolving knowledge should

trouble any dispassionate observer not only about the abortion decisions, but about a number of other areas in which the Court unhesitatingly steps into the realm of social policy under the guise of constitutional adjudication.

Today's Laws

For many years, Gallup has conducted an elaborate and consistent series of public opinion polls regarding abortion,[54] and the percentage of pro-life advocates passed pro-choice advocates for the first time late in 2008. In 1996, 56% were pro-choice and 33% were pro-life. More impressively, the latest data indicates that only 24% believe abortion should be legal under any circumstances, 19% believe it should be illegal in all circumstances, and 54% believe that it should be legal only under certain circumstances. This provides a 73% proportion of people who will favor limitations that will significantly serve the interest of the unborn.

Wikipedia's article on late-term abortions list the following statistics: In 2003, 6.2% of abortions in the U.S. were conducted from 13 to 15 weeks, 4.2% from 16 to 20 weeks, and 1.4% at or after 21 weeks.[55]

The State of Arizona has one of the more elaborate sets of abortion laws in the nation to protect both the mother and the child. I encourage readers to compare these laws with those statutes in your jurisdiction. I examined the laws in many states and found that the protection of a fetus is sorely lacking. The State of California, for instance, vaguely references protection of a viable fetus, but provides no method to ensure enforcement. I will lastly provide proposals for the future that each of you can offer to your state and federal legislators. If enough people ask, they will be bound to respond; their jobs depend on it!

Arizona Laws

Reference to Arizona laws are in numerical order for convenience.

Title 13, Sections 1102 through 1105 describe crimes causing death and include negligent homicide, manslaughter, second degree murder and first degree murder, in that order. The first two specifically state "applies to an unborn child in the womb at any stage of development." 1104 and 1105 include unborn children, but are not clear at what stage the crimes arise, which may be interpreted either to be the point of viability or the point of conception.

First degree murder can also be charged if any of a long list of crimes leads to the death of an unborn child.

13-3603.01 criminalizes partial-birth abortions as a class 6 felony and imposes fines, imprisonment, or both. It provides an exception for a partial-birth abortion that is necessary to save the life of the mother.

13-3604 criminalizes solicitation by a woman to get a drug or substance, or who submits to an operation, or to the use of any means whatever with intent to procure a miscarriage, unless it is necessary to preserve her life.

13-3605 criminalizes advertisement of any medicine or means for producing or facilitating a miscarriage or abortion.

15-1630 prohibits abortion at any educational facility unless it is necessary to save the life of a woman.

35-196.02: "Notwithstanding any provisions of law to the contrary, no public funds nor tax monies of this state or any political subdivision of this state nor any federal funds passing through the state treasury or the treasury of any political

subdivision of this state may be expended for payment to any person or entity for the performance of any abortion unless the abortion is necessary to save the life of the woman having the abortion."

36-329 requires any medical facility or practitioner to submit a completed fetal death certificate within seven days for any fetus after a gestation period of 20 weeks or that weighs more than 350 grams (a little more than 12 ounces).

36-449.03 "Abortion clinics; rules" provides a detailed list of regulations for a facility to hold itself out as an abortion clinic. It mandates ultrasound equipment in all facilities that provide abortions after 12 weeks' gestation *and requires an ultrasound evaluation for all patients who elect to have an abortion after 12 weeks' gestation.* It further obligates the attendant physician to estimate the gestational age and to write the estimate in the patient's medical history.

36-2152 addresses the parental consent requirement for an abortion performed on a minor and includes the exception for a superior court judge to make the decision. It also provides exceptions for a medical emergency or when the pregnant minor certifies that the pregnancy resulted from sexual conduct with a relative or a person who lives in the same household.

36-2153 demands informed consent from the patient. It requires that the woman know the name of the physician, the nature of the treatment, immediate and long-term medical risks, alternatives to the treatment, notice of probable gestational age of the child(ren), probable anatomical and physiological characteristics of the unborn child, and medical risks associated with carrying the child to term. It further demands that at least 24 hours before the operation the physician who will perform the procedure *personally* inform the woman of the availability of medical assistance benefits for prenatal care, childbirth, and neonatal care; that the father of the child is liable for the support; that public and private agencies and services are available to assist her both before and after birth, including adoption. She must be informed that it is unlawful for any person to coerce her to undergo an abortion and that she is free at any time to withdraw her consent to the operation without any fear of loss of any available state or federally funded benefits to which she may otherwise be entitled. She must sign a statement avowing that all of the information has been provided to her.

36-2153 goes on to demand that no medication regarding the abortion may be prescribed for or provided to the patient for at least twenty-four hours and that no person may coerce or intimidate any person to obtain an abortion. A physician who violates any of this section is subject to license revocation or suspension. Any violation of the section will provide cause for civil claims by the woman, the father of the unborn if married, and the unborn's maternal grandparents.

36-2154 provides the right to refuse to participate in any abortion, abortion medication, or emergency contraception to any hospital, pharmacy, physician, or any other medical personnel.

36-2301 is entitled "Duty to promote life of fetus or embryo delivered alive" and specifically states:

> If an abortion is performed and a human fetus or embryo is delivered alive, it is the duty of the physician performing such abortion and any additional physician in attendance as required by section 36-2301.01 to see that all available means and medical skills are used to promote, preserve and maintain the life of such fetus or embryo.

36-2301.01 is entitled, "Abortion of a viable fetus; requirements; definitions" and provides:

A. A physician shall not knowingly perform an abortion on a viable fetus unless:

1. The physician states in writing before the abortion is performed that the abortion is necessary to preserve the life or health of the woman, specifying the medical indications for and the probable health consequences of the abortion. The physician shall attach a copy of this statement to any fetal death report.

2. The physician uses the available method or technique of abortion most likely to preserve the life or health of the fetus, unless the use of such method or technique would present a greater risk to the life or health of the woman.

4. In addition to the physician performing the abortion, there is another physician in attendance who shall take control of and provide immediate care for a living child born as a result of the abortion.

This statute goes on to provide: "'Viable fetus' means in the judgment of the attending physician on the particular facts of the case, there is a reasonable probability of the fetus' sustained survival outside the uterus, with or without artificial support." This language provides great deference to the opinion of the attending physician and denies the newly born infant any guarantee of the best available treatment. For this reason, codification of a 16-week or lesser term of presumed viability will give every infant a chance, no matter how small, to survive. We will gain great comfort in spending thousands of hours of wasted effort on hopeless victims when we are successful in saving just one. It is worth the price.

36-2301.02 provides detailed instruction concerning the performance, care, recording, and distribution of ultrasound examinations after twelve weeks' gestation of any fetus. It then details the review of each analysis to ensure that the doctor's estimate of period of gestation is consistently accurate.

36-2302 prohibits any experimentation on a human fetus or embryo and provides no exception for any physician-patient privilege.

36-2907 and 36-2989 describe government covered health and medical services but specifically deny abortion or abortion counseling.

What You Can Do

These statutes are very strong, and I am grateful for the work the Arizona State legislators have done. Nevertheless, I am not yet satisfied with what we have, and I know that many of you in other states are embarrassed by the condition of your laws. I therefore ask that you impress upon each of your legislators their duties to protect both the unborn and the expectant mothers. Please use Arizona's statutes as starting points and offer the following as ways to make further progress:

1. The state of Nebraska enacted a statute banning abortion after 20 weeks. Utah has similar laws. These are codifications of viability at that time. We can expect that these laws will be challenged but that doesn't mean that we should sit and wait. I urge every state's legislature to push the envelope to 16 weeks. I further urge that companion statutes be enacted that mirror the 16-week standard with periods of 10, 12, 14, 18, and 20 weeks. We won't know what we can do until we try.

2. *Santana v. Zilog* referenced previously evinces a sincere lack of legal standing for nonviable fetuses. We have a duty to give those unborn children the ability to make civil claims against those whose actions cause them harm. Only six states have enacted legislation in this area. We need every state on board!

3. All work by any state or federal legislative body is bound to give professional courtesy to doctors and assume that their actions are reasonable and prudent. We nevertheless know that many of these abortion doctors tend to provide little care for the newborn "accidents" that are intended to be lifeless. Our legislatures have a duty to enact a system of monitoring for all abortion procedures including records of gestational periods and a detailed description of each abortion. We need statutory limitations to the number of late-term and D&E abortions performed by each doctor. When a physician's work is proportionately higher than a preset standard for these procedures, that doctor's abortion practice must cease, pending administrative review by the State's Department of Health Services. Any argument of denial of necessary medical services for patients will be answered with a list of physicians whose records comply with the guidelines.

4. The doctor performing an abortion before viability must do everything medically possible to limit the pain and suffering of the fetus. This standard applies to every abortion from the point of conception without regard to any proof that the fetus can or cannot feel pain at any particular stage of development.

5. No post-viability abortion can be performed unless a second physician is on hand with the ability to provide care for the aborted fetus. The abortion must be performed in the manner that will most likely protect the fetus and allow him/her the opportunity to survive the operation. Only when it is necessary to ensure the health of the mother can the infant's care be compromised.

These are only suggestions. I ask all readers to use your creativity to see what you can put on your legislator's desk. We have the momentum and we have the responsibility to do everything we can for the defenseless children. Please remember the three rules:

(1) Our legislatures are growing wiser.

(2) The courts are growing tired of the onslaught of challenges to abortion laws.

(3) Public opinion is a powerful force that will affect all three branches of government, especially at the polling places!

You can make a difference. Every child that is rescued is a victory. Please don't be discouraged that the *Roe v. Wade* ruling is still the law. Every legislative act passing constitutional muster will save hundreds, if not thousands. Momentum is on our side.

The Federal Budget

The word "budget" in reference to any government institution's spending plan is a gross misuse of the term. You may as well refer to a firing squad as a "health care plan." The concept of a budget involves an itemized summary of probable income and expenditures for a given period, usually consisting of a systematic plan or schedule for meeting those expenses. Notice I mentioned income before expenditures—a concept that Congress has yet to grasp. The U.S. government's current fiscal year of 2010 began on October 1, 2009 and will end September 30, 2010.

The federal budget for fiscal year 2011 projects expenses of $3.8339 trillion based on total revenue of $2.5672 trillion.[1] This plan results in the government spending about $1.50 for every dollar it brings in. These numbers are based upon estimates, which are historically conservative.

The 2011 budget estimates gross domestic product (GDP) of $15.299 trillion and gross public debt (GPD) of $15.144 trillion. The 2012 budget estimates GDP of $16.203.3 and GPD of $16.335.7 trillion. By my guesstimate, the federal government will owe more than the entire income of every person, corporation, or other entity for the entire year on or about October 31, 2011.

Happy Halloween! Remember this debt is only the "due and payables" and does not reflect continuing obligations that become due every day including Social Security and Medicare.

In the current economic environment it is understandable for individuals to be more focused on personal budgets than a federal budget that seems totally out of control. However, it is important for you to recognize a few major differences in how the federal budget process differs from your personal one and also how it impacts your own budget.

Frequently, congressional candidates campaign on promises of expenditures for special projects. Candidates assume that the number of votes they will get from those supporting the expenditures will outweigh the number of votes they may lose by those who oppose the expenditures. Voters must remember that Congress and the executive branch spend money they do not have to earn.

Citizens Against Government Waste is an organization that researches and exposes the pork projects.[2] Their "2010 Congressional Pig Book Summary" exposes $16.5 billion in pork expenditures and names the responsible legislators. That is about .43% of the 2010 budget and it cost 308.9 million Americans a little more than $50 apiece.

The figure .43% may not be much, but it is a start. In this chapter I am going to give you two major considerations. First, I will describe how we can cut federal spending by more than 45%. Secondly, I'll outline a plan for our U.S. government to gain the most possible income at the least inconvenience to its citizens. With my plan, the budget will be balanced and we will be paying off the national debt. Unemployment will be well below 5%, the economy will be booming, and everyone will have virtually everything that they want. No, I am not fantasizing and I am not a candidate making hollow promises. America recovered from economic disaster in the mid-1920s with Presidents Harding and Coolidge. John F. Kennedy and Ronald Reagan both cut taxes with huge economic benefits. However, once we were on the right path, we became greedy and forgot how we had prospered. We repeated the same mistakes and got the same results: inflation, unemployment, and higher taxes. We need to elect candidates willing to learn from the past and get us back on track.

Spending Cuts

I created some rules for my assessment of the federal budget. Every line item in the federal budget will get severe cuts. I will go line-by-line according to the worksheet that follows. Some of the cutting is based on what was discussed in the preceding chapters; the remainder is based on what is provided by the Cato Institute[3] and The Heritage Foundation.[4] Some of the numbers listed in the federal budgets are inclusive of other departments' expenditures and others are not all-inclusive. Therefore I may appear to be cutting more from some areas than the budget appears to allow because the money is actually coming from a different department.

Pensions

No budget cuts can be made for current obligations. Nevertheless, Congress has the opportunity to open the market for privatization of retirement accounts for public employees. There is no way to estimate how much could be saved by privatizing pension accounts, but we can then be certain that the government is protected from abuses that drag us deeper into the hole. According to William W. Beach of American Heritage, Social Security has been collecting more than necessary to finance retirement benefits since 1983.[5] That money

was then "borrowed" by the federal government to finance other government programs with treasury bonds. It was the ultimate borrowing from Peter to pay Paul when Peter and Paul are in fact the same person. The treasury bonds will have to be honored but where will the money will come from?

Health Care

Federal health care coverage has more than doubled since 2002 and Obamacare is nuclear fuel for the rocket. My prior discussion of Health Savings Accounts must be expanded to apply to Medicare as well. Practically speaking, we must install an incentive to earn benefits by foregoing wasted abuse of medical services. Under no circumstances can care be denied to senior citizens and others who enjoy public health care, but it cannot be a casual treat. I believe that proper incentives will allow us to improve from where we were in 2002 at $427.4 billion. At that time senior care cost $230.9 billion, welfare services cost $172.6 billion, and public health services/research and development health cost $24 billion. Multiply those numbers by inflation of 19.3% and the increased population of citizens over 65 at 11.24% and we get $567.2 billion; assuming that the other factors have similar growth patterns. Proper legislation to protect the medical care providers and stimulate conservative use will bring us to approximately $400 billion. That provides each public health care beneficiary with unlimited necessary care but saves us the expense of frivolous abuse of the system. Look at it this way: we have 39,570,590 U.S. citizens aged 65 and over. They account for 55.1 percent of the federal health dole. That will give us approximately $5,571 per year per senior for health care. That is a manageable fund with proper legislation. This does not take into account the public health care savings generated by reduced unemployment and the stimulus of group heath care plans by small businesses.

Education

Welcome to the private school of your choice, the Department of Education is eliminated. Total spending cuts are $140,900,000,000.

Defense

Almost half of all military spending in the world, 47 percent, is done by the United States. All the nations of Europe combined last year spent $289 billion, less than one-third of our $895 billion investment in 2010. Yet we look at the numbers from 1960 and 1962 and see that we spent, respectively, 54.8% and 59.6% of our total federal budget on defense. Yet in 2010 and 2011 we spent 24.1% and 24.2% of the total federal budget on defense. Compare that with total government spending's share of the gross domestic product for each of those years: 18.48%, 18.23%, 25.44%, and 25.06%, and we see that defense spending has been significantly reduced.

Our problem is that we need to spend more wisely. At this time, U.S. military is spread all over the world and neglecting our priorities. The rules of engagement in Afghanistan are atrocious; the enemy can fire on us and step into a crowd of innocent civilians. We are taking years to accomplish what could be done in months. America needs to get the job done and come home; we cannot afford to simply play around waiting for progress. We need to put our troops in the best strategic areas in the world and bring home the ones who are wasting their time.

My proposal is this:

1) Start a big surge in Afghanistan to get the job done by annihilating Al-Qaeda, the Taliban, Hamas, or whoever they claim to be on that day. Then we can move on to better places.

2) We have a proper strategic advantage to be in the Middle East. Israel will welcome us setting up a military base and will probably provide funding for it. The message to Iran and its friends: "You mess with them and you mess with us."

3) Bringing troops home will enable us to fortify the southern border to protect us from the criminal element that is using the flood of illegal immigrants as a decoy. Once we stop the incentives for illegals we can open fire on the drug lords and terrorists.

4) Stop the wasteful spending. While I admit that $19 billion in responsibilities are being transferred from the Department of Energy (see below), the Department of Defense is overrun with pork-barrel spending. It is reasonable to expect that moving our soldiers back home and putting them to work where we need them can trim 25% of the current budget.

5) Moving the troops home will bring the money home, which is a boost for our economy.

Welfare

The plan that worked like a Swiss watch to boost our economy by cutting taxes (Harding, Coolidge, Kennedy, Reagan) will reduce all needs by at least 50%.

Protection

We are well aware the criminal element of the illegal alien population occupies 28% of our federal prisons. There is no immediate financial benefit to securing our border in this area, but we will be able to greatly reduce the future influx. I make no adjustment to the budget now, but we know that we will save money in the future.

Transportation

States need to fund their highways. Cities will make much wiser decisions concerning urban transit. Air Traffic Control should be commercialized similar to Canada's system. Amtrak is an absolute waste that would be in better hands as a private company. High-speed rail is a loser all over the world; stop the insanity! Total spending cuts $84,888,000,000.

General Government

We can all tighten our belts. I am cutting 10% from the executive, legislative, finance department, and 20% from general services.

Other Spending

(a) The "Basic Research" expense includes a great deal of the pork-barrel spending discussed in the 2010 Congressional Pig Book Summary by Citizens Against Government Waste. It must be eliminated and research projects that have merit will be the responsibilities of the respective department(s).

(b) Agriculture: The Department of Agriculture is the source of billions of dollars in subsidies to people and business entities that don't need them. We give money to farms to compensate for overproduction of products, and we give money to farms as compensation for not growing anything. Most of these farms are owned by large corporations. They really don't need any money from the government. In 1984 the nation of New Zealand cut off its subsidy program. The farms responded by looking at the market and producing the best marketable products. They are now flourishing without any government assistance and we enjoy their kiwi!

(c) The Department of Agriculture also handles Food Stamps (SNAP), a Nutrition Program (WIC), and school lunch and related programs. These are all wasted and abused. They need to be the responsibilities of states and communities that are better able to manage their local needs.

(d) The Forest Service (also under the Department of Agriculture) can be properly managed and funded by charging reasonable rates for enjoyment of the facilities, parks, and wilderness areas. Local management would be far more efficient and privatization would allow the market to determine fair prices. Total spending cuts for the Department of Agriculture are $131,255,000,000.

(e) The Department of Commerce provides many valuable services but they include unnecessary funding of subsidies for economic development. Total spending cuts are $2,117,000,000.

(f) Housing and Urban Development (HUD) is the responsibility of local government. It can be done much more cheaply, and the savings from reformatting education alone will cover the expenses. Total spending cuts are $62,518,000,000.

(g) The Department of Energy is serving us in ways that will be better managed by the Department of Defense (nuclear safety, defense environmental clean-up, and uranium-related activities). Transfer $19,303,000,000 of their responsibilities to Defense and cut the remaining $18,975,000,000.

(h) Pollution abatement is better the responsibility of the local government.

	1960	1962	2010	2011	CUTS	*2012*
Pensions	11.70	11.70	774.30	787.60		787.6
Sickness and Disability		0.70	8	6.90		
Old Age	11.70	11.10	766.30	780.80		
Fed. Employee Retmt. & Disability	0.90	2	120.60	123.50		
Social Security	10.80	14.40	721.50	736.30		
Employer Share (on-budget)		-5	-60.90	-63.50		
Employer Share (off-budget)		-0.20	-14.90	-15.60		
Health Care	1.50	1.20	829.50	898	498	400
Medical Service (Seniors)			457.20	497.30		
Medical Service	1.50					
Public Health Services		0.10	4.40	4.50		
R&D Health		0.60	32.70	38.50		
Vendor Payments (Welfare)			335.20	357.70		
Education	1.60	1.70	157	140.90	140.90	0
Pre-Primary thru Secondary		0.50	84.10	61		
Tertiary		0.30	20.40	31.30		
Education Not Definable by Level	1.60	0.90	52.50	48.60		
Defense	53.30	63.60	895	928.50	241.625	686.875
Military Defense	41.30	52.30	719.20	749.70	187.425	
Veterans	4.40	5.60	124.70	124.50	0	
Foreign Military Aid		2	9.90	10.10	10.10	
Foreign Economic Aid	7.60	3.70	41.20	44.10	44.10	
Welfare	3	6.60	557.30	464.60	359.45	105.15
Family & Children		0.30	99.30	103.50	51.75	
Unemployment	0.60	3.80	194.30	106.60	53.30	
Housing	0.30	0.20	77	64.10	64.10	
Social Exclusion n.e.c.	2.10	2.30	186.80	190.30	190.30	
Protection	0.20	0.40	55	57.30		57.30
Police Services	0.20	0.30	28.80	30		
Law Courts		0.10	18.40	18.90		
Prisons			7.70	8.30		
Transportation	4.40	4.30	106.50	104.2	84.888	19.312
General Government	0.70	1.30	30.60	29	18.49	
Executive, Legislative, Finance	0.70	1.10	18.50	19.90	1.99	
General Services		0.20	12.20	9.10	1.82	
Other Spending	9.60	9	109	151.40	436.965	-285.565
Basic Research		1.20	18.60	17.10	17.10	
General Economic, Commercial & Labour		-0.40	-26.60	4.20	2.117	
Agriculture, Forestry, Fishing & Hunting	5.90	3.70	33.20	32.40	131.255	
Fuel & Energy		0.60	15.40	17.60	18.975	
Communication	3.70	0.80	1	-1.20		
Economic Affairs (n.e.c.)		0.40	-55.90	15.40	15.40	
Pollution Abatement		0.10	11.50	11.40	11.40	
Protection of Biodiversity & Landscape		0.40	12.50	11.70	11.70	
Housing Development		0.70	55.70	-0.50	62.518	
Community Development		0.50	28.50	32		
Water Supply		1.30	12.40	8.50	8.50	
Recreational & Sporting Services		0.10	4	4.10	4.10	
General Public Services n.e.c.		-0.30	-1.40	-1.40		
Interest	7.70	6.90	187.80	250.70		250.70
Balance	3.50	0	18.70	21.70		21.70
Total Spending	97.30	106.80	3,720.70	3,833.90		2,043.07
Total Revenue	-99.80	-99.70	-2,165.10	-2,567.20		-2,567.20
Federal Deficit	-2.50	7.10	1,555.60	1,266.70		-524.13
Gross Public Debt	286.30	298.20	13,786.60	15,144		
Gross Domestic Product	526.40	585.70	14,623.90	15,299		
Population (in millions)	179.30	183.90	308.90	311.60		

Before I go on to discuss income we need to understand a number of details. The adjustments to the federal budget include the assignment of approximately $106.3 billion in obligations for Agriculture, Housing, and Pollution to the states. Conversion of our system of education will save states approximately $500 billion based on the proviso that a well-managed administration of private schools with vouchers for tuition will reduce the total education costs for all levels. Many of the other adjustments are based on limited information and data in the hands of internal government administrative offices.

The bottom line is that some of my suggestions may be too strong, but many may be too weak. The Internal Revenue Service itself appears to cost approximately $11 billion for 2010 and that can be drastically reduced or eliminated, as you will see. The problem is that the deeper we dive into the federal government's accounting system, the harder it is to determine where everything fits.

Maximizing Income

In December 1974, economist Arthur Laffer was sitting for dinner with President Gerald Ford, Donald Rumsfeld, and Dick Cheney at the Two Continents Restaurant in the Washington Hotel, Washington, D.C. They were discussing President Ford's "WIN" (Whip Inflation Now) proposal that depended on tax increases. Legend has it that Mr. Laffer took a napkin and drew a graph representing "The Laffer Curve" based upon the following premise: A government's tax income is based upon the percentage of income that is taxed. The higher the tax rate, the more government income, *assuming* the taxpayers' income is constant. The problem is that taxpayers are less stimulated to gain income as the portion they are allowed to retain decreases. If the government was taxing at 100%, nobody would work and the government would get nothing. If the government's tax rate were 0%, everybody would work their fingers to the bone and the government would get nothing. Somewhere in between a 0% and 100% tax rate is the perfect number to stimulate the economy and more importantly, give the government the most that it can get.

This is an absolute law that works every time, but there are some details. Different demographic groups will have different "sweet spots" on the Laffer Curve. People desperate for income may be more inclined to do the work despite higher taxes. Those with high incomes may also have a higher pain threshold, but we can't write tax laws to suit every particular individual. The logical solution is to find the sweet spot that in the overall population gains the most income for the government. The perfect sweet spot will stimulate the economy and eliminate all but marginal unemployment. More money will change hands and the government will get its share of each transaction.

In 1913, the federal progressive income tax rate's highest bracket was 7%. World War I caused that rate for those who made more than a million dollars to peak at 77% in 1918. During those years inflation-adjusted revenues *declined* by an average of 9.2% per year. After the war, Presidents Harding and Coolidge gradually cut the top marginal tax rate to 25% and revenues *increased* at .1%. Bear in mind that the total of taxes paid by those earning more than $100,000 per year went from 29.9% in 1920 to 62.2% in 1929. That means that cutting the tax to less than one-third of its previous rate more than doubled the tax income. More importantly: Real GDP growth went from an average of 2.0% to 3.4% and unemployment fell from 6.5% to 3.1%.

The Depression and World War II caused Congress to raise the tax rate ceiling to 94% in 1944 and 1945. That rate remained above 90% until John F. Kennedy cut it to 70% in 1965. The four years preceding the tax cut saw total government income tax revenue increasing at an average of 2.1% per year. From 1965 through 1968, tax revenue increased an average of 8.6% per year.

In August 1981, President Reagan signed the Economic Recovery Tax Act (ERTA, aka the Kemp-Roth Tax Cut). It slashed marginal income tax rates by 25% across the board over a three-year period. As a result, government income tax revenue increased at an average of 3.5% per year and unemployment fell from 9.7% in 1982 to 5.3% when President Reagan left office in January 1989.

Income tax is not the only revenue horse in the government's barn. Capital gains taxes impede people from making trades that result in income. In 1981 the capital gains tax rate was reduced from 28% to 20% and tax revenues jumped from $12.5 billion in 1980 to $18.7 billion in 1983. We need to determine what the proper capital gains tax rate is to stimulate trading and maximize the government's income.

Estonia suffered from a declining economy for many years until it converted to a 26% flat tax in 1994. Since then its economic growth has averaged 5.2% per year. Latvia's real GDP had shrunk more than 50% in the five years preceding its adoption of a 25% flat tax. Since then it has grown an average of 3.8% per year. Lithuania followed suit with a 33% flat tax and experienced similar results.

Russia instituted a 13% personal and 24% corporate flat tax on January 1, 2001 and January 1, 2002, respectively. Tax revenues were:

2000: 965 billion rubles;
2001: 1,461 billion rubles;

2002: 1,696 billion rubles; and
2003: 1,892 billion rubles.

These are all evidences of the successes of two economic stimuli: reduced taxes and conversion to a flat tax system, the latter of which will be much easier to manage and could eliminate the IRS altogether. The necessary conclusion is based on our current recession-laden economy: the U.S. government estimates $15.299 trillion dollars as GDP for 2011. A 15% flat tax on that depressed output will yield $2.29 trillion dollars, and the oil tax referenced in chapter four will yield $236 billion for a total of $2.526 trillion, almost a mirror image of the federal budget's current estimate of income.

We are sitting on a gold mine that a number of members of Congress understand and are working to implement, but the great majority of our legislators turn a blind eye to the problem and the solution. On April 30, 2008, a number of Representatives attempted to move in the right direction by proposing an amendment to the U.S. Constitution that would work toward a balanced budget. It was summarily laughed off the floor.[6] We need the last laugh in the voting booths.

Conclusion

The reality is that we have all of the knowledge from experience but are afraid to use it. The estimates I have made demonstrate that we can recover in every area, even based upon the dismal circumstance of our current economy. A simple reduction of our tax rate may easily cause GDP to grow to $20 trillion, and a flat tax of 10% will create a balanced budget without any help from Social Security taxation. The 2011 budget only calls for $1,418 billion in income taxes, $933 billion in Social Security taxes, and $144 billion in ad valorem taxes. In other words, the lowest flat tax rate in the world with a little help from oil tax could pay for all governmental obligations, eliminate federal debt, and ensure a booming economy.

Needless to say, these numbers are going to require some work. A blanket assumption of a flat tax on the entire GDP is not quite realistic. Some of the GDP would not be subject to the tax. It is entirely conceivable that we may have to copy Russia and assign a different flat tax to corporations. These are details that we leave to the accountants. The good part is these are simply the details. We know for a fact that our economy will recover by lowering taxes and the recovery will be accelerated by a flat tax. The exact numbers of the tax rates are not necessary. We simply need to act. When you are going the wrong way on a street, you will eventually turn around. Please elect a Congress willing to grab the steering wheel.

The Candidates

Arizona Representative John Shadegg spoke recently at an election law seminar. He described his excitement about the work he planned to do during his first term in office. Then came the rude awakening. He learned newly elected members are perfectly free to do their work on the house floor, but their first obligation is to seek donations for their political party.

This is not really news to most, but it helps us gain a perspective on politics. Elected representatives cannot begin work until they are in office. Even those with great plans of action are handcuffed to the trying ordeal of running for the office. It all boils down to advertising crafted to appeal to each particular segment of voters. Candidates campaigning in retirement communities will be sure to tout their protection of the Social Security and Medicare accounts, while the next day they will be in Hispanic communities berating SB 1070. Just look at the campaign brochures: "I will protect our borders," "I will work to recall the Health Care Act." On and on the promises go. They are bullet points designed to gain support and have little to do with what the candidates actually will do if they are elected. Candidates are not alone in the campaign; news media will edit the content of their reporting to cater to those they perceive will protect their chosen interests. This leaves American voters with distorted propaganda and leads them to make uninformed decisions at the ballot box.

This chapter provides an unbiased bird's-eye view of those candidates who are currently in office. I reviewed and evaluated every bill on the floor of either house of Congress since 2004 but am only discussing those since 2008. I determined whether a "yes" or "no" vote was contributory to each of the seven interests addressed in this book. Those seven issues are: (1) health care, (2) education, (3) immigration and border control, (4) oil, (5) housing and the U.S. economy, (6) freedom of religion and (7) abortion. I provide the name of each bill and, when the name is not enough, a brief description of the content. Many names and even the descriptions are misleading. What may appear to demand a "yes" vote can be very counterproductive to the issue at hand, thereby demanding a "no" just to keep the options open for future consideration. Other bills address multiple issues and have a much greater impact on something not contemplated in the title of the bill. Some of the votes relate only to consideration of a measure rather than a vote on the measure itself because the final vote was almost unanimous, thereby indicating the real difference was settled by the bill being brought to the floor.

I found 58 Senate votes and 27 House votes that directly affect the issues.[1] This means 104 senators and 444 representatives could have cast 18,020 votes, although some held office only temporarily. Following this chapter, you'll find tables that provide a set of three numbers per category for each legislator. The first number is for the number of positive votes, the second number is the number of negative votes, and the third is the total number of votes the legislator participated in. Senators score extra points for sponsorship of a bill, but I did not provide points for sponsorship in the House because the scores would have been skewed based on the limited volume of legislation in that venue.

As discussed in the freedom of religion chapter, the white cross located in the Mojave National Preserve was the subject of many efforts to save a symbol that was, on its face, a violation of the Establishment Clause. On September 24, 2003, the House voted on H.R. 2658: Department of Defense Appropriations for fiscal year 2004. This bill included Section 8121: a provision to transfer the property in the Mojave National Preserve designated as a national World War I memorial. Fifteen representatives voted "nay" on this legislation. Those nays were from: John Conyers, Jr. of Michigan, Sam Farr of California, Bob Filner of California, Jesse L. Jackson, Jr. Of Illinois, Dennis J. Kucinich of Ohio, Barbara Lee of California, Jim McDermott of Washington, James L. Oberstar of Minnesota, Major R. Owens of New York, Ron Paul of Texas, Bernard Sanders of Vermont, Janice D. Schakowsky of Illinois, Fortney Pete Stark of California, Maxine Waters of California, and Lynn C. Woolsey of California.

I need to install a disclaimer. My work in this chapter is objective in the sense that it is derived entirely from the votes cast by each member of Congress. Nevertheless, my determination of which bills are relevant is entirely subjective. Any other researcher may discard some of the records that I choose and/ or include other measures. In any case, I strongly believe that the final numbers assigned to each legislator validly reflect that person's record concerning each of the issues addressed. I strongly urge you to look into the details of every bill if you have any questions. The more that you know, the better you are prepared for the voting booth.

I. SENATE

Health Care

2010-105 (*This means that this was the 105ᵗʰ vote in the 2010 session of the Senate*); March 25, 2010; H.R. 4872; (Health Care and Education Reconciliation Act of 2010): An act to provide for reconciliation pursuant to Title II of the concurrent resolution on the budget for fiscal year 2010 (Senate Congressional Resolution 13).

2010-104; March 25, 2010; S. Amdmt. 3712 to H.R. 4872: To give states incentives to reduce fraud, waste, and abuse in their Medicaid programs.

2010-99; March 25, 2010; S. Amdmt. 3665 to H.R. 4872: To prevent the new government entitlement program from further increasing an unsustainable deficit.

2010-96; March 25, 2010; S. Amdmt. 3698 to H.R. 4872: To ensure that health care reform reduces health care costs for American families, small businesses, and taxpayers.

2010-93; March 25, 2010; S. Amdmt. 3593 to H.R. 4872: To improve access to pro bono care for medically underserved or indigent individuals by providing limited medical liability protections.

2010-87; March 25, 2010; S. Amdmt. 3681 to H.R. 4872: To allow individuals to opt out of the Medicare part A benefits.

2010-84; March 24, 2010; S. Amdmt. 3553 to H.R. 4872: To repeal the government takeover of health care.

2010-74; March 24, 2010; S. Amdmt. 3608 to H.R. 4872: To protect the right of states to opt out of a federal health care takeover.

2009-368; December 7, 2009; S. Amdmt. 2942 to S. Amdmt. 2786 to H.R. 3590 (Service Members Home Ownership Tax Act of 2009): To prevent Medicare from being raided for new entitlements and to use Medicare savings to save Medicare. (The 2010-65 bill was based on the sweetheart deals that drew votes from specific legislators for special financial benefits to their constituents at a direct cost to taxpayers.)

2009-360; December 4, 2009; S. Amdmt. 2901 to S. Amdmt. 2786 to H.R. 3590: To eliminate entitlement programs and limit the government control over the health care of American families.

2009-356; December 3, 2009; S. Amdmt. 2836 to S. Amdmt. 2786 to H.R. 3590: To ensure patients receive doctor recommendations for preventive health services, including mammograms and cervical cancer screening, without interference from government or insurance company bureaucrats.

2009-355; December 3, 2009; S. Amdmt. 2791 to S. Amdmt. 2786 to H.R. 3590: To clarify provisions relating to first dollar coverage for preventive services for women.

2009-23; January 28, 2009; S. Amdmt. 77 to H.R. 2 (Children's Health Insurance Program Reauthorization Act of 2009): To provide for the development of best practice recommendations and to ensure coverage of children from low-income families.

Immigration/Border Control/Terrorism

2010-167; May 27, 2010; S. Amdmt. 4202 to H.R. 4899 (Supplemental Appropriations Act, 2010): To make appropriations to improve border security, with an offset from unobligated appropriations under division A of Public Law 111-5.

2010-166; May 27, 2010; S. Amdmt. 4228 to S. Amdmt. 4202 to H.R. 4899: To appropriate $200,000,000 to increase resources for the Department of Justice and the Judiciary to address illegal crossings of the southwest border, with an offset.

2010-165; May 27, 2010; S. Amdmt. 4214 to H.R. 4899: To provide for National Guard support to secure the southern land border of the United States.

2010-95; March 25, 2010; S. Amdmt. 3701 to H.R. 4872 (Health Care and Education Reconciliation Act of 2010): To ensure that Americans are not required to pay for the health benefits for those here illegally by requiring the use of an effective eligibility verification system, consistent with existing law for other federal health-related programs, and also to maintain the current and well-established requirement of law, that legal immigrants should not become a "public charge" or burden to the American taxpayers, to reduce the cost of this bill, and to reduce the deficit and for other purposes.

2009-347; November 17, 2009; S. Amdmt. 2774 to S. Amdmt. 2730 to H.R. 3082 (Military Construction and Veterans Affairs Appropriations Act, 2010): To prohibit the use of funds appropriated or otherwise made available by this act to construct or modify a facility in the United States or its territories to permanently or temporarily hold any individual held at Guantanamo Bay, Cuba.

2009-338; November 5, 2009; S. Amdmt. 2669 to H.R. 2847 (Commerce, Justice, Science, and Related Agencies Appropriations Act, 2010): To prohibit the use of funds for the prosecution in Article III courts of the United States of individuals involved in the September 11, 2001 terrorist attacks.

2009-316; October 7, 2009; S. Amdmt. 2630 to H.R. 2847: To prohibit funds from being used in contravention of Section 642(a) of the Illegal Immigration Reform and Immigrant Responsibility Act of 1996.

2009-239; July 22, 2009; S. Amdmt. 1597 to S. 1390 (National Defense Authorization Act for Fiscal Year 2010): To express the sense of the Senate that the Secretary of State should redesignate North Korea as a state sponsor of terrorism.

2009-220; July 8, 2009; S. Amdmt. 1399 to S. Amdmt. 1373 to H.R. 2892 (Department of Homeland Security Appropriations Act, 2010): To require the completion of at least 700 miles of reinforced fencing along the southwest border by December 31, 2010.

2009-219; July 8, 2009; S. Amdmt. 1371 to S. Amdmt. 1373 to H.R. 2892: To make the pilot program for employment eligibility confirmation for aliens permanent and to improve verification of immigration status of employees.

2009-150; April 2, 2009; S. Amdmt. 969 to S. Con. Res. 13: To provide for a point of order against any appropriations bill that fails to fully fund the construction of the southwest border fence.

2009-93; March 10, 2009; S. Amdmt. 604 to H.R. 1105 (Omnibus Appropriations Act, 2009): To extend the pilot program for employment eligibility confirmation established in title IV of the Illegal Immigration Reform and Immigrant Responsibility Act of 1966 for 6 years.

2009-88; March 9, 2009; S. Amdmt. 631 to H.R. 1105: To require the Secretary of State to certify that funds made available for reconstruction efforts in Gaza will not be diverted to Hamas or entities controlled by Hamas.

Oil

2010-188; June 15, 2010; S. Amdmt. 4312 to S. Amdmt. 4301 to H.R. 4213 (American Workers, State, and Business Relief Act of 2010): To ensure that any new revenues to the Oil Spill Liability Trust Fund will be used for the purposes of the fund and not used as a budget gimmick to offset deficit spending.

2010-187; June 15, 2010; S. Amdmt. 4318 to S. Amdmt. 4301 to H.R. 4213: To amend the Internal Revenue Code of 1986 to eliminate big oil and gas company tax loopholes, and to use the resulting increase in revenues to reduce the deficit and to invest in energy efficiency and conservation.

2009-295; September 24, 2009; S. Amdmt. 2549 to H.R. 2996 (Department of the Interior, Environment, and Related Agencies Appropriations Act, 2010): To ensure that the Assistant to the President for Energy and Climate Change (commonly known as the "White House Climate Change Czar") is not directing actions of departments and agencies funded by this act.

2009-126; April1, 2009; S. Amdmt. 735 to S. Con. Res. 13: To prohibit the use of reconciliation in the Senate for climate change legislation involving a cap and trade system.

Housing/Economy

2010-153; May 18, 2010; S. Amdmt. 4051 to S. Amdmt. 3739 to S. 3217 (Restoring American Financial Stability Act of 2010): To prohibit taxpayer bailouts of fiscally irresponsible state and local governments.

2010-151; May 17, 2010; S. Amdmt. 4020 to S. Amdmt. 3739 to S. 3217: To limit further bailouts of Fannie Mae and Freddie Mac, to enhance the regulation and oversight of such enterprises, and for other purposes.

2010-142; May 12, 2010; S. Amdmt. 3955 to S. Amdmt. 3739 to S. 3217: To provide for a study of the asset-backed securitization process and for residential mortgage underwriting standards.

2010-141; May 12, 2010; S. Amdmt. 3962 to S. Amdmt. 3739 to S. 3217: To prohibit certain payments to loan originators and to require verification by lenders of the ability of consumers to repay loans.

2010-140; May 11, 2010; S. Amdmt. 3839 to S. Amdmt. 3739 to S. 3217: To provide for enhanced regulation of, and to establish a term certain for the conservatorships of Fannie Mae and Freddie Mac, to provide conditions for continued operation of such enterprises, to provide for the wind down of such operations and the dissolution of such enterprises, and to address budgetary treatment of such enterprises.

2010-139; May 11, 2010; S. Amdmt. 3938 to S. Amdmt. 3739 to S. 3217: To require the Secretary of the Treasury to conduct a study on ending the conservatorship of Fannie Mae and Freddie Mac, and reforming the housing finance system.

2010-60; March 18, 2010; S. Amdmt. 3475 to S. Amdmt. 3452 to H.R. 1586: To prohibit earmarks in years in which there is a deficit.

2009-281; September 16, 2009; S. Amdmt. 2361 to H.R. 3288 (Transportation, Housing and Urban Development, and Related Agencies Appropriations Act, 2010): To prohibit the use of stimulus funds for self-congratulatory signage that allows lawmakers to promote their spending of taxpayer dollars on stimulus projects.

2009-267; August 6, 2009; S. Amdmt. 2303 to H.R. 3435: To provide for a date certain for termination of the Troubled Asset Relief Program.

2009-244; July 29, 2009; S. Amdmt. 1862 to S. Amdmt. 1813 to H.R. 3183 (Energy and Water Development and Related Agencies Appropriations Act, 2010): To limit disbursement of additional funds under the Troubled Asset Relief Program to certain automobile manufacturers, to impose fiduciary duties on the Secretary of the Treasury with respect to shareholders of such automobile manufacturers, to require the issuance of shares

of common stock to eligible taxpayers which represent the common stock holdings of the United States government in such automobile manufacturers, and for other purposes.

2009-192; May 13, 2009; S. Amdmt. 1085 to S. Amdmt. 1058 to H.R. 627 (Credit Cardholders' Bill of Rights Act of 2009): To enhance public knowledge regarding the national debt by requiring the publication of the facts about the national debt on IRS instructions, federal websites, and in new legislation.

2009-181; May 5, 2009; S. Amdmt. 1026 to S. Amdmt. 1018 to S. 896 (Helping Families Save Their Homes Act of 2009): To prohibit the use of Troubled Asset Relief Program funds for the purchase of common stock, and for other purposes.

2009-179; May 5, 2009; S. Amdmt. 1030 to S. Amdmt. 1018 to S. 896: To require the Secretary of the Treasury to use any amounts repaid by a financial institution that is a recipient of assistance under the Troubled Assets Relief Program to reduce the authorization level under the TARP.

2009-174; April 30, 2009; S. Amdmt. 1014 to S. 896: To prevent mortgage foreclosures and preserve home values.

2009-148; April 2, 2009; S. Amdmt. 965 to S. Con. Res. 13: To prevent taxpayer-funded bailouts for auto manufacturers.

2009-39; February 4, 2009; S. Amdmt. 238 to S. Amdmt. 98 to H.R. 1 (American Recovery and Reinvestment Act of 2009): To ensure that the $1 trillion spending bill is not used to expand the scope of the federal government by adding new spending programs.

Abortion

2009-369; December 8, 2009; S. Amdmt. 2692 to S. Amdmt. 2786 to H.R. 3590 (Service Members Home Ownership Tax Act of 2009): To prohibit the use of federal funds for abortions.

2009-111; March 25, 2009; S. Amdmt. 715 to S. Amdmt. 692 to S. Amdmt. 687 to H.R. 1388: To clarify that nonprofit organizations assisted under the Nonprofit Capacity Building Program include certain crisis pregnancy centers and organizations that serve battered women or victims of rape or incest.

2009-81; March 5, 2009; S. Amdmt. 607 to H.R. 1105 (Omnibus Appropriations Act, 2009): To require that amounts appropriated for the United Nations Population Fund are not used by organizations which support coercive abortion or involuntary sterilization.

2009-26; January 29, 2009; S. Amdmt. 80 to H.R. 2 (Children's Health Insurance Program Reauthorization Act of 2009): To codify regulations specifying that an unborn child is eligible for child health assistance.

2009-19; January 28, 2009; S. Amdmt. 65 to H.R. 2: To restore the prohibition on funding of nongovernmental organizations promoting abortion as a method of birth control (the "Mexico City Policy").

Freedom of Religion

2009-47; February 5, 2009; S. Amdmt. 189 to S. Amdmt. 98 to H.R. 1 (American Recovery and Reinvestment Act of 2009): To allow the free exercise of religion at institutions of higher education receiving funding under section 803 of division A.

Other

2009-289; September 17, 2009; S. Amdmt. 2394 to H.R. 2996 (Department of the Interior, Environment, and Related Agencies

Appropriations Act, 2010): Prohibiting use of funds to fund the Association of Community Organizations for Reform Now (ACORN).

2009-114; March 26, 2009; S. Amdmt. 705 to S. Amdmt. 687 to H.R. 1388 (GIVE Act): To prohibit ACORN, or organizations affiliated or co-located with ACORN, from receiving assistance under this act.

2009-80; March 4, 2009; S. Amdmt. 623 to H.R. 1105 (Omnibus Appropriations Act, 2009): To prohibit taxpayer dollars from being earmarked to fourteen clients of a lobbying firm under federal investigation for making campaign donations in exchange for political favors for the group's clients.

2009-56; February 26, 2009; S. Amdmt. 107 to S. Amdmt. 98 to H.R. 1 (American Recovery and Reinvestment Act of 2009): Prohibiting direct or indirect use of funds to fund the Association of Community Organizations for Reform Now (ACORN).

2009-11; January 22, 2009; S. Amdmt. 31 to S. 181 (Lilly Ledbetter Fair Pay Act of 2009): To preserve and protect the free choice of individual employees to form, join, or assist labor organizations, or to refrain from such activities.

II. House

Reporting procedures in the House are different from those in the Senate. The descriptions for each bill noted above were part of the voting records. The House does not include descriptions and I provide brief excerpts of the summaries available in the Congressional Records when I see that an explanation is necessary.

Health Care

2010-167; March 21, 2010; H.R. 4872; Health Care and Education Reconciliation Act of 2010: The bill makes a number of health-related financing and revenue changes to the Patient Protection and Affordable Care Act enacted by H.R. 3590 and modifies higher education assistance provisions.

2010-165; March 21, 2010; H.R. 3590: Patient Protection and Affordable Care Act.

2010-60; February 24, 2010; H. Res. 1098: Providing for consideration of the bill (H.R. 4626) to restore the application of the Federal antitrust laws to the business of health insurance to protect competition and consumers.

2009-909; November 19, 2009; H.R. 3961: Medicare Physician Payment Reform Act of 2009.

2009-887; November 7, 2009; H.R. 3962; Affordable Health Care for America Act: Preservation of Access to Care for Medicare Beneficiaries and Pension Relief Act of 2010.

2009-16; January 14, 2009; H.R. 2; Children's Health Insurance Program Reauthorization Act of 2009: Allows certain state plans under titles XIX (Medicaid) or XXI (State Children's Health Insurance Program) (SCHIP, referred to in this act as CHIP) of the Social Security Act (SSA) that require state legislation to meet additional requirements imposed by this act additional time to make required plan changes.

Immigration/Border Control/Terrorism

2009-875; November 6, 2009; H.R. 2868; Chemical Facility Anti-Terrorism Act of 2009: Authorizes the Secretary of Homeland Security (DHS) to designate any chemical substance as a

substance of concern and establish the threshold quantity for each such substance after considering the potential extent of death, injury, and serious adverse effects that could result from a chemical facility terrorist incident.

Education

2009-719; September 17, 2009; H.R. 3221; Student Aid and Fiscal Responsibility Act of 2009: Amends the Higher Education Act of 1965 (the Act) to authorize and appropriate such sums as may be necessary to fully fund maximum Pell Grant amounts, beginning in FY2010.

Oil

2010-255; May 6, 2010; H.R. 5019; Home Star Energy Retrofit Act: Requires the Secretary of Energy to establish: (1) the Home Star Retrofit Rebate Program to provide rebates to contractors to be passed through as discounts to homeowners who retrofit their homes to achieve energy savings; (2) a Federal Rebate Processing System to enable rebate aggregators to submit claims for reimbursement; and (3) a national retrofit website and public information campaign to provide information on the program.

2009-943; December 9, 2009; H.R. 4213; Tax Extenders Act of 2009: Amends the Internal Revenue Code to extend through 2010: (1) the alternative motor vehicle tax credit for hybrid vehicles that are medium and heavy trucks; (2) tax credits for biodiesel and renewable diesel as fuel; (3) tax credits for producing electricity from open-loop biomass facilities and from refined coal facilities; (4) tax credits for the production of low sulfur diesel fuel and the production of fuel from coke or coke gas; (5) tax credit for new energy-efficient home expenditures; (6) excise tax credits and payments for alternative fuels; (7)

tax deferral rules for sales or dispositions by a qualified electric utility; and (8) the suspension of the taxable income limitation on percentage depletion for oil and gas from marginal wells.

2009-709; September 16, 2009; H.R. 3246; Advanced Vehicle Technology Act: Authorizes appropriations to the Secretary of Energy for research, development, demonstration, and commercial application of vehicles and related technologies for FY2010-FY2014.

2009-477; June 26, 2009; H.R. 2454; American Clean Energy and Security Act of 2009: Sets forth provisions concerning clean energy, energy efficiency, reducing global warming, pollution, transitioning to a clean energy economy, and providing for agriculture and forestry related offsets. Includes provisions: (1) creating a combined energy efficiency and renewable electricity standard and requiring retail electrical suppliers to meet 20% of their demand through renewable electricity and electricity savings by 2020; (2) setting a goal of, and requiring a strategic plan for, improving overall U.S. energy productivity by at least 2.5% per year by 2012 and maintaining that improvement rate through 2030; and (3) establishing a cap-and-trade system for greenhouse gas (GHG) emissions and setting goals for reducing such emissions from covered resources by 83% of 2005 levels by 2050.

Housing/Economy

2010-359; June 15, 2010; H.R. 5486 and H.R. 5297; The Small Business Jobs Tax Relief Act and the Small Business Lending Funds Act: Providing for consideration of the bill (H.R. 5486) to amend the Internal Revenue Code of 1986 to provide tax incentives for small business job creation, and for other purposes; and providing for consideration of the bill (H.R. 5297)

to create the Small Business Lending Fund Program to direct the Secretary of the Treasury to make capital investments in eligible institutions in order to increase the availability of credit for small businesses, and for other purposes.

2010-340; June 9, 2010; H. Res. 1424; Providing for consideration of the bill H.R. 5072, the FHA Reform Act.

2010-225; April 27, 2010; H.R. 5017; Rural Housing Preservation and Stabilization Act: Amends the Housing Act of 1949 and the Doug Bereuter Section 502 Single Family Housing Loan Guarantee Act to increase from up to 1% to up to 4% the guarantee fee on loans for housing and building on adequate farms.

2010-190; March 25, 2010; H.R. 1586: To impose an additional tax on bonuses received from TARP recipients, and for other purposes.

2010-188; March 25, 2010; H.R. 1586: Providing for consideration of the Senate amendments to H. R. 1586 to impose an additional tax on bonuses received from TARP recipients, and for other purposes.

2010-173; March 23, 2010; H. Res. 1205: Providing for consideration of the bill (H.R. 4849) to amend the Internal Revenue Code of 1986 to provide tax incentives for small business job creation, extend the Build America Bonds program, provide for other infrastructure job creation tax incentives, and for other purposes.

2010-90; March 4, 2010; H.R. 2847; Hiring Incentives to Restore Employment Act.

2010-48; February 4, 2010; H.J. Res. 45; Statutory Pay-As-You-Go Act: Increases the statutory limit of the public debt from $12.394 trillion to $14.294 trillion.

2009-968; December 11, 2009; H.R. 4173: The Wall Street Reform and Consumer Protection Act of 2009.

2009-612; July 22, 2009; H.R. 2920; Statutory Pay-As-You-Go-Act of 2009: (Sec. 4) Requires a Pay-As-You-Go (PAYGO) Act to include by reference an estimate of its budgetary effects as determined by the Congressional Budget Act of 1974 (CBA), if timely submitted for printing in the Congressional Record by the chairs of the congressional budget committees (chairs) before they vote on it.

2009-242; May 7, 2009; H.R. 1728: Mortgage Reform and Anti-Predatory Lending Act.

2009-143; March 19, 2009; H.R. 1586: To impose an additional tax on bonuses received from certain TARP recipients.

2009-104; March 5, 2009; H.R. 1106: Helping Families Save Their Homes Act of 2009.

2009-26; January 21, 2009; H.R. 384: TARP Reform and Accountability Act.

Other

2010-391; June 24, 2010; H.R. 5175; Democracy is Strengthened by Casting Light on Spending in Elections Act or the DISCLOSE Act: Title I: Regulation of Certain Political Spending (Sec. 101) Amends the Federal Election Campaign Act (FECA) to prohibit: (1) independent expenditures and payments for electioneering communications by government contractors if the value of the contract is at least $10 million; (2) recipients of assistance under the Troubled Asset Relief Program (TARP) of the Emergency Economic Stabilization Act of 2008 (EESA) from making any contribution to any political party, committee, or candidate for public office, or to any other person for any political purpose or use, or from making any independent expenditure or disbursing any funds for an electioneering communication; and (3) persons who enter into negotiations for an oil or gas exploration, development, or production lease under the Outer Continental Shelf Lands Act from making any contribution to any political party, committee, or candidate for public office or to any person for any political purpose or use, or from making an independent expenditure or disbursing any funds for an electioneering communication.

Valuable Information

Thus far, I have only discussed incumbents' voting records. That is like assuming there is only one book in the library.

1. If you are not certain who your representative is, you can go to www.vote-smart.com and find the names of your lawmakers based on your zip code.

2. Your senators' and representatives' biographies, lists of committees they serve on, telephone numbers, addresses, and some Facebook and Twitter accounts can be found via links at www.senate.gov and www.house.gov.

3. The Center for Responsive Politics at www.opensecrets. org analyzes where candidates get their campaign funding and how it is spent. Click on "Politicians & Elections" and follow the menu options.

4. The Center for Responsive Politics also provides annual personal financial disclosure information for each lawmaker as derived from their required disclosures to the Clerk of the House and Secretary of the Senate. Click on "Politicians & Elections" and then "personal finances."

5. Another source for information concerning all incumbents' voting is www.opencongress.org.

6. Who pays for legislators' trips? Go to www.legistorm.com/trip.html and follow the menu options.

7. All of the bills each legislator has sponsored are listed at the Library of Congress: http://thomas.loc.gov.

8. How each representative spends his/her budget is posted in quarterly expense reports at http://disbursements.house.gov/. The Senate information is not yet available.

9. Interest groups rate each lawmaker and post it at www.vote-smart.com. Click on "Congress" and select your lawmaker.

10. C-SPAN ranks each lawmaker by the number of days that they speak on the floor of the House or Senate and provides links to each appearance: www.c-spanarchives.org/congress/.

Final Word

This chapter is intended to be a tool to assist voters in preparing for the coming elections. The fact that any candidate may have a perfect or an imperfect score is simply something to be weighed against other relevant factors. The Congressional Records are valuable sources of information providing insight that may not otherwise be available in campaign rhetoric or from the media.

For example, take a look at Nancy Pelosi's voting record. She voted only 11 of the 27 times when matters relevant to issues addressed in this book were on the floor. Another interesting fact is that the records of every vote list the "Aye," "Nay," "Present," and "Not Voting" members. Despite this, I never found any record that listed Ms. Pelosi as "Not Voting" because, being the Speaker, she elected not to have that as part of the record.

Another interesting detail concerns Jeff Flake of Arizona. In all of my research, I noticed he was proposing amendments to almost every piece of legislation. I looked at those amendments and they all had the words "prohibit funding," "prohibit earmarks," or something of that nature. He attacked government expenditures of as little as $90,000 all the way up into the billions. He even objected to some funding for pork-barrel projects in the State of Arizona. It is sometimes considered to be politically suicidal to reduce funding to your state. If every member of Congress were that careful about deficit spending, we might not be in such a financial crisis.

In 2008, I ran for Justice of the Peace in the newly formed Desert Ridge Precinct of Maricopa County, Arizona. I lost that election because I ran a very poor political campaign. I had the naive belief that voters would be interested in the candidates' backgrounds, abilities, and most importantly, their plans to serve the electorate. I didn't use postcards with catch phrases like "I will protect our borders" or "I will be strict on crime." My postcard was a relatively detailed discussion of my plans to accelerate the criminal court's administration, to make the court system and forms more user-friendly, and to create better online access for the convenience of the public. I was endorsed by almost every police organization in the cities, county, state, and federal government. I was the only Justice of the Peace candidate in the state endorsed by Arizona Right to Life and by Arizona's 2006 Republican gubernatorial candidate Len Munsil. I lost that election because I didn't really understand how the advertising and marketing of candidates works. I gave a detailed dissertation to questions that demanded a "yes" or "no" answer. Today is different. I believe that the electorate is very interested in learning about what each candidate is willing to do for our nation's future.

I wrote this book based on the belief that America has awakened from its placid status quo. A huge share of our population is crying for what is right. The Tea Party is not a temporary fit of anger but a force to be reckoned with. My goal is to enable enough voters to understand the truth and vote effectively to serve our nation's needs. An even greater goal is one that is shared with me by a number of congressional candidates; we need to keep pushing for the reforms that only Congress can provide. My vision of having every state in the union pass legislation to give unborn fetuses a legislative conclusion of viability at 8, 10, 12, 14, 16, 18 and 20 weeks is only one example. We don't know what we can do until we give it a try, and we need to elect congresspersons who are willing to ply their labors.

The viability legislation for the unborn is only one of the tasks before us. Every chapter of this book demands action by the electorate. Members of Congress are our employees and they answer to us! Our decayed system of education needs repair. The health care environment needs a reform stimulated by Health Savings Accounts and protecting the medical community from frivolous litigation. Congress must address immigration by doing away with entitlements to illegal aliens and protection for those who are productive members of our communities. We must stimulate the harvesting of our nation's oil reserves and provide the foundation for a strong economy.

You, the electorate, are the only ones to hold our legislators accountable. Be well-informed and cast your votes wisely!

God bless America!

SENATE	OVERALL	HEALTH CARE	IMMIGRATION	OIL	HOUSING/ECONOMY	ABORTION	RELIGION	OTHER
AL-Sessions	60-0-55	14-0-14	17-0-13	4-0-4	15-0-15	5-0-4	1-0-1	4-0-4
AL-Shelby	59-1-58	14-0-14	13-0-13	4-0--4	17-1-16	5-0-5	1-0-1	5-0-5
AK-Begich	6-51-56	1-12-13	1-12-13	3-1-4	0-16-15	0-5-5	0-1-1	1-4-5
AK-Murkowski	51-8-54	16-0-14	10-3-10-	4-0-4	13-2-15	3-2-5-	1-0-1	4-1-5-
AZ-Kyl	65-0-58	14-0-14	18-0-13	4-0-4	17-0-16	6-0-5	1-0-1	5-0-5
AZ-McCain	69-0-58	16-0-14	17-0-13	4-0-4	19-0-16	6-0-5	1-0-1	6-0-5
AR-Lincoln	20-36-56	3-11-14-	8-5-13-	2-2-4-	5-9-14-	0-5-5	0-1-1	2-3-5-
AR-Pryor	17-41-58	1-13-14-	8-5-13-	2-2-4-	4-12-16-	1-4-5-	0-1-1	1-4-5-
CA-Boxer	6-53-57	0-14-13	4-9-13-	0-4-4	1-16-16-	0-5-5	0-1-1	1-4-5-
CA-Feinstein	6-52-58	0-14-14	4-9-13-	0-4-4	2-14-16-	0-5-5	0-1-1	0-5-5
CO-Bennett	8-50-58	0-14-14	1-12-13-	2-2-4-	3-13-16-	0-5-5	0-1-1	2-3-5-
CO-Udall	6-51-57	1-12-13-	1-12-13-	1-3-4-	2-14-16-	0-5-5	0-1-1	1-4-5-
CT-Dodd	2-60-58	0-15-14	0-13-13	1-3-4-	0-19-16	0-5-5	0-1-1	1-4-5-
CT-Lieberman	12-47-58	1-13-14-	8-6-13-	2-2-4-	0-16-16	0-5-5	0-1-1	1-4-5-
DE-Carper	4-54-58	2-12-14-	0-13-13	0-4-4	1-15-16-	0-5-5	0-1-1	1-4-5-
DE-Kaufman	2-55-57	0-14-14	0-13-13	0-4-4	0-15-15	1-4-5-	0-1-1	1-4-5-
FL-Lemieux	33-0-31	14-0-13	7-0-7	1-0-1	9-0-8	1-0-1		1-0-1
FL-Martinez	21-6-25	1-0-1	4-2-6-	1-0-1	5-3-8-	6-0-4	1-0-1	3-1-4-
FL-Nelson	7-51-58	0-14-14	4-9-13-	0-4-4	1-15-16-	0-5-5	0-1-1	2-3-5-
GA-Chambliss	58-0-56	14-0-14	12-0-11	4-0-4	17-0-16	5-0-5	1-0-1	5-0-5
GA-Isakson	54-0-48	7-0-5	13-0-12	4-0-4	17-0-16	6-0-5	1-0-1	6-0-5
HI-Akaka	0-58-58	0-14-14	0-13-13	0-4-4	0-16-16	0-5-5	0-1-1	0-5-5-
HI-Inouye	1-57-58	0-14-14	0-13-13	0-4-4	0-16-16	0-5-5	0-1-1	1-4-5-
ID-Crapo	62-0-58	15-0-14	13-0-13	4-0-4	18-0-16	6-0-5	1-0-1	5-0-5
ID-Risch	59-0-58	14-0-14	13-0-13	4-0-4	16-0-16	6-0-5	1-0-1	5-0-5
IL-Burris	0-57-57	0-14-14	0-13-13	0-4-4	0-16-16	0-5-5	0-1-1	0-4-4
IL-Durbin	0-59-58	0-14-14	0-13-13	0-4-4	0-17-16	0-5-5	0-1-1	0-5-5
IN-Bayh	28-31-58	3-11-14-	9-5-13-	2-2-4-	8-8-16-	2-3-5-	1-0-1	3-2-5-
IN-Lugar	47-11-58	13-1-14	9-4-13-	4-0-4	10-6-16-	5-0-5	1-0-1	5-0-5
IA-Grassley	59-2-58	14-0-14	13-0-13	5-0-4	14-2-16	7-0-5	1-0-1	5-0-5
IA-Harkin	0-58-56	0-15-14	0-12-12	0-4-4	0-16-15	0-5-5	0-1-1	0-5-5-
KS-Brownback	65-1-58	14-0-14	14-0-13	5-0-4	15-1-16	9-0-5	2-0-1	6-0-5
KS-Roberts	63-1-56	14-0-14	14-0-13	4-0-2	17-1-16	7-0-5	1-0-1	6-0-5
KY-Bunning	63-1-57	14-0-13	13-0-13	5-0-4	15-1-16	8-0-5	2-0-1	6-0-5
KY-MccONNELL	57-1-58	14-0-14	13-0-13	4-0-4	15-1-16	5-0-5	1-0-1	5-0-5
LA-Landrieu	9-46-55	1-12-13-	4-9-13-	3-1-4-	1-15-16-	0-4-4	0-1-1	0-4-4
LA-Vitter	71-1-58	15-1-14	14-0-13	5-0-4	18-0-16	9-0-5	2-0-1	8-0-5
ME-Collins	45-15-58	13-2-14	11-2-13-	4-0-4	13-4-16	0-5-5	0-1-1	4-1-5-
ME-Snowe	41-19-58	12-3-14-	11-2-13-	3-1-4-	11-6-16-	0-5-5	0-1-1	4-1-5-
MD-Cardin	2-57-58	0-15-14	0-13-13	0-4-4	1-15-16-	0-5-5	0-1-1	1-4-5-
MD-Mikulski	1-54-54	0-15-14	0-12-12	0-4-4	0-13-13	0-5-5	0-1-1	1-4-5-
MA-Brown	20-5-22	9-1-9-	4-0-4	2-0-2	5-4-7			
MA-Kennedy								
MA-Kerry	2-58-58	0-15-14	0-13-13	1-3-4-	0-17-16	0-5-5	0-1-1	1-4-5-
MA-Kirk	0-8-8	0-4-4	0-3-3			0-1-1		
MI-Levin	2-57-58	0-14-14	0-13-13	1-3-4-	0-17-16	0-5-5	0-1-1	1-4-5-
MI-Stabenow	3-56-58	0-15-14	1-12-13-	1-3-4-	0-16-16	0-5-5	0-1-1	1-4-5-
MN-Franken	1-39-38	0-14-13	0-10-10	0-3-3	0-11-10	0-1-1		1-0-1
MN-Klobuchar	13-46-58	1-13-14-	6-7-13-	1-3-4-	3-14-16-	0-5-5	0-1-1	2-3-5-
MS-Cochran	55-3-58	14-0-14	11-2-13-	4-0-4	15-1-16	5-0-5	1-0-1	5-0-5
MS-Wicker	60-1-58	14-0-14	13-0-13	4-0-4	15-1-16	8-0-5	1-0-1	5-0-5
MO-Bond	54-4-56	12-0-12	13-0-13	4-0-4	14-3-16	6-0-5	1-0-1	4-1-5-

SENATE	OVERALL	HEALTH CARE	IMMIGRATION	OIL	HHOUSING/ ECONOMY	ABORTION	RELIGION	OTHER
MO-McCaskill	14-44-58	2-12-14-	6-7-13-	2-2-4-	3-13-16-	0-5-5	0-1-1	1-4-5-
MT-Baucus	12-45-57	1-13-14-	5-8-13-	2-2-4-	2-13-15-	0-5-5	0-1-1	2-3-5-
MT-Tester	12-47-58	0-15-14	5-8-13-	2-2-4-	3-13-16-	0-5-5	0-1-1	2-3-5-
NE-Johanns	61-2-54	17-0-14	11-0-11	5-0-4	16-1-16	7-0-4	1-0-1	4-1-4-
NE-Nelson	39-21-58	8-6-14-	10-3-13-	4-0-4	6-10-16-	7-0-5	1-0-1	3-2-5-
NV-Ensign	60-1-58	15-0-14	12-1-13-	4-0-4	16-0-16	7-0-5	1-0-1	5-0-5
NV-Reid	1-58-58	0-14-14	0-13-13	0-4-4	0-17-16	0-5-5	0-1-1	1-4-5-
NH-Gregg	62-4-55	15-0-14	14-1-13	4-0-4	20-2-15	6-0-5		3-1-4-
NH-Shaheen	4-53-56	0-15-14	0-12-12	0-4-4	3-12-15-	0-5-5	0-1-1	1-4-5-
NJ-Lautenberg	1-58-57	0-14-13	0-13-13	0-5-4	0-16-16	0-5-5	0-1-1	1-4-5-
NJ-Menendez	1-58-58	0-14-14	0-13-13	0-5-4	0-16-16	0-5-5	0-1-1	1-4-5-
NM-Bingaman	3-55-58	1-13-14-	0-13-13	2-2-4-	0-16-16	0-5-5	0-1-1	0-5-5
NM-Udall	2-56-58	0-14-14	0-13-13	1-3-4-	0-16-16	0-5-5	0-1-1	1-4-5-
NY-Gillibrand	2-56-57	0-15-14	0-13-13	0-4-4	2-14-16-	0-5-5	0-1-1	0-4-4
NY-Schumer	3-59-58	0-15-14	1-12-13-	0-5-4	1-17-16-	0-5-5	0-1-1	1-4-5-
NC-Burr	64-1-58	17-0-14	13-0-13	4-0-4	18-1-16	5-0-5	1-0-1	6-0-5
NC-Hagan	7-50-57	0-14-14	1-11-12-	3-1-4-	1-15-16-	0-5-5	0-1-1	2-3-5-
ND-Conrad	11-45-56	0-14-14	2-11-13-	3-1-4-	2-14-16-	2-2-4-	1-0-1	1-3-4-
ND-Dorgan	11-46-57	0-14-14	2-11-13-	3-1-4-	3-13-16-	1-4-5-	1-0-1	1-3-4-
OH-Brown	1-58-58	0-15-14	0-13-13	0-4-4	0-16-16	0-5-5	0-1-1	1-4-5-
OH-Voinovich	45-13-58	13-1-14	8-5-13-	4-0-4	11-5-16-	5-0-5	1-0-1	3-2-5-
OK-Coburn	68-1-58	17-0-14	14-0-13	4-0-4	17-1-16	9-0-5	1-0-1	6-0-5
OK-Inhofe	65-1-58	14-0-14	14-0-13	5-0-4	15-1-16	9-0-5	2-0-1	6-0-5
OR-Merkley	4-55-58	0-14-14	2-11-13-	1-3-4-	0-17-16	0-5-5	0-1-1	1-4-5-
OR-Wyden	3-56-58	0-14-14	2-11-13-	0-5-4	0-16-16	0-5-5	0-1-1	1-4-5-
PA-Casey	7-53-58	0-14-14	0-13-13	1-3-4-	0-16-16	6-1-5-	0-1-1	0-5-5
PA-Specter	12-46-56	0-16-14	3-10-13-	1-3-4-	3-11-14-	1-4-5-	1-0-1	3-2-5-
RI-Reed	1-57-58	0-14-14	0-13-13	0-4-4	0-16-16	0-5-5	0-1-1	1-4-5-
RI-Whitehouse	0-59-57	0-14-14	0-13-13	0-5-4	0-16-15	0-5-5	0-1-1	0-5-5
SC-DeMint	67-0-58	14-0-14	14-0-13	4-0-4	18-0-16	8-0-5	2-0-1	7-0-5
SC-Graham	61-0-58	14-0-14	15-0-13	4-0-4	16-0-16	6-0-5	1-0-1	5-0-5
SD-Johnson	2-53-55	0-14-14	0-13-13	0-3-3	1-13-14-	0-5-5	0-1-1	1-4-5-
SD-Thune	68-0-58	16-0-14	13-0-13	4-0-4	18-0-16	9-0-5	2-0-1	6-0-5
TN-Alexander	57-3-58	15-0-14	13-0-13	4-0-4	15-2-16	5-0-5	1-0-1	4-1-5-
TN-Corker	59-5-58	15-0-14	11-2-13-	4-0-4	16-3-16	7-0-5	1-0-1	5-0-5
TX-Cornin	66-0-58	17-0-14	16-0-13	4-0-4	16-0-16	7-0-5	1-0-1	5-0-5
TX-Hutchison	63-2-56	16-0-14	14-0-12	4-0-4	16-2-16	7-0-5	1-0-1	5-0-4
UT-Bennett	61-2-55	13-0-13	14-0-12	4-0-4	16-2-15	7-0-5	1-0-1	6-0-5
UT-Hatch	59-2-58	14-0-14	14-0-13	4-0-4	14-2-16	7-0-5	1-0-1	5-0-5
VT-Leahy	0-58-57	0-15-14	0-13-13	0-4-4	0-15-15	0-5-5	0-1-1	0-5-5
VT-Sanders	0-59-58	0-14-14	0-13-13	0-5-4	0-16-16	0-5-5	0-1-1	0-5-5
VA-Warner	6-52-58	1-13-14-	1-12-13-	2-2-4-	1-15-16-	0-5-5	0-1-1	1-4-5-
VA-Webb	14-46-58	3-11-14-	8-7-13-	2-2-4-	0-16-16	0-5-5	0-1-1	1-4-5-
WA-Cantwell	4-53-57	0-13-13	1-12-13-	1-3-4-	1-15-16-	0-5-5	0-1-1	1-4-5-
WA-Murray	1-56-56	0-15-14	0-13-13	1-3-4-	0-15-15	0-5-5	0-1-1	0-4-4
WV-Byrd	5/20/25	0-5-5	0-3-3	1-0-1	1-5-6-	0-4-4	0-1-1	3-2-5-
WV-Rockefeller	4-48-52	0-14-14	2-11-13-	1-3-4-	0-10-10	0-5-5	0-1-1	1-4-5-
WI-Feingold	12-46-58	1-13-14-	1-12-13-	1-3-4-	7-9-16-	0-5-5	0-1-1	2-3-5-
WI-Kohl	5-53-58	0-14-14	1-12-13-	1-3-4-	2-14-16-	0-5-5	0-1-1	1-4-5-
WY-Barrasso	65-0-58	15-0-14	13-0-13	5-0-4	18-0-16	7-0-5	1-0-1	6-0-5
WY-Enzi	68-0-57	17-0-14	13-0-13	5-0-4	18-0-16	8-0-4	2-0-1	5-0-5

HOUSE	OVERALL	HEALTH CARE	IMMIGRATION	EDUCATION	OIL	HOUSING/ECONOMY	OTHER
AL 4th-Aderholt	23-3-26	6-0-6		1-0-1	3-1-4	12-2-14	1-0-1
AL 6th-Bachus	24-2-26	6-0-6	1-0-1	1-0-1	3-1-4	12-1-13	1-0-1
AL 1st-Bonner	24-2-26	6-0-6	1-0-1	1-0-1	2-1-3	13-1-14	1-0-1
Al 2nd-Bright	17-10-27	5-1-6	1-0-1	0-1-1	1-3-4	9-5-14	1-0-1
AL 7th-Davis, Artur	4-18-22	3-3-6	0-1-1	0-1-1	1-2-3	0-10-10	0-1-1
AL 5th-Griffith	16-11-27	4-2-6	1-0-1	0-1-1	2-2-4	8-6-14	1-0-1
AL 3rd-Rogers, Mike	22-5-27	5-1-6	1-0-1	1-0-1	3-1-4	11-3-14	1-0-1
AK Young, D.	19-6-25	5-1-6	1-0-1	1-0-1	3-1-4	8-4-12	1-0-1
AR 1st-Berry	6-19-25	2-4-6	1-0-1	0-1-1	1-3-4	2-10-12	0-1-1
AR 3rd-Boozman	25-2-27	6-0-6	1-0-1	1-0-1	4-0-4	12-2-14	1-0-1
AR 4th-Ross	6-21-27	3-3-6	1-0-1	0-1-1	1-3-4	1-13-14	0-1-1
AR 2nd-Snyder	1-25-26	0-5-5	0-1-1	0-1-1	0-4-4	1-13-14	0-1-1
AZ 6th-Flake	26-0-26	6-0-6	1-0-1	1-0-1	3-0-3	14-0-14	1-0-1
AZ 2nd-Franks	27-0-27	6-0-6	1-0-1	1-0-1	4-0-4	14-0-14	1-0-1
AZ 8th-Giffords	2-24-26	1-5-6	0-1-1	0-1-1	0-4-4	1-12-13	0-1-1
AZ 7th-Grijalva	2-25-27	0-6-6	0-1-1	0-1-1	0-4-4	2-12-14	0-1-1
AZ 1st-Kirkpatrick	9-18-27	0-6-6	0-1-1	0-1-1	2-2-4	7-7-14	0-1-1
AZ 5th-Mitchell	12-15-27	1-5-6	0-1-1	0-1-1	2-2-4	8-6-14	1-0-1
AZ 4th-Pastor	3-24-27	0-6-6	0-1-1	0-1-1	0-4-4	3-11-14	0-1-1
AZ 3rd-Shadegg	27-0-27	6-0-6	1-0-1	1-0-1	4-0-4	14-0-14	1-0-1
CA 43rd-Baca	0-26-26	0-6-6	0-1-1	0-1-1	0-4-4	0-13-13	0-1-1
CA 31st-Becerra	0-26-26	0-6-6	0-1-1	0-1-1	0-4-4	0-13-13	0-1-1
CA 28th-Berman	0-27-27	0-6-6	0-1-1	0-1-1	0-4-4	0-14-14	0-1-1
CA 50th-Bilbray	21-6-27	6-0-6	1-0-1	1-0-1	2-2-4	10-4-14	1-0-1
CA 45th-Bono Mack	21-6-27	5-1-6	1-0-1	1-0-1	3-1-4	10-4-14	1-0-1
CA 44th-Calvert	23-3-26	6-0-6	1-0-1	1-0-1	3-1-4	11-2-13	1-0-1
CA 48th-Campbell	22-1-23	6-0-6	1-0-1	1-0-1	3-0-3	10-1-11	1-0-1
CA 23rd-Capps	0-24-24	0-6-6	0-1-1	0-1-1	0-3-3	0-12-12	0-1-1
CA 18th-Cardoza	3-24-27	0-6-6	1-0-1	0-1-1	0-4-4	2-12-14	0-1-1
CA 32nd-Chu	0-21-21	0-5-5	0-1-1	0-1-1	0-3-3	0-10-10	0-1-1
CA 20th-Costa	4-22-26	0-6-6	1-0-1		1-3-4	2-12-14	0-1-1
CA 53rd-Davis, Susan	0-27-27	0-6-6	0-1-1	0-1-1	0-4-4	0-14-14	0-1-1
CA 26th-Dreier	25-2-27	6-0-6	1-0-1	1-0-1	4-0-4	12-2-14	1-0-1
CA 14th-Eshoo	0-26-26	0-6-6	0-1-1	0-1-1	0-4-4	0-13-13	0-1-1
CA 17th-Farr	0-27-27	0-6-6	0-1-1	0-1-1	0-4-4	0-14-14	0-1-1
CA 51st-Filner	2-24-26	0-6-6	0-1-1	0-1-1	0-3-3	2-12-14	0-1-1
CA 24th-Gallegly	25-2-27	6-0-6	1-0-1	1-0-1	4-0-4	12-2-14	1-0-1
CA 10th-Garamendi	0-18-18	0-5-5	0-1-1		0-2-2	0-9-9	0-1-1
CA 36th-Harman	0-25-25	0-6-6	0-1-1	0-1-1	0-4-4	0-12-12	0-1-1
CA 2nd-Herger	26-1-27	6-0-6	1-0-1	1-0-1	4-0-4	13-1-14	1-0-1
CA 15th-Honda	0-26-26	0-6-6	0-1-1	0-1-1	0-4-4	0-13-13	0-1-1
CA 52nd-Hunter	27-0-27	6-0-6	1-0-1	1-0-1	4-0-4	14-0-14	1-0-1

HOUSE	OVERALL	HEALTH CARE	IMMIGRATION	EDUCATION	OIL	HOUSING/ ECONOMY	OTHER
CA 49th-Issa	26-1-27	6-0-6	1-0-1	1-0-1	4-0-4	13-1-14	1-0-1
CA 9th-Lee, Barbara	2-25-27	0-6-6	0-1-1	0-1-1	0-4-4	2-12-14	0-1-1
CA 41st-Lewis, Jerry	26-1-27	6-0-6	1-0-1	1-0-1	4-0-4	13-1-14	1-0-1
CA 16th-Lofgren	0-26-26	0-6-6	0-1-1	0-1-1	0-4-4	0-13-13	0-1-1
CA 3rd-Lungren	25-2-27	6-0-6	1-0-1	1-0-1	4-0-4	12-2-14	1-0-1
CA 5th-Matsui	0-27-27	0-6-6	0-1-1	0-1-1	0-4-4	0-14-14	0-1-1
CA 22nd-McCarthy, K.	25-1-26	6-0-6	1-0-1	1-0-1	3-0-3	13-1-14	1-0-1
CA 4th-McClintock	26-1-27	6-0-6	1-0-1	1-0-1	4-0-4	13-1-14	1-0-1
CA 25th-McKeon	26-1-27	6-0-6	1-0-1	1-0-1	4-0-4	13-1-14	1-0-1
CA 11th-McNerney	1-26-27	0-6-6	0-1-1	0-1-1	0-4-4	1-13-14	0-1-1
CA 42nd-Miller, Gary	21-3-24	6-0-6	1-0-1	1-0-1	3-1-4	9-2-11	1-0-1
CA 7th-Miller, George	0-26-26	0-5-5	0-1-1	0-1-1	0-4-4	0-14-14	0-1-1
CA 38th-Napolitano	0-26-26	0-6-6	0-1-1	0-1-1	0-4-4	0-13-13	0-1-1
CA 21st-Nunes	26-0-26	6-0-6	1-0-1		4-0-4	14-0-14	1-0-1
CA 8th-Pelosi	0-11-11	0-4-4		0-1-1	0-1-1	0-4-4	0-1-1
CA 19th-Radanovich	20-1-21	5-0-5	1-0-1		3-0-3	10-1-11	1-0-1
CA 37th-Richardson	1-25-26	0-6-6	0-1-1	0-1-1	0-4-4	1-12-13	0-1-1
CA 46th-Rohrabacher	23-4-27	6-0-6	1-0-1	1-0-1	3-1-4	11-3-14	1-0-1
CA 34th-Roybal-Allard	0-27-27	0-6-6	0-1-1	0-1-1	0-4-4	0-14-14	0-1-1
CA 40th-Royce	26-1-27	6-0-6	1-0-1	1-0-1	4-0-4	13-1-14	1-0-1
CA 39th-Sanchez, Linda	0-26-26	0-6-6		0-1-1	0-4-4	0-14-14	0-1-1
CA 47th-Sanchez, Loretta	0-26-26	0-6-6	0-1-1	0-1-1	0-3-3	0-14-14	0-1-1
CA 29th-Schiff	0-27-27	0-6-6	0-1-1	0-1-1	0-4-4	0-14-14	0-1-1
CA 27th-Sherman	0-26-26	0-5-5	0-1-1	0-1-1	0-4-4	0-14-14	0-1-1
CA 32nd-Solis							
CA 12th-Speier	0-27-27	0-6-6	0-1-1	0-1-1	0-4-4	0-14-14	0-1-1
CA 13th-Stark	2-21-23	0-5-5	0-1-1	0-1-1	1-3-4	1-10-11	0-1-1
CA 10th-Tauscher	0-6-6	0-1-1			0-1-1	0-4-4	
CA 1st-Thompson, M.	0-27-27	0-6-6	0-1-1	0-1-1	0-4-4	0-14-14	0-1-1
CA 35th-Waters	4-22-26	0-6-6		0-1-1	0-4-4	3-11-14	1-0-1
CA 33rd-Watson	0-26-26	0-6-6	0-1-1	0-1-1	0-4-4	0-13-13	0-1-1
CA 30th-Waxman	0-27-27	0-6-6	0-1-1	0-1-1	0-4-4	0-14-14	0-1-1
CA 6th-Woolsey	0-27-27	0-6-6	0-1-1	0-1-1	0-4-4	0-14-14	0-1-1
CO 6th-Coffman	26-0-26	6-0-6	1-0-1	1-0-1	4-0-4	13-0-13	1-0-1
CO 1st-DeGette	0-26-26	0-6-6	0-1-1	0-1-1	0-3-3	0-14-14	0-1-1
CO 5th-Lamborn	27-0-27	6-0-6	1-0-1	1-0-1	4-0-4	14-0-14	1-0-1
CO 4th-Markey, B.	3-24-27	1-5-6	1-0-1	0-1-1	0-4-4	1-13-14	0-1-1
CO 7th-Perlmutter	0-27-27	0-6-6	0-1-1	0-1-1	0-4-4	0-14-14	0-1-1
CO 2nd-Polis	2-25-27	0-6-6	0-1-1	0-1-1	1-3-4	1-13-14	0-1-1
CO 3rd-Salazar	1-26-27	0-6-6	0-1-1	0-1-1	1-3-4	0-14-14	0-1-1
CT 2nd-Courtney	0-27-27	0-6-6	0-1-1	0-1-1	0-4-4	0-14-14	0-1-1
CT 3rd-DeLauro	0-27-27	0-6-6	0-1-1	0-1-1	0-4-4	0-14-14	0-1-1

HOUSE	OVERALL	HEALTH CARE	IMMIGRATION	EDUCATION	OIL	HOUSING/ECONOMY	OTHER
CT 4th-Himes	1-26-27	0-6-6	0-1-1	0-1-1	1-3-4	0-14-14	0-1-1
CT 1st-Larson	0-27-27	0-6-6	0-1-1	0-1-1	0-4-4	0-14-14	0-1-1
CT 5th-Murphy, C.	0-27-27	0-6-6	0-1-1	0-1-1	0-4-4	0-14-14	0-1-1
DE Castle	15-12-27	5-1-6	1-0-1	1-0-1	1-3-4	7-7-14	0-1-1
FL 9th-Bilirakis	22-3-25	6-0-6	1-0-1	1-0-1	4-0-4	9-3-12	1-0-1]
FL 2nd-Boyd	4-20-24	1-5-6	0-1-1	1-0-1	0-3-3	1-11-12	1-0-1
FL 3rd-Brown, Corrine	1-24-25	0-6-6	0-1-1	0-1-1	0-3-3	1-12-13	0-1-1
FL 5th-Brown-Waite	21-4-25	5-0-5	1-0-1	1-0-1	4-0-4	9-4-13	1-0-1
FL 13th-Buchanan	20-7-27	5-1-6	1-0-1	0-1-1	4-0-4	9-5-14	1-0-1
FL11th-Castor	0-27-27	0-6-6	0-1-1	0-1-1	0-4-4	0-14-14	0-1-1
FL 4th-Crenshaw	25-2-27	6-0-6	1-0-1	1-0-1	4-0-4	12-2-14	1-0-1
FL 19th-Deutch	0-4-4				0-1-1	0-2-2	0-1-1
FL 21st-Diaz-Balart, L.	19-8-27	5-1-6	1-0-1	1-0-1	3-1-4	8-6-14	1-0-1
FL 25th-Diaz-Balart, M.	19-8-27	5-1-6	1-0-1	1-0-1	3-1-4	8-6-14	1-0-1
FL 8th-Grayson	0-27-27	0-6-6	0-1-1	0-1-1	0-4-4	0-14-14	0-1-1
FL 23rd-Hastings, A.	2-24-26	0-6-6	0-1-1	0-1-1	0-3-3	1-13-14	1-0-1
FL 22nd-Klein	1-26-27	0-6-6	0-1-1	0-1-1	1-3-4	0-14-14	0-1-1
FL 24th-Kosmas	3-24-27	2-4-6	0-1-1	0-1-1	0-4-4	1-13-14	0-1-1
FL 14th-Mack	27-0-27	6-0-6	1-0-1	1-0-1	4-0-4	14-0-14	1-0-1
FL 17th-Meek	0-27-27	0-6-6	0-1-1	0-1-1	0-4-4	0-14-14	0-1-1
FL 7th-Mica	26-1-27	6-0-6	1-0-1	1-0-1	4-0-4	13-1-14	1-0-1
FL 1st-Miller, Jeff	26-0-26	6-0-6	1-0-1	1-0-1	4-0-4	13-0-13	1-0-1
FL 15th-Posey	25-2-27	6-0-6	1-0-1	1-0-1	3-1-4	13-1-14	1-0-1
FL 12th-Putnam	24-3-27	6-0-6	1-0-1	1-0-1	3-1-4	12-2-14	1-0-1
FL 16th-Rooney	25-2-27	6-0-6	1-0-1	1-0-1	4-0-4	12-2-14	1-0-1
FL 18th-Ros-Lehtinen	20-7-27	5-1-6	1-0-1	0-1-1	3-1-4	10-4-14	1-0-1
FL 6th-Stearns	25-2-27	6-0-6	1-0-1	1-0-1	4-0-4	12-2-14	1-0-1
FL 20th-Wasserman Schultz	0-27-27	0-6-6	0-1-1	0-1-1	0-4-4	0-14-14	0-1-1
FL 19th-Wexler	1-13-15	0-3-3	0-1-1	0-1-1	1-2-3	0-6-6	
FL 10th-Young, C. W. Bill	21-5-26	5-1-6	1-0-1	1-0-1	4-0-4	9-4-13	1-0-1
GA 12th-Barrow	5-22-27	3-3-6	0-1-1	0-1-1	1-3-4	0-14-14	1-0-1
GA 2nd-Bishop, Jr., Sanford D.	1-27-28	0-6-6	0-1-1	0-1-1	0-4-4	0-14-14	1-0-1
GA 10th-Broun	27-0-27	6-0-6	1-0-1	1-0-1	4-0-4	14-0-14	1-0-1
GA 9th-Deal	19-0-19	6-0-6	1-0-1	1-0-1	3-0-3	8-0-8	
GA 11th-Gingrey	27-0-27	6-0-6	1-0-1	1-0-1	4-0-4	14-0-14	1-0-1
GA 9th-Graves, T.	2-0-2					1-0-1	1-0-1
GA 4th-Johnson, H.	1-26-27	0-6-6	0-1-1	0-1-1	0-4-4	1-13-14	0-1-1
GA 1st-Kingston	27-0-27	6-0-6	1-0-1	1-0-1	4-0-4	14-0-14	1-0-1
GA 5th-Lewis, John	0-25-25	0-6-6	0-1-1	0-1-1	0-3-3	0-13-13	0-1-1
GA 7th-Linder	24-0-24	6-0-6	1-0-1	1-0-1	4-0-4	11-0-11	1-0-1
GA 8th-Marshall	9-18-27	4-2-6	1-0-1	0-1-1	2-2-4	1-13-14	1-0-1
GA 6th-Price, T.	26-0-26	6-0-6	1-0-1	1-0-1	4-0-4	13-0-13	1-0-1

HOUSE	OVERALL	HEALTH CARE	IMMIGRATION	EDUCATION	OIL	HOUSING/ ECONOMY	OTHER
GA 13th-Scott, D.	0-27-27	0-6-6	0-1-1	0-1-1	0-4-4	0-14-14	0-1-1
GA 3rd-Westmoreland	27-0-27	6-0-6	1-0-1	1-0-1	4-0-4	14-0-14	1-0-1
HI 1st-Abercrombie	0-15-15	0-4-4	0-1-1		0-3-3	0-7-7	
HI 1st-Djou	3-0-3					2-0-2	1-0-1
HI 2nd-Hirono	0-27-27	0-6-6	0-1-1	0-1-1	0-4-4	0-14-14	0-1-1
ID 1st-Minnick	13-14-27	4-2-6	1-0-1	0-1-1	1-3-4	6-8-14	1-0-1
ID 2nd-Simpson	23-4-27	5-1-6	1-0-1	1-0-1	4-0-4	11-3-14	1-0-1
IL 8th-Bean	4-22-26	0-6-6	0-1-1	0-1-1	1-3-4	2-11-13	1-0-1
IL 13th-Biggert	20-7-27	6-0-6	1-0-1	0-1-1	2-2-4	10-4-14	1-0-1
IL 12th-Costello	2-25-27	0-6-6	0-1-1	0-1-1	2-2-4	0-14-14	0-1-1
IL 7th-Davis, Danny K.	2-24-26	0-6-6	0-1-1	0-1-1	0-4-4	1-12-13	1-0-1
IL 14th-Foster	1-25-27	0-6-6	0-1-1	0-1-1	1-3-4	0-14-14	0-1-1
IL 4th-Gutierrez	0-26-26	0-6-6	0-1-1	0-1-1	0-4-4	0-13-13	0-1-1
IL 11th-Halvorson	4-23-27	0-6-6	1-0-1	0-1-1	0-4-4	3-11-14	0-1-1
IL 17th-Hare	1-26-27	0-6-6	1-0-1	0-1-1	0-4-4	0-14-14	0-1-1
IL 2nd-Jackson, Jr.	1-26-27	0-6-6	0-1-1	0-1-1	0-4-4	1-13-14	0-1-1
IL 15th-Johnson, T.	21-6-27	6-0-6	1-0-1	0-1-1	3-1-4	10-4-14	1-0-1
IL 10th-Kirk	20-7-27	5-1-6	1-0-1	1-0-1	2-2-4	10-4-14	1-0-1
IL 3rd-Lipinski	2-25-27	2-4-6	0-1-1	0-1-1	0-4-4	0-14-14	0-1-1
IL 16th-Manzullo	24-2-26	6-0-6	1-0-1	1-0-1	4-0-4	11-2-13	1-0-1
IL 5th-Quigley	1-22-23	0-5-5	0-1-1	0-1-1	0-4-4	1-10-11	0-1-1
IL 6th-Roskam	26-1-27	6-0-6	1-0-1	1-0-1	4-0-4	13-1-14	1-0-1
IL 1st-Rush	2-25-27	0-6-6	0-1-1	0-1-1	0-4-4	1-13-14	1-0-1
IL 9th-Schakowsky	0-27-27	0-6-6	0-1-1	0-1-1	0-4-4	0-14-14	0-1-1
IL 18th-Schock	22-5-27	6-0-6	1-0-1	1-0-1	3-1-4	10-4-14	1-0-1
IL 19th-Shimkus	24-3-27	6-0-6	1-0-1	1-0-1	4-0-4	11-3-14	1-0-1
IN 5th-Burton	26-1-27	6-0-6	1-0-1	1-0-1	4-0-4	13-1-14	1-0-1
IN 4th-Buyer	20-3-23	5-0-5	1-0-1	1-0-1	3-1-4	9-2-11	1-0-1
IN 7th-Carson	0-27-27	0-6-6	0-1-1	0-1-1	0-4-4	0-14-14	0-1-1
IN 2nd-Donnelly	2-25-27	0-6-6	0-1-1	0-1-1	1-3-4	0-14-14	1-0-1
IN 8th-Ellsworth	4-22-26	1-5-6	0-1-1	0-1-1	1-3-4	2-11-13	0-1-1
IN 9th-Hill	8-19-27	1-5-6	0-1-1	0-1-1	0-4-4	6-8-14	1-0-1
IN 6th-Pence	26-0-26	6-0-6	1-0-1	1-0-1	4-0-4	14-0-14	
IN 3rd-Souder	18-3-21	6-0-6	1-0-1	1-0-1	3-1-4	7-2-9	
IN 1st-Visclosky	3-23-26	0-6-6	0-1-1	0-1-1	1-3-4	2-12-14	
IA 3rd-Boswell	0-27-27	0-6-6	0-1-1	0-1-1	0-4-4	0-14-14	0-1-1
IA 1st-Braley	0-27-27	0-6-6	0-1-1	0-1-1	0-4-4	0-14-14	0-1-1
IA 5th-King,S.	27-0-27	6-0-6	1-0-1	1-0-1	4-0-4	14-0-14	1-0-1
IA 4th-Latham	23-4-27	6-0-6	1-0-1	1-0-1	4-0-4	10-4-14	1-0-1
IA 2nd-Loebsack	0-27-27	0-6-6	0-1-1	0-1-1	0-4-4	0-14-14	0-1-1
KS 2nd-Jenkins	23-4-27	6-0-6	1-0-1	1-0-1	3-1-4	11-3-14	1-0-1
KS 3rd-Moore, D.	0-27-27	0-6-6	0-1-1	0-1-1	0-4-4	0-14-14	0-1-1

HOUSE	OVERALL	HEALTH CARE	IMMIGRATION	EDUCATION	OIL	HOUSING/ ECONOMY	OTHER
KS 1st-Moran, Jerry	22-5-27	5-1-6	1-0-1	1-0-1	4-0-4	10-4-14	1-0-1
KS 4th-Tiahrt	23-2-25	6-0-6	1-0-1	1-0-1	4-0-4	10-2-12	1-0-1
KY 6th-Chandler	4-21-25	3-3-6		0-1-1	0-3-3	1-13-14	0-1-1
KY 4th-Davis, Geoff	24-3-27	6-0-6	1-0-1	1-0-1	3-1-4	12-2-14	1-0-1
KY 2nd-Guthrie	24-2-26	6-0-6	1-0-1	1-0-1	3-0-3	12-2-14	1-0-1
KY 5th-Rogers, H.	24-3-27	6-0-6	1-0-1	1-0-1	3-1-4	12-2-14	1-0-1
KY 1st-Whitfield	22-4-26	6-0-6	1-0-1	1-0-1	2-1-3	11-3-14	1-0-1
KY 3rd-Yarmuth	0-26-26	0-6-6	0-1-1	0-1-1	0-4-4	0-13-13	0-1-1
LA 5th-Alexander	25-2-27	6-0-6	1-0-1	1-0-1	4-0-4	12-2-14	1-0-1
LA 7th-Boustany Jr.	25-1-26	6-0-6	1-0-1	1-0-1	4-0-4	12-1-13	1-0-1
LA 2nd-Cao	15-11-26	4-2-6	1-0-1	0-1-1	1-3-4	9-4-13	0-1-1
LA 6th-Cassidy	24-2-26	6-0-6	1-0-1	1-0-1	4-0-4	11-2-13	1-0-1
LA 4th-Fleming	26-1-27	6-0-6	1-0-1	1-0-1	4-0-4	13-1-14	1-0-1
LA 3rd-Melancon	5-19-24	3-2-5	0-1-1	0-1-1	1-2-3	1-12-13	0-1-1
LA 1st-Scalise	26-0-26	6-0-6	1-0-1	1-0-1	4-0-4	13-0-13	1-0-1
ME 1st-Pingree	0-27-27	0-6-6	0-1-1	0-1-1	0-4-4	0-14-14	0-1-1
MD 6th-Bartlett	23-4-27	6-0-6	1-0-1	1-0-1	2-2-4	12-2-14	1-0-1
MD 7th-Cummings	0-27-27	0-6-6	0-1-1	0-1-1	0-4-4	0-14-14	0-1-1
MD 4th-Edwards, D.	2-25-27	0-6-6	0-1-1	0-1-1	0-4-4	1-13-14	1-0-1
MD 5th-Hoyer	0-27-27	0-6-6	0-1-1	0-1-1	0-4-4	0-14-14	0-1-1
MD 1st-Kratovil, Jr.	7-20-27	3-3-6	0-1-1	0-1-1	0-4-4	3-11-14	1-0-1
MD 2nd-Ruppersberger	0-26-26	0-6-6	0-1-1	0-1-1	0-4-4	0-13-13	0-1-1
MD 3rd-Sarbanes	0-27-27	0-6-6	0-1-1	0-1-1	0-4-4	0-14-14	0-1-1
MD 8th-Van Hollen	0-27-27	0-6-6	0-1-1	0-1-1	0-4-4	0-14-14	0-1-1
MA 8th-Capuano	0-27-27	0-6-6	0-1-1	0-1-1	0-4-4	0-14-14	0-1-1
MA 10th-Delahunt	0-25-25	0-6-6	0-1-1	0-1-1	0-3-3	0-13-13	0-1-1
MA 4th-Frank	0-26-26	0-6-6	0-1-1		0-4-4	0-14-14	0-1-1
MA 9th-Lynch	1-25-26	1-5-6	0-1-1	0-1-1	0-4-4	0-13-13	0-1-1
MA 7th-Markey,E.	0-27-27	0-6-6	0-1-1	0-1-1	0-4-4	0-14-14	0-1-1
MA 3rd-McGovern	0-27-27	0-6-6	0-1-1	0-1-1	0-4-4	0-14-14	0-1-1
MA 2nd-Neal	0-26-26	0-6-6	0-1-1	0-1-1	0-4-4	0-13-13	0-1-1
MA 1st-Olver	0-27-27	0-6-6	0-1-1	0-1-1	0-4-4	0-14-14	0-1-1
MA 6th-Tierney	0-26-26	0-6-6	0-1-1	0-1-1	0-4-4	0-13-13	0-1-1
MA 5th-Tsongas	0-27-27	0-6-6	0-1-1	0-1-1	0-4-4	0-14-14	0-1-1
MI 4th-Camp	21-6-27	6-0-6	1-0-1	1-0-1	2-2-4	10-4-14	1-0-1
MI 1st-Childers	9-18-27	4-2-6	0-1-1	0-1-1	1-3-4	3-11-14	1-0-1
MI 14th-Conyers	1-24-25	0-6-6	0-1-1		0-4-4	1-12-13	0-1-1
MI 15th-Dingell	0-26-26	0-5-5	0-1-1	0-1-1	0-4-4	0-14-14	0-1-1
MI 3rd-Ehlers	14-10-24	5-1-6		1-0-1	2-2-4	5-7-12	1-0-1
MI 3rd-Harper	27-0-27	6-0-6	1-0-1	1-0-1	4-0-4	14-0-14	1-0-1
MI 2nd-Hoekstra	16-3-19	5-0-5	1-0-1	1-0-1	2-1-3	7-2-9	
MI 5th-Kildee	0-27-27	0-6-6	0-1-1	0-1-1	0-4-4	0-14-14	0-1-1

HOUSE	OVERALL	HEALTH CARE	IMMIGRATION	EDUCATION	OIL	HOUSING/ ECONOMY	OTHER
MI 13t-Kilpatrick	3-22-25	0-6-6	0-1-1	0-1-1	0-4-4	2-10-12	1-0-1
MI 12th-Levin	0-27-27	0-6-6	0-1-1	0-1-1	0-4-4	0-14-14	0-1-1
MI 11th-McCotter	20-7-27	5-1-6	1-0-1	1-0-1	3-1-4	9-5-14	1-0-1
MI 10th-Miller, C.	19-7-26	5-1-6	1-0-1	1-0-1	3-1-4	8-5-13	1-0-1
MI 9th-Peters	1-26-27	0-6-6	0-1-1	0-1-1	0-4-4	1-13-14	0-1-1
MI 8th-Rogers, Mike	21-5-26	6-0-6		1-0-1	3-1-4	10-4-14	1-0-1
MI 7th-Schauer	1-26-27	0-6-6	0-1-1	0-1-1	1-3-4	0-14-14	0-1-1
MI 1st-Stupak	3-23-26	0-6-6	0-1-1	0-1-1	0-4-4	3-10-13	0-1-1
MI 6th-Upton	20-7-27	5-1-6	1-0-1	1-0-1	3-1-4	9-5-14	1-0-1
MN 6th-Bachmann	26-1-27	6-0-6	1-0-1	1-0-1	4-0-4	13-1-14	1-0-1
MN 5th-Ellison	0-26-26	0-6-6	0-1-1	0-1-1	0-4-4	0-13-13	0-1-1
MN 2nd-Kline	26-1-27	6-0-6	1-0-1	1-0-1	4-0-4	13-1-14	1-0-1
MN 4th-McCollum	0-26-26	0-6-6	0-1-1	0-1-1	0-3-3	0-14-14	0-1-1
MN 2nd-Michaud	0-27-27	0-6-6	0-1-1	0-1-1	0-4-4	0-14-14	0-1-1
MN 8th-Oberstar	0-26-26	0-6-6	0-1-1	0-1-1	0-4-4	0-13-13	0-1-1
MN 3rd-Paulsen	24-3-27	5-1-6	1-0-1	1-0-1	3-1-4	13-1-14	1-0-1
MN 7th-Peterson	6-21-27	4-2-6	0-1-1	0-1-1	0-4-4	1-13-14	1-0-1
MN 1st-Walz	0-27-27	0-6-6	0-1-1	0-1-1	0-4-4	0-14-14	0-1-1
MS 2d-Akin	27-0-27	6-0-6	1-0-1	1-0-1	4-0-4	14-0-14	1-0-1
MS 7th-Blunt	22-2-24	5-0-5	1-0-1	1-0-1	4-0-4	11-2-13	
MS 3rd-Carnahan	0-27-27	0-6-6	0-1-1	0-1-1	0-4-4	0-14-14	0-1-1
MS 1st-Clay Jr.	2-23-25	0-5-5	0-1-1	0-1-1	0-4-4	2-11-13	0-1-1
MS 5th-Cleaver	1-25-26	0-6-6		0-1-1	0-4-4	1-13-14	0-1-1
MS 8th-Emerson	21-6-27	5-1-6	1-0-1	1-0-1	3-1-4	10-4-14	1-0-1
MS 6th-Graves, S.	26-1-27	6-0-6	1-0-1	1-0-1	4-0-4	13-1-14	1-0-1
MS 9th-Luetkemeyer	26-1-27	6-0-6	1-0-1	1-0-1	4-0-4	13-1-14	1-0-1
MS 4th-Taylor	16-11-27	4-2-6	1-0-1	0-1-1	2-2-4	8-6-14	1-0-1
MS 2nd-Thompson, B.	2-24-26	0-6-6	0-1-1	0-1-1	0-4-4	1-12-13	1-0-1
MO 4th-Skelton	5-22-27	3-3-6	1-0-1	0-1-1	0-4-4	1-13-14	0-1-1
MT Rehberg	24-3-27	5-1-6	1-0-1	1-0-1	4-0-4	12-2-14	1-0-1
NE 1st-Fortenberry	24-2-26	6-0-6	1-0-1	1-0-1	4-0-4	11-2-13	1-0-1
NE 3rd-Smith, Adrian	25-2-27	6-0-6	1-0-1	1-0-1	3-1-4	13-1-14	1-0-1
NE 2nd-Terry	23-4-27	6-0-6	1-0-1	1-0-1	3-1-4	11-3-14	1-0-1
NV 1st-Berkley	0-26-26	0-6-6	0-1-1	0-1-1	0-4-4	0-13-13	0-1-1
NV 2nd-Heller	24-2-26	6-0-6	1-0-1	1-0-1	4-0-4	11-2-13	1-0-1
NV 3rd-Titus	0-27-27	0-6-6	0-1-1	0-1-1	0-4-4	0-14-14	0-1-1
NH 2nd-Hodes	0-26-26	0-6-6	0-1-1	0-1-1	0-4-4	0-13-13	0-1-1
NH 1st-Shea-Porter	0-27-27	0-6-6	0-1-1	0-1-1	0-4-4	0-14-14	0-1-1
NJ 3rd-Adler	4-22-26	3-3-6	0-1-1	0-1-1	0-4-4	1-12-13	0-1-1
NJ 1st-Andrews	0-27-27	0-6-6	0-1-1	0-1-1	0-4-4	0-14-14	0-1-1
NJ 11th-Frelinghuysen	23-4-27	5-1-6	1-0-1	1-0-1	3-1-4	12-2-14	1-0-1
NJ 5th-Garrett	27-0-27	6-0-6	1-0-1	1-0-1	4-0-4	14-0-14	1-0-1

HOUSE	OVERALL	HEALTH CARE	IMMIGRATION	EDUCATION	OIL	HOUSING/ ECONOMY	OTHER
NJ 12t-Holt	0-26-26	0-6-6	0-1-1	0-1-1	0-4-4	0-13-13	0-1-1
NJ 7th-Lance	19-8-27	5-1-6	1-0-1	1-0-1	2-2-4	9-5-14	1-0-1
NJ 2nd-LoBiondo	20-7-27	5-1-6	1-0-1	1-0-1	2-2-4	10-4-14	1-0-1
NJ 6th-Pallone, Jr.	0-26-26	0-6-6	0-1-1	0-1-1	0-4-4	0-13-13	0-1-1
NJ 8th-Pascrell, Jr.	0-27-27	0-6-6	0-1-1	0-1-1	0-4-4	0-14-14	0-1-1
NJ 10th-Payne	2-25-27	0-6-6	0-1-1	0-1-1	0-4-4	1-13-14	1-0-1
NJ 9th-Rothman	0-26-26	0-6-6	0-1-1	0-1-1	0-4-4	0-14-14	
NJ 13th-Sires	1-26-27	0-6-6	0-1-1	0-1-1	0-4-4	1-13-14	0-1-1
NJ 4th-Smith, Chris	20-7-27	5-1-6	1-0-1	1-0-1	2-2-4	10-4-14	1-0-1
NM 1st-Heinrich	0-27-27	0-6-6	0-1-1	0-1-1	0-4-4	0-14-14	0-1-1
NM 3rd-Lujan	1-26-27	0-6-6	0-1-1	0-1-1	0-4-4	1-13-14	0-1-1
NM 2nd-Teague	7-20-27	3-3-6	1-0-1	0-1-1	1-3-4	2-12-14	0-1-1
NY 5th-Ackerman	0-27-27	0-6-6	0-1-1	0-1-1	0-4-4	0-14-14	0-1-1
NY 24th-Arcuri	3-24-27	2-4-6	0-1-1	0-1-1	1-3-4	0-14-14	0-1-1
NY 1st-Bishop, Timothy	0-27-27	0-6-6	0-1-1	0-1-1	0-4-4	0-14-14	0-1-1
NY 11th-Clarke	2-25-27	0-6-6	0-1-1	0-1-1	0-4-4	1-13-14	1-0-1
NY 7th-Crowley	0-26-26	0-6-6	0-1-1	0-1-1	0-4-4	0-13-13	0-1-1
NY 17th-Engel	1-26-27	0-6-6	0-1-1	0-1-1	0-4-4	1-13-14	0-1-1
NY 20th-Gillibrand	0-2-2	0-1-1				0-1-1	
NY 19th-Hall, J.	0-27-27	0-6-6	0-1-1	0-1-1	0-4-4	0-14-14	0-1-1
NY 27th-Higgins	0-26-26	0-5-5	0-1-1	0-1-1	0-4-4	0-14-14	0-1-1
NY 22nd-Hinchey	1-24-25	0-6-6	0-1-1	0-1-1	0-3-3	1-12-13	0-1-1
NY 2nd-Israel	0-27-27	0-6-6	0-1-1	0-1-1	0-4-4	0-14-14	0-1-1
NY 3rd-King, P.	22-5-27	5-1-6	1-0-1	1-0-1	3-1-4	11-3-14	1-0-1
NY 26th-Lee, Christopher	22-5-27	5-1-6	1-0-1	1-0-1	3-1-4	11-3-14	1-0-1
NY 18th-Lowey	0-26-26	0-6-6	0-1-1	0-1-1	0-4-4	0-13-13	0-1-1
NY 25th-Maffei	2-25-27	0-6-6	0-1-1	0-1-1	1-3-4	1-13-14	0-1-1
NY 14th-Maloney	0-27-27	0-6-6	0-1-1	0-1-1	0-4-4	0-14-14	0-1-1
NY 29th-Massa	4-12-16	1-3-4	0-1-1	0-1-1	1-2-3	2-5-7	
NY 4th-McCarthy, C.	1-25-26	0-6-6	0-1-1	0-1-1	0-4-4	0-13-13	1-0-1
NY 23rd-McHugh	1-5-6	0-1-1			0-1-1	1-3-4	
NY 13th-McMahon	6-21-27	4-2-6	0-1-1	1-0-1	0-4-4	1-13-14	0-1-1
NY 6th-Meeks	0-25-25	0-5-5	0-1-1	0-1-1	0-4-4	0-13-13	0-1-1
NY 20th-Murphy, S.	4-19-23	2-3-5	0-1-1	0-1-1	0-4-4	2-9-11	0-1-1
NY 8th-Nadler	0-26-26	0-6-6	0-1-1	0-1-1	0-4-4	0-13-13	0-1-1
NY 23rd-Owens	1-17-18	0-5-5	0-1-1		0-2-2	0-9-9	1-0-1
NY 15th-Rangel	0-26-26	0-6-6	0-1-1	0-1-1	0-4-4	0-13-13	0-1-1
NY 16th-Serrano	0-27-27	0-6-6	0-1-1	0-1-1	0-4-4	0-14-14	0-1-1
NY 28th-Slaughter	0-25-25	0-6-6	0-1-1	0-1-1	0-4-4	0-12-12	0-1-1
NY 21st-Tonko	0-27-27	0-6-6	0-1-1	0-1-1	0-4-4	0-14-14	0-1-1
NY 10th-Towns	1-25-26	0-5-5	0-1-1	0-1-1	0-4-4	1-13-14	0-1-1
NY 12th-Velazquez	0-27-27	0-6-6	0-1-1	0-1-1	0-4-4	0-14-14	0-1-1

HOUSE	OVERALL	HEALTH CARE	IMMIGRATION	EDUCATION	OIL	HOUSING/ ECONOMY	OTHER
NY 9th-Weiner	2-25-27	0-6-6	0-1-1	0-1-1	0-4-4	2-12-14	0-1-1
NC 1st-Butterfield	1-26-27	0-6-6	0-1-1	0-1-1	0-4-4	0-14-14	1-0-1
NC 6th-Coble	25-2-27	6-0-6	1-0-1	1-0-1	3-1-4	13-1-14	1-0-1
NC 2nd-Etheridge	0-27-27	0-6-6	0-1-1	0-1-1	0-4-4	0-14-14	0-1-1
NC 5th-Foxx	27-0-27	6-0-6	1-0-1	1-0-1	4-0-4	14-0-14	1-0-1
NC 3rd-Jones	21-6-27	6-0-6	1-0-1	1-0-1	2-2-4	10-4-14	1-0-1
NC 8th-Kissell	6-21-27	3-3-6	0-1-1	0-1-1	1-3-4	2-12-14	0-1-1
NC 10th-McHenry	26-1-27	6-0-6	1-0-1	1-0-1	4-0-4	13-1-14	1-0-1
NC 7th-McIntyre	9-28-27	3-3-6	0-1-1	0-1-1	1-3-4	4-10-14	1-0-1
NC 13th-Miller, B.	0-27-27	0-6-6	0-1-1	0-1-1	0-4-4	0-14-14	0-1-1
NC 9th-Myrick	26-0-26	6-0-6	1-0-1	1-0-1	4-04	13-0-13	1-0-1
NC 4th-Price, D.	0-27-27	0-6-6	0-1-1	0-1-1	0-4-4	0-14-14	0-1-1
NC 11th-Shuler	9-18-27	4-2-6	0-1-1	0-1-1	0-4-4	5-9-14	0-1-1
NC 12th-Watt	2-25-27	0-6-6	0-1-1	0-1-1	0-4-4	1-13-14	1-0-1
ND Pomeroy	1-26-27	0-6-6	0-1-1	0-1-1	1-3-4	0-14-14	0-1-1
OH 7th-Austria	13-14-27	5-1-6	1-0-1	1-0-1	3-1-4	2-12-14	1-0-1
OH 16th-Boccieri	2-25-27	1-5-6	1-0-1	0-1-1	0-4-4	0-14-14	0-1-1
OH 8th-Boehner	26-1-27	6-0-6	1-0-1	1-0-1	4-0-4	13-1-14	1-0-1
OH 1st-Driehaus	1-26-27	0-6-6	0-1-1	0-1-1	0-4-4	1-13-14	0-1-1
OH 11th-Fudge	2-24-26	0-6-6	0-1-1	0-1-1	0-3-3	1-13-14	1-0-1
OH 4th-Jordan	26-0-26	6-0-6	1-0-1	1-0-1	4-0-4	13-0-13	1-0-1
OH 9th-Kaptur	1-24-25	0-6-6	0-1-1	0-1-1	0-3-3	1-12-13	0-1-1
OH 15th-Kilroy	0-27-27	0-6-6	0-1-1	0-1-1	0-4-4	0-14-14	0-1-1
OH 10th-Kucinich	5-22-27	1-5-6	0-1-1	0-1-1	1-3-4	3-11-14	0-1-1
OH 14th-LaTourette	20-7-27	5-1-6	1-0-1	1-0-1	3-1-4	9-5-14	1-0-1
OH 5th-Latta	26-1-27	6-0-6	1-0-1	1-0-1	4-0-4	13-1-14	1-0-1
OH 17th-Ryan, T.	0-27-27	0-6-6	0-1-1	0-1-1	0-4-4	0-14-14	0-1-1
OH 2nd-Schmidt	26-1-27	6-0-6	1-0-1	1-0-1	4-0-4	13-1-14	1-0-1
OH 18th-Space	5-22-27	2-4-6	1-0-1	0-1-1	0-4-4	2-12-14	0-1-1
OH 13th-Sutton	0-27-27	0-6-6	0-1-1	0-1-1	0-4-4	0-14-14	0-1-1
OH 12th-Tiberi	20-6-26	5-1-6	1-0-1	1-0-1	3-1-4	9-4-13	1-0-1
OH 3rd-Turner	19-8-27	5-1-6	1-0-1	1-0-1	3-1-4	8-6-14	1-0-1
OH 6th-Wilson, C.	1-25-26	0-6-6	0-1-1	0-1-1	1-3-4	0-13-13	0-1-1
OK 2nd-Boren	11-16-27	4-2-6	1-0-1	0-1-1	2-2-4	3-11-14	1-0-1
OK 4th-Cole	25-2-27	6-0-6	1-0-1	1-0-1	4-0-4	12-2-14	1-0-1
OK 5th-Fallin	24-0-24	6-0-6	1-0-1	1-0-1	4-0-4	11-0-11	1-0-1
OK 3rd-Lucas	25-2-27	6-0-6	1-0-1	1-0-1	3-1-4	13-1-14	1-0-1
OK 1st-Sullivan	24-1-25	5-0-5	1-0-1	1-0-1	3-0-3	13-1-14	1-0-1
OR 3rd-Blumenauer	0-26-26	0-6-6	0-1-1	0-1-1	0-3-3	0-14-14	0-1-1
OR 4th-DeFazio	1-26-27	0-6-6	0-1-1	0-1-1	1-3-4	0-14-14	0-1-1
OR 5th-Schrader	4-23-27	0-6-6	0-1-1	0-1-1	1-3-4	3-11-14	0-1-1
OR 2nd-Walden	24-3-27	6-0-6	1-0-1	1-0-1	4-0-4	11-3-14	1-0-1

HOUSE	OVERALL	HEALTH CARE	IMMIGRATION	EDUCATION	OIL	HOUSING/ECONOMY	OTHER
OR 1st-Wu	0-27-27	0-6-6	0-1-1	0-1-1	0-4-4	0-14-14	0-1-1
PA 4th-Altmire	5-22-27	3-3-6	0-1-1	0-1-1	1-3-4	1-13-14	0-1-1
PA 1st-Brady,Robert	0-27-27	0-6-6	0-1-1	0-1-1	0-4-4	0-14-14	0-1-1
PA 10th-Carney	2-25-27	0-6-6	0-1-1	0-1-1	1-3-4	1-13-14	0-1-1
PA 12th-Critz	1-2-3					0-2-2	1-0-1
PA 3rd-Dahlkemper	4-22-26	1-5-6	0-1-1	0-1-1	1-3-4	1-12-13	1-0-1
PA 15th-Dent	21-6-27	5-1-6	1-0-1	1-0-1	3-1-4	10-4-14	1-0-1
PA 14th-Doyle	0-27-27	0-6-6	0-1-1	0-1-1	0-4-4	0-14-14	0-1-1
PA 2nd-Fattah	0-27-27	0-6-6	0-1-1	0-1-1	0-4-4	0-14-14	0-1-1
PA 6th-Gerlach	21-6-27	5-1-6	1-0-1	1-0-1	3-1-4	10-4-14	1-0-1
PA 17th-Holden	7-20-27	3-3-6	0-1-1	0-1-1	1-3-4	2-12-14	1-0-1
PA 11th-Kanjorski	2-25-27	0-6-6	0-1-1	1-0-1	1-3-4	0-14-14	0-1-1
PA 8th-Murphy, Patrick	0-26-26	0-6-6		0-1-1	0-4-4	0-14-14	0-1-1
PA 18th-Murphy, Tim	19-8-27	5-1-6	1-0-1	1-0-1	2-2-4	9-5-14	1-0-1
PA 12th-Murtha	0-13-13	0-3-3	0-1-1	0-1-1	0-2-2	0-6-6	
PA 16th-Pitts	23-2-25	5-0-5	1-0-1	1-0-1	2-1-3	13-1-14	1-0-1
PA 19th-Platts	20-7-27	5-1-6	1-0-1	0-1-1	3-1-4	10-4-14	1-0-1
PA 13th-Schwartz	0-26-26	0-6-6	0-1-1	0-1-1	0-4-4	0-13-13	0-1-1
PA 7th-Sestak	0-26-26	0-6-6	0-1-1	0-1-1	0-3-3	0-14-14	0-1-1
PA 9th-Shuster	25-2-27	6-0-6	1-0-1	1-0-1	3-1-4	13-1-14	1-0-1
PA 5th-Thompson, G.	23-3-26	5-1-6	1-0-1	1-0-1	4-0-5	11-2-13	1-0-1
RI 1st-Kennedy	0-23-23	0-5-5	0-1-1	0-1-1	0-3-3	0-12-12	0-1-1
RI 2nd-Langevin	0-27-27	0-6-6	0-1-1	0-1-1	0-4-4	0-14-14	0-1-1
SC 3d-Barrett	17-0-17	5-0-5	1-0-1		1-0-1	10-0-10	
SC 1st-Brown, Henry	23-1-24	5-0-5	1-0-1	1-0-1	4-0-4	12-1-13	
SC 6th-Clyburn	0-27-27	0-6-6	0-1-1	0-1-1	0-4-4	0-14-14	0-1-1
SC 4th-Inglis	25-1-26	6-0-6	1-0-1	1-0-1	3-1-4	13-0-13	1-0-1
SC 5th-Spratt	0-26-26	0-5-5	0-1-1	0-1-1	0-4-4	0-14-14	0-1-1
SC 2nd-Wilson, J.	26-1-27	6-0-6	1-0-1	1-0-1	4-0-4	13-1-14	1-0-1
SD Herseth Sandlin	11-16-27	4-2-6	1-0-1	1-0-1	1-3-4	3-11-14	1-0-1
TN 7th-Blackburn	26-0-26	6-0-6	1-0-1	1-0-1	3-0-3	14-0-14	1-0-1
TN 9th-Cohen	2-25-27	0-6-6	0-1-1	0-1-1	0-4-4	2-12-14	0-1-1
TN 5th-Cooper	1-26-27	0-6-6	0-1-1	0-1-1	0-4-4	1-13-14	0-1-1
TN 4th-Davis, Lincoln	8-16-24	3-3-6	1-0-1	0-1-1	1-3-4	2-9-11	1-0-1
TN 2nd-Duncan Jr.	24-3-27	6-0-6	1-0-1	1-0-1	4-0-4	11-3-14	1-0-1
TN 6th-Gordon	2-25-27	1-5-6	0-1-1	0-1-1	0-4-4	1-13-14	0-1-1
TN 1st-Roe	25-2-27	6-0-6	1-0-1	1-0-1	4-0-4	12-2-14	1-0-1
TN 8th-Tanner	6-19-25	3-3-6	0-1-1		1-2-3	2-12-14	0-1-1
TN 3rd-Wamp	19-2-21	6-0-6	1-0-1	1-0-1	2-1-3	9-1-10	
TX 6th-Barton	23-3-26	6-0-6	1-0-1	1-0-1	2-1-3	12-2-14	1-0-1
TX 8th-Brady, Kevin	26-0-26	5-0-5	1-0-1	1-0-1	4-0-4	14-0-14	1-0-1
TX 26th-Burgess	25-2-27	5-1-6	1-0-1	1-0-1	4-0-4	13-1-14	1-0-1

HOUSE	OVERALL	HEALTH CARE	IMMIGRATION	EDUCATION	OIL	HOUSING/ ECONOMY	OTHER
TX 31st-Carter	23-0-23	5-0-5		1-0-1	3-0-3	13-0-13	1-0-1
TX 11th-Conaway	26-0-26	6-0-6		1-0-1	4-0-4	14-0-14	1-0-1
TX 28th-Cuellar	1-26-27	0-6-6	0-1-1	0-1-1	0-4-4	1-13-14	0-1-1
TX 7th-Culberson	25-1-26	6-0-6	1-0-1	1-0-1	4-0-4	12-1-13	1-0-1
TX 25th-Doggett	1-26-27	0-6-6	0-1-1	0-1-1	0-4-4	1-13-14	0-1-1
TX 17th-Edwards, C.	7-20-27	4-2-6	0-1-1	0-1-1	1-3-4	2-12-14	0-1-1
TX 1st-Gohmert	23-2-25	6-0-6	1-0-1	1-0-1	3-1-4	11-1-12	1-0-1
TX 20th-Gonzalez	0-26-26	0-6-6	0-1-1	0-1-1	0-4-4	0-13-13	0-1-1
TX 12th-Granger	26-0-26	6-0-6	1-0-1	1-0-1	3-0-3	14-0-14	1-0-1
TX 9th-Green, Al	1-26-27	0-6-6	0-1-1	0-1-1	0-4-4	1-13-14	0-1-1
TX 29th-Green, Gene	0-26-26	0-6-6	0-1-1	0-1-1	0-4-4	0-13-13	0-1-1
TX 4th-Hall, R.	23-4-27	6-0-6	1-0-1	1-0-1	2-2-4	12-2-14	1-0-1
TX 5th-Hensarling	27-0-27	6-0-6	1-0-1	1-0-1	4-0-4	14-0-14	1-0-1
TX 15th-Hinojosa	0-26-26	0-6-6	0-1-1	0-1-1	0-4-4	0-13-13	0-1-1
TX 18th-Jackson, Lee	11-16-27	0-6-6	0-1-1	0-1-1	0-4-4	11-3-14	0-1-1
TX 30th-Johnson, E. B.	0-27-27	0-6-6	0-1-1	0-1-1	0-4-4	0-14-14	0-1-1
TX 3rd-Johnson, Sam	27-0-27	6-0-6	1-0-1	1-0-1	4-0-4	14-0-14	1-0-1
TX 24th-Marchant	27-0-27	6-0-6	1-0-1	1-0-1	4-0-4	14-0-14	1-0-1
TX 10th-McCaul	24-2-26	5-0-5	1-0-1	1-0-1	4-0-4	12-2-14	1-0-1
TX 19th-Neugebauer	25-1-26	6-0-6	1-0-1	1-0-1	4-0-4	12-1-13	1-0-1
TX 22nd-Olson	25-1-26	6-0-6	1-0-1	1-0-1	4-0-4	12-1-13	1-0-1
TX 27th-Ortiz	1-26-27	0-6-6	0-1-1	0-1-1	1-3-4	0-14-14	0-1-1
TX 14th-Paul	26-0-26	6-0-6	1-0-1		4-0-4	14-0-14	1-0-1
TX 2nd-Poe	26-0-26	6-0-6	1-0-1	1-0-1	4-0-4	13-0-13	1-0-1
TX 16th-Reyes	0-26-26	0-6-6	0-1-1	0-1-1	0-4-4	0-13-13	0-1-1
TX 23rd-Rodriguez	1-26-27	0-6-6	0-1-1	0-1-1	1-3-4	0-14-14	0-1-1
TX 32nd-Sessions	26-0-26	6-0-6	1-0-1	1-0-1	4-0-4	13-0-13	1-0-1
TX 21st-Smith, Lamar	25-2-27	6-0-6	1-0-1	1-0-1	4-0-4	12-2-14	1-0-1
TX 13th-Thornberry	26-1-27	6-0-6	1-0-1	1-0-1	4-0-4	13-1-14	1-0-1
UT 1st-Bishop, Rob	27-0-27	6-0-6	1-0-1	1-0-1	4-0-4	14-0-14	1-0-1
UT 3rd-Chaffetz	27-0-27	6-0-6	1-0-1	1-0-1	4-0-4	14-0-14	1-0-1
UT 2nd-Matheson	5-22-27	3-3-6	0-1-1	0-1-1	1-3-4	1-13-14	0-1-1
VT Welch	0-27-27	0-6-6	0-1-1	0-1-1	0-4-4	0-14-14	0-1-1
VA 9th-Boucher	5-20-25	3-2-5	0-1-1	0-1-1	0-4-4	2-11-13	0-1-1
VA 7th-Cantor	25-1-26	6-0-6	1-0-1	1-0-1	4-0-4	12-1-13	1-0-1
VA 11th-Connolly	0-27-27	0-6-6	0-1-1	0-1-1	0-4-4	0-14-14	0-1-1
VA 4th-Forbes	24-3-27	6-0-6	1-0-1	1-0-1	4-0-4	11-3-14	1-0-1
VA 6th-Goodlatte	25-2-27	6-0-6	1-0-1	1-0-1	4-0-4	12-2-14	1-0-1
VA 8th-Moran, Jim	1-24-25	0-6-6	0-1-1	0-1-1	0-3-3	1-12-13	0-1-1
VA 2nd-Nye III	8-19-27	3-3-6	0-1-1	0-1-1	1-3-4	3-11-14	1-0-1
VA 5th-Perriello	3-23-26	0-6-6	1-0-1	0-1-1	0-4-4	2-11-13	0-1-1
VA 3rd-Scott, R.	0-27-27	0-6-6	0-1-1	0-1-1	0-4-4	0-14-14	0-1-1

HOUSE	OVERALL	HEALTH CARE	IMMIGRATION	EDUCATION	OIL	HOUSING/ ECONOMY	OTHER
VA 1st-Wittman	23-4-27	6-0-6	1-0-1	1-0-1	4-0-4	10-4-14	1-0-1
VA 10th-Wolf	20-7-27	5-1-6	1-0-1	1-0-1	3-1-4	9-5-14	1-0-1
WA 3rd-Baird	3-24-27	2-4-6	1-0-1	0-1-1	0-4-4	0-14-14	0-1-1
WA 6th-Dicks	0-27-27	0-6-6	0-1-1	0-1-1	0-4-4	0-14-14	0-1-1
WA 4th-Hastings, D.	26-0-26	6-0-6	1-0-1	1-0-1	3-0-3	14-0-14	1-0-1
WA 1st-Inslee	0-27-27	0-6-6	0-1-1	0-1-1	0-4-4	0-14-14	0-1-1
WA 2nd-Larsen	0-27-27	0-6-6	0-1-1	0-1-1	0-4-4	0-14-14	0-1-1
WA 7th-McDermott	1-24-25	0-6-6		0-1-1	0-4-4	1-12-13	0-1-1
WA 5th-McMorris Rodgers	25-2-27	6-0-6	1-0-1	1-0-1	4-0-4	12-2-14	1-0-1
WA 8th-Reichert	17-7-24	4-1-5	1-0-1	1-0-1	2-2-4	8-4-12	1-0-1
WA 9th-Smith, Adam	2-24-26	1-5-6	0-1-1	0-1-1	1-3-4	0-13-13	0-1-1
WV 2nd-Capito	21-6-27	5-1-6	1-0-1	1-0-1	3-1-4	10-4-14	1-0-1
WV 1st-Mollohan	1-24-25	0-6-6	0-1-1	0-1-1	1-2-3	0-13-13	0-1-1
WV 3rd-Rahall	1-26-27	0-6-6	0-1-1	0-1-1	1-3-4	0-14-14	0-1-1
WI 2d-Baldwin	0-25-25	0-6-6	0-1-1	0-1-1	0-3-3	0-13-13	0-1-1
WI 8th-Kagen	0-27-27	0-6-6	0-1-1	0-1-1	0-4-4	0-14-14	0-1-1
WI 3rd-Kind	1-23-24	0-6-6	0-1-1	0-1-1	0-4-4	1-10-11	0-1-1
WI 4th-Moore, G.	1-22-23	0-5-5	0-1-1	0-1-1	0-4-4	1-10-11	0-1-1
WI 7th-Obey	0-26-26	0-6-6	0-1-1	0-1-1	0-3-3	0-14-14	0-1-1
WI 6th-Petri	22-5-27	5-1-6	1-0-1	0-1-1	4-0-4	11-3-14	1-0-1
WI 1st-Ryan, P.	26-1-27	6-0-6	1-0-1	1-0-1	4-0-4	13-1-14	1-0-1
WI 5th-Sensenbrenner	27-0-27	6-0-6	1-0-1	1-0-1	4-0-4	14-0-14	1-0-1
WY Lummis	27-0-27	6-0-6	1-0-1	1-0-1	4-0-4	14-0-14	1-0-1

Notes

Chapter 1: Health Care

1. U.S. Dept. of Health and Human Services, Center for Medicare & Medicaid Services, "National Health Expenditures 2008 Highlights," http://www.cms.hhs.gov/NationalHealthExpendData/02_NationalHealthAccountsHistorical.asp.

   See also: U.S. Dept. of Health and Human Services, "The Nation's Health Dollar, Calendar Year 2008: Where it Came From and Where it Went," http://www.cms.gov/NationalHealthExpendData/downloads/PieChartSourcesExpenditures2008.pdf.

   U.S. Dept. of Health and Human Services, "Table 1: National Health Expenditures, by Source of Funds and Type of Expenditure: Calendar Year 2008," http://www.cms.gov/NationalHealthExpendData/downloads/tables.pdf.

2. InflationData.com, "Inflation - Historical," http://inflationdata.com/inflation/Inflation_Rate/Historical/Inflation.aspx?.

3. PricewaterhouseCoopers, "The Factors Fueling Rising Health Care Costs 2008," http://www.ahip.org/content/default.aspx?docid=25123.

   California Health Care Foundation, "Health Care Costs 101," http://www.chcf.org/documents/insurance/HealthCareCosts06.pdf.

4. Tillinghast Towers Perrin, "Medical Malpractice Costs 1975-2004, Adjusted for Inflation," *U.S. Tort Costs and Cross-Border Perspectives: 2005 Update,*

http://www.towersperrin.com/tillinghast/publications/
reports/2005_Tort_Cost/2005_Tort.pdf
(Accessed August 16, 2010).

5. Newsbatch.com, "Lawyers Per 100,000 Population,"
http://www.newsbatch.com/tort-lawyerinc.html.
(Accessed August 16, 2010).

   See also: Congressional Budget Office, "Medical
   Malpractice Tort Limits and Healthcare Spending,"
   April 2006, http://www.cbo.gov/showdoc.
   cfm?index=7174&sequence=0.

6. Tillinghast Towers Perrin. "Tort Costs as Percentage
   of GDP 1950-2004," *U.S. Tort Costs and Cross-Border
   Perspectives: 2005 Update*, http://www.towersperrin.
   com:80/tillinghast/publications/reports/
   2005_Tort_Cost/2005_Tort.pdf (Accessed August 16, 2010).

7. Newsbatch.com, "Inflation Adjusted Increase in Per Capita
   Tort Costs 1950-2004," http://www.newsbatch.com/tort-
   dolinc.html.

   See also: Tillinghast Towers Perrin, *U.S. Tort Costs
   and Cross-Border Perspectives: 2005 Update*,
   http://www.towersperrin.com/tillinghast/publications/
   reports/2005_Tort_Cost/2005_Tort.pdf
   (Accessed August 16, 2010).

8. Newsbatch.com, "Malpractice Costs as a Percentage of
   Revenues for Physician Specialties," *USA Today* (March 5,
   2003): http://www.newsbatch.com/tort-malbyspec.html.

9. Kathleen Doheny, "Malpractice Premiums, Rate of
   C-Sections Rise Together," *HealthDay* (May 5, 2008):
   http://www.washingtonpost.com/wpdyn/content/
   article/2008/05/05/AR2008050501308.html
   (Accessed August 16, 2010).

See also: Jim McElhatton, "Without Tort Reform, Doctors Say They'll Leave," *The Washington Times* (March 16, 2005): http://www.washingtontimes.com/news/2005/mar/16/20050316-102510-3112r//print/ (Accessed August 16, 2010).

10. Trial Lawyers Inc., "Malpractice Maladies: Doctors continue to flee states with out-of-control medical-injury verdicts," *Trial Lawyers Inc. Health Care: The Lawsuit Industry's Effect on American Health 2005*, http://www.triallawyersinc.com/healthcare/print05.html (Accessed August 16, 2010).

11. American College of Obstetricians and Gynecologists, Medical Liability Survey (2004), http://www.acog.org/from_home/publications/press_releases/nr07-16-04.cfm.

12. Troyen A. Brennan, et al., "Incidence of Adverse Events and Negligence in Hospitalized Patients: Results of the Harvard Medical Practice Study I & II," *New England Journal of Medicine* 324, 370-84 (1991).

See also: Richard Anderson, "An "Epidemic" of Medical Malpractice? A Commentary on the Harvard Medical Practice Study," Manhattan Inst. Center for Legal Policy (July 1996): http://www.manhattaninstitute.org/html/cjm_27.htm.

13. Medical Malpractice, "National Medical Malpractice Statistics," http://www.medicalmalpractice.com /national-medical-malpractice-facts.cfm.

14. Wikipedia, the free encyclopedia, "Medical Malpractice," http://en.wikipedia.org/wiki/Medical_malpractice.

15. Phillips RL, Bartholemew LA, Dovey SM, Fryer GE,

Miyoshi TJ, Green LA, "Learning from malpractice claims about negligent, adverse events in primary care in the United States," *Quality and Safety in Health Care* 13 (April 2004): http://qshc.bmj.com/content/13/2/121.long (Accessed August 16, 2010).

16. Medical News Today, "In Hospital Deaths from Medical Errors at 195,000 per Year USA," (Aug. 9 2004): http://www.medicalnewstoday.com/medicalnews.php?newsid=11856

17. Alex Nussbaum, "Malpractice Lawsuits are 'Red Herring" in Obama Plan (Update1)," Bloomberg.com, http://www.bloomberg.com/apps/news?pid=20601087&sid=az9qxQZNmf0o.

18. Newsbatch.com, "Effect of Damage Caps and Insurance Reform on California Medical Malpractice Insurance 1975-2001," http://www.newsbatch.com/tort-calmalrates.html.

19. Paul Henning, "The Ballad of Jed Clampett," 1962; performed by Scoggins, Flatt, and Scruggs, 1963, CBS, Columbia Records.

20. Newsbatch.com, "States With Significant Limits on Contingency Fees in Medical Malpractice Cases," Source: American Tort Reform Association, http://www.newsbatch.com/tort-contfeereg.html

21. Newsbatch.com, "Caps on Damages for Medical Malpractice," Source: U.S. Congress, "Impact of Legal Reforms on Medical Malpractice Costs" 1993, updated with data from American Tort Reform Association, http://www.newsbatch.com/tort-maldamcaps.html.

22. MSN Money, "Know Your Emergency Room Rights," By Insure.com, http://articles.moneycentral.msn.com/

Insurance/KnowYourRights KnowYourEmergency RoomRights.aspx.

See also: Robert Longley, "Is the US Really That Uninsured? Health Insurance Statistics You Need to Know," About.com, US Government Info, http://usgovinfo.about. com/od/medicarehealthinsurance/a/insurancestats.htm.

23. U.S. Dept. of Health and Human Services, Center for Medicare & Medicaid Services, "National Health Expenditures 2008 Highlights," http://www.cms.hhs.gov/ NationalHealthExpendData/02_NationalHealth AccountsHistorical.asp.

24. Centers for Disease Control and Prevention, "Health Insurance Coverage," http://www.cdc.gov/nchs/fastats/ hinsure.htm.

25. FactCheck.org, "The 'Real' Uninsured," http://www.factcheck.org/2009/06/the-real-uninsured/.

See also: Kaiser Family Foundation, "The Uninsured: A Primer," Oct. 2008, http://www.kff.org/uninsured/ upload/7451.pdf (Accessed August 16, 2010).

26. Julia A. Seymour, "Health Care Lie: '436 Million Uninsured Americans' –Michael Moore, politicians and the media use inflated numbers of those without health insurance to promote universal coverage," Business & Media Institute, http://www.businessandmedia.org printer/2007/ 20070718153509.aspx.

27. U.S. Census Bureau, "Current Population Survey, 2007 and 2008 Annual Social and Economic Supplements. Table 6. People Without Health Insurance Coverage by Selected Characteristics: 2006 and 2007," http://www.census.gov/ hhes/www/hlthin07/p60no235_table6.pdf.

28. Kaiser Commission Report #7613, "Medicaid and the Uninsured," http://www.kff.org/uninsured/upload/7613.pdf.

   See also: Medicine Plus, "Over 45 Million Americans Now Lack Health Insurance," www.nlm.nih.gov/medicineplus/print/news/fullstory_93076.html.

   HealthPac online, "Health Care Statistics in the United States," http://www.healthpaconline.net/health-care-statistics-in-the-united-states.htm.

   Blue Cross and Blue Shield Association, "The Uninsured in America," http://www.coverageforall.org/pdf/BC-BS_Uninsured-America.pdf.

29. Lisa Dubay, John Holahan and Allison Cook, "The Uninsured And The Affordability Of Health Insurance Coverage," *Health Affairs* 26, no. 1 (2007): w22-w30, http://content.healthaffairs.org/cgi/reprint/26/1/w22?maxtoshow=&hits=10&RESULTFORMAT=&fulltext=Uninsured+Affordability+insurance&andorexactfulltext=and&searchid=1&FIRSTINDEX=0&resourcetype=HWCIT.

   See also: National Review Institute, "Why That 48 Million Uninsured Number is Wrong," http://nrinstitute.org/mediamalpractice/?p=134.

30. Steven Hayward & Erik Peterson, "The Medicare Monster—A Cautionary Tale," Reason.com, http://reason.com/archives/1993/01/01/the-medicare-monster.

31. U.S. Department of Health and Human Services, Centers for Medicare and Medicaid Services, "2008 Annual Report of the Boards of Trustees of the Federal Hospital Insurance and Federal Supplementary Medical Insurance Trust Funds," http://www.cms.hhs.gov/ReportsTrustFunds/downloads/tr2008.pdf.

See also: U.S. Social Security Administration, "Trust Fund Data—Social Security & Medicare Tax Rates," http://www.ssa.gov/OACT/ProgData/taxRates.html.

32. Carl Campanile, "Medicaid Cops Bare Eye-Popping Scams," *New York Post,* http://www.nypost.com/p/news/regional/medicaid_cops_bare_eye_popping_scams_e2FlWbSaeWIb0P2CB9q6HM (Accessed Aug. 16, 2010).

33. Liz Kowalczyk, "ER visits, costs in Mass. Climb: Questions raised about healthcare law's impact on overuse," *Boston Globe,* (April 24, 2009): http://www.boston.com/news/local/massachusetts/articles/2009/04/24/er_visits_costs_in_mass_climb/ (Accessed Aug. 18, 2010).

34. Melissa Scott, "Healthy in Cuba, Sick in America? John Stossel Takes on Michael Moore, Examines Government-Run Health Care," ABC News, http://abcnews.go.com/print?id=3568278.

    See also: SiCKO the Movie, "SiCKO Factual Backup," http://sickothemovie.com/checkup/ (Accessed Aug. 17, 2010).

35. Msnbc.com, "Some U.K. patients denied costly cancer meds: Drugs more readily available in U.S. but patients often pay part of price," www.msnbc.msn.com/id/30106986 (Accessed Aug. 17, 2010).

36. Gardiner Harris, "British Balance Benefit vs. Cost of Latest Drugs," *New York Times* (Dec. 2, 2008): www.nytimes.com/2008/12/03/health/03nice.html?_r=1.

37. Ibid.

38. Daniel Martin, "Four-hour wait for a life-saving ambulance trip," *Mail Online* (Jan. 2009): http://www.dailymail.co.uk/health/article-1112207/Four-hour-wait-lifesaving-ambulance-trip.html (Accessed Aug. 17, 2010).

39. Daniel Martin, "Hard-up hospital orders staff: Don't wash sheets-turn them over," *Mail Online* (April 2007): http://www.dailymail.co.uk/health/article-448395/Hard-hospital-orders-staff-Don't-wash-sheets--turn-over.html (Accessed Aug. 17, 2010).

40. Matthew Moore and agencies, "Sufferers pull out teeth due to lack of dentists," *Telegraph*, October 2007, http://www.telegraph.co.uk/news/uknews/1566241/Sufferers-pull-out-teeth-due-to-lack-of-dentists.html (Accessed Aug. 17, 2010).

41. Celia Hall, "Patients wait year for hip surgery," *Telegraph*, December 2006, http://www.telegraph.co.uk/news/uknews/1537385/Patients-wait-year-for-hip-surgery.html (Accessed Aug. 17, 2010).

42. The Glenn Beck Program, "Glenn Beck: Brits running out of $$$," www.glennbeck.com/content/articles/article/196/23233/.

See also: Cato Institute, "American Cancer Society Wants Gov't to Run Health Care," *Opposing Views* (May 2009): www.opposingviews.com /i/american-cancer-society-wants-gov-t-to-run-health-care (Accessed Aug. 17, 2010).

43. CBC News, "Indepth: Health Care," www.cbc.ca/news/background/healthcare/.

44. Steffie Woolhandler, M.D., M.P.H., Terry Campbell, M.H.A., and David Himmelstein, M.D., "Cost of Health Care Administration in the United States and Canada," *The New England Journal of Medicine*, http://content.nejm.org/cgi/content/short/349/8/768.

See also: Wikipedia, "Comparison of Canadian and American health care systems," http://en.wikipedia.org/wiki/Comparison_of_Canadian_and_American_health_care_systems

45. Michael Tanner, "The Grass Is Not Always Greener: A Look at National Health Care Systems Around the World," Cato Institute, www.cato.org/pubs/pas/pa-613.pdf (Accessed Aug. 17, 2010).

46. Ibid.

47. Gary Claxton, Bianca DiJulio, Benjamin Finder and Eric Becker, "Employer Health Benefits 2007 Annual Survey," Kaiser Family Foundation, http://www.kff.org/insurance/7672/upload/76723.pdf.

48. Cato Institute, "Medicaid's Soaring Costs: Time to Step on the Brakes," Featuring Sen. Judd Gregg (R-NH), Jagadeesh Gokhale, Cato Institute, and John Holahan, Urban Institute (July 2007): http://www.cato.org/event.php?eventid=3947.

49. SiCKO the Movie, "Michael Moore's Health Care Proposal," http://sickothemovie.com/health-care-proposal/ (Accessed Aug. 17, 2010).

    See also: Physicians for A National Health Program, http://www.pnhp.org (Accessed Aug. 17, 2010).

50. Cato Institute, "Medicaid's Soaring Costs," (July 2007).

51. SiCKO the Movie, "SiCKO Factual Backup," http://sickothemovie.com/checkup/ (Accessed Aug. 17, 2010). World Health Organization, "The World Health Organization Assesses the World's Health Systems." WHO World Health Report (June 2000): http://www.who.int/inf-pr-2000/en/pr2000-44.html (Accessed Aug. 17, 2010).

52. Ibid.

53. U.S. Census Bureau, "Average Life Expectancy at Birth by State For 2000," 2000 Census, http://www.census.gov/population/www/projections/files/MethTab2.xls (Accessed Aug. 17, 2010).

54. Robert L. Ohsfeldt and John E. Schneider, *The Business of Health: The Role of Competiiton, Markets, and Regulation* (Washington: American Enterprise Institute Press, 2006).

55. Organisation for Economic Cooperation and Development, "OECD Health Data, 2007 Statistics and Indicates for 30 Countries" (Paris: OECD, July 2007). Note: this web address provides same data for 2010: http://www.oecd.org/document/30/ 0,3343,n_2649_34631_12968734_1_1_1_37407,00.html.

56. Victor Rodwin, "The Health Care System under French National Health Insurance: Lessons for Health Reform in the United States," *American Journal of Public Health* 93, no. 1 (2003): 34.

57. "Deficit-Saddled France under Fire over Budget," *Reuters*, July 5, 2007. Members of the Eurozone are required to keep budget deficits below 3 percent of GDP. And "French Health Care Is Badly Run," *BBC News*, Aug. 8, 2006.

58. Thomas Buchmueller and Agnes Cuffinhal, "Private Health Insurance in France," OECD Health Working Paper no. 12, 2004. *And* Francesca Columbo and Nicole Tapay, "Private Health Insurance in the OECD Countries: The Benefits and Costs for Individuals and Health Systems," Health Working Paper no. 15, 2004.

59. OECD, "OECD Health Data 2007: Statistics and Indicators for 30 Countries." (See note 55).

60. Paul Dutton, "Health Care in France and the United States: Learning from Each Other," Brookings Institution, July 2002. *And* Rodwin, "The Health Care System under French National Health Insurance."

61. High Council for the Future of Health Insurance, "L'Avenir de l'Assurance Maladie: L'Urgence d'un Redressment par la Qualite' " (Paris, Ministry of Health, 2004). *And Valentin* Petkantchin, "The Ineffectiveness of Health Cost Containment Policies in France," *Economic Note* (Brussels: Institut Economique Molinari, 2007) http://www.institutmolinari.org/pubs/note20073.pdf.

62. D. Benamouzig and R. Launois, "Rationing Health Care in Europe-France," in *Rationing Health Care in Europe: An Empirical Study*, eds. J. Matthias Graf von der Schulenberg and Michael Blanke (Amsterdam: IOS Press, 2004), p. 16. *And* Helen Disney et al., *Impatient for Change: European Attitudes to Healthcare Reform* (London: Stockholm Network, 2004), pp. 69-86.

63. Ezra Klein, "The Health of Nations—Here's How Canada, France, Germany, and our Own Veterans Health Administration Manage to Cover Everybody at Less Cost and with Better Care than We Do," *American Prospect*, April 24, 2007.

64. Source: OECD, "OECD Health Data 2007: Statistics and Indicators for 30 Countries." (See note 55).

65. Michael F. Cannon, "Health Savings Accounts Work," Cato Institute, (Feb. 5, 2006): http://www.cato.org/pub_display. php?pub_id=5482.

66. U.S. Department of the Treasury, "Health Savings Accounts (HSAs)" http://www.treas.gov/offices/public-affairs/hsa/

See also: Nina Owcharenko, "Health Savings Accounts: How to Broaden Health Coverage for Working Families," The Heritage Foundation, April 16, 2004, WebMemo #481, http:www.heritage.org/research/healthcare/wm481.

cfm?renderforprint=1.

Michael F. Cannon, "Tax Treatment of Health Care," *Cato Handbook for Policymakers*, 7th ed. (Washington, D.C.: Cato Institute, 2009), 14.

67. Devon M. Herrick, "Health Care Entrepreneurs: The Changing Nature of Providers," National Center For Policy Analysis Policy Report No. 318, http://www.ncpa.org/pub/st318.

68. Walmartstores.com, "Wal-Mart Launches Phase Three of $4 Prescription Program" http://walmartstores.com/FactsNews/NewsRoom/8248.aspx.

See also: The Associated Press, "Wal-Mart Expands Program Providing Drug Discounts," *New York Times*, http://query.nytimes.com/gst/fullpage.html?res=9B0CE5D71431F935A35756C0A96E9C8B63&scp=1&sq=Wal-Mart%20Expands%20Program%20Providing%20Drug%20Discounts&st=cse (Accessed Aug. 17, 2010).

Shannon Pettypiece, "Generic-Pill Spending Dips in 'Fierce' U.S. Price War (Update3)" Bloomberg.com, http://www.bloomberg.com/apps/news?pid=20670001&sid=a_tiY4.EFggo.

69. http://www.teladoc.com

70. U.S. Department of Health and Human Services, Centers for Medicare & Medicaid Services, "National Health Expenditure Data," http://www.cms.gov/NationalHealthExpendData/downloads/nhe2008.zip.

See also: Cohen RA, Martinez ME. "Health insurance coverage: Early release of estimates from the National Health Interview Survey, 2008. National Center for Health Statistics," June 2009, http://www.cdc.gov/nchs/nhis/

released200906.htm.

71. U.S. Department of the Treasury, "Health Savings Accounts (HSAs)," http://www.treas.gov /offices/public-affairs/hsa/.

72. Economic Policy Institute, "Employer-Sponsored Health Insurance Erosion Continues," By Elise Gould, http://epi.3cdn.net/6356d48ae59f625af6_xxm6bnyn2.pdf

73. Economic Policy Institute, research and ideas for "Shared Prosperity," http://www.epi.org (Accessed Aug. 17, 2010).

74. Small Business Majority, "State Surveys Highlight Small Business Support for Healthcare Reform," http://www. smallbusinessmajority.org/pdfs/state_research_ averages_91709.pdf.

75. The O'Leary Report, "Small Business Owners and Stockholders Agree on Ten Crucial Health Care Reform Issues, According to Zogby/O'Leary Poll," http://www. olearyreport.com/files/HealthCarePoll-SmallBusiness.cfm.

Chapter 2: Education

1. National Center for Education Statistics, U.S. Department of Education. "Current expenditure per pupil in fall enrollment in public elementary and secondary schools; Selected years 1961-62 through 2005-06," *Digest of Education Statistics, 2008*, Chapter 2 and Table 179, http://nces.ed.gov/fastfacts/ display.asp?id=66.

2. U.S. Census Bureau, "Public Education Finances 2007," Figures 1a, 1b, 2, and 3, 2007 Census of Governments Survey of Local Government Finances - School Systems, http://www2.census.gov/govs/school/07f33pub.pdf (Accessed Aug. 17, 2010).

3. Government Spending in the United States of America. "U.S. Federal Budget Pie Chart for FY11," http://www. usgovernmentspending.com/us_budget_pie_chart (Accessed Aug. 17, 2010).

4. U.S. Census Bureau, "Public Education Finances 2007," Table 18: Population, Enrollment, and Personal Income by State: 2006 and 2007, http://www2.census.gov/govs/ school/07f33pub.pdf.

5. Public Broadcasting Services. "The Department of Education," http://www.pbs.org/newshour/backgrounders/ department_of_education.html.

6. Veronica de Rugy and Marie Gryphon, "Individual Liberty, Free Markets, and Peace—Elimination Lost: What happened to Abolishing the Department of Education?," Cato Institute (Feb. 11, 2004): http://cato.org/research/ articles/gryphon-040211.html.

7. Devvy Kidd, "Department of Education must be abolished," *World Net Daily* (Dec. 7, 2004): http://www.wnd.com/news/ article.asp?ARTICLE_ID=41802.

8. Working Californians, "Obama Announces Support for Teacher Merit Pay," (July 5, 2007): http:// workingcalifornians.com/2008_presidential_issues/ education.

9. John Stossel and Andrew Sullivan, "Ron Paul Unplugged," ABC News, http://abcnews.go.com/print?id=3970818.

10. Department of Education, "The Federal Role in Education," http://www2.ed.gov/print/about/overview/fed/role.html.

11. Anonymous, "The Real Cost of Public Schools," *The Washington Post*, (April 6, 2008): http://pqasb.pqarchiver.

com/washingtonpost/access/1457491551.html?FMT=ABS
&FMTS=ABS:FT&date=Apr+6%2C+2008&author=Anony
mous&pub=The+Washington+Post&edition=&startpage
=B.8&desc=The+Real+Cost+Of+Public+Schools.

12. Education Bug, "Public Schools vs. Private Schools,"
http://www.educationbug.org/a/public-schools-vs–private-
schools.html.

Education Bug, "Charter Schools vs. Magnet Schools,"
http://www.educationbug.org/a/charter-schools-vs–
magnet-schools.html.

Education Bug, "Charter Schools,"
http://www.educationbug.org/a/charter-schools.html.

Education Bug, "Magnet Schools,"
http://www.educationbug.org/a/magnet-schools.html.

Education Bug, "Public School vs. Christian School,"
http://www.educationbug.org/a/public-school-vs–christian-
school.html.

13. Council for American Private Education, "Facts and
Studies—Private School Statistics at a Glance," http://
www.capenet.org/facts.html.

14. Government Spending in the U.S, "Total Budgeted
Government Spending Expenditure GDP," (2010):
http://www.usgovernmentspending.com/.

15. Answers.com, WikiAnswers, "What is the national average
cost per student in private schools?," http://wiki.answers.
com/Q/What_is_the_national_average_cost_per_student_
in_private_schools.

16. Free by 50, "What does private school cost?," http://www.
freeby50.com/2009/10/what-does-private-school-cost.html
(Accessed Aug. 17, 2010).

See also: The Independent Institute, "Surprise! Median Private School Tuition Beats Per Pupil Expenditure at Government Schools, Says Institute," (March 1, 2002): http://www.independent.org/newsroom/news_detail. asp?newsID=10.

17. GreatSchools.org, "Private versus public," http://www. greatschools.org/find-a-school/defining-your-ideal/ private-vs-public-schools.gs?content=59&print= true&fromPage=1.

18. Patrick L. Anderson, Richard D. McLellan, Joseph P. Overton, and Gary L. Wolfram, "Private School Costs vs. Public School Costs," *Mackinac Center for Public Policy* (Nov. 13, 1997): http://www.mackinac.org/article. aspx?ID=1118&print=yes.

19. Ibid.

20. Ibid.

21. Henry Braun, Frank Jenkins, and Wendy Grigg, "Comparing Private Schools and Public Schools Using Hierarchical Linear Modeling," National Center for Education Statistics, The Nation's Report Card (July 14, 2006): http://nces.ed.gov/nationsreportcard/ pubs/studies/2006461.asp (Accessed Aug. 17, 2010).

22. National Center for Education Statistics, "NAEP Overview—NAEP: A Common Yardstick," http://nces. ed.gov/nationsreportcard/about/.

23. National Education Association, "Public Schools: As Good or Better Than Charter, Private Schools," http://www.nea.org/home/18142.htm.
See also: Teresa Mendez, "Public Schools: Do they outperform private ones?," *Christian Science Monitor,*

(May 10, 2005): http://www.csmonitor.com/2005/0510/
p11s01-legn.html (Accessed Aug. 17, 2010).

24. Paul E. Peterson and Elena Llaudet, "On the Public-Private
School Achievement Debate," Harvard University
(Aug. 2006): http://www.hks.harvard.edu/pepg/PDF/
Papers/PEPG06-PetersonLlaudet.pdf.

25. John Cloud, "Are Private Schools Really Better?," *TIME*, in
partnership with CNN, http://www.time.com/time/nation/
article/0,8599,1670063,00.html.

26. Shanea Watkins, "Are Public or Private Schools doing
Better? How the NCES Study Is Being Misinterpreted," The
Heritage Foundation, http://www.heritage.org/Research/
Reports/2006/09/Are-Public-or-Private-Schools-Doing-
Better-How-the-NCES-Study-Is-Being-Misinterpreted.

27. Ibid.

28. Elena Llaudet and Paul E. Peterson, "The NCES Private-
Public School Study: Findings are other than they seem,"
Education next, http://educationnext.org/the-nces-
privatepublic-school-study/.

29. U.S. Bureau of Labor Statistics, "May 2008 Occupational
Employment and Wage Estimates," http://www.bls.gov/
oes/oes_dl.htm (Accessed Aug. 17, 2010).

30. Rancho Solano Private Schools, "Test Scores—Student
Achievement Assessment," http://www.ranchosolano.com/
AboutRanchoSolano/tests.stml.

31. Braun, Jenkins, Grigg, "Comparing Private Schools and
Public Schools..." (July 14, 2006).

32. Council for American Private Education, "Facts and
Studies: Private School Statistics at a Glance,"
http://www.capenet.org/facts.html.

33. Nicole C. Focareto, B.A., Marietta College 2006, Master's Examination Committee Dr. William M. Bauer, Advisor, "Private vs. Non-Private: A Correlational Study Between ACT and GPA," http://etd.ohiolink.edu/send-pdf.cgi/ FocaretoNicole.pdf?acc_num=marietta1147440821.

34. Marcia Manna, "Great Schools," *San Diego Magazine*, (July 2006): http://www.sandiegomagazine.com/media/ San-Diego-Magazine/July-2006/Great-Schools/.

35. Dan Lips and Matthew Ladner, "Policy Report No. 227— Demography Defeated: Florida's K-12 Reforms and Their Lessons for the Nation," Goldwater Institute, (2008): http://www.goldwaterinstitute.org/article/2577.

36. Ibid.

37. National Center for Education Statistics, *Digest of Education Statistics: 2007*, U.S. Department of Education, Office of Educational Research and Improvement, Table 174.

38. Lips and Ladner, "Demography Defeated," (2008).

39. Greg Forster, "Lost Opportunity: An Empirical Analysis of How Vouchers Affected Florida Public Schools," Friedman Foundation for Educational Choice, March 2008.

40. Cecilia Elena Rouse, "Feeling the Florida Heat? How Low-Performing Schools Respond to Voucher and Accountability Pressure," Urban Institute Working Paper No. 13, Nov. 2007.

41. Greg Forster, "Lost Opportunity," 2008.

42. Yes; these numbers are not quite accurate. Exhibit E shows that Massachusetts spends $18,794 while Florida spends $17,189. Nevertheless, this article's analysis is directly on point.

43. Lips and Ladner, "Demography Defeated," (2008): 16.

44. John Stossel, "John Stossel's 'Stupid in America'," *ABC News* (Jan. 13, 2006): http://abcnews.go.com/2020/Stossel/story?id=1500338&CMP=OTC-RSSFeeds0312.

45. Ibid.

46. Ibid.

47. Matthew Ladner, "Policy Brief No. 09-04—Freedom From Responsibility: A Survey of Civic Knowledge Among Arizona High School Students," Goldwater Institute (June 30, 2009): http://www.goldwaterinstutute.org/article/3211.

48. Matthew Ladner, "Policy Brief No. 09-06—Tough Crowd: Arizona High School Students Evaluate Their Schools," Goldwater Institute (Sept. 10, 2009): http://www.goldwaterinstitute.org/article/3657.

Chapter 3: Immigration

1. U.S. Department of State Foreign Affairs, "7 FAM 1100—Acquisition and Retention of U.S. Citizenship and Nationality," *Manual Volume 7: Consular Affairs* (Aug. 21, 2009): http://www.state.gov/documents/organization/86755.pdf.

   See also: Dual Citizenship FAQ, "U.S. law relating to dual citizenship," http://www.richw.org/dualcit/law.html (Accessed Aug. 17, 2010).

2. The Ladders, "The Ladders Tennis TV commercial," (Jan. 28, 2008): http://www.theladders.com/video-audio-clip/theladders-tennis-tv-commercial (Accessed Aug. 17, 2010).

3. GlobalSecurity.org, "US-Mexico Border Fence / Great Wall

of Mexico," http://www.globalsecurity.org/security/systems/
mexico-wall.htm.

4. Jon Feere and Jessica Vaughan, "Taking Back the Streets:
ICE and Local Law Enforcement Target Immigrant Gangs,"
Center for Immigration Studies (Sept. 2008): http://www.cis.
org/ImmigrantGangs.

5. National Alliance of Gang Investigators Association, "2005
National Gang Threat Assessment," http://www.ojp.usdoj.
gov/BJA/what/2005_threat_assesment.pdf.

National Drug Intelligence Center, U.S. Dept. of Justice,
"National Drug Threat Assessment 2006," (Jan. 2006):
http://www.usdoj.gov/ndic/pubs11/18862/index.htm.

6. U.S. Federal Bureau of Investigation, "Violent Gangs,"
http://www.fbi.gov/hq/cid/ngic/violent_gangs.htm.

7. U.S. House of Representatives International Relations
Committee, Subcommittee on the Western Hemisphere,
Statement of Chris Swecker, Assistant Director, Criminal
Investigative Division, FBI, 109th Cong., 1st sess., (April 20,
2005): http://www.fbi.gov/congress/congress05/
swecker042005.htm.

8. National Drug Intelligence Center, "Drugs and Gangs Fast
Facts," http://www.usdoj.gov/ndic/pubs11/13157/index.htm.

9. Claude Arnold, "Immigration Authorities and Gang
Enforcement," *U.S. Attorneys' Bulletin 47* (May 2006):
http://www.usdoj.gov/usao/eousa/foia_reading_room/
usab5403.pdf (Accessed Aug. 17, 2010).

Claire Ribando, *Gangs in Central America*, Congressional
Research Service, May 10, 2005.

∽

10. Arnold, "Immigration Authorities and Gang Enforcement," (May 2006).

11. Celinda Franco, *The MS-13 and 18th Street Gangs: Emerging Transnational Gang Threats?*, Congressional Research Service, (Nov. 2, 2007).

    See also: Diego Cevallos, "MEXICO: Spread of Central American Youth Gangs Uncurbed," *Inter Press Service News Agency*, (Nov. 3, 2007).

    Ana Arena, "How the Street Gangs Took Central America," *Foreign Affairs*, (May/June, 2005).

12. David McLemore, "MS-13 Gang Seen as a Growing Threat: Authorities Target Group in Texas and Across U.S." *Dallas Morning News*, (Oct. 29, 2006).

13. U.S. House Judiciary Committee, Subcommittee on Crime, Terrorism, and Homeland Security, "A Hearing On Youth Violence," 110th Cong., 1st sess., (Feb. 15, 2007): http://judiciary.house.gov/hearings/pdf/Memo091202.pdf.

    See also: U.S. House Committee on the Judiciary, Subcommittee on Immigration, Border Security, and Claims, Congressional Testimony. Kris W. Kobach. "The Scope of the Illegal Alien Street Gang Problem." 109th Cong., 1st sess., (June 28, 2005): http://judiciary.house.gov/hearings/pdf/Memo091202.pdf.

    See also: www.ice.gov/pi/news/insideice/articles/insideice_032805_Web1.htm.

14. Sara A. Carter and Mason Stockstill, "Report: MS-13 Gang Hired to Murder Border Patrol," *Daily Bulletin* (San Bernardino, CA), (Jan. 10, 2006).

15. Statement of First Assistant Chief David O'Neal Brown, Dallas Police Department, at a Department of Homeland

Security press conference (March 10, 2006): http://www.dhs.gov/xnews/releases/press_release_0879.shtm.

See also: Clare Ribando, *Gangs in Central America.* Congressional Research Service. (May 10, 2005) *and* Victor J. Blue, "Gangs Without Borders," *San Francisco Chronicle,* (April 2, 2006).

16. Amy Gardner, "Gang Crimes Have Fallen in Fairfax," *The Washington Post* (Sept. 22, 2007): http://www.washingtonpost.com/wp-dyn/content/article/2007/09/21/AR2007092102223.html (Accessed Aug. 17, 2010).

17. Associated Press, "U.S. Turns Over Mexican Man Accused in 1998 Massacre," *The Maui News* (Aug. 24, 2008): http://www.mauinews.com/page/content.detail/id/57874.html?isap=1&nav=5023 (Accessed Aug. 17, 2010).

18. K. Jack Riley, "Border Control," Rand Corporation (2006): www.rand.org/pubs/reprints/2008/RAND_RP1216.pdf.

19. settleinamerica.com, "Securing U.S. Borders Against Illegal Immigration Raises Controversy," http://www.settleinamerica.com/immigration-articles/illegal-immigration-statistics.htm.

20. VOANews.com, "US Border Patrol Facing New Illegal Immigration Problem," *VOANews* (June 30, 2005): http://www1.voanews.com/english/news/a-13-2005-06-30voa100-66387907.html.

21. Ibid.

22. Foxnews.com, "Border Patrol: U.S.-Mexico Border Deaths Up 7 Percent," (April 8, 2009): www.foxnews.com/printer_friendly_story/0,3566,513359,00.html.

23. Blas Nunez-Neto, "Border Security: The Role of the U.S. Border Patrol," Open CRS, *CRS Report RL32562* (Nov. 20, 2008): http://opencrs.com/document/RL32562/2008-11-20/ (Accessed Aug. 18, 2010).

24. Ibid.

25. Jeremy Schwartz, "In Eagle Pass, divided view of border fence," *American-Statesman,* http://www.statesman.com/news/texas/in-eagle-pass-divided-view-of-border-fence-326471.html?cxtype=rss_ece_frontpage (Accessed Aug. 18, 2010).

26. Robert Rector and Christine Kim, "The Fiscal Cost of Low-Skill Immigrants to the U.S. Taxpayer," The Heritage Foundation, (May 21, 2007): www.heritage.org/research/immigration/sr14.cfm.

   See also: Mary Fitzgerald, "Illegal Immigrants' Cost to Government Studied," *The Washington Post,* (Aug. 26, 2004): http://www.washingtonpost.com/ac2/wp-dyn/A33783-2004Aug25?l... (Accessed Aug. 18, 2010).

27. Wikipedia, "Illegal Immigration to the United States," http://en.wikipedia.org/wiki/Illegal_immigration_to_the_United_States.

   See also: Jeffrey S. Passel, "The Size and Characteristics of the Unauthorized Migrant Population in the U.S.: Estimates Based on the March 2005 Current Population Survey," Pew Hispanic Center (March 7, 2006): http://pewhispanic.org/files/reports/61.pdf.

28. Jeffrey Passel, Randolph Capps, and Michael Fix, "Undocumented Immigrants," Urban Institute (Jan. 12, 2004): http://www.urban.org/publications/1000587.html (Accessed Aug. 18, 2010).

29. This estimate from Heritage is comparatively conservative. Another study performed by Robert Rector of the Heritage Foundation found that the average low-skill household received $22,449 more in benefits than taxes paid each year:

Byron York, "What Does Illegal Immigration Cost?," *National Review Online* (April 10, 2007): http://article. nationalreview.com/311221/what-does-illegal-immigration-cost/byron-york (Accessed Aug. 18, 2010).

30. US Debt Clock.org, "US Population," http://usdebtclock.org.

31. usgovernmentspending.com, "U.S. Federal Budget Pie Chart for FY11," http://www.usgovernmentspending.com/ budget_pie_gs.php?span=usgs302&year=2011&view= 1&expand=0002&expandC=&units=b&fy=fy11&local= undefined&state=US#usgs302, (Accessed Aug. 18, 2010).

32. Jeffrey S. Passel, "The Size and Characteristics of the Unauthorized Migrant Population in the U.S.: Estimates Based on the March 2005 Current Population Survey," Pew Hispanic Center (March 7, 2006).

33. Robert Rector and Christine Kim, "The Fiscal Cost of Low-Skill Immigrants," 2007.

34. SolutionsAbroad.com, "Cost of Living in Mexico," http://www.solutionsabroad.com/index2.php?option= com_content&task=view&id=865&pop=1&page= 0&Itemid=129.

35. UCAN Enterprises, "Mexico," http://www.ucanstudy.com/ english/index.php?parent_id=42.

36. Jeffrey S. Passel, Randolph Capps, and Michael E. Fix, "Undocumented Immigrants: Facts and Figures," Urban Institute, (Jan. 12, 2004): www.urban.org/url.cfm?ID= 1000587&renderforprint=1 (Accessed August 18, 2010).

See also: Steven A. Camarota, "Immigration, both legal and illegal, puts huge strain on the country," *North County Times* (Calif.), Center for Immigration Studies, http://www.cis.org/node/464 (Accessed Aug. 18, 2010).

37. Robert Longley, "US Government Info - Illegal Immigration Costs California Over Ten Billion Annually - State's "cheap labor" costs average household $1,183 a year," About.com, http://usgovinfo.about.com/od/immigrationnaturalizatio/a/caillegals.htm.

38. Michael Arnold Glueck, M.D. & Robert J. Cihak, M.D., "High Cost of Medical Care for Illegal Immigrants," Newsmax.com, (Dec. 27, 2005): http://archive.newsmax.com/archives/articles/2005/12/26/170334.shtml (Accessed Aug. 18, 2010).

39. John Rabe, "Calculating the Social Cost of Illegal Immigration," National Public Radio, (April 27, 2009): http://www.npr.org/templates/story/story.php?storyId=5366515.

40. Timothy Noah, "The Nativism Tax," *Slate,* (Nov. 20, 2009): http://www.slate.com/id/2236288/.

41. Judicial Watch, "Illegal Immigration Costs U.S. Hundreds of Billions," www.judicialwatch.org /blog/illegal-immigration-costs-u-s-hundreds-of-billions.

42. Anna Gorman, "U.S. funding for jailing illegal immigrants falls far short of costs," *Los Angeles Times* (Feb. 5, 2010): http://articles.latimes.com/2010/feb/05/local/la-me-immig-jails5-2010feb05.

43. Arizona State Legislature, State of Arizona Senate, "Bill Status Overview: House Engrossed Senate Bill 1070," Forty-ninth Legislature, Second Regular Session 2010,

Chapter 113, http://www.azleg.gov/FormatDocument.
asp?inDoc=/legtext/49leg/2r/bills/sb1070o.asp
(Accessed Aug. 18, 2010).

44. United States Code Title 8, secs. 1324a, 1373, and 1644,
http://uscode.house.gov.

45. Ibid.

46. Arizona Senate Bill 1070. Title 11, Chapter 7, Article 8.
"Enforcement of Immigration Laws," Section 11-1051,
http://www.azleg.gov/legtext/49leg/2r/bills/sb1070s.pdf.

47. United States Code Title 8, sec. 1324, http://uscode.house.
gov.

48. Arizona Senate Bill 1070. Title 11, Chapter 7, Article 8.
"Enforcement of Immigration Laws," Section 11-1051,
http://www.azleg.gov/legtext/49leg/2r/bills/sb1070s.pdf.

49. Albor Ruiz, "Hispanic voters say immigration's No. 1," *New
York Daily News*, (May 20, 2009): http://www.nydailynews.
com/ny_local/2009/05/21/2009-05-21_hispanic_voters_say_
immigrations_no_1.html (Accessed Aug. 18, 2010).

50. The Federation for American Immigration Reform (FAIR),
"Poll Data Hispanics," http://www.fairus.org /site/
PageServer?pagename=research_polldataHisp.

51. Randal C. Archibold and Megan Thee-Brenan, "Poll
Shows Most in U.S. Want Overhaul of Immigration Laws,"
New York Times (May 3, 2010): http://www.nytimes.
com/2010/05/04/us/04poll.html?scp=1&sq=Poll%20
Shows%20Most%20in%20U.S.%20Want%20Overhaul%20
of%20Immigration%20Laws&st=cse.

52. Rasmussen Reports, "Arizona Voters Favor Welcoming Immigration Policy, 64% Support New Immigration Law," (April 28, 2010): http://www.rasmussenreports.com/public_content/politics/general_state_surveys/arizona/arizona_voters_favor_welcoming_immigration_policy_64_support_new_immigration_law.

See also: Jeffrey M. Jones, "More Americans Favor Than Oppose Arizona Immigration Law," Gallup,   http://www.gallup.com/poll/127598/Americans-Favor-Oppose-Arizona-Immigration-Law.aspx.

53. *The Christian Science Monitor*, "Immigration reform rests on a national worker ID," (March 9, 2010): http://www.csmonitor.com/Commentary/the-monitors-view/2010/0309/Immigration-reform-rests-on-a-national-worker-ID.

Chapter 4: Oil

1. Wikipedia, "1970s energy crisis," http://en.wikipedia.org/wiki/1970s_energy_crisis (Accessed Aug 13, 2010).

2. Wikipedia, "Deepwater Horizon Oil Spill," http://en.wikipedia.org/wiki/BP_Oil_Spill (Accessed Aug 13, 2010).

3. U.S. Energy Information Administration, "Frequently Asked Questions: Crude Oil," http://tonto.eia.gov/ask/crudeoil_faqs.asp.

See also: U.S. Energy Information Administration, "Petroleum Statistics," http://tonto.eia.doe.gov/energyexplained/index.cfm?page=oil_home#tab2 (Accessed Aug. 13, 2010).

4. The Organization of the Petroleum Exporting Countries (OPEC), "Brief History," http://www.opec.org/aboutus/ history/history.htm (Accessed Aug. 13, 2010).

5. Mark Wieczorek, "Global Oil Production and Consumption," Mark Wieczorek's Weblog, http://www.marktaw.com/culture_ and_media/politics/GlobalOil.html (Accessed Aug. 13, 2010).

6. Bernard A. Gelb, "Caspian Oil and Gas: Production and Prospects," Open CRS, *CRS Report for Congress RS21190*, (April 9, 2002): www.opencrs.com/document/RS21190/ 2002-04-09/download/1005/   (Accessed Aug. 13, 2010).

7. Wikipedia, "Oil Reserves," http://en.wikipedia.org/wiki/Oil_ reserves.com (Accessed Aug. 13, 2010).

8. Wikipedia, "Arctic Refuge Drilling Controversy," (Jan. 31, 2005): http://en.wikipedia.org/wiki/Arctic_Refuge_drilling_ controversy (Accessed Aug. 13, 2010).

9. Gary L. Galemore, "CRS Report for Congress: President Clinton's Vetoes," Open CRS, (Oct. 7, 2000): http://assets. opencrs.com/rpts/98-147_20001007.pdf (Accessed Aug. 13, 2010)

10. Jeffrey Kluger, "Going Green: The Eco Vote," *Time*, Nov. 2, 2007, 123.

11. U.S. Department of the Interior, U.S. Geological Survey, "3 to 3.4 Billion Barrels of Technically Recoverable Oil Assessed in North Dakota and Montana's Bakken Formation - 25 Times More Than 1995 Estimate," (April 10, 2008): http://www.usgs.gov/newsroom/article.asp?ID=1911.

12. Snopes.com, "Bakken Formation, Mixture of True and False Information," (March 27, 2009): http://www.snopes. com/politics/gasoline/bakken.asp.

13. Christopher J. Petherick, "U.S. Has Massive Oil Reserves,
    Shale Remains Untapped After Decades of Failure,"
    American Free Press, no. 20 (May 15, 2006): http://www.
    americanfreepress.net/html/u_s__has_massive_oil.html.

14. Jim Ostroff, "The U.S.' Untapped Oil Bounty," *Kiplinger
    Business Resource Center* (June 30, 2008): http://www.
    kiplinger.com/printstory.php?pid=14201.

15. James T. Bartis and others, *Oil Shale Development in the
    United States*, (Santa Monica, CA: Rand Corporation,
    2005), http://www.rand.org /pubs/monographs/MG414/.

16. U.S. Energy Information Administration, "Crude Oil
    Production," http://www.eia.doe.gov/neic/infosheets/
    crudeproduction.html.

    See also: U.S. Energy Information Administration, "Country
    Energy Profiles," http://tonto.eia.doe.gov/country/index.cfm.

17. U.S. Energy Information Administration, "Oil: Crude and
    Petroleum Products Explained," http://tonto.eia.doe.gov/
    energyexplained/print.cfm?page=oil_home.

18. Shehal, "Energy: Cost of Oil Production," Kanabona.com,
    (Jan. 31, 2008): http://www.kanabona.com/ kanabona/
    ?q=energy_cost_of_oil_production#1
    (Accessed Aug. 13, 2010).

19. U.S. Energy Information Administration, "Annual U.S.
    Field Production of Crude Oil (Thousand Barrels per Day),"
    http://tonto.eia.doe.gov/dnav/pet/hist/LeafHandler.
    ashx?n=pet&s=mcrfpus2&f=a (Accessed Aug. 13, 2010).

    U.S. Energy Information Administration, "Petroleum
    Navigator: Crude Oil Production," http://tonto.eia.doe.gov/
    dnav/pet/pet_crd_crpdn_adc_mbbl_a.htm
    (Accessed Aug. 13, 2010).

20. Kimberly Amadeo, "U.S. Economy - Gas and Oil Prices - How Oil Prices Affect Gas Prices," *About.com*, http://useconomy.about.com/od/supply/p/oil_gas_prices.htm (Accessed Aug. 18, 2010).

21. WTRG Economics, "Oil Price History and Analysis - OPEC's Failed Meeting: Price vs. Market Share," http://www.wtrg.com/opec.html.

22. Inflationdata.com, "Inflation Adjusted Monthly Crude Oil Prices (1946-Present) in January 2010 Dollars Updated 3/11/2010," www.inflationdata.com/inflation/images/charts/Oil/Inflation_Adj_Oil_Prices_Chart.htm.

23. Geohive, "Energy: oil consumption (in millions tonnes)," http://www.xist.org/charts/en_oilcons.aspx.

See also: Central Intelligence Agency, "The World Factbook: Country Comparison: Oil-Proved Reserves," (January 2009): https://www.cia.gov/library/publications/the-world-factbook/rankorder/2178rank.html (Accessed Aug. 18, 2010).

24. U.S. Energy Information Administration, "Table 11.5 World Crude Oil Production, 1960-2008 (Million Barrels per Day)," http://www.eia.doe.gov/emeu/aer/txt/ptb1105.html.

25. Planete-energies.com, "Production and consumption of oil," http://www.planete-energies.com/content/oil-gas/companies/world/consumption-oil-production-statistics.html.

See also: Yahoo Education, "World Factbook: Oil Production and Consumption Country Comparison Table," http://education.yahoo.com/reference/factbook/countrycompare/oil/la.html.

26. U.S. Energy Information Administration, "Annual U.S. Imports of Crude Oil (Thousand Barrels per Day)," http://tonto.eia.doe.gov/dnav/pet/hist/LeafHandler. ashx?n=PET&s=MCRIMUS2&f=A.

27. U.S. Energy Information Administration, "Petroleum Navigator—Exports," http://www.eia.gov/dnav/pet/ pet_move_exp_dc_NUS-Z00_mbbl_m.htm.

28. InflationData.com, "Historical Crude Oil Prices (Table)," http://www.inflationdata.com/inflation/Inflation_Rate/ Historical_Oil_Prices_Table.asp.

   See also: James K. Jackson, "U.S. Trade Deficit and the Impact of Rising Oil Prices," Open CRS, *CRS Report for Congress RS22204* (June 10, 2008): http://opencrs.com/ document/RS22204/2006-11-14/download/1009/.

29. U.S. Census Bureau, Foreign Trade Division, "U.S. Trade in Goods and Services - Balance of Payments (BOP) Basis, Value in Millions of Dollars, 1960 thru 2008," http://www. census.gov/foreign-trade/statistics/historical/gands.pdf.

30. U-S-History.com, "U.S. Population, 1790-2000," http://www.u-s-history.com/pages/h980.html.

31. US Debt Clock.org, http://usdebtclock.org/ (Accessed Aug. 13, 2010).

32. Bureau of Economic Analysis, "National Economic Accounts: Current-dollar GDP," http://bea.gov/ newsreleases/national/gdp/gdpnewsrelease.htm.

33. Cornell University School of Law, "U.S. Code: Title 11, Chapter 1, Section 109(e): Who may be a debtor," http:// www4.law.cornell.edu/uscode/11/usc_sec_11_00000109---- 000-.html (Accessed Aug. 18, 2010).

34. U.S. Government, Executive Branch, "Budget of the United States Government: Browse Fiscal Year 2010," http://www.gpoaccess.gov/usbudget/fy10/browse.html;

    U.S. Government, Executive Branch, "Budget of the United States Government: Browse Fiscal Year 2011," http://www.gpoaccess.gov/usbudget/fy11/index.html.

35. Energy Efficiency News, "Electric vehicle battery research in US gets $11 million," (June 17, 2009): http://www.energyefficiencynews.com/i/2183/.

    See also: TruGroup.com, "Lithium Fibre Battery," http://www.trugroup.com/Lithium-fibre-Battery.html (Accessed Aug. 14, 2010).

36. Jennifer Macey, "Battery breakthrough could make electric cars practical," Adapted from a report by Jennifer Macey for PM, *ABC News* (March 12, 2009): http://www.abc.net.au/news/stories/2009/03/12/2514848.htm (Accessed Aug. 18, 2010).

37. John Timmer, "Lithium breakthrough could charge batteries in 10 seconds," *ars technica*, (March 11, 2009): http://arstechnica.com/science/news/2009/03/lithium-breakthrough-could-charge-batteries-in-10-seconds.ars (Accessed Aug. 18, 2010).

    See also: Tyler Hamilton, "Betting on a Metal-Air Battery Breakthrough," *Technology Review* (Nov. 5, 2009): http://www.technologyreview.com/energy/23877/ (Accessed Aug. 18, 2010);

    mydigitallife.info, "Ionic Battery Technology Breakthrough with Higher Energy Density Targeted for Future Electric Vehicles," (Nov. 8, 2009): http://www.mydigitallife.

info/2009/11/08/ionic-battery-technology-breakthrough-with-higher-energy-density-targeted-for-future-electric-vehicles/ (Accessed Aug. 18, 2010).

38. Chris Morrison, "30 electric cars companies ready to take over the road," *GreenBeat*, (Jan. 10, 2008): http://green.venturebeat.com/2008/01/10/27-electric-cars-companies-ready-to-take-over-the-road/?obref=obinsite (Accessed Aug. 18, 2010);

Tom Slater, "21 companies that will lead the green car charge," *GreenBeat*, (Dec. 31, 2009): http://green.venturebeat.com/2009/12/31/21-companies-that-will-lead-the-green-car-charge/ (Accessed Aug. 18, 2010);

Pure Energy Systems Wiki, "Directory: Electric Cars," http://peswicki.com/index.php/Directory:Electric_Cars; Tesla Motors, http://www.teslamotors.com.

39. Nissan, "Leaf Electric Car," http://www.nissanusa.com/leaf-electric-car/;

Chuck Squatriglia, "Nissan Turns Over An Electric Leaf," *Wired*, (Aug. 2, 2009): http://www.wired.com/autopia/2009/08/nissan-electric-leaf/ (Accessed Aug. 18, 2010);

edmunds.com, "2011 Chevrolet Volt Review," http://www.edmunds.com/chevrolet/volt/2011/review.html (Accessed Aug. 18, 2010);

Shawn Maynard, "Subaru's Electric Car On Sale Next Year," *Automobile.com*, http://www.automobile.com/subarus-electric-car-on-sale-next-year.html (Accessed Aug. 18, 2010).

40. Hybrid Cars, "Top 7 Issues for an Electric Car Conversion," (June 2, 2009):

http://www.hybridcars.com/decision-process/top-7-issues-electric-car-conversion-25839.html (Accessed Aug. 18, 2010).

41. Kimberly Amadeo, "U.S. Economy - Gas and Oil Prices - How Prices Affect Gas Prices," *About.com*, http://useconomy.about.com/od/supply/p/oil_gas_prices.htm (Accessed Aug. 18, 2010). Note: this analysis transposes its estimates of oil use by the U.S. and the EU.

42. U.S. Energy Information Administration, "Gasoline Components History," http://tonto.eia.doe.gov/oog/info/gdu/gaspump.html (Accessed Aug. 14, 2010).

43. U.S. Energy Information Administration, "Oil: Crude and Petroleum Products Explained; Petroleum Statistics," (2008): http://www.eia.doe.gov/energyexplained/index.cfm?page=oil_home#tab2 (Accessed Aug. 14, 2010).

44. US Debt Clock.org, http://usdebtclock.org/.

Chapter 5: Housing and the U.S. Economy

1. Answers.com, "Community Reinvestment Act of 1977," http://www.answers.com/topic/community-reinvestment-act-of-1977 (Accessed July 23, 2010).

2. U.S. Department of Housing and Urban Development, "HUD Historical Background," (May 18, 2007): http://www.hud.gov/offices/adm/about/admguide/history.cfm#top (Accessed Aug. 7, 2010).

Data from multiple sources, including:
U.S. Department of Housing and Urban Development, "HUD Historical Background," (May 18, 2007), http://www.hud.gov/offices/adm/about/admguide/history.cfm (Accessed July 23, 2010).

Allie Mae, "History of Fannie Mae" (2004): http://www.alliemae.org/historyoffanniemae.html.

Allie Mae, "Ginnie Mae" (2004): http://www.alliemae.org/ginniemae.html.

U.S. Department of Housing and Urban Development, Data Sets, "Low-Income Housing Tax Credits," http://www.huduser.org/portal/datasets/lihtc.html (Accessed July 23, 2010).

4. Kitco, "Charts and Data," Historical Chart for Gold, http://www.kitco.com/scripts/hist_charts/monthly_graphs.plx (Accessed July 23, 2010).

5. Data gathered from multiple sources.

For inflation data: InflationData.com, "Historical U.S. Inflation Rate 1914–Present," Inflation: Historical, http://inflationdata.com/inflation/Inflation_Rate/HistoricalInflation.aspx.

For mean household income: Catherine Mulbrandon, "Average Income in the United States (1913-2006)," *Visualizing Economics*, (May 4, 2008): http://www.visualizingeconomics.com/2008/05/04/average-income-in-the-united-states-1913-2006/ (Accessed Aug. 18, 2010).

For home prices: Economagic.com, Economic Time Series, "US: Average Prices of Houses Actually Sold," http://www.economagic.com/em-cgi/data/exe/cenc25/c25q07 (Accessed July 23, 2010).

For Dow Jones averages: New York Stock Exchange, "Dow Jones Industrial Average History: 1900–Present," Week-Ending Close Value (2009), http://www.nyse.tv/dow-jones-industrial-average-history-djia.htm.

For gold averages: Kitco, "Charts and Data," Yearly Gold Charts, http://www.kitco.com/charts/historicalgold.html (Accessed July 23, 2010).

6. U.S. Census Bureau, "Table F-3. Mean Income Received by Each Fifth and Top 5 Percent of Families," http://www. census.gov/hhes/www/income/data/historical/ families/ (Accessed Aug. 7, 2010).

Chapter 6: Freedom of Religion

1. U.S. Constitution, amend I, http://www.usconstitution.net/ const.html#Am1 (Accessed July 17, 2010).

2. *Lemon v. Kurtzman* 403 U.S. 602; 91 Sup.Ct. 105; 29 L.Ed. 2d 745 (1971).

3. *Lamb's Chapel v. Center Moriches Sch. Dist.*, 508 U.S. 384 (1993).

4. *Salazar v. Buono*, No. 08-472 (U.S. 4/28/2010).

5. "The Magna Carta," *University of Oklahoma College of Law*, http://www.law.ou.edu/ushistory/magnacarta.shtml (Accessed July 15, 2010).

6. "The Second Virginia Charter May 23, 1609," *University of Oklahoma College of Law*, http://www.law.ou.edu/ushistory/ vchart2.shtml (Accessed July 15, 2010).

7. "The Third Virginia Charter March 12, 1612," *University of Oklahoma College of Law*, http://www.law.ou.edu/ ushistory/vchart3.shtml (Accessed July 15, 2010).

8. "Mayflower Compact 1620," *Yale Law School, Lillian Goldman Law Library, The Avalon Project*, http://avalon.

law.yale.edu/17th_century/mayflower.asp (Accessed July 15, 2010).

9. "The 1629 Charter of Massachusetts Bay," *University of Oklahoma College of Law*, http://www.law.ou.edu/hist/massbay.html (Accessed July 15, 2010).

10. "The Fundamental Orders of Connecticut, January 14, 1639," *University of Oklahoma College of Law*, http://www.law.ou.edu/hist/orders.html (Accessed July 15, 2010).

11. "Connecticut Colony Charter of 1662," *University of Oklahoma College of Law*, http://www.law.ou.edu/ushistory/colony.shtml (Accessed July 15, 2010).

12. "William Penn: Frame of Government of Pennsylvania, 1682," *Constitution Society*, http://www.constitution.org/bcp/frampenn.htm (Accessed July 15, 2010).

13. "Pennsylvania Charter of Privileges, 28 October, 1701," *Constitution Society*, http://www.constitution.org/bcp/penncharpriv.htm (Accessed July 15, 2010).

14. "Resolutions of the Stamp Act, October 19, 1765," *University of Oklahoma College of Law*, http://www.law.ou.edu/ushistory/stamp.shtml (Accessed July 15, 2010).

15. "The First Thanksgiving Proclamation," University of Oklahoma College of Law, http://www.law.ou.edu/hist/thanksgiv.html (Accessed July 15, 2010).

16. "The Thanksgiving Story," *Wilstar*, http://wilstar.com/holidays/thankstr.htm (Accessed June 5, 2010).

See also: "Thanksgiving," *The History Channel,* http://www. history.com/topics/thanksgiving (Accessed June 5, 2010);

"History of Thanksgiving," *The Holiday Spot,* http://www. theholidayspot.com/thanksgiving/history.htm (Accessed June 5, 2010);

"George Washington's 1789 Thanksgiving Proclamation," *Wilstar,* http://wilstar.com/holidays/wash_thanks.html (Accessed June 5, 2010); and

"Lincoln's Thanksgiving Proclamation," *Wilstar,* http://wilstar. com/holidays/thanksproc2.htm (Accessed June 5, 2010).

17. "The Declaration of Rights and Grievances," *The U.S. Constitution Online,* http://www.usconstitution.net/intol. html (Accessed June 5, 2010).

18. "Declaration of the Causes and Necessity of Taking Up Arms," *The University of Oklahoma Law Center,* http:// www.law.ou.edu/hist/arms.html (Accessed June 5, 2010).

19. "The Virginia Declaration of Rights," *The U.S. Constitution Online,* http://www.usconstitution.net/vdeclar.html (Accessed June 5, 2010).

See also: "The Virginia Declaration of Rights, June 12, 1776," *The University of Oklahoma Law Center,* http://www.law. ou.edu/hist/vadeclar.html (Accessed June 5, 2010).

20. "Signers of The Declaration of Independence," *The U.S. Constitution Online,* http://www.usconstitution.net/ declarsigndata.html (Accessed June 5, 2010).

21. "Declaration of Independence," *The University of Oklahoma Law Center,* http://www.law.ou.edu/hist/ decind.html (Accessed June 5, 2010).

See also: "Constitutional Topic: The Declaration of Independence," *The U.S. Constitution Online,* http://www.usconstitution.net/consttop_decl.html (Accessed June 5, 2010).

22. "The Articles of Confederation," *The University of Oklahoma Law Center* http://www.law.ou.edu/hist/artconf.html (Accessed June 5, 2010).

   See also: "Constitutional Topic: Articles of Confederation," *The U.S. Constitution Online,* http://www.usconstitution.net/consttop_arti.html (Accessed June 5, 2010).

23. "Signers of the Articles of Confederation," *The U.S. Constitution Online,* http://www.usconstitution.net/artsigndata.html (Accessed June 5, 2010).

24. "Jefferson's 1777 Draft of a Bill for Religious Freedom," *Religious Tolerance.org* http://www.religioustolerance.org/virg_bil.htm (Accessed June 5, 2010).

   See also: Wikipedia, "Thomas Jefferson and Religion," http://en.wikipedia.org/wiki/Thomas_Jefferson_and_religion (Accessed June 5, 2010).

25. "Jefferson's Wall of Separation Letter," *The U.S. Constitution Online,* http://www.usconstitution.net/jeffwall.html (Accessed June 7, 2010).

26. "To James Madison 1 - Thomas Jefferson, The Works, vol. 5 (Correspondence 1786-1789) [1905]," *The Online Library of Liberty,* http://oll.libertyfund.org/?option=com_staticxt&staticfile=show.php%3Ftitle=802&chapter=86687&layout=html&Itemid=27 (Accessed June 7, 2010).

27. "Thomas Jefferson and John Adams—Requiem for an American President," *Home of Heroes,* http://www.

homeofheroes.com/profiles/profiles_jeffadams.html (Accessed June 7, 2010).

28. "Data on the Framers of the Constitution," *The U.S. Constitution Online*, http://www.usconstitution.net/ constframedata.html (Accessed June 7, 2010).

29. *Lemon v. Kurtzman*, 403 U.S. 602; 91 Sup.Ct. 105; 29 L.Ed.2d 745 (1971).

30. *Walz v. Tax Commission*, 397 U.S. 664, 668; 90 Sup.Ct. 1409; 1411, 25 L.Ed.2d 697 (1970).

31. *Board of Education v. Allen*, 392 U.S. 236, 243; 88 Sup.Ct. 1923, 1926; 20 L.Ed.2d 1060 (1968).

32. *Zorach v. Clauson*, 343 U.S. 306, 312; 72 Sup.Ct. 679, 683; 96 L.Ed. 954 (1952).

See also: Sherbert v. Verner, 374 U.S. 398, 422; 83 Sup.Ct. 1790, 1803; 10 L.Ed.2d 965 (1963).

33. *Lemon v. Kurtzman*, 403 U.S. 602; 91 Sup.Ct. 105; 29 L.Ed.2d 745 (1971).

34. *Everson v. Board of Education*, 330 U.S. 1, 67; Sup. Ct. 504; 91 L.Ed. 711 (1947).

35. Ibid.

36. *Thomas v. Review Board Of the Indiana Employment Security Division*, 450 U.S. 707; 101 Sup.Ct. 1425; 67 L. Ed.2d 624 (1981).

37. *Sherbert v. Verner*, 374 U.S. 398; 83 Sup.Ct. 1790; 10 L.Ed.2d 965 (1963).

38. *Marsh v. Chambers*, 463 U.S. 783 (1983).

39. *Zorach v. Clauson*, 343 U.S. 306, 313 (1952).

40. *Marsh v. Chambers*, 463 U.S. 783 (1983).

41. *Lynch v. Donnelly*, 465 U.S. 668, 688; 104 Sup.Ct. 1355; 79 L.Ed.2d 604 (1984).

42. Ibid.

43. *Stone v. Graham*, 449 U.S. 39; 101 Sup.Ct. 192; 66 L.Ed.2d 199 (1980).

44. *Zorach v. Clauson*, 343 U.S. 306, 314; 72 S.Ct. 679; 96 L.Ed. 954 (1952).

45. *Edwards v. Aguillard*, 482 U.S. 578; 107 Sup.Ct 2573; 96 L.Ed.2d 510 (1987).

46. Louisiana *Revised Statutes, Annotated* (West 1982)17:286.2.

47. *Stone v. Graham*, 449 U.S. 39; 101 Sup.Ct. 192; 66 L.Ed.2d 199 (1980).

48. *County of Allegheny v. American Civil Liberties Union Greater Pittsburgh Chapter*, 492 U.S. 573; 109 S.Ct. 3086; 106 L.Ed.2d 472 (1989).

49. Clint Eastwood, "Clint Eastwood Quotes," *ThinkExist. com*, http://thinkexist.com/quotation/-a_good_man_always_knows_his/340230.html, (Accessed June 9, 2010).

50. American Center for Law & Justice, "About Chief Counsel," http://www.aclj.org/About/Default.aspx?Section=11 (Accessed June 9, 2010).

51. Ibid.

52. *Board of Education v. Mergens*, 406 U.S. 226; 110 Sup.Ct. 2356; 110 L.Ed.2d 191 (1990).

53. *Widmar v. Vincent*, 454 U.S. 263; 102 Sup.Ct. 269; 70 L.Ed2d 440 (1981).

54. Ibid.

55. United States Code, Title 20, Sections 4071(a) and (b), "Equal Access Act," http://frwebgate.access.gpo.gov/ cgibin/usc.cgi?ACTION=RETRIEVE&FILE= $$xa$$busc20.wais&start=6541259&SIZE=3835&TYPE= PDF (Accessed July 18, 2010).

56. *McDaniel v. Paty*, 435 U.S. 618, 641; 98 Sup.Ct. 1322, 1335; 55 L.Ed.2d 593 (1978).

57. *Lamb's Chapel v. Center Moriches Sch. Dist.*, 508 U.S. 384 (1993).

58. *Cornelius v. NAACP Legal Defense & Ed. Fund, Inc.*, 473 U.S. 788, 800 (1985);

Perry Ed. Assn. v. Perry Local Educators' Assn., 460 U.S. 37, 46 (1983);

Postal Service v. Council of Greenburgh Civic Assns., 453 U.S. 114, 129-130 (1981);

Greer v. Spock, 424 U.S. 828, 836 (1976); *Adderly v. Florida*, 385 U.S. 39, 47 (1966).

59. *Lamb's Chapel v. Center Moriches Sch. Dist.*, 508 U.S. 384 (1993).

60. *Rosenburger v. University of Va.*, 515 U.S. 819 (1995).

61. *Police Dept. Of Chicago v. Mosley*, 408 U.S. 92, 96, (1972).

62. *Turner Broadcasting System, Inc. v. FCC*, 512 U.S. 622, (1994).

63. *Cornelius v. NAACP Legal Defense & Ed. Fund*, 473 U.S. 788, 806 (1985).

See also: Perry Ed. Assn. v. Perry Local Educators' Assn., 460 U.S. 37, 46 (1983).

64. *Widmar v. Vincent*, 454 U.S. 263; 102 Sup.Ct. 269; 70 L.Ed. 440 (1981).

65. *Board of Ed. of Kiryas Joel Village School Dist. v. Grumet*, 512 U.S. 687 (1994).

66. *Witters v. Washington Dept. Of Services for Blind*, 474 U.S. 481 (1986).

67. Super Bowl History, "Super Bowl History 2000-2008," http://www.superbowlhistory.net/superbowl/2000s.php (Accessed June 10, 2010).

68. U.S. District Court, M.D. Alabama, Northern Division, *Glassroth v. Moore*, 229 F.Supp.2d 1290 at 1319, (M.D.Ala. 2002) and U.S. District Court, M.D. Alabama, Northern Division, *Glassroth v. Moore*, 242 F.Supp.2d 1067, (M.D. Ala. 2002).

69. *Glassroth v. Moore*, 335 F.3d 1282 (11th Cir. 2003).

70. U.S. Constitution, art. II, sec. 2. "Powers of the President."

Chapter 7: Abortion

1. *National Abortion Federation v. Gonzales*, 437 F.3d 278 (2nd Cir. 2006).

2. *Gonzales v. Carhart*, 550 U.S. 124; 127 Sup.Ct. 1610; 167 L.Ed.2d 480 (2007).

3. U.S. Senate Judiciary Committee, *Partial-birth Abortion Ban Act of 2003: Hearings on H.R. 760*, 108th Cong., 1st sess., 3 April 2003. http://www.congress.gov/cgi-bin/ cpquery/T?&report=hr058&dbname=108&.

4. *Women's Medical Professional Corporation v. Taft*, 353 F.3d 436 (6th Cir. 2003).

5. *Ayotte v. Planned Parenthood of Northern New England,* 546 U.S. 320; 126 Sup.Ct. 961; 163 L.Ed.2d 812 (2006).

6. Ibid.

7. *Roe v. Wade,* 410 U.S. 113 (1973).

8. *Doe v. Bolton,* 410 U.S. 179 (1973).

9. Exodus 21:22-25, *The Holy Bible, New International Version.*

10. *County of Santa Clara v. Southern Pac. Co.,* 118 U.S. 394; 6 S.Ct. 1132; 30 L.Ed. 118 (1886).

11. *Sweatt v. Painter,* 339 U.S. 629 (1950).

12. RTE News, "World's earliest live birth baby goes home," (Feb. 20, 2007): http://www.rte.ie/news/2007/0220/baby.html, (Accessed June 21, 2010).

See also: Jill Stanek, "World's youngest surviving baby born in Miami," (Feb. 20, 2007): http://www.jillstanek.com/aborted-alive/worlds-youngest.html (Accessed June 21, 2010).

13. Vanessa Allen and Andrew Levy, "Doctors told me it was against the rules to save my premature baby," *Mail Online,* (Sept. 10, 2009): http://www.dailymail.co.uk/news/article-1211950/Premature-baby-left-die-doctors-mother-gives-birth-just-days-22-week-care-limit.html, (Accessed June 21, 2010).

14. *Diamond v. Charles,* 476 U.S. 54 (1986).

15. *Catholic League v. Women's Health Center,* 469 U.S. 1303 (1984).

16. *Thornburgh v. American Coll. Of Obst. & Gyn.,* 476 U.S. 747 (1986).

17. *FEC v. Massachusetts Citizens For Life, Inc.*, 479 U.S. 238 (1986).

18. *Doe v. Smith*, 486 U.S. 1308 (1988).

19. *Webster v. Reproductive Health Services*, 492 U.S. 490 (1989).

20. *Hodgson v. Minnesota*, 497 U.S. 417 (1990).

    See also: Ohio v. Akron Center, 497 U.S. 502 (1990), in which the Supreme Court validated an Ohio statute that made it criminal for a physician or any other person to perform an abortion on an unemancipated minor without a parent's consent.

21. *Rust v. Sullivan*, 500 U.S. 173 (1991).

22. *Planned Parenthood of Southeastern Pa. v. Casey*, 505 U.S. 833 (1992).

23. Ibid.

24. *Akron v. Akron Center for Reproductive Health, Inc.*, 462 U.S. 416; 103 Sup.Ct. 2481; 76 L.Ed.2d 687 (1983).

25. *Bray v. Alexandria Clinic*, 506 U.S. 263 (1993).

26. *National Organization for Women, Inc. v. Scheidler*, 510 U.S. 249 (1994); and *National Organization for Women, Inc. v. Scheidler*, 547 U.S. 9, 126; Sup.Ct. 1264; 164 L.Ed.2d 10 (2006).

27. U.S. House Committee on the Judiciary. U.S. Senate Subcommittee on Civil and Constitutional Rights. *Abortion Clinic Violence*, Statement by Joseph M. Scheidler, Executive Director, Pro-Life Action League. 99th Cong., 1st and 2d sess., 1987, 55.

28. *National Organization for Women, Inc. v. Scheidler*, 547 U.S. 9; 126 Sup.Ct. 1264; 164 L.Ed.2d 10 (2006).

29. *Madsen v. Women's Health Center, Inc.*, 512 U.S. 753; 114 Sup.Ct. 2516; 129 L.Ed.2d 593 (1994).

30. *Dalton v. Family Planning Services*, 516 U.S. 474; 116 Sup. Ct. 1063; 134 L.Ed.2d 115 (1996).

31. *Santana v. Zilog*, 95 F.3d 780 (9th Cir. 1996).

32. *Causeway Medical Suite v. Ieyoub*, 109 F.3d 1096 (5th Cir. 1997).

33. *Women's Med Prof v. Voinovich*, 130 F.3d 187 (6th Cir. 1997)

34. As referenced in *Leavitt v. Jane L., et al*, 518 U.S. 137; 116 Sup. Ct. 2068, 135 L.Ed. 443 (1996).

35. *Leavitt v. Jane L., et al*, 518 U.S. 137; 116 Sup. Ct. 2068; 135 L.Ed. 443 (1996).

36. *Coe v. County of Cook, et al.*, 162 F.3d 491 (7th Cir. (Ill.) 1998).

37. *Planned Parenthood of Wisconsin v. Doyle*, 162 F.3d 463 (7th Cir. (Wis.) 1998).

38. Ibid.

39. *Carhart v. Stenberg*, 530 U.S. 914; 120 Sup.Ct. 2597; 147 L.Ed.2d 743 (2000).

See also: Carhart v. Stenberg, 192 F.3d 1142 (8th Cir. 1999).

40. *Planned Parenthood v. Farmer*, 220 F.3d 127 (3rd Cir. 2000).

41. *Richmond Medical Center For Women v. Gilmore*, 224 F.3d 337 (4th Cir. 2000).

42. *Women's Medical Professional Corporation v. Taft*, 353 F.3d 436 (6th Cir. 2003).

43. *Richmond Medical Center for Women v. Hicks*, 409 F.3d 619 (Fed. 4th Cir. 2005) and *Richmond Medical Center for Women v. Hicks*, 422 F.3d 160 (Fed. 4th Cir. 2005).

44. *Carhart v. Gonzales*, 413 F.3d 791 (Fed. 8th Cir., 2005).

45. *National Abortion Federation v. Alberto Gonzales*, 437 F.3d 278 (2d Cir. 2006).

46. Ibid.

47. U.S. Code, title 18, sec. 1531, "Partial-Birth Abortion Ban Act of 2003," (2000 ed., Supp. IV): http://www.gpoaccess. gov/uscode/index.html.

48. *Richmond Medical Center for Women v. Herring*, 570 F.3d 165 (4th Cir., 2009).

49. Louisiana *Liability for Termination of a Pregnancy, Revised Statute*, (1997) sec. 9.2800.12.

    See also: Louisiana *Acts* (1997) no. 825, sec. 1.

50. *Okpalobi v. Foster*, 244 F.3d 405 (5th Cir. 2001).

51. *Planned Parenthood v. American Coalition of Life Activists*, 244 F.3d 1007 (9th Cir. 2000).

52. *Cano v. Baker*, 435 F.3d 1337 (11th Cir., 2006).

53. *McCorvey v. Hill*, 385 F.3d 846 (5th Cir., 2004).

54. Gallup Polls, "Abortion," (1975-2010) http://www.gallup. com/poll/1576/Abortion.aspx (Accessed June 25, 2010).

55. Wikipedia, "Late-term abortion," http://en.wikipedia.org/ wiki/Late-term_abortion (Accessed June 28, 2010).

Chapter 8: The Federal Budget

1. Christopher Chantrill, "United States Federal State and Local Government Spending Fiscal Year 2011 in $ billion," USGovernmentSpending.com, US Budget FY11, http://www.usgovernmentspending.com/budget_pie_gs.php?span=usgs302&year=2011&view=1&expand=0002&expandC=&units=b&fy=fy11&local=undefined&state=US#usgs302 .

2. David E. Williams, Sean Kennedy, and MacMillin Slobodien, ed. Thomas A. Schatz, "2010 Congressional Pig Book Summary," Citizens Against Government Waste, http://www.cagw.org.

3. Chris Edwards, "Cato Handbook For Congress," Cato Institute, http://www.cato.org/pubs/handbook/hb108/hb108-23.pdf.

See also: Chris Edwards, Tad DeHaven, and Randal O'Toole and others. "Downsizing the Federal Government," Cato Institute, http://www.downsizinggovernment.org.

4. Brian M. Reidl, The Heritage Foundation, "Federal Spending—By the Numbers," (Feb. 6, 2006): http://www.heritage.org/Research/Reports/2006/02/Federal-Spending-By-the-Numbers.

See also: William Beach, "The 2009 Index of Dependence on Government," The Heritage Foundation, (March 4, 2010): http://www.heritage.org/Research/Reports/2010/03/The-2009-Index-of-Dependence-on-Government.

The Heritage Foundation, "2010 Budget Chart Book," http://www.heritage.org/BudgetChartBook/.

5. William Beach, "The 2009 Index of Dependence on Government," The Heritage Foundation, (March 4, 2010): p.15; http://www.heritage.org/Research/Reports/2010/03/The-2009-Index-of-Dependence-on-Government.

6. Proposing an Amendment to the Constitution of the United States to Control Spending, 110th Cong., 2d sess., H.J.R. 81. Note: Sponsored by Mr. Campbell of California with 34 co-sponsors. Accessing this bill requires access to the Library of Congress at http://thomas.loc.gov and then going through a number of steps to see the bill. See http://thomas.loc.gov/cgibin/query/z?c110:H.J.RES.81.

Chapter 9: The Candidates

1. Legislation and Votes, *Office of the Clerk, U.S. House of Representatives*, http://clerk.house.gov/legislative/legvotes.html; and

Legislation and Records, *United States Senate*, http://www.senate.gov/pagelayout/legislative/a_three_sections_with_teasers/votes.htm.